JOURNAL FOR THE STUDY OF THE NEW TESTAMENT
SUPPLEMENT SERIES
191

Executive Editor
Stanley E. Porter

Sheffield Academic Press

The Criteria for Authenticity
in Historical-Jesus Research

Previous Discussion and New Proposals

Stanley E. Porter

Journal for the Study of the New Testament
Supplement Series 191

This monograph is dedicated to my loving mother,

Lorraine De Haan Porter

Published by
Sheffield Academic Press Ltd
Mansion House
19 Kingfield Road
Sheffield S11 9AS
England

Typeset by Sheffield Academic Press
and
Printed on acid-free paper in Great Britain
by Bookcraft Ltd
Midsomer Norton, Somerset

British Library Cataloguing in Publication Data

A catalogue record for this book is available
from the British Library

ISBN 1 84127 089 X

CONTENTS

LIST OF TABLES

PREFACE

This book began as a lengthy essay, some of which was delivered at the Symposium on 'The Historical Jesus' on 1 April 1999 as part of the 650th anniversary celebration of the founding of Charles University in Prague. This Symposium was held in conjunction with the celebration of the founding of the Centre for Biblical Studies by the Comenius Protestant Theological Faculty, Charles University, the Institute for Classical Antiquity, and the Czech Academy of Sciences. A shorter form of the essay upon which this monograph is based, and which prompted this more detailed and extended discussion, is to be published in Petr Pokorný and Jirí Mrázek (eds.), *The Historical Jesus in Recent Discussion* (JSNTSup; Sheffield: Sheffield Academic Press, forthcoming). An earlier draft of the excursus of Chapter 4 has also been accepted for publication in the *Bulletin for Biblical Research*, and will appear in volume 10 in 2000. Professor Pokorný has reminded me, as well as the others who were in attendance at this Symposium, of the tremendous significance of the fact that such a Centre for Biblical Studies has been founded in Charles University. What he held before 1989 as only a private dream, and one that he never expected to see realized in his lifetime (and probably did not dare to breathe to others), has now been brought to fruition by the Czech Academy of Sciences giving its formal and tangible support to a centre for the academic study of theology. This Centre was inconceivable under the previous, oppressive regime. I believe that I represent the opinion of all of those involved in the Symposium, as well as numerous academics elsewhere, in wishing the Centre tremendous success in the years ahead as it helps to chart the course of theological discussion and education in the Czech Republic for the twenty-first century.

I wish to thank Professor Dr Petr Pokorný for the invitation to deliver the original paper at this stimulating and satisfying Symposium. I wish also to thank his colleagues in the Protestant Theological Faculty for their work and effort in the planning of this occasion. This Symposium, one of several that took place at this time of celebration, was held in conjunction with commemoration of the eightieth anniversary of the founding of the Faculty, in 1919. I was honoured to be a guest at this moving commendatory celebration also. The formalized scholarly, academic and social links between the Protestant Theological Faculty and Roehampton Institute London (now the University of Surrey Roehampton) have helped to make these mutually enjoyed occasions possible. All of those who have helped to maintain these associations, including Peter Stephens and the International Office at the Protestant Theological Faculty, deserve thanks for their efforts.

The context of the Symposium provided much stimulation for further thought on this topic, and this monograph is the inadequate result. The manuscript has since gone through several stages of development, as well as alteration of my perspective at several significant points. I trust that it is now a better piece of work than it was originally, and one that makes a contribution to the debate in historical-Jesus research. If there is merit in what I say, at least some of the credit must go to a number of those who heard, read and responded to it at earlier stages. I wish first of all to thank my fellow speakers at the Symposium for their stimulating and insightful papers, as well as their questions and comments on my paper. These include not only Professor Pokorný, but Professor Dr Hermann Lichtenburger of the University of Tübingen, Professor Dr Markus Wolter of the University of Bonn, Dr Anders Ekenberg of Uppsala University, Sweden, and Professor J. Keith Elliott of the University of Leeds. Those in attendance as well helped all of us to think more clearly about the topic of the Symposium and our individual contributions to it. I wish to note especially Dr Peter Balla of the Károli Gáspár Reformed University of Budapest, Professor Dr Peter Pilhofer of the University of Greifswald, Germany, and Dr Moises Mayordomo of the University of Bern, Switzerland. Several times throughout the Symposium we were able to engage in discussion of the papers, but several more casual social occasions led to exploration of a variety of other issues and topics (including the piano playing of Glenn Gould, a subject of great interest to me). The conversations and times of sociability that we were able to enjoy outside of the Symposium proper helped to make the occasion even more satisfying. As usual, Professor Pokorný and his wife were instrumental in these rewarding sociable times, with their invitation to several of us to enjoy an evening in their home.

The fuller draft of the paper that I delivered at the Symposium was presented at the Biblical Studies Research Cluster of the Centre for Advanced Theological Research at Roehampton Institute London. The paper benefited immensely from the insightful comments of those who were present, and, I hope, will lead to further exploration of this topic, of which this monograph is only the beginning. This is the first of my authored books to be devoted to questions regarding the historical Jesus. I am not intending it to be my last effort in this area—in fact, it has generated much creative discussion among my colleagues regarding further areas of exploration. In particular regarding this volume, I wish to thank my colleagues, Mr Arthur Gibson, Professor Craig Evans, Mr Brook Pearson, Dr Anthony Cross, Cynthia Westfall, and Mr Matthew Brook O'Donnell, for their trenchant observations, willingness to tackle this subject in new and different ways, and general scholarly support (including pointing out helpful bibliography). Matt especially has devoted serious further effort to refining my arguments and presentation, and I look forward to working on further projects on this topic with him. It will come as no surprise to those who know him to discover that the tables at the end of Chapters 1 and 2 and the tables in Chapter 4 came about as a result of his gentle prodding, as well as industry. I am pleased that the debate over various elements of the programme of historical-Jesus research has led several of us in the Centre for Advanced Theological Research now of the University of Surrey Roehampton toward formal plans to explore further dimensions of this topic.

As always, my wife, Wendy, my co-worker and a scholar in her own right, but more importantly my friend and companion, has been my greatest support and help in the development of this monograph during a time of exceptional busyness and transition. Her attention to the detail of this monograph has been invaluable.

ABBREVIATIONS

AB	Anchor Bible
ABD	David Noel Freedman (ed.), *The Anchor Bible Dictionary* (New York: Doubleday, 1992)
ABRL	Anchor Bible Reference Library
AGJU	Arbeiten zur Geschichte des antiken Judentums und des Urchristentums
AJP	*American Journal of Philology*
ANRW	Hildegard Temporini and Wolfgang Haase (eds.), *Aufstieg und Niedergang der römischen Welt: Geschichte und Kultur Roms im Spiegel der neueren Forschung* (Berlin: W. de Gruyter, 1972–)
ASNU	Acta seminarii neotestamentici upsaliensis
ATANT	Abhandlungen zur Theologie des Alten und Neuen Testaments
ATR	*Anglican Theological Review*
BARev	*Biblical Archaeology Review*
BASOR	*Bulletin of the American Schools of Oriental Research*
BBB	Bonner biblische Beiträge
BBR	*Bulletin for Biblical Research*
BENT	Beiträge zur Einleitung in das Neue Testament
BETL	Bibliotheca ephemeridum theologicarum lovaniensium
BEvT	Beiträge zur evangelischen Theologie
BHT	Beiträge zur historischen Theologie
Bib	*Biblica*
BibSem	The Biblical Seminar
BIS	Biblical Interpretation Series
BJRL	*Bulletin of the John Rylands University Library of Manchester*
BJS	Brown Judaic Studies
BLG	Biblical Languages: Greek
BNTC	Black's New Testament Commentaries
BR	*Biblical Research*
BWANT	Beiträge zur Wissenschaft vom Alten und Neuen Testament
CBQ	*Catholic Biblical Quarterly*
ConBNT	Coniectanea biblica, New Testament
CR	*Currents in Research*
CRINT	Compendia rerum iudaicarum ad Novum Testamentum

CSR	*Christian Scholar's Review*
CThL	Crown Theological Library
CTL	Cambridge Textbooks in Linguistics
CTQ	*Concordia Theological Quarterly*
DBSup	*Dictionnaire de la Bible, Supplément*
DJD	Discoveries in the Judaean Desert
EB	Etudes bibliques
EFN	Estudios de Filología Neotestamentaria
EILS	Explorations in Language Study
ELS	English Language Series
EncJud	*Encyclopaedia Judaica*
ETL	*Ephemerides theologicae lovanienses*
EvT	*Evangelische Theologie*
ExpTim	*Expository Times*
FN	*Filología neotestamentaria*
FRLANT	Forschungen zur Religion und Literatur des Alten und Neuen Testaments
GBS	Guides to Biblical Scholarship
GNS	Good News Studies
GRBS	*Greek, Roman, and Byzantine Studies*
HNT	Handbuch zum Neuen Testament
HNTC	Harper's New Testament Commentaries
HTS	Harvard Theological Studies
HUCA	*Hebrew Union College Annual*
IBS	*Irish Biblical Studies*
ICC	International Critical Commentary
IEJ	*Israel Exploration Journal*
IRT	Issues in Religion and Theology
JAAR	*Journal of the American Academy of Religion*
JBL	*Journal of Biblical Literature*
JBLMS	*Journal of Biblical Literature* Monograph Series
JBR	*Journal of Bible and Religion*
JETS	*Journal of the Evangelical Theological Society*
JGRChJ	*Journal of Greco-Roman Christianity and Judaism*
JQR	*Jewish Quarterly Review*
JR	*Journal of Religion*
JRS	*Journal of Roman Studies*
JSNT	*Journal for the Study of the New Testament*
JSNTSup	*Journal for the Study of the New Testament*, Supplement Series
JSOTSup	*Journal for the Study of the Old Testament*, Supplement Series
JSP	*Journal for the Study of the Pseudepigrapha*
JSPSup	*Journal for the Study of the Pseudepigrapha*, Supplement Series
JTS	*Journal of Theological Studies*

KD	*Kerygma und Dogma*
LCL	Loeb Classical Library
LJ	Lives of Jesus
LLL	Longman Linguistics Library
LSLS	Language in Social Life Series
MeyerK	H.A.W. Meyer (ed.), Kritisch-exegetischer Kommentar über das Neue Testament
Neot	*Neotestamentica*
NewDocs	*New Documents Illustrating Early Christianity* (1976–)
NICNT	New International Commentary on the New Testament
NIGTC	The New International Greek Testament Commentary
NovT	*Novum Testamentum*
NovTSup	*Novum Testamentum*, Supplements
NTG	New Testament Guides
NTL	New Testament Library
NTOA	Novum Testamentum et orbis antiquus
NTS	*New Testament Studies*
NTTS	New Testament Tools and Studies
OBS	Oxford Bible Series
QD	Quaestiones disputatae
RB	*Revue biblique*
RevQ	*Revue de Qumran*
RGG	*Religion in Geschichte und Gegenwart*
RILP	Roehampton Institute London Papers
RSR	*Recherches de science religieuse*
SBG	Studies in Biblical Greek
SBLDS	Society of Biblical Literature Dissertation Series
SBLMS	Society of Biblical Literature Monograph Series
SBLRBS	Society of Biblical Literature Resources for Biblical Study
SBLSCS	Society of Biblical Literature Septuagint and Cognate Studies
SBLSP	Society of Biblical Literature Seminar Papers
SBT	Studies in Biblical Theology
SD	Studies and Documents
SHJ	Studying the Historical Jesus
SJT	*Scottish Journal of Theology*
SNT	Studien zum Neuen Testament
SNTG	Studies in New Testament Greek
SNTSMS	Society for New Testament Studies Monograph Series
SNTU	Studien zum Neuen Testament und seiner Umwelt
SNTW	Studies of the New Testament and its World
SP	Sacra Pagina
ST	*Studia theologica*
THKNT	Theologischer Handkommentar zum Neuen Testament
TLZ	*Theologische Literaturzeitung*
TMEA	Travaux et mémoires: Etudes anciennes

TRu	*Theologische Rundschau*
TTL	Theological Translation Library
TTZ	*Trierer theologische Zeitschrift*
TU	Texte und Untersuchungen
TynBul	*Tyndale Bulletin*
UBSMS	United Bible Societies Monograph Series
UTb	Uni-Taschenbücher
VTSup	*Vetus Testamentum*, Supplements
WBC	Word Biblical Commentary
WUNT	Wissenschaftliche Untersuchungen zum Neuen Testament
ZAW	*Zeitschrift für die alttestamentliche Wissenschaft*
ZNW	*Zeitschrift für die neutestamentliche Wissenschaft*
ZTK	*Zeitschrift für Theologie und Kirche*

INTRODUCTION

The Purpose and Approach of this Study

Books on the historical Jesus abound. More books on this topic are being written all of the time and there is no perceivable sense of this trend abating.[1] One does not have to be particularly astute or involved in this subject to realize that Jesus research has become a growth industry in its own right (in fact, this was the case for most of the twentieth century, if not the one before as well), with many scholars taking up the challenge of writing another book or article on what Jesus may have said and done, or not. Many of these volumes make noteworthy contributions to scholarship—especially regarding scholarly understanding of particular passages or pericopes—and raise interesting issues regarding the historical Jesus. Many of these issues merit more significant extended discussion. This volume is not a book on the historical Jesus in this sense, however. In other words, in this monograph, I do not attempt to write a life of Jesus or even, on any significant scale, establish what the historical Jesus may have said or done. I am certainly concerned with such issues, as the ensuing chapters will make clear, but only within the confines of a small area of the discussion, and that related to the use of the Greek language as providing the basis for new criteria for establishing authentic sayings of Jesus. Neither do I attempt to outline a complete programme that shows how one might proceed to such a task as writing a life of Jesus. (I leave it to others to debate the merits of such a task.) Nevertheless, the criteria that are developed in this volume are designed to be suggestive of how and where further research could be undertaken by those who utilize such methods. I do not pretend to have

---

1. A very useful bibliography is to be found in C.A. Evans, *Life of Jesus Research: An Annotated Bibliography* (NTTS, 24; Leiden: E.J. Brill, rev. edn, 1996).

When citing works that originally appeared in languages other than English, when there is an English translation known to me I cite its page numbers, rather than the original, except where a point regarding the translation is being made.

treated exhaustively the several passages to which these criteria might apply, or to have uncovered the full range of passages that might potentially be involved in such a discussion. Those tasks remain for further research.

To the contrary, this volume has quite narrow aims and intentions. These revolve primarily around certain fixed questions of method in recent historical-Jesus research, specifically those questions related to the so-called criteria for authenticity. Not formally labelled as criteria in much of the discussion of the historical Jesus throughout the first half of the twentieth century, their use nevertheless goes back to many of the formative thinkers regarding this topic, and has been continued in current research to varying degrees. The history of Jesus-research is currently dominated by a number of figures who have made significant contributions to the larger discussion. Several of the most recent and influential are E.P. Sanders, John Meier, and Tom Wright.[2] They follow in a long line of others who have preceded them in discussion, however. The two arguably most well known are Albert Schweitzer and Rudolf Bultmann.[3] In several ways, Schweitzer and Bultmann strike me as two of the most potentially misunderstood yet fundamentally important biblical scholars of the twentieth century. Sometimes Schweitzer is treated as if he were something other than a seminal figure in New Testament

2.   See E.P. Sanders, *Jesus and Judaism* (London: SCM Press; Philadelphia: Fortress Press, 1985); *idem, The Historical Figure of Jesus* (London: Allen Lane/ Penguin, 1993); J.P. Meier, *A Marginal Jew: Rethinking the Historical Jesus* (3 vols.; ABRL; New York: Doubleday, 1991–); and N.T. Wright, *Jesus and the Victory of God* (Minneapolis: Fortress Press, 1996). This does not include those members of the Jesus Seminar, such as J.D. Crossan, *The Historical Jesus: The Life of a Mediterranean Jewish Peasant* (San Francisco: HarperSanFrancisco, 1992) and M.J. Borg, *Jesus in Contemporary Scholarship* (Valley Forge, PA: Trinity Press International, 1994), esp. pp. 18-43. I am only incidentally concerned with the Jesus Seminar in this volume, as will become apparent. There are many assessments of the results of the Jesus Seminar now being written. For a recent attempt, see M.A. Powell, *Jesus as a Figure in History: How Modern Historians View the Man from Galilee* (Louisville, KY: Westminster/John Knox Press, 1998), pp. 65-81, followed by discussion of Crossan (pp. 83-99) and Borg (pp. 101-12). Since I live in the UK, I am in no position to judge the grass roots impact of the Jesus Seminar especially on North America, but my impression is that it has proved far more stimulating to a small group of scholars than it has to the public that it sought to influence.

3.   On these two seminal figures, among many studies, see J.C. O'Neill, *The Bible's Authority: A Portrait Gallery of Thinkers from Lessing to Bultmann* (Edinburgh: T. & T. Clark, 1991), pp. 248-65, 284-309.

studies, and is seen as more of a descriptive nay-sayer, who brought the so-called 'old quest' to an abrupt halt. I attempt to qualify this picture in Chapter 1, regarding research on the historical Jesus.[4] Likewise, Bultmann is sometimes caricatured as merely a creature of his time, governed and controlled by the mechanistic and post-Enlightenment world of the nineteenth century, with the implication that his work is now dated and irredeemably flawed by this fact. His work on Jesus is sometimes consequently seen as having little resulting interest today, except as a chronicle of its time. There is of course the obvious sense in which every person is bound by his or her own time (how is it even possible to think of someone being outside of one's own time?), but Bultmann's sincere struggle to come to terms with experience within a theological context can only be commended, and seen as an example of intellectual honesty that others could benefit from by emulating.[5] Nevertheless,

---

4.   It is true that Schweitzer, who held earned doctorates in theology, philosophy and medicine, was expert in academic areas other than biblical studies (e.g. his work on Bach is one of the two fundamental modern interpretations of the great composer; see his *J.S. Bach* [Leipzig: Breitkopf & Härtel, 1951 (1908); ET *J.S. Bach* (trans. E. Newman; 2 vols.; Leipzig: Breitkopf & Härtel, 1911)]; and his work on Kantian philosophy is still highly regarded; see his *Die Religionsphilosophie Kants* [Tübingen: Mohr Siebeck, 1899]), and this says nothing of his Nobel-prize winning humanitarian work. Nevertheless, his work in New Testament deserves further recognition than it has recently received. This includes not only his *Von Reimarus zu Wrede: Eine Geschichte der Leben-Jesu-Forschung* (Tübingen: Mohr Siebeck, 1906; 2nd edn, 1910; 6th edn, 1951; ET *The Quest of the Historical Jesus: A Critical Study of its Progress from Reimarus to Wrede* [trans. W. Montgomery; London: A. & C. Black, 1910]) and his *Das Messianitäts- und Leidensgeheimnis: Eine Skizze des Lebens Jesu* (Tübingen: Mohr Siebeck, 1901; 3rd edn, 1956; ET *The Mystery of the Kingdom of God: The Secret of Jesus' Messiahship and Passion* [trans. W. Lowrie; London: A. & C. Black, 1925]), both of which are discussed in Chapter 1, but also his still important and useful *Geschichte der paulinischen Forschung* (Tübingen: Mohr Siebeck, 1911; ET *Paul and his Interpreters: A Critical History* [trans. W. Montgomery; London: A. & C. Black, 1912]) and his *Die Mystik des Apostels Paulus* (Tübingen: Mohr Siebeck, 1930; ET *The Mysticism of Paul the Apostle* [trans. W. Montgomery; London: A. & C. Black, 1931]), among several others.

5.   See, e.g., R. Bultmann 'Neues Testament und Mythologie: Das Problem der Entmythologisierung der neutestamentlichen Verkündigung', in H.W. Bartsch (ed.), *Kerygma und Mythos: Ein theologisches Gespräch* (Hamburg: H. Reich, 1948; 2nd edn, 1951), pp. 15-48; ET 'New Testament and Mythology: The Mythological Element in the Message of the New Testament and the Problem of its Re-Interpretation', in H.W. Bartsch (ed.), *Kerygma and Myth: A Theological Debate* (trans.

these two figures still rightly loom large on the landscape of much contemporary biblical studies, not least in their work in the area of his-torical-Jesus research. Both were truly great men, who excelled in much beyond the narrow confines of this area. Such prominence can too often result in what might be called the star factor. The star factor is not con-fined to those in Hollywood or politics, but is also, unfortunately, some-thing by which even those in academic disciplines, such as biblical studies, can be afflicted. In disciplines that pride themselves on being academically and intellectually rigorous in their approach, it is regret-table to find that simply invoking a name can often result in a lack of such critical analysis with regard to the nature and extent of their con-tribution. This is often the fault not of those such as a Schweitzer and a Bultmann, but of those who have misread or misappropriated their work, or used it as a short-cut to understanding of the subject at hand. Such appears to be the case with respect to some of the contributions in his-torical-Jesus research. Thus, in a very real sense, before I can put for-ward my proposals regarding how one might utilize knowledge of the Greek language in the first century as a criterion in historical-Jesus research, there is some ground-clearing that must take place. Some of this involves Schweitzer and Bultmann, but it encompasses much more than them as well. It requires a re-examination of a number of the facts and trends that have come to be normative and determinative for cur-rent historical-Jesus research. Not all of these trends and movements are well grounded, or at the very least they often mask some of the assump-tions that drive their investigations, especially in terms of the criteria for authenticity.

Discussion of these criteria relies upon some knowledge of the histori-cal background and context in which their development has taken place.

R.H. Fuller; London: SPCK, 1953; 2nd edn, 1964), pp. 1-44. Much of his scholar-ship still rewards serious consideration, including, I suggest, his *Die Geschichte der synoptischen Tradition* (FRLANT, 29; Göttingen: Vandenhoeck & Ruprecht, 1921; 2nd edn, 1931; 6th edn, 1957; ET *History of the Synoptic Tradition* [trans. J. Marsh; Oxford: Basil Blackwell, 1963; 2nd edn, 1968]), which will be discussed especially in Chapter 2, his *Theologie des Neuen Testaments* (Tübingen: Mohr Siebeck, 1948; 7th edn ed. O. Merk, 1977; ET *Theology of the New Testament* [2 vols.; trans. K. Grobel; London: SCM Press; New York: Charles Scribner's Sons, 1951, 1955]), and his *Das Evangelium des Johannes* (MeyerK; Göttingen: Vandenhoeck & Rup-recht, 1947; 2nd edn, 1964; supplement 1966; ET *The Gospel of John: A Com-mentary* [trans. G.R. Beasley-Murray; Oxford: Basil Blackwell, 1971]), among many others, some of which are treated in this volume.

That is what I concentrate upon in Part 1 of this study. The survey is not meant to be more than a thumbnail sketch of the history of research. Recent research into the historical Jesus has begun to speak more intensively about a 'third quest'. This follows on from two previous ones, the first in the nineteenth century and into the beginning of the twentieth, and the second beginning in the 1950s, with an intervening period in which the quest was said to be non-existent, or at least stagnant. I begin with discussion of what it means when certain scholars invoke this 'third quest' as defining their interpretive task, especially in terms of the criteria that they use for establishing the authenticity of sayings of Jesus. This initial analysis leads me to survey briefly the history of historical-Jesus research. I end up questioning the entire system of characterizing and labelling the various quests as distinctive periods in historical-Jesus research, in the light of the range of research represented over the last 100 or so years (Chapter 1). I then attempt to isolate and define the major criteria for authenticity, and their relationship to the development of New Testament form criticism in the first half of the twentieth century, as well as redaction criticism in the second half (Chapter 2). As might be expected, it is in Chapter 2 that the criterion of Semitic (Aramaic) language and Palestinian environment is briefly scrutinized. Many scholars have examined the history of discussion of historical-Jesus research, and even more scholars have written firmly within the various supposed epochs of the several quests. Far fewer, it turns out, have been as concerned with the criteria for authenticity, at least until very recently. Two especially noteworthy major recent attempts—one by an American scholar, John Meier, and the other by a German scholar, Gerd Theissen (with compatriots)[6]—to define and re-define these criteria have been made. They merit special attention, if for no other reason than to see that not as much progress has been made in this discussion as one might have thought or hoped for (Chapter 3).

---

6. Meier, *Marginal Jew*, I, pp. 167-95; G. Theissen, 'Historical Scepticism and the Criteria of Jesus Research *or* My Attempt to Leap across Lessing's Yawning Gulf', *SJT* 49 (1996), pp. 147-76; G. Theissen and A. Merz, *Der historische Jesus: Ein Lehrbuch* (Göttingen: Vandenhoeck & Ruprecht, 1996; ET *The Historical Jesus: A Comprehensive Guide* [trans. J. Bowden; London: SCM Press; Minneapolis: Fortress Press, 1998]), esp. pp. 115-18; G. Theissen and D. Winter, *Die Kriterienfrage in der Jesusforschung: Vom Differenzkriterium zum Plausibilitätskriterium* (NTOA, 34; Freiburg: Universitätsverlag; Göttingen: Vandenhoeck & Ruprecht, 1997), esp. pp. 175-232.

As a result of the tracing of this historical background into the quests for the historical Jesus especially in terms of the criteria for authenticity, several shortcomings in method emerge. Although several volumes could easily be written to address these issues, I choose instead to focus upon discussion of criteria related to matters of language in Jesus research. It may come as a surprise to some that discussion of the issues of Jesus' use of Aramaic, Greek and possibly Hebrew have lagged behind other areas of study regarding the historical Jesus, especially when the so-called Aramaic language hypothesis has been so widely and thoroughly used in New Testament studies for over 100 years.[7] In the last few years, however, there have been several publications that have addressed many of these issues, often from differing and even conflicting standpoints. I must confess that much of my interest in historical-Jesus research stems from work on the use of Greek in Palestine and surrounding areas in the first century. This has raised the eyebrows of at least one contemporary scholar, whose response to some of my work I analyse in the second part of this study. In the second part of this volume, I scrutinize some of this recent work on the language of Jesus as a prelude to developing several new criteria that attempt to address some of these issues and to move forward discussion of the criteria.

These three criteria have been labelled below as the criterion of Greek language and its context (Chapter 4), the criterion of textual variance (Chapter 5), and the criterion of discourse features (Chapter 6). The criterion of Greek language and its context reiterates and, I hope, expands and contextualizes work by myself and others on the Greek of the New Testament, and possibly of Jesus, and integrates it into discussion of questions of authenticity with regard to the sayings of the historical Jesus. Discussion of the possible use of Greek by Jesus is an area that was once a fruitful domain of scholarly interest, but has in recent years been greatly overshadowed by the pursuit of Aramaic language studies. This section attempts to begin to redress this balance, not by excluding

---

7.   One cannot help but note that my article on language is the only one in the recent volume that surveys the state of historical-Jesus research: 'Jesus and the Use of Greek in Galilee', in B. Chilton and C.A. Evans (eds.), *Studying the Historical Jesus: Evaluations of the State of Current Research* (NTTS, 19; Leiden: E.J. Brill, 1994), pp. 123-54. I am currently working on a volume, *The Language of Jesus and his Contemporaries* (SHJ; Grand Rapids: Eerdmans, in preparation), which will survey the multilingualism of Palestine in the first century, providing reference to and examples of numerous primary texts.

discussion of Aramaic as a language of Jesus, but by attempting to factor his possible use of Greek into the equation. The criterion of textual variance is a modification and expansion of recent work by myself and a colleague on textual variants in the words of Jesus.[8] Again, although much historical-Jesus research is concerned with determining what Jesus may have said or whether he said something that approximates what is recorded in the Gospels (the so-called *ipsissima vox*)—and this often suffices as 'authentic' Jesus material[9]—little of it is concerned with the actual wording that he may have used (the *ipsissima verba*) (since it is maintained by many of these scholars that the words were uttered in Aramaic, but are now found in Greek Gospels). In many instances, this wording, as now recorded in the Gospels, evidences variation in the textual tradition. This criterion begins from this recognition and attempts to construct a criterion that will appreciate the similarities and differences in the Greek textual tradition of the words of Jesus. The third criterion attempts to transform a major area of recent scholarly research, discourse analysis or textlinguistics,[10] into a usable tool for historical-Jesus research. One must be careful in attempting such integration, because a new or un(der)-utilized method runs the risk of alienating potential users by its introduction of strange or technical vocabulary,[11] as well

8. My colleague, Matthew Brook O'Donnell, and I have written 'The Implications of Textual Variants for Authenticating the Words of Jesus', in B. Chilton and C.A. Evans (eds.), *Authenticating the Words of Jesus* (NTTS, 28.1; Leiden: E.J. Brill, 1998), pp. 97-133; cf. also our 'The Implications of Textual Variants for Authenticating the Activities of Jesus', in B. Chilton and C.A. Evans (eds.), *Authenticating the Activities of Jesus* (NTTS, 28.2; Leiden: E.J. Brill, 1998), pp. 121-51.

9. Theissen and Winter, *Die Kriterienfrage in der Jesusforschung*, p. 201.

10. The literature in this field is growing immensely, including work that is applying it to New Testament studies. Some of these works are noted in Chapter 6. For an introductory survey of the topic from a New Testament perspective, see S.E. Porter, 'Discourse Analysis and New Testament Studies: An Introductory Survey', in S.E. Porter and D.A. Carson (eds.), *Discourse Analysis and Other Topics in Biblical Greek* (JSNTSup, 113; SNTG, 2; Sheffield: JSOT Press, 1995), pp. 14-35.

11. There is a regrettable tendency among New Testament scholars to shun the use of technical vocabulary from other disciplines. This strikes me as strange for several reasons. The first is that New Testament studies itself certainly has its own technical vocabulary, including the use of words from a variety of languages (e.g. note even in English-language scholarship the contrast made between *Geschichte* and *Historie*, the numerous *geschichtliches* that we throw around, and the ever-useful *Sitz im Leben*). The second is that the learning of technical vocabulary must surely be a matter of the will, rather than one of inherent difficulty. Today, virtually

as by appearing to utilize data that are not accessible or recognized by all within the field. I have attempted to avoid these problems by defining all relevant terms and utilizing data gathered by previous scholars who have been engaged in compatible and related, though fundamentally different, research. In each of these three chapters of Part 2, I attempt to develop a criterion that can stand independently of others, yet that is compatible in its formulation and utilization with the widely recognized criteria discussed in the first part of this study. My hope is that, by the suggestion and preliminary development of these criteria, there can be an opening up of discussion of the whole realm of criteria that are often invoked in historical-Jesus research.

Several further methodological points must also be mentioned here. This study functions within the boundaries of much, if not most, conventional historical-Jesus research, as it is currently being practised. In other words, I do not raise for serious discussion, although I do mention in passing, the kinds of issues that are suggested by Luke Johnson and others in their recent work on how the Jesus of the Church relates to the Jesus of the Gospels and the supposed historical Jesus.[12] Many have acknowledged the strength of the arguments that Johnson has put forward, but without wishing to concede the nature of their more narrowly confined historical task.[13] The result in many circles has been to con-

every schoolchild has a mastery of a great deal of technical vocabulary regarding computers that would have been completely alien even a decade ago (and is still alien to many of these children's parents!). The third is that technical vocabulary is simply a necessary part of any discipline, and reflects one's knowledge of it. D.A. Black has recently noted the irony of the situation if one were to take an automobile to a mechanic and the mechanic were not to have technical names for the parts, but to point and call them 'whatchamacallits', 'doodads', 'thingamabobs', 'doohickeys' or 'gizmos' (*It's Still Greek to Me: An Easy-to-Understand Guide to Intermediate Greek* [Grand Rapids: Baker Book House, 1998], p. 19). Few would want to take a car to such a mechanic.

12. L.T. Johnson, *The Real Jesus: The Misguided Quest for the Historical Jesus and the Truth of the Traditional Gospels* (San Francisco: HarperCollins, 1996); cf. H. Schwarz, *Christology* (Grand Rapids: Eerdmans, 1998). An insightful set of reviews of Johnson's book, with Johnson's and others' responses, is found in *BBR* 7 (1997), pp. 225-57. Cf. also R. Morgan, 'The Historical Jesus and the Theology of the New Testament', in L.D. Hurst and N.T. Wright (eds.), *The Glory of Christ in the New Testament: Studies in Christology* (Festschrift G.B. Caird; Oxford: Clarendon Press, 1987), pp. 187-206.

13. See, e.g., B. Chilton and C.A. Evans, *Jesus in Context: Temple, Purity, and Restoration* (AGJU, 39; Leiden: E.J. Brill, 1997), p. 1 n. 1.

tinue historical-Jesus research in virtually the same mode and vein as before. This is not the place to discuss these issues, but it seems to me that if Johnson is right—and some scholars wish to acknowledge that much of what he says is along the right lines, while continuing their work unaltered—then business cannot continue as usual. This volume takes as a working assumption the methods of historical-Jesus research as currently practised, bracketing out the question for the time being of the validity of this assumption. It is also worth noting that much, though certainly not all, of the recent discussion of the criteria for authenticity in historical-Jesus research has been developed in North America. As a result, I tend to concentrate upon the secondary literature in English, without, I hope, neglecting much of importance in other language traditions. Any attempt at a thorough or complete survey of the available literature on this topic would result in a much, much larger book, but one that would not, I hope, result in significantly different results. With such a wealth of material available, I have nevertheless had to be highly selective. It may not appear that I have been so, when the size of the annotations are considered. But much of the popular-level writing has been excluded from the analysis, unless there is an important reason for including it, such as its containing a discussion not found elsewhere, or having a provenness that can only come through years of use by subsequent scholars.

The study of the historical Jesus is clearly one that has interested many scholars for much of this past century, and more. One of the surprising results of my investigation is how, in some ways, much of that study, at least in so far as criteria for authenticity are concerned, has not moved forward at the same pace as other dimensions of the research, or as other areas of New Testament studies as a whole. My hope is that my survey of this research will provide some impetus for opening up this discussion once again. However, a more important goal is to inject some new life into the discussion by taking a different approach altogether than has usually been taken. I attempt to do this by discussing the possible use of Greek by Jesus as providing a new set of criteria for discussing the authenticity of certain of his sayings. This is very much a work in progress, for which I assert very few, if any, final conclusions, but which I hope will prompt others to enter the discussion and debate.

Part I

PREVIOUS DISCUSSION

Chapter 1

THE 'THIRD QUEST' FOR THE HISTORICAL JESUS
AND THE CRITERIA FOR AUTHENTICITY

1. *Introduction*

In his lengthy supplementary chapter to Stephen Neill's classic work on interpretation of the New Testament, originally published in 1964 and revised and expanded for publication in 1988, Tom Wright labels what he sees as the latest developments in historical-Jesus research as a 'third quest'.[1] When Neill wrote the first edition of the book 25 years earlier, Jesus research, Wright says, was just getting under way, but now, fortified by Jewish material and using historical methods, 'This movement of scholarship has become so pronounced that it is not fanciful to talk in terms of a "Third Quest"'.[2] One scholar goes so far as to say recently that 'The twentieth century will be remembered for two world wars, but in New Testament studies for no less than three quests of the historical Jesus'.[3] The comment by Wright, subject to numerous qualifications (and hyperbolically characterized by Rosner), as will be shown below, appears to be the earliest reference in the secondary scholarly literature to a 'third quest' of the historical Jesus, following on from a previous two quests.[4] A label such as this might not, at first glance, appear to be that significant, and far from determinative for the course of a disci-

---

1. S. Neill and T. Wright, *The Interpretation of the New Testament 1861–1986* (Oxford: Oxford University Press, 2nd edn, 1988 [1964]), pp. 379-403.

2. Neill and Wright, *Interpretation of the New Testament*, p. 379.

3. B.S. Rosner, 'Looking Back on the 20th Century 1. New Testament Studies', *ExpTim* 110 (1999), pp. 316-20 (317).

4. Contra M.A. Powell, *Jesus as a Figure in History: How Modern Historians View the Man from Galilee* (Louisville, KY: Westminster/John Knox Press, 1998), who makes the apparently mistaken statement on p. 22 that 'N.T. Wright coined the term Third Quest in 1992' (in his 'Quest for the Historical Jesus', *ABD* 3 [1992], pp. 796-802).

pline. However, Wright's and others' use of such terminology, as well as the surrounding discourse in which it is embedded, implies a number of issues regarding the previous history of discussion of Jesus, and what Wright sees as the course to pursue for further work regarding this supposed 'third quest'. Since the term 'third quest' appears to be Wright's, I will concentrate below on his arguments for the appropriateness of this label, after turning to related issues of importance regarding the other quests for the historical Jesus raised by such analysis.

This is not the place to offer a full and complete history of the development of historical-Jesus research. Numerous accounts, with varying amounts of detail, are readily available elsewhere, with more of them being written all the time as this topic continues to capture the imagination of scholars and others alike.[5] What I wish to present here in this chapter is a basic summary of what seem to me to be the fundamental trends and movements in previous historical-Jesus research, which will enable me to develop the context necessary for this monograph (see the Excursus at the end of this chapter, for an encapsulation of what is described in the discourse of this chapter).[6] In other words, I wish briefly

5.   Throughout this volume, I am deeply indebted to the useful bibliography of C.A. Evans, *Life of Jesus Research: An Annotated Bibliography* (NTTS, 24; Leiden: E.J. Brill, rev. edn, 1996); cf. also *idem*, *Jesus* (IBR Bibliographies, 5; Grand Rapids: Baker Book House, 1992), for a shorter form of much the same bibliography. The larger bibliography surveys the material both by historical periods and by topics, enabling ready access to discussion from a number of perspectives. Although there is a fairly significant amount of duplication in the entries especially between the two major sections, his entries total over 2000—even then he is not comprehensive, since in the course of my research I have come across numerous other sources that probably need to be included in such a tool. Other useful volumes are J. Reumann, *Jesus in the Church's Gospels: Modern Scholarship and the Earliest Sources* (Philadelphia: Fortress Press, 1968; London: SPCK, 1970), esp. pp. 492-513; and *idem*, 'Jesus and Christology', in E.J. Epp and G.W. MacRae (eds.), *The New Testament and its Modern Interpreters* (The Bible and its Modern Interpreters; Atlanta: Scholars Press, 1989), pp. 501-64, esp. pp. 525-64 for bibliography; and W.G. Kümmel, *Dreissig Jahre Jesusforschung (1950–80)* (BBB, 60; ed. H. Merklein; Bonn: Hanstein, 1985); and for the years since, *idem*, 'Jesusforschung seit 1981', *TRu* 53 (1988), pp. 229-49; 54 (1989), pp. 1-53; 55 (1990), pp. 21-45; 56 (1991), pp. 27-53, 391-420. For selections from many of the major writers on the topic up to the 1960s, see the useful collection of H.K. McArthur (ed.), *In Search of the Historical Jesus* (New York: Charles Scribner's Sons, 1969); and the representative articles in C.A. Evans and S.E. Porter (eds.), *The Historical Jesus: A Sheffield Reader* (BibSem, 33; Sheffield: Sheffield Academic Press, 1995).

to show how it is that historical-Jesus research has progressed in order to arrive at the place that it is today. I will concentrate on a few of the basic facts and trends, as a necessary prelude to making new proposals for its further development, especially in the area of criteria for authen-

6.   Accounts of the history of discussion of the various so-called quests for the historical Jesus are almost as plentiful as the reconstructed lives or portions of lives of Jesus himself. Attempts include those of N.A. Dahl, 'Der historische Jesus als geschichtswissenschaftliches und theologisches Problem', *KD* 1 (1955), pp. 104-32; ET 'The Problem of the Historical Jesus', in C.E. Braaten and R.A. Harrisville (eds.), *Kerygma and History: A Symposium on the Theology of Rudolf Bultmann* (Nashville: Abingdon Press, 1962), pp. 138-71; repr. in N.A. Dahl, *The Crucified Messiah and Other Essays* (Minneapolis: Augsburg, 1974), pp. 48-89, 173-74, esp. pp. 50-63; H.G. Wood, *Jesus in the Twentieth Century* (London: Lutterworth, 1960), pp. 62-151; Neill and Wright, *Interpretation of the New Testament*, pp. 252-312; E. Trocmé, *Jésus de Nazareth vu par les témoins de sa vie* (Neuchâtel: Delachaux & Niestlé, 1972; ET *Jesus and his Contemporaries* [trans. R.A. Wilson; London: SCM Press, 1973]), pp. 1-13; J. Roloff, 'Auf der Suche nach einem neuen Jesusbild: Tendenzen und Aspekte der gegenwärtigen Diskussion', *TLZ* 98 (1973), cols. 561-72; I.H. Marshall, *I Believe in the Historical Jesus* (Grand Rapids: Eerdmans, 1977), pp. 109-142; B.F. Meyer, *The Aims of Jesus* (London: SCM Press, 1979), pp. 25-59; R. Morgan with J. Barton, *Biblical Interpretation* (OBS; Oxford: Oxford University Press, 1988), pp. 62-132 *passim*; Reumann, 'Jesus and Christology', esp. pp. 501-508; C. Brown, 'Historical Jesus, Quest of', in J.B. Green, S. McKnight and I.H. Marshall (eds.), *Dictionary of Jesus and the Gospels* (Downers Grove, IL: InterVarsity Press, 1992), pp. 326-41 (whose perspective perhaps comes the closest to the one at which I have arrived); J.K. Riches, *A Century of New Testament Study* (Cambridge: Lutterworth, 1993), esp. pp. 1-69, 89-124; B. Witherington, *The Jesus Quest: The Third Search for the Jew of Nazareth* (Downers Grove, IL: InterVarsity Press, 1995), esp. pp. 9-13; G. Theissen and D. Winter, *Die Kriterienfrage in der Jesusforschung: Vom Differenzkriterium zum Plausibilitätskriterium* (NTOA, 34; Freiburg: Universitätsverlag; Göttingen: Vandenhoeck & Ruprecht, 1997), pp. 1-8; Powell, *Jesus as a Figure in History*, esp. pp. 12-23; and two fine summaries and studies: C.J. den Heyer, *Wie is Jezus? Balans van 150 jaar onderzoek naar Jesus* (Zoetermeer, The Netherlands: Uitgeverij Meinema, 1996; ET *Jesus Matters: 150 Years of Research* [trans. J. Bowden: London: SCM Press, 1996]) and H. Schwarz, *Christology* (Grand Rapids: Eerdmans, 1998), pp. 7-71. Cf. also the selective but insightful treatments of W.R. Telford, 'Major Trends and Interpretive Issues in the Study of Jesus', in B. Chilton and C.A. Evans (eds.), *Studying the Historical Jesus: Evaluations of the State of Current Research* (NTTS, 19; Leiden: E.J. Brill, 1994), pp. 33-74, esp. pp. 55-61; and C.A. Evans, 'The Historical Jesus and Christian Faith: A Critical Assessment of a Scholarly Problem', *CSR* 18 (1988), pp. 48-63; *idem, Jesus and his Contemporaries: Comparative Studies* (AGJU, 25; Leiden: E.J. Brill, 1995), pp. 1-13. On some of the earlier figures in this discussion, see J.C.

ticity. In the course of my research, I have arrived at what appears to me to be a different perspective on the course of research than is typically reflected in the scholarly discussion. Nevertheless, I believe that this historical reconstruction is worth offering, because it brings clarity to a number of issues often raised in the course of historical-Jesus research, especially in terms of the development of the criteria for authenticity. This reconstruction also casts some shadows on what are typically seen as clear lines of demarcation in historical-Jesus research. This can only be a portrait drawn in outline, but the rough lines themselves reveal several dimensions that are worth noting and that sometimes get lost in the current debate.

2. *The Quest for the Historical Jesus*

Scholarship today typically, and almost unanimously, claims to find at least three major periods in the quest for the historical Jesus, at least two of these periods often being called quests in their own right.[7] For example, one often finds scenarios in which the 'first quest' or 'old quest' is dated from the late eighteenth century. This 'first' or 'old quest' is typically defined as being concerned with questions regarding such issues as the historical or supernatural elements in the Gospels concerning Jesus, the relation of the Synoptic Gospels to the Gospel of John, the eschatological dimension of Jesus' life and teaching, and the relation of Christology to the historical elements in the Gospel accounts. The so-called 'no quest' period is virtually always tied to Albert Schweitzer's[8] and then Rudolf Bultmann's[9] influence, during which the de-

O'Neill, *The Bible's Authority: A Portrait Gallery of Thinkers from Lessing to Bultmann* (Edinburgh: T. & T. Clark, 1991), *passim*, who discusses Herder, Lessing, Strauss, Kähler, Harnack, Schweitzer and Bultmann, among others.

7.   For a useful dissenting position, comparing the so-called 'first quest' with that of recent work, see S.E. Fowl, 'Reconstructing and Deconstructing the Quest of the Historical Jesus', *SJT* 42 (1989), pp. 319-33, although I do not draw the boundaries in the same way that Fowl does.

8.   A. Schweitzer, *Von Reimarus zu Wrede: Eine Geschichte der Leben-Jesu-Forschung* (Tübingen: Mohr Siebeck, 1906; 2nd edn, 1910; 6th edn, 1951; ET *The Quest of the Historical Jesus: A Critical Study of its Progress from Reimarus to Wrede* [trans. W. Montgomery; London: A. & C. Black, 1910]).

9.   Among many important publications, several of which are discussed below, see R. Bultmann, *Jesus* (Berlin: Deutsche Bibliothek, 1926; 2nd edn, 1934; ET *Jesus and the Word* [trans. L.P. Smith and E. Huntress; New York: Charles Scribner's

velopment of form criticism showed that all of the Gospels are influenced by the later Church, and that a biography of Jesus following nineteenth-century presuppositions is impossible to write. With a famous lecture in 1953 by Ernst Käsemann,[10] the 'second' or 'new quest' of the historical Jesus was supposedly inaugurated, which corresponded to the development of redaction criticism.[11] This brief summary leads to the major question of this chapter—whether we have now entered a 'third quest'. However, this broad summary of the course of historical-Jesus research masks at least as much as it reveals. The actual story of research into the life of Jesus, as evidenced by the history of publication on the topic, indicates that this scenario is only partially true, and that there is much more to be said when the full extent of the evidence is examined. Before we can answer the question of whether we are in a 'third quest', we need to examine the nature of the supposed previous quests, and even ask the question of whether these quests have really existed in quite the way that they are often portrayed. Rather than categorize the history of this debate by periods or quests, however, I will divide the course of debate into chronological periods, which I believe are a more accurate and revealing way to characterize and classify the discussion.

a. *1778–1906*
The so-called 'first' or 'old quest' of the historical Jesus, from the late-eighteenth to the earliest years of the twentieth centuries, is virtually always described as being marked by numerous descriptions of Jesus in terms of the highly romanticized sociopolitical issues of the day, as well as reflecting post-Enlightenment critical scepticism. Thus, some writers of the time were rationalistically optimistic in their treatments

Sons, 1934; London: Ivor Nicholson & Watson, 1935]).

10. E. Käsemann, 'Das Problem des historischen Jesus', *ZTK* 51 (1954), pp. 125-53 (repr. in *idem*, *Exegetische Versuche und Besinnungen*, I [Göttingen: Vandenhoeck & Ruprecht, 2nd edn, 1960], pp. 187-214); ET 'The Problem of the Historical Jesus', in *idem*, *Essays on New Testament Themes* (trans. W.J. Montague; SBT, 41; London: SCM Press, 1964; Philadelphia: Fortress Press, 1982), pp. 15-47.

11. The above discussion paraphrases and adapts the handy scheme presented by Reumann, 'Jesus and Christology', p. 502, which seems to be widely recognized in the discussion.

of the Gospel sources. Scholars such as J.G. Herder and H.E.G. Paulus in their assessments combined rationalism, in particular a desire to explain the miraculous, with a romanticized idealism that one could recover such non-supernatural material from all four of the Gospels.[12] Others during this period, however, practised a form of Jesus research that some might be tempted to disparagingly call pre-critical, but which might be better labelled traditional in its approach, often utilizing harmonization of the Gospel accounts. Accounts of Jesus' life such as those by such major scholars as Alfred Edersheim, Bernhard Weiss and William Sanday, often overlooked in current discussion in an apparent attempt to find a consistent characterization for this so-called 'first quest', represent this approach (among other such writers).[13] An examination of these scholars' works, however, reveals that they are informed of the critical issues of their day, and address these issues in their research, without necessarily agreeing with them or capitulating to their method —and this is perhaps the single most important reason for their neglect in current scholarly discussion.

Those writers of this period, however, who have had the most enduring impact—at least on the scholarly community—responded in more pessimistic ways regarding the Gospels as sources for the life of Jesus.

---

12. See J.G. Herder, *Vom Erlöser der Menschen: Nach unsern drei ersten Evangelien* (Riga: Hartknoch, 1796); *idem, Von Gottes Sohn, der Welt Heiland: Nach Johannes Evangelium* (Riga: Hartknoch, 1797); and H.E.G. Paulus, *Das Leben Jesu, als Grundlage einer reinen Geschichte des Urchristentums* (2 vols.; Heidelberg: Winter, 1828).

13. A. Edersheim, *The Life and Times of Jesus the Messiah* (2 vols.; London: Longmans, Green; New York: Randolph, 1883; 7th edn, 1892), a volume that obviously was popular in its day if the number of editions is any indication; B. Weiss, *Das Leben Jesu* (2 vols.; Berlin: Wilhelm Herz, 1888); W. Sanday, *Outlines of the Life of Christ* (Edinburgh: T. & T. Clark, 1905), an expanded reprint of his 1899 article 'Jesus Christ', in J. Hastings (ed.), *A Dictionary of the Bible* (5 vols.; Edinburgh: T. & T. Clark, 1898–1904), II, pp. 603-53; and his *The Life of Christ in Recent Research* (New York: Oxford University Press, 1907), esp. pp. 37-118, where he critically analyses the work of such German scholars as Schweitzer (see below). It is worth noting the shift in approach from Sanday's earlier to his later work, in the light of Schweitzer, recognizing the influence of German criticism, even though he clearly does not accept many of its conclusions. Riches (*Century of New Testament Study*, p. 27) notes that Sanday is 'sympathetic to Schweitzer' in *Life of Christ in Recent Research*, but he does not note Sanday's earlier work.

This is even though these scholars remained optimistic about writing accounts of the life of Jesus, ones that they often depicted as penetrating to the essence of his being and purpose. A progression in thought can be found among many of the major figures who took this approach. A brief summary of the thrust of their work is instructive to a history of discussion. Hermann Samuel Reimarus is usually seen as instigating modern critical research about Jesus, with the publication of his fragments in 1778 by the philosopher Gotthold Lessing. Reimarus made a distinction between the historical Jesus and the Jesus of the Gospels. Much of the Gospel material, he claimed, was confessional and contradicted the historical facts, and thus hid the fact that Jesus was a political revolutionary.[14] In some ways consistent with but in other ways departing from Reimarus was the work of David Friedrich Strauss. Also responding to forms of the rationalism of his time, he was influenced by Deism. As a result, he subjected the Gospels to critical scrutiny and found that they portrayed a mythological Jesus.[15] Ernest Renan, rejecting supernaturalism altogether, presented an altogether human and in many ways sympathetic Jesus, in some ways mirroring his own personal life.[16] Wilhelm Bousset, the notable history-of-religions scholar,

14. H.S. Reimarus, *Von dem Zwecke Jesu und seiner Jünger: Noch ein Fragment des Wolfenbüttelschen Ungenannten* (Fragment 7; ed. G.E. Lessing; Braunschweig: n.p., 1778; ET *Reimarus: Fragments* [ed. C.H. Talbert; trans. R.S. Fraser; LJ; Philadelphia: Fortress Press, 1970; London: SCM Press, 1971]). This English edition also contains a translation of §§38-40 (pp. 44-57) of D.F. Strauss, *Hermann Samuel Reimarus und seine Schutzschrift für die vernünftigen Verehrer Gottes* [*Hermann Samuel Reimarus and his Apology*] (Bonn: Strauss, 2nd edn, 1877 [1862]), with his own verdict on Reimarus's views, including comments on their being time-bound, somewhat naive, and superseded. One wonders of whom this could not be said, especially 100 years later.

15. D.F. Strauss, *Das Leben Jesu kritisch bearbeitet* (2 vols.; Tübingen: Osiander, 1835–36; 4th edn, 1840; ET *The Life of Jesus, Critically Examined* [3 vols.; trans. G. Eliot; London: Chapman, 1846; repr. Philadelphia: Fortress Press, 1972; London: SCM Press, 1973]). Cf. also D.F. Strauss, *Das Leben Jesu für das deutsche Volk bearbeitet* (Leipzig: Brockhaus, 1864; 3rd edn, 1874; ET *A New Life of Jesus* [London: Williams & Norgate, 1865]); *idem, Der Christus des Glaubens und der Jesus der Geschichte: Eine Kritik des Schleiermacher'schen Lebens Jesu* (Berlin: Duncker, 1865; ET *The Christ of Faith and the Jesus of History: A Critique of Schleiermacher's Life of Jesus* [trans. L.E. Keck; Philadelphia: Fortress Press, 1977]).

16. E. Renan, *La vie de Jésus* (Paris: Lévy, 1863; ET *The Life of Jesus* [London: Trübner, 1864]).

gave his reading of Jesus as a somewhat confused visionary, a figure found in other religious traditions.[17] Although many other scholars and their works of this time could be mentioned,[18] a last work from the close of this period is that of Adolf Harnack, a work said to 'represent the fine flower of this enterprise' of historical-Jesus research.[19] Harnack characterized the teaching of Jesus in terms of romanticized humanistic values. These included such things as the fatherhood of God and the infinite value of the human soul, the commandment of love, and the power of the gospel in relation to a variety of social problems of the day, such as poverty.[20]

Although in later discussion of this so-called 'first quest' the focus is usually upon the work of Reimarus, Strauss and Renan, the above brief survey shows that there are many other works from the period worth considering as well. Some of this work followed the tradition of Reimarus, Strauss and Renan, with its sceptical and rationalistic approach, but some of this research did not attempt to distance itself from the tradition of the Church, a feature that characterized many of these more sceptical studies. Besides that, there is a considerable amount of diversity even in the approaches of Reimarus, Strauss and Renan, as noted above. In many ways, the work of Harnack is as descriptive of the highly critical scholarly nineteenth-century approach as is to be found, and as pivotal in the history of discussion as any other single work. This is especially worth noting, since it comes from a scholar whose work in many ways, especially on the development of Christianity, has

17. W. Bousset, *Jesus* (Halle: Gebauer-Schwetschke, 1904; 3rd edn, Tübingen: Mohr Siebeck, 3rd edn, 1907; ET *Jesus* [CThL; trans. J.P. Trevelyan; London: Williams & Norgate; New York: Putnam's Sons, 1906]); cf. *idem*, *Kyrios Christos: Geschichte des Christusglaubens von den Anfängen des Christentums bis Irenaeus* (FRLANT, 4; Göttingen: Vandenhoeck & Ruprecht, 1913; 5th edn, 1964; ET *Kyrios Christos: A History of the Belief in Christ from the Beginnings of Christianity to Irenaeus* [trans. J.E. Steely; Nashville: Abingdon Press, 1970]).

18. See Evans, *Life of Jesus Research*, pp. 16-19, 251-55.

19. R.H. Fuller, *The New Testament in Current Study: Some Trends in the Years 1941–1962* (New York: Charles Scribner's Sons, 1962; London: SCM Press, rev. edn, 1963), p. 34.

20. A. Harnack, *Das Wesen des Christentums* (Leipzig: J.C. Hinrichs, 1900; ET *What is Christianity?* [trans. T.B. Saunders; CThL; London: Williams & Norgate; New York: Putnam's Sons, 1900; 3rd edn, 1904]).

continued to have importance for contemporary New Testament scholarship to a proportion not often found for scholars of this era.[21] Although later scholarship has called this the 'first' or 'old quest' of the historical Jesus, and many of the most well-known works did have certain anti-supernaturalist presuppositions in common, there is also a surprising amount of diversity as well, with some of it not sharing in such negative presuppositions.

b. *1906–1953*

The purported demise of the so-called 'first quest' for the historical Jesus is typically attributed to the work of Albert Schweitzer and, to a lesser and later extent, of Rudolf Bultmann.[22] It is true that Schweitzer had a major role to play in the re-thinking of the validity of the quest that was based on a highly romanticized world-view. However, the picture is far more complex even than that. In many ways, it appears to be the case that all that was really brought to an end by Schweitzer and others was quests that remained optimistic of writing romanticized and overly psychologized lives of Jesus along anti-supernatural lines (and usually in German). Attempts to write lives of Jesus along more tradi-

---

21. This is not the place to chronicle Harnack's contribution to modern New Testament scholarship, except to note the continuing importance of such a work as his *Mission und Ausbreitung des Christentums in den ersten drei Jahrhunderten* (Leipzig: J.C. Hinrichs, 1902; 4th edn, 1924; ET *The Mission and Expansion of Christianity in the First Three Centuries* [TTL; trans. J. Moffatt; 2 vols.; London: Williams & Norgate; New York: Putnam's Sons, 1908]), as well as his volumes on Luke–Acts: *Lukas der Arzt: Der Verfasser des dritten Evangeliums und der Apostelgeschichte* (BENT, 1; Leipzig: Hinrichs, 1906; ET *Luke the Physician: The Author of the Third Gospel and the Acts of the Apostles* [CThL; trans. J.R. Wilkinson; London: Williams & Norgate; New York: Putnam, 1907]), *Die Apostelgeschichte* (BENT, 3; Leipzig: J.C. Hinrichs, 1908; ET *The Acts of the Apostles* [CThL; trans. J.R. Wilkinson; London: Williams & Norgate; New York: Putnam's Sons, 1909]), and *Zur Apostelgeschichte und zur Abfassungszeit der synoptischen Evangelien* (BENT, 4; Leipzig: J.C. Hinrichs, 1911; ET *The Date of the Acts and of the Synoptic Gospels* [CThL; London: Williams & Norgate; New York: Putnam's Sons, 1911]).

22. For a selective, yet balanced view of this period of Jesus research, see Riches, *Century of New Testament Study*, pp. 14-30. W.P. Weaver's *The Historical Jesus in the Twentieth Century: 1900–1950* (Harrisburg, PA: Trinity Press International, 1999) arrived too late for my consideration.

tional historical lines do not appear to have been curtailed, only made more aware of the critical issues involved in such attempts, critical issues usually directly addressed in such treatments.

Even for those scholars of the so-called first optimistic and romanticized quest—if many of the diverse scholars mentioned above can be conveniently lumped together for the purposes of discussion and critique—their efforts were brought to an end by a confluence of criticism of such attempts. Not all of the criticism brought against the romanticized quests was similarly conceived or addressed the same issues, since much of it emerged over the course of about 15 or 20 years. Thus, Martin Kähler, writing 15 years before Schweitzer, observed what he saw as the discrepancy between nineteenth-century historical reconstructions of Jesus and the Church's theological confession. As a result, he argued that a biography could not be written of Jesus on the basis of the information available. In fact, he called 'the entire Life-of-Jesus movement' (as the 'first quest' came to be characterized) a 'blind alley'.[23] Pursuing a different line of thought, Johannes Weiss rejected the social basis for analysing Jesus' preaching, and claimed that Jesus preached an eschatological message, in which God's kingdom was expected as imminent.[24] Weiss's eschatological position had a major impact upon contemporary and subsequent scholarship, which has continued to debate the nature of the kingdom of God and the relation of Jesus' teaching to it.[25] William Wrede concurred in seeing Jesus as a

23. M. Kähler, *Der sogenannte historische Jesus und der geschichtliche, biblische Christus* (Leipzig: Deichert, 1892; 2nd edn, 1896; repr. Theologische Bücherei, 2; Munich: Chr. Kaiser Verlag, 1956; ET *The So-Called Historical Jesus and the Historic, Biblical Christ* [trans. C.E. Braaten; Philadelphia: Fortress Press, 1964]), esp. pp. 46-71 (46).

24. J. Weiss, *Die Predigt Jesu vom Reiche Gottes* (Göttingen: Vandenhoeck & Ruprecht, 1892; 2nd edn, 1900; ET *Jesus' Proclamation of the Kingdom of God* [trans. R.H. Hiers and D.L. Holland; LJ; Philadelphia: Fortress Press; London: SCM Press, 1971]).

25. The amount of secondary literature on the debate over the nature of the kingdom, especially in its temporal dimension and its relation to the proclamation of Jesus, is immense, and cannot be cited here. To be noted, however, is how this discussion has continued throughout the century, regardless of the so-called 'quest' of the historical Jesus of the time. For a history of discussion, see W. Willis (ed.), *The Kingdom of God in 20th-Century Interpretation* (Peabody, MA: Hendrickson, 1987); and B. Chilton, 'The Kingdom of God in Recent Discussion', in Chilton and Evans (eds.), *Studying the Historical Jesus*, pp. 255-80. Among the most informative and

teacher, but also as a healer and exorcist, not as a messianic claimant.[26] The most devastating and damaging blow to the 'first quest' was indeed delivered by the great polymath Albert Schweitzer. As we have just seen, however, many of Schweitzer's ideas had already been anticipated by others. Much of the strength of his critique was instead provided by his thorough, comprehensive and enthusiastic analysis of much of the previous historical-Jesus research (at least that in the German-speaking world, with reference to some work in French),[27] categorizing and then moving through many of the most important writers on the topic.[28] In some respects Schweitzer's most lasting comment is his noting that the characterizations of Jesus often had an uncanny ability to look much

significant studies, besides those of Weiss and Schweitzer (see below), see C.H. Dodd, *The Parables of the Kingdom* (London: Nisbet, 1935; New York: Charles Scribner's Sons, rev. edn, 1961), pp. 21-59 (on pp. 28-30 he makes his classic mistake regarding the verb φθάνω); W.G. Kümmel, *Verheissung und Erfüllung* (Zürich: Zwingli-Verlag, 1956; ET *Promise and Fulfilment: The Eschatological Message of Jesus* [trans. D.M. Barton; London: SCM Press, 1957]); R. Schnackenburg, *Gottes Herrschaft und Reich* (Freiburg: Herder, 1963; 4th edn, 1965; ET *God's Rule and Kingdom* [trans. J. Murray; London: Burns & Oates, 1963; 2nd edn, 1968]); N. Perrin, *The Kingdom of God in the Teaching of Jesus* (London: SCM Press, 1963); G.E. Ladd, *Jesus and the Kingdom: The Eschatology of Biblical Realism* (Grand Rapids: Eerdmans, 1964; London: SPCK, 1966); G.R. Beasley-Murray, *Jesus and the Kingdom of God* (Grand Rapids: Eerdmans; Exeter: Paternoster Press, 1986); B. Chilton, *Pure Kingdom: Jesus' Vision of God* (SHJ; Grand Rapids: Eerdmans; London: SPCK, 1996); and S. McKnight, *A New Vision for Israel: The Teachings of Jesus in National Context* (SHJ; Grand Rapids: Eerdmans, 1999), pp. 70-155. For a sample of shorter studies, see B. Chilton (ed.), *The Kingdom of God in the Teaching of Jesus* (IRT, 5; Philadelphia: Fortress Press; London: SPCK, 1984).

26. W. Wrede, *Das Messiasgeheimnis in den Evangelien: Zugleich ein Beitrag zum Verständnis des Markusevangeliums* (Göttingen: Vandenhoeck & Ruprecht, 1901; ET *The Messianic Secret* [trans. J.C.G. Greig; Cambridge: J. Clarke, 1971]).

27. See Brown, 'Historical Jesus, Quest of', p. 332.

28. At the time, Schweitzer's work was characterized by Sanday (*Life of Christ in Recent Research*, p. 45) as 'one-sided, but he glories in his one-sidedness. He takes the line that only by the pursuit of a relentless logic is it possible to arrive at the truth. His own logic is relentless, and he does at least succeed in presenting that side of the truth which he wishes to bring out in a very vivid and impressive manner.'

like the characterizers.[29] It is perhaps worth noting that, in many ways, Schweitzer was also a part of the very quest that he so categorically dismissed. Previous to his critique of the movement, he had put forward his own view of Jesus as a thoroughgoing or proleptic, but nevertheless thwarted, eschatologist, with his beliefs rooted in Jewish apocalypticism.[30] In one sense, Schweitzer's own critique was as applicable to his own work as to that of others, although he did not seem to realize this. In another sense, as Brown states, Schweitzer 'presented a massive critique of the views of the theological establishment, set out in such a way as to show that all paths but Schweitzer's proved to be dead ends'.[31] Nevertheless, even though Kähler had already declared the previous attempts a blind alley and Weiss led the way in suggesting the eschatological viewpoint, it was Schweitzer's thorough and complete dismissal of the previous research and his grounding of eschatology in Jewish apocalypticism that has come to be identified with this position, and much of the research on the historical Jesus in the first half of the twentieth century.

The influence on subsequent scholarship of such critical study in the early years of the twentieth century, however, was far more complex

---

29. Schweitzer, *Quest of the Historical Jesus*, esp. pp. 396-401.

30. See A. Schweitzer, *Das Messianitäts- und Leidensgeheimnis: Eine Skizze des Lebens Jesu* (Tübingen: Mohr Siebeck, 1901; 3rd edn, 1956; ET *The Mystery of the Kingdom of God: The Secret of Jesus' Messiahship and Passion* [trans. W. Lowrie; London: A. & C. Black, 1925]). This proleptic eschatology has even been discussed as providing a criterion for authenticity of the words of Jesus (see R.N. Longenecker, 'Literary Criteria in Life of Jesus Research: An Evaluation and Proposal', in G.F. Hawthorne [ed.], *Current Issues in Biblical and Patristic Interpretation* [Festschrift M.C. Tenney; Grand Rapids: Eerdmans, 1975], pp. 217-29, esp. p. 220; S. McKnight, *Interpreting the Synoptic Gospels* [Guides to New Testament Exegesis; Grand Rapids: Baker Book House, 1988], pp. 61-62; Evans, *Life of Jesus Research*, pp. 144-46). For a highly critical assessment of Schweitzer's influence in this regard, see T.F. Glasson, 'Schweitzer's Influence: Blessing or Bane?', *JTS* NS 28 (1977), pp. 289-302; repr. in Chilton (ed.), *The Kingdom of God in the Teaching of Jesus*, pp. 107-20. In many ways Glasson has been Schweitzer's biggest critic, although many of Glasson's works remain neglected. See also T.F. Glasson, *The Second Advent: The Origin of the New Testament Doctrine* (London: Epworth Press, 1945; 2nd edn, 1947); *idem, His Appearing and his Kingdom: The Christian Hope in the Light of its History* (London: Epworth Press, 1953); *idem, Greek Influence in Jewish Eschatology* (London: SPCK, 1961).

31. Brown, 'Historical Jesus, Quest of', p. 332.

than is often apparently realized and certainly as often depicted.[32] Rather than following a single cause, the ensuing scholarly research was clearly bifurcated, with some scholars accepting the demise of the nineteenth-century quest for the historical Jesus (so-called Life-of-Jesus research), but with many others rejecting such a pessimistic end to all such research and continuing to engage in it. Thus, Walker baldly states, 'And of course, there are many who have never abandoned the old quest'.[33] A significant number of scholars, especially in English-speaking circles, continued to believe that knowledge of the historical Jesus could, through proper critical means, be found in the Gospels, perhaps at least in part because Schweitzer's critique had not been directed at English-language scholarship on Jesus. This English-language work was in several respects a direct continuation of the approach of Sanday already mentioned above.[34] Sanday wrote both before and after the work of Schweitzer, taking into account Schweitzer's perspective, but continuing to engage in critical study of the life of Jesus, even if he and other scholars did not as optimistically believe one could write the same kinds of Life of Jesus argued for in the nineteenth century.[35] This major trend continued to varying degrees throughout the entire twentieth century, and should not be neglected in any truly critical study of the period (see below on the 'new quest' for the historical Jesus). Many of the scholars who wrote about Jesus during this period continue to be influential in other areas of New Testament scholarship, as well as in other areas of study of the Gospels, with a few even playing crucial roles in historical-Jesus research, such as the development of criteria for authenticity, as subsequent discussion below will show. Scholars such as A.C. Headlam, F.C. Burkitt, William Manson, A.M. Hunter, and Vincent Taylor, among others, continued to write what amounted to critical lives of Jesus, usually following a harmonistic and chronologically based format.[36] This means of investigating and writing about the life of Jesus

32. See Trocmé, *Jesus and his Contemporaries*, pp. 1-2.

33. W.O. Walker, 'The Quest for the Historical Jesus: A Discussion of Methodology', *ATR* 51 (1969), pp. 38-56 (52); cf. also Brown, 'Historical Jesus, Quest of', pp. 334-35.

34. As noted above, Sanday's earlier work appeared in 1899, and was reprinted in book form in 1905, both before Schweitzer's work appeared, and his third appeared in 1907, directly responding to Schweitzer.

35. See Theissen and Winter, *Die Kriterienfrage in der Jesusforschung*, p. 5.

36. See A.C. Headlam, *The Life and Teaching of Jesus the Christ* (London: John

was far from being confined to English scholars, however. The French scholars, M.-J. Lagrange and F.-M. Braun, also worked in this vein,[37] as did the American scholars, A.T. Robertson and E.J. Goodspeed,[38] and the Jewish scholar J. Klausner.[39] It is all too easy to dismiss such studies as anachronistic, and they are for the most part now ignored in much current discussion of historical-Jesus research. This is perhaps because they are seen to utilize what many consider an outmoded historical method. This method relies upon the Gospels as the primary sources for the life of Jesus, even if they are used critically, rather than rigorously applying the canons of higher criticism, and especially of form criticism, which was developing at much the same time. Or perhaps it is because they do not conveniently fit within the concise divisions of the quests for the historical Jesus into a number of neatly labelled categories. An examination of the better examples of these works on Jesus, however, shows that these scholars were well aware of the critical issues

Murray, 1923; 2nd edn, 1927); F.C. Burkitt, *Jesus Christ: An Historical Outline* (London: Blackie, 1932); W. Manson, *Jesus the Messiah: The Synoptic Tradition of the Revelation of God in Christ with Special Reference to Form-Criticism* (London: Hodder & Stoughton, 1943; Philadelphia: Westminster Press, 1946); A.M. Hunter, *The Work and Words of Jesus* (Philadelphia: Westminster Press, 1950; London: SCM Press, 1951); and V. Taylor, *The Work and Words of Jesus* (London: Macmillan, 1950); *idem, The Life and Ministry of Jesus* (London: Macmillan, 1954; Nashville: Abingdon Press, 1955); cf. *idem, Jesus and his Sacrifice: A Study of the Passion-Sayings in the Gospels* (London: Macmillan, 1937). See also G. Ogg, *The Chronology of the Public Ministry of Jesus* (Cambridge: Cambridge University Press, 1940), who obviously believes that reliable facts can be gleaned about the life of Jesus from the Gospels, since he uses them to write a chronology.

37. M.-J. Lagrange, *L'évangile de Jésus-Christ* (Paris: J. Gabalda, 1928; ET *The Gospel of Jesus Christ* [2 vols.; London: Burns, Oates & Washbourne, 1938]); F.M. Braun, *Jésus: Histoire et critique* (Tournai: Casterman, 1947). Cf. also H. Daniel-Rops, *Jésus en son temps* (Paris: Fayard, 1945; ET *Jesus in his Time* [trans. R.W. Millar; London: Eyre & Spottiswoode, 1955; 2nd edn, 1956]).

38. A.T. Robertson, *Epochs in the Life of Jesus: A Study of Development and Struggle in the Messiah's Work* (London: Hodder & Stoughton, 1908); and E.J. Goodspeed, *A Life of Jesus* (New York: Harper & Brothers, 1950).

39. J. Klausner, *Jesus of Nazareth: His Life, Times, and Teaching* [Hebrew 1925] (trans. H. Danby; London: George Allen & Unwin, 1925), for whom over half of the book is devoted to discussion of the sources and the historical period, before considering Jesus' life and teaching.

at play and often devoted considerable attention to discussing them They nevertheless thought that their historically based method was able to penetrate the sources so as to be able to provide a reliable life of Jesus. Again, as Walker states, 'It is highly significant, however, that they seek to recover the historical Jesus through the general methods of secular historiography and, at least in theory, are unwilling to allow their theological convictions to govern their historical conclusions'.[40]

Others, such as the classicist T.R. Glover, T.W. Manson, C.H. Dodd, C.J. Cadoux, G.S. Duncan, and H.A. Guy, again a significant group of scholars (note the contributions of some of them, discussed later in this chapter and in others below), relied upon the Gospels as the basis of presenting the message and teaching of Jesus.[41] Like those above who

---

40. Walker, 'Quest for the Historical Jesus', p. 52, who also attempts to develop such a method. It would be invidious to mention a number of lesser examples that fail to meet such exacting historical-critical standards, but there are a number that one must be aware of in such a discussion.

41. See T.R. Glover, *The Jesus of History* (London: SCM Press, 1917); *idem*, *Jesus of Nazareth* (York: William Sessions, 1912; repr. from *idem*, *The Conflict of Religions in the Early Roman Empire* [London: Methuen, 1909], pp. 113-40); T.W. Manson, *The Teaching of Jesus: Studies of its Form and Content* (Cambridge: Cambridge University Press, 1931; 2nd edn, 1935); *idem*, *The Sayings of Jesus* (London: SCM Press, 1949 [first published in H.D.A. Major, T.W. Manson and C.J. Wright, *The Mission and Message of Jesus: An Exposition of the Gospels in the Light of Modern Research* (London: Ivor Nicholson & Watson, 1937), pp. 301-639]); *idem*, 'The Life of Jesus: A Study of the Available Materials', *ExpTim* 53 (1942), pp. 248-51 and 'The Quest of the Historical Jesus—Continued', both in *idem*, *Studies in the Gospels and Epistles* (ed. M. Black; Manchester: Manchester University Press, 1962), pp. 13-27, 3-12 respectively; *idem*, *The Servant-Messiah: A Study of the Public Ministry of Jesus* (Cambridge: Cambridge University Press, 1953); *idem*, 'The Life of Jesus: Some Tendencies in Present-day Research', in W.D. Davies and D. Daube (eds.), *The Background of the New Testament and its Eschatology* (Festschrift C.H. Dodd; Cambridge: Cambridge University Press, 1954), pp. 211-21; C.H. Dodd, 'The Framework of the Gospel Narrative (1932)', in *idem*, *New Testament Studies* (Manchester: Manchester University Press, 1953), pp. 1-11; *idem*, *The Apostolic Preaching and its Developments* (London: Hodder & Stoughton, 1936); *idem*, *The Parables of the Kingdom*; *idem*, *The Founder of Christianity* (New York: Macmillan, 1970; London: Collins, 1971); C.J. Cadoux, *The Historic Mission of Jesus: A Constructive Reexamination of the Eschatological Teaching in the Synoptic Gospels* (London: Lutterworth, 1941); G.S. Duncan, *Jesus, Son of Man: Studies Contributory to a Modern Portrait* (London: Nisbet, 1947); and H.A. Guy, *The Life of Christ: Notes on the Narrative and Teaching in the*

attempted to write a life of Jesus, these scholars were very familiar with the issues in higher criticism related to the study of Jesus (and other discussions of the ancient world), with some of them being significant contributors to formation of such methods. For example, Glover used the canons of classical historical scholarship in his presentation of Jesus and his teaching within the ancient world. Manson utilized form criticism, but without linking its results with determination of authenticity. Dodd saw underlying the Gospel accounts an account of the life of Jesus. And Cadoux explored Jesus' eschatological perspective in terms of other Jewish teaching of the time. Thus, on the one hand distancing himself from the efforts of the previous century, Duncan can state that 'Scholars no longer attempt to write a "Life of Jesus". The materials for a biography do not exist',[42] yet on the other hand, he can write what he called a modern portrait of Jesus. Nevertheless, many of those mentioned above never reflected the severe lack of belief in the availability of historical information regarding Jesus in the Gospels that came to typify the attitude of many other of the prominent scholars of the day.[43] To be fair, despite what must have been significant academic and intellectual pressure, even in German scholarship of this time there were those of this era who continued to have varying degrees of optimism

---

Gospels (London: Macmillan, 1957). See Wood, *Jesus in the Twentieth Century*, pp. 111-30.

42. Duncan, *Jesus, Son of Man*, p. vii.

43. The social-gospel movement in the United States also produced during this time some lives/teachings of Jesus, e.g., S. Matthews, *The Social Teaching of Jesus: An Essay in Christian Sociology* (New York: Macmillan, 1902); S.J. Case, *The Historicity of Jesus* (Chicago: University of Chicago Press, 1912; 2nd edn, 1928); *idem*, *Jesus: A New Biography* (Chicago: University of Chicago Press, 1927); W. Rauschenbusch, *A Theology of the Social Gospel* (New York: Macmillan, 1922); F.G. Peabody, *The Social Teaching of Jesus Christ* (Philadelphia: University of Pennsylvania Press, 1924). These lives tended to resemble the position taken by Harnack, with its emphasis upon romanticized and idealistic notions about human character. Nevertheless, they were efforts to write accounts of the lives and teachings of Jesus, which persisted well into the 1920s, and later with such popular treatments as H.E. Fosdick, *The Man from Nazareth as his Contemporaries Saw Him* (New York: Harper, 1949). Cf. R.A. Harrisville, 'Representative American Lives of Jesus', in C.E. Braaten and R.A. Harrisville (eds.), *The Historical Jesus and the Kerygmatic Christ: Essays on the New Quest of the Historical Jesus* (Nashville: Abingdon Press, 1964), pp. 172-96.

regarding one's ability to discover the original teaching or facts regarding Jesus. These scholars included a number of highly significant
scholars in various dimensions of Jesus research (several of which are
mentioned in subsequent chapters), including Heinrich Soden, Adolf
Schlatter, Joachim Jeremias, Ethelbert Stauffer, Leonhard Goppelt, and
even, at the beginning of the supposed period in question, K.L. Schmidt
and Martin Dibelius.[44] There was also a joint project by a number of
German and English scholars, sponsored by the World Council of
Churches, that resulted in a volume entitled *Mysterium Christi*.[45] In the

44. H.F. Soden, *Die wichtigsten Fragen im Leben Jesu* (Leipzig: J.C. Hinrichs,
2nd edn, 1909); A. Schlatter, *Die Geschichte des Christus* (Stuttgart: Calwer Verlag,
1921; 2nd edn, 1923; ET *The History of the Christ: The Foundation for New Testament Theology* [trans. A.J. Köstenberger; Grand Rapids: Baker Book House, 1997]);
J. Jeremias, *Die Abendmahlsworte Jesu* (Göttingen: Vandenhoeck & Ruprecht,
1935; 3rd edn, 1960; ET *The Eucharistic Words of Jesus* [trans. A. Ehrhardt; Oxford:
Basil Blackwell, 1955]); *idem, Die Gleichnisse Jesu* (Zürich: Zwingli-Verlag, 1947;
Göttingen: Vandenhoeck & Ruprecht, 10th edn, 1984; ET *The Parables of Jesus*
[trans. S.H. Hooke; London: SCM Press, 3rd edn, 1972]); *idem, The Prayers of Jesus*
(trans. J. Bowden, C. Burchard and J. Reumann; SBT, 2.6; London: SCM Press,
1967) (which consists of selections from *Abba: Studien zur neutestamentlichen
Theologie und Zeitgeschichte* [Göttingen: Vandenhoeck & Ruprecht, 1966]); *idem,
Neutestamentliche Theologie. I. Die Verkündigung Jesu* (Gütersloh: Gerd Mohn,
1971; ET *New Testament Theology. I. The Proclamation of Jesus* [trans. J. Bowden;
NTL; London: SCM Press; New York: Charles Scribner's Sons, 1971]), a fitting
contrast to Bultmann's theology, in that this volume is devoted to Jesus, whereas
Bultmann only devoted the first 32 pages in his *Theology of the New Testament* (see
below); E. Stauffer, *Jesus: Gestalt und Geschichte* (Bern: Francke, 1957; ET *Jesus
and his Story* [trans. R. Winstone and C. Winston; London: SCM Press; New York:
Knopf, 1960]); *idem*, 'Jesus, Geschichte und Verkündigung', *ANRW* 2.25.1, pp. 3-
130; L. Goppelt, *Theologie des Neuen Testaments. I. Jesu Wirken in seiner theologischen Bedeutung* (ed. J. Roloff; Göttingen: Vandenhoeck & Ruprecht, 1975; ET
*Theology of the New Testament. I. The Ministry of Jesus in its Theological Sig-
nificance* [trans. J.E. Alsup; Grand Rapids: Eerdmans, 1981]), esp. pp. 251-81,
where similar comments as are made regarding Jeremias's theology also apply here;
K.L. Schmidt, 'Jesus Christus', *RGG*, III (Tübingen: Mohr–Siebeck, 2nd edn, 1929),
cols. 110-51; and M. Dibelius, *Jesus* (Sammlung Göschen; Berlin: W. de Gruyter,
1939; ET *Jesus* [trans. C.B. Hedrick and F.C. Grant; Philadelphia: Westminster
Press, 1949; London: SCM Press, 1963]).
    45. G.K.A. Bell and A. Deissmann (eds.), *Mysterium Christi: Christological
Studies by British and German Theologians* (London: Longmans, Green; Berlin:
Furche-Verlag, 1930), which contains a range of essays on the topic, with various
approaches, by such scholars as Deissmann, G. Kittel, C.H. Dodd, E.C. Hoskyns,

light of the role that Dibelius played with Bultmann in the development of form criticism (see Chapter 2), it is perhaps surprising that he and Bultmann came to very different conclusions regarding what one could know of Jesus through the Gospel sources. A recognition of the issues involved, as well as the diversity of opinion evidenced in the work during this period, is found in the comments of no less a scholar than Goodspeed. In 1950, apparently recognizing the situation that I have depicted above, he stated that ' "The life of Jesus cannot be written". This has long been a commonplace with historians and biographers... And yet what life has been so often written?' He himself then goes on to offer his 'sketch' of the ministry of Jesus.[46]

In many circles, especially German ones, however, as a result of the work of Schweitzer and others, there was indeed both a serious dampening of the optimism that often accompanied the romanticized 'first quest' and the establishment of the belief that Jesus was seen to be an/ the eschatological prophet. This model apparently dominated German depictions of Jesus for the first half of the twentieth century. The results of such an orientation were found in the work of scholars such as Bultmann, who were highly sceptical of attempts to find the historical Jesus in documents produced by Christian faith—at least in the terms of the romanticized notions of the nineteenth century. This has become known in many circles as the 'no-quest' period,[47] but in the light of the number of lives of various sorts that were written during this time elsewhere, several of which have been noted above, it is questionable whether this label should really be used, since it was far from a period of no questing. One may well note that numerous presuppositions held by a number of the scholars of the time regarding this task were altered from those of before, but attempts to write even if modified lives of Jesus still abounded. In retrospect, this negative 'no-quest' position has come to be used to characterize most, if not all, historical-Jesus research during this period—probably wrongly in the light of the evidence to be found in scholarly production during this time. Bultmann is all too well known for his statement that 'I think that we can now know almost noth-

---

and H. Sasse, among others. Form criticism is only mentioned once (on p. 71 of Hoskyns's essay).

46. Goodspeed, *Life of Jesus*, pp. 11, 12.

47. See Reumann, 'Jesus and Christology', p. 502.

ing concerning the life and personality of Jesus, since the early Christian sources show no interest in either, are moreover fragmentary and often legendary; and other sources about Jesus do not exist'.[48] Nevertheless, this did not prevent even Bultmann from producing a book on Jesus. I think the key to understanding Bultmann's statement is his rejection of trying to find the deep-seated personality of Jesus in the Gospels, something that was sought by many of the lives written in the nineteenth century,[49] although he then goes much further in another

---

48. Bultmann, *Jesus*, p. 8; cf. his comments at the outset of his *Theologie des Neuen Testaments* (Tübingen: Mohr Siebeck, 1948; 7th edn ed. O. Merk, 1977; ET *Theology of the New Testament* [2 vols.; trans. K. Grobel; London: SCM Press; New York: Charles Scribner's Sons, 1951, 1955], I, p. 3: 'The message of Jesus is a presupposition for the theology of the New Testament rather than a part of that theology itself... But Christian faith did not exist until there was a Christian kerygma... He was first so proclaimed in the kerygma of the earliest Church, not in the message of the historical Jesus, even though that Church frequently introduced into its account of Jesus' message, motifs of its own proclamation.' His programme was directly pursued by R.H. Fuller, *The Mission and Achievement of Jesus: An Examination of the Presuppositions of New Testament Theology* (SBT, 12; London: SCM Press, 1954). 'Minimalist' interpretations of Jesus (though certainly not necessarily short treatments!) written during this period that reflect this more negative perspective include M. Goguel, *La vie de Jésus* (Paris: Payot, 1932; ET *The Life of Jesus* [trans. O. Wyon; London: George Allen & Unwin; New York: Macmillan, 1933]); A. Loisy, *La naissance du christianisme* (Paris: Nourry, 1933; ET *The Birth of the Christian Religion* [trans. L.P. Jacks; London: George Allen & Unwin, 1948]), pp. 61-87; R.H. Lightfoot, *History and Interpretation in the Gospels* (London: Hodder & Stoughton; New York: Harper, 1935); *idem, The Gospel Message of St Mark* (Oxford: Clarendon Press, 1950); and N. Perrin, *Rediscovering the Teaching of Jesus* (NTL; London: SCM Press; New York: Harper & Row, 1967); among others. The number of volumes written does not appear to be as many as those written by scholars with other presuppositions—but this is understandable in the light of the assumptions of the method. For a moderating and enlightening view of Bultmann and his programme, see J.K. Riches, *Jesus and the Transformation of Judaism* (London: Darton, Longman & Todd; New York: Seabury, 1980), pp. 44-61; and on other writers of this time, see Wood, *Jesus in the Twentieth Century*, pp. 96-110.

49. Bultmann, *Jesus*, pp. 6, 8. In responding to his critics in 1962, Bultmann attempts to clarify his position, when he says that 'from the discrepancy which I emphasize between the historical Jesus and the Christ of the kerygma it does not at all follow that I destroy continuity between the historical Jesus and the primitive Christian proclamation' (R. Bultmann, *Das Verhältnis der urchristlichen Christusbotschaft zum historischen Jesus* [Sitzungsberichte der Heidelberger Akademie der Wissenschaften phil.-hist. Klasse; Heidelberg: Winter, 1960; 3rd edn, 1962]; ET

direction in his own characterization. He and others also argued for an eschatological Jesus. These factors indicate that Bultmann and others were rejecting what they saw as unrealistic methods, both rationalistic and romanticized, from the nineteenth century as much as anything. In this sense, the rubric 'no quest' describes an abandonment in some, perhaps mostly German, circles of the agenda of some nineteenth-century questing after Jesus, but it can hardly be used as an adequate label for the entire period of research on Jesus in the first half of the twentieth century.

c. *1953–1988*

The analysis that I am offering of a much more multi-faceted development of historical-Jesus research perhaps makes it more understandable how it was that Bultmann's student, Ernst Käsemann, could appear to some to rejuvenate debate regarding the historical Jesus by means of his 1953 lecture. As will be seen in the next chapter, Käsemann, using very similar methods as those of Bultmann and others instrumental in the development of form criticism, asked again whether there was not still historical information about Jesus that could be gleaned from the Gospel sources.[50] However, Käsemann had a clear approach in mind when he issued this challenge, looking to form criticism, which he saw as a particularly German type of critical method, as the only proper means of investigating the life of Jesus. Many of the scholars mentioned above had never quit asking Käsemann's question, and using historical methods to answer it, as noted above, but they had not all used form criti-

---

'The Primitive Christian Kerygma and the Historical Jesus', in Braaten and Harrisville [eds.], *The Historical Jesus and the Kerygmatic Christ*, pp. 15-42 [18]).

50. Käsemann, 'Problem of the Historical Jesus', pp. 15-47. Cf. Käsemann's own earlier essay, which is in some ways part of the more sceptical, earlier period in German scholarship: 'Zum Thema der Nichtobjektivierbarkeit', *EvT* 12 (1952–53), pp. 455-66 (repr. in *idem*, *Exegetische Versuche and Besinnungen*, I, pp. 224-36); ET 'Is the Gospel Objective?', in *idem*, *Essays on New Testament Themes*, pp. 48-62. Käsemann himself did not pursue further the agenda that he set down in his 'Problem of the Historical Jesus': see his 'Die neue Jesus-Frage', in J. Dupont (ed.), *Jésus aux origines de la christologie* (BETL, 40; Gembloux: Duculot, 1975; Leuven: Leuven University Press/Peeters, 2nd edn, 1989), pp. 47-57. For a different reading of the role of Käsemann, see Theissen and Winter, *Die Kriterienfrage in der Jesusforschung*, p. 5.

cism, even as this interpretive tool became more widely known. Confirmation for the perspective that I have taken in this chapter comes, of all places, from Käsemann himself. In an essay by Käsemann that deserves to be better known in this discussion, in a section noteworthily entitled 'The Continuation of the Old Type of "Life of Jesus" Study', he states the following: 'The old type of "Life of Jesus" study still blooms richly, if somewhat autumnally, wherever dialectical theology, thorough-going eschatology and the form-critical method—that strange, peculiarly German combination of questionings, rejected for the most part on the rest of the European continent—have not succeeded in penetrating'.[51] Käsemann's called-for peculiarly German form-critical investigation has been seen by some scholars to mark the beginning of what has been called a 'new' or 'second quest' of historical-Jesus research.[52]

51. E. Käsemann, 'Sackgassen im Streit um den historischen Jesus', in *idem*, *Exegetische Versuche und Besinnungen*, II (Göttingen: Vandenhoeck & Ruprecht, 1964; 2nd edn, 1965), pp. 31-68; ET 'Blind Alleys in the "Jesus of History" Controversy', in *idem*, *New Testament Questions of Today* (trans. W.J. Montague; London: SCM Press, 1969), pp. 23-65 (24). The major writer of this old-fashioned life of Jesus that Käsemann singles out for criticism, however, is not an English-speaking scholar, but the German scholar Joachim Jeremias, in particular in his 'Der gegenwärtige Stand der Debatte um das Problem des historischen Jesus', in H. Ristow and K. Matthiae (eds.), *Der historische Jesus und der kerygmatische Christus: Beiträge zum Christusverständnis in Forschung und Verkündigung* (Berlin: Evangelische Verlagsanstalt, 1960), pp. 12-25; ET 'The Present Position in the Controversy Concerning the Problem of the Historical Jesus', *ExpTim* 69 (1957–58), pp. 333-39.

52. For an early accounting of this so-called 'new quest' (and the work that gave this movement its name), see J.M. Robinson, *A New Quest of the Historical Jesus* (SBT, 25; London: SCM Press, 1959; Missoula, MT: Scholars Press, 1979). Much like today regarding the supposed 'third quest', some were not convinced then. See, e.g., V.A. Harvey and S.M. Ogden, 'How New is the "New Quest of the Historical Jesus"?', in Braaten and Harrisville (eds.), *The Historical Jesus and the Kerygmatic Christ*, pp. 197-242; Walker, 'Quest for the Historical Jesus', p. 51, who calls the 'new quest' a 'halfway house' between scepticism and uncritical naiveté; cf. F. Hahn, 'Methodologische Überlegungen zur Rückfrage nach Jesus', in K. Kertelge (ed.), *Rückfrage nach Jesus: Zur Methodik und Bedeutung der Frage nach dem historischen Jesus* (QD, 63; Freiburg: Herder, 1974), pp. 11-77; ET 'Methodological Reflections on the Historical Investigation of Jesus', in F. Hahn, *Historical Investigation and New Testament Faith: Two Essays* (trans. R. Maddox; Philadelphia: Fortress Press, 1983), pp. 35-105; J.I.H. McDonald, 'New Quest—Dead End? So What about the Historical Jesus', in E.A. Livingstone (ed.), *Studia Biblica 1978. II. Papers on the Gospels. Sixth International Congress on Biblical Studies*

In the light of my above historical survey of Jesus research in the first half of the twentieth century, essentially confirmed by Käsemann (see the Excursus at the end of this chapter for a graphic display of this research), Käsemann's perspective seems to be in many ways nothing more than a rallying call for a particularly German type of scholarship for investigating the life of Jesus. Käsemann's published lecture of 1953 seems in retrospect merely to have given permission for some German scholars, especially those most heavily influenced by the German research in the first half of the century, to re-enter what was in fact already an ongoing discussion of the historical Jesus—but to do so by using form criticism.

On the basis of the survey offered above, there is no doubt that the terms and methods of discussion of the historical Jesus had continued to develop throughout the first half of the century, so that Morton Enslin can state with regard to the orientation of the supposed 'old' or 'first quest' that 'This book is in no sense a Life of Jesus. To write such is impossible... We simply do not have the materials'—even though he then proceeds to write about Jesus as prophet.[53] But as Käsemann was forced to admit, this is only part of the story. There were many who had written accounts of the life and teachings of Jesus in the first half of the century, and they were now joined more actively by German scholars. In continuity with the ongoing quest for the historical Jesus that had never really ceased (as we have already seen above), a number of the most prominent New Testament scholars, both German and otherwise, have gone on to make various types of contributions to and identified their work with the debate over the last 50 or so years of the twentieth century (often called the 'new' or 'second quest'), arguing for various results in the light of this supposed re-opening of the question of the historical Jesus. What is often cited as probably the classic treatment of Jesus written during this period is that by Günther Bornkamm,[54] but

---

(JSNTSup, 2; Sheffield: JSOT Press, 1980), pp. 151-70.

53. M.S. Enslin, *The Prophet from Nazareth* (New York: McGraw–Hill, 1961), p. 1.

54. G. Bornkamm, *Jesus von Nazareth* (Urban-Bücher, 19; Stuttgart: W. Kohlhammer, 1956; 10th edn, 1975; ET *Jesus of Nazareth* [trans. I. McLuskey and F. McLuskey with J.M. Robinson; London: Hodder & Stoughton, 1960]). Marshall has noted that in substance Bornkamm's volume is very similar to the earlier one of Dibelius, the difference being that Bornkamm's life of Jesus was written by a student of Bultmann (Marshall, *I Believe in the Historical Jesus*, p. 131).

there have been other particularly noteworthy contributions as well. The range of acceptance and scepticism with regard to the reliability of the Gospel tradition is manifestly large, with the major recognizable difference in the last half of the century from the first half being that both sides and the middle at least appear to be part of the same general debate. However, within this broad range, there are still a number of perceivable differences in the treatments, especially on the basis of whether they utilize form criticism or not, and hence whether they conform to the expectations of the 'new' or 'second quest' as defined by German scholarship.[55] Nevertheless, there has been no sign of interest

55. Other treatments include: H. Conzelmann, 'Jesus Christus', *RGG*, III (Tübingen: Mohr Siebeck, 3rd edn, 1959), cols. 619-53; ET *Jesus* (trans. J.R. Lord; Philadelphia: Fortress Press, 1973); *idem*, 'Zur methode der Leben-Jesu-Forschung', *ZTK* 56 (1959), pp. 2-13; ET 'The Method of the Life-of-Jesus Research', in Braaten and Harrisville (eds.), *The Historical Jesus and the Kerygmatic Christ*, pp. 54-68; W. Grundmann, *Die Geschichte Jesu Christi* (Berlin: Evangelische Verlagsanstalt, 1956; 2nd edn, 1959); E. Fuchs, *Zur Frage nach dem historischen Jesus* (Tübingen: Mohr Siebeck, 1960; ET *Studies of the Historical Jesus* (trans. A. Scobie; SBT, 42; London: SCM Press, 1964); H. Zahrnt, *Es begann mit Jesus von Nazareth: Die Frage nach dem historischen Jesus* (Stuttgart: Kreuz, 1960; ET *The Historical Jesus* [trans. J.S. Bowden; London: Collins; New York: Harper & Row, 1963]), esp. pp. 43-54; H. Ristow and K. Matthiae (eds.), *Der historische Jesus und der kerygmatische Christus: Beiträge zum Christusverständnis in Forschung und Verkündigung* (Berlin: Evangelische Verlagsanstalt, 1962), with essays by J. Jeremias, W.G. Kümmel, H. Conzelmann, B. Reicke, R. Bultmann, O. Cullmann, G. Bornkamm, W. Michaelis, H. Schürmann, and E. Fuchs; J. Knox, *The Church and the Reality of Christ* (New York: Harper & Row, 1962; London: Collins, 1963); E.C. Colwell, *Jesus and the Gospel* (New York: Oxford University Press, 1963); J.A. Baird, *The Justice of God in the Teaching of Jesus* (Philadelphia: Westminster Press, 1963); *idem, Audience Criticism and the Historical Jesus* (NTL; Philadelphia: Westminster Press; London: SCM Press, 1969); H. Anderson, *Jesus and Christian Origins: A Commentary on Modern Viewpoints* (New York: Oxford University Press, 1964); O. Betz, *Was Wissen wir von Jesus?* (Stuttgart: Kreuz, 1965; ET *What Do We Know about Jesus?* [trans. M. Kohl; London: SCM Press, 1968]); W. Neil, *The Life and Teaching of Jesus* (London: Hodder & Stoughton; Philadelphia: Lippincott, 1965); C.K. Barrett, *Jesus and the Gospel Tradition* (London: SPCK, 1967); D. Flusser, *Jesus in Selbstzeugnissen und Bilddocumenten* (Rowohlts Monographien, 140; Hamburg: Rowohlt, 1968; ET *Jesus* [in collaboration with R.S. Notley; New York: Herder & Herder, 1969; Jerusalem: Magnes Press, rev. edn, 1997]); E. Schweizer, *Jesus Christus im vielfältigen Zeugnis des Neuen Testaments* (Munich: Siebenstern, 1968; ET *Jesus* [trans. D.E. Green; London: SCM Press; Atlanta: John Knox Press, 1971]); Reumann, *Jesus in the Church's*

in this discussion of the life of Jesus flagging, and indeed many signs of its further flourishing.[56] In the next chapter, some of the dimensions of this characterization of the 'new' or 'second quest' will be scrutinized in more detail, especially regarding the development and use of the criteria for authenticity.

d. *1988–Present*

The question here, however, is whether more recent developments merit the term 'third quest' as Wright uses it. Before attempting to answer that question, one cannot help but note that there is a great deal of

---

Gospels, passim; H. Braun, *Jesus: Der Mann aus Nazareth und seine Zeit* (Berlin: Kreuz-Verlag, 1969); H.C. Kee, *Jesus in History: An Approach to the Study of the Gospels* (New York: Harcourt Brace Jovanovich, 1970; 2nd edn, 1977); L.E. Keck, *A Future for the Historical Jesus: The Place of Jesus in Preaching and Theology* (Nashville: Abingdon Press, 1971; London: SCM Press, 1972); S. Schulz, 'Die neue Frage nach dem historischen Jesus', in H. Baltensweiler and B. Reicke (eds.), *Neues Testament und Geschichte: Historisches Geschehen und Deutung im Neuen Testament* (Festschrift O. Cullmann; Zürich: Theologischer Verlag; Tübingen: Mohr Siebeck, 1972), pp. 33-42; *idem*, 'Der historische Jesus: Bilanz der Fragen und Lösungen', in G. Strecker (ed.), *Jesus Christus in Historie und Theologie* (Festschrift H. Conzelmann; Tübingen: Mohr Siebeck, 1975), pp. 3-25; G. Vermes, *Jesus the Jew: A Historian's Reading of the Gospels* (London: Collins; Philadelphia: Fortress Press, 1973); G. Aulén, *Jesus i nutida historisk forskning* (Stockholm: Verbum, 1973; 2nd edn, 1974; ET *Jesus in Contemporary Historical Research* [trans. I.H. Hjelm; Philadelphia: Fortress Press, 1976]); Trocmé, *Jesus and his Contemporaries, passim*; C.L. Mitton, *Jesus: The Fact behind the Faith* (Grand Rapids: Eerdmans, 1973; London: Mowbrays, 1975); W. Kasper, *Jesus der Christus* (Mainz: Matthias-Grünewald Verlag, 1974; ET *Jesus the Christ* [trans. V. Green; London: Burns & Oates; New York: Paulist Press, 1976]), esp. pp. 26-40; G.N. Stanton, *Jesus of Nazareth in New Testament Preaching* (SNTSMS, 27; Cambridge: Cambridge University Press, 1974); *idem, The Gospels and Jesus* (OBS; Oxford: Oxford University Press, 1989); Marshall, *I Believe in the Historical Jesus, passim*; R.H. Stein, *The Method and Message of Jesus' Teachings* (Philadelphia: Westminster Press, 1978; Louisville, KY: Westminster/John Knox Press, rev. edn, 1994); H. Carpenter, *Jesus* (Past Masters; Oxford: Oxford University Press, 1980), esp. pp. 1-20; J.R. Michaels, *Servant and Son: Jesus in Parable and Gospel* (Atlanta: John Knox Press, 1981); J. Marsh, *Jesus in his Lifetime* (London: Sidgwick & Jackson, 1981); Riches, *Jesus and the Transformation of Judaism, passim*; G. O'Collins, *Interpreting Jesus* (Geoffrey Chapman Theology Library; London: Chapman, 1983); J.S. Bowden, *Jesus: The Unanswered Questions* (London: SCM Press, 1988); among many others, several more of which are cited below and in subsequent chapters.

56. See Evans, *Life of Jesus Research*, pp. 16-109.

evidence that there has always been just one multi-faceted quest for the historical Jesus. This quest has certainly undergone development in a number of ways and in different circles, though not all in the same way or to the same degree. As the above survey of research shows, this cannot be denied. However, this quest is also unified by a fundamental underlying attempt to discover the proper means to be able to speak of the historical Jesus. This unbroken line of scholarly investigation reveals more than a century of ongoing research, one that cannot be easily dismissed. If anything, utilizing the signposts of such figures as Reimarus, Schweitzer, Bultmann and Käsemann shows only that the tripartite characterization of the quests for the historical Jesus so often cited by scholars has perhaps more of a basis in German scholarship, or perhaps even one kind of German scholarship, than it does in being a fair general characterization of the diverse and multi-faceted quest as it has been practised by a wider range of scholars worldwide. As Banks so aptly stated nearly 20 years ago, 'Despite Schweitzer's strictures, there has been an unbroken interest in the "quest for the historical Jesus" in Anglo-Saxon circles, while the return of concern among German scholars, first heralded in Ernst Käsemann's well-known essay, has now proceeded for more than twenty-five years'.[57]

As a result of this smoothing out of the divides between the several epochs in the quest for the historical Jesus, it should not come as a surprise that the kind of radical division that Wright's statements above anticipate between the so-called 'second' and 'third quests' is, to my mind, simply not to be found. In none of the four important works that had formed the high point of the 'third quest' to the point of his writing, according to Wright, had the term 'third quest' even been used.[58] He

57. R.J. Banks, 'Setting "The Quest for the Historical Jesus" in a Broader Framework', in R.T. France and D. Wenham (eds.), *Gospel Perspectives: Studies of History and Tradition in the Four Gospels*, II (Sheffield: JSOT Press, 1981), pp. 61-82 (61).

58. These four include: Meyer, *The Aims of Jesus*; A.E. Harvey, *Jesus and the Constraints of History* (London: Gerald Duckworth; Philadelphia: Westminster Press, 1982); M.J. Borg, *Conflict, Holiness and Politics in the Teachings of Jesus* (Lewiston, NY: Edwin Mellen Press, 1984; repr. Harrisburg, PA: Trinity Press International, 1998), and E.P. Sanders, *Jesus and Judaism* (London: SCM Press; Philadelphia: Fortress Press, 1985) (J.D.G. Dunn, 'Can the Third Quest Hope to Succeed?', in B. Chilton and C.A. Evans [eds.], *Authenticating the Activities of Jesus* [NTTS, 28.2; Leiden: E.J. Brill, 1998], pp. 31-48, esp. p. 35, attributes the beginning of the 'third quest' to Sanders). In subsequent work, Wright has engaged in

describes four distinguishing features of this 'third quest' in relation to the 'second quest' (or the 'new quest'): (1) locating Jesus firmly in terms of his Jewish background, (2) asking the question of why Jesus was crucified rather than simply noting the fact that he was, (3) integrating political and theological issues rather than distinguishing them, and (4) bringing together scholars with various backgrounds.[59] As a result of Wright's and others' scholarly work, after roughly ten years it is fairly common to see and hear reference to the 'third quest' in both the scholarly and more popular discussion.[60] Clearly not all have been convinced by these supposed distinguishing features of this 'third quest', however.[61] At the time of the publication of Wright's revision of Neill's book, in a review, I noted my scepticism over the term, seeing much greater continuity between the supposed 'second' and 'third quests' than

what appears to be his own form of historical revisionism, reading his 'third quest' back even much earlier. In his *Jesus and the Victory of God* (Minneapolis: Fortress Press, 1996), he cites 20 scholars as particularly important to the 'third quest' from the year 1965 to the present, although most date to the 1970s and 1980s (p. 84)! This seems to be more than a slightly hyperbolic view of the so-called 'third quest'. Nevertheless, it helps to establish my point that there is little in this 'third quest' that cannot be seen in continuity with previous questing after the historical Jesus.

59. Neill and Wright, *Interpretation of the New Testament*, pp. 397-98. See also Wright, *Jesus and the Victory of God*, pp. 89-121, where these are reiterated and expanded to include the questions of what Jesus' aims were and of the origins of the Church.

60. Besides Wright, see Evans, *Life of Jesus Research*, p. 3; M.J. Borg, *Jesus in Contemporary Scholarship* (Valley Forge, PA: Trinity Press International, 1994), p. ix; Witherington, *The Jesus Quest*; J. Beker, *Jesus von Nazaret* (Berlin: W. de Gruyter, 1995), esp. pp. 10-11; Theissen and Winter, *Die Kriterienfrage in der Jesusforschung*, pp. 1-8; B. Chilton, 'Assessing Progress in the Third Quest', in B. Chilton and C.A. Evans (eds.), *Authenticating the Words of Jesus* (NTTS, 28.1; Leiden: E.J. Brill, 1998), pp. 15-25; P. Pokorný, *Jesus in the Eyes of his Followers: Newly Discovered Manuscripts and Old Christian Confessions* (Dead Sea Scrolls and Christian Origins Library; North Richland Hills, TX: Bibal Press, 1998), pp. 14-21; L.M. McDonald and S.E. Porter, *Early Christianity and its Sacred Literature* (Peabody, MA: Hendrickson, forthcoming 2000), Chapter 4; among many others.

61. For example, in their surveys of the state of research: Reumann, 'Jesus and Christology', esp. p. 502; Telford, 'Major Trends and Interpretive Issues', pp. 55-61; M. Bockmuehl, *This Jesus: Martyr, Lord, Messiah* (Edinburgh: T. & T. Clark; Downers Grove, IL: InterVarsity Press, 1994), p. 6; R.H. Stein, *Jesus the Messiah: A Survey of the Life of Christ* (Downers Grove, IL: InterVarsity Press, 1996), p. 13.

Wright seems to have recognized.[62] This is even though his formulation is in terms of the 'third quest' clearly building upon the 'second'—for example, in being concerned to join the kerygma to its historical context, and relying upon the crucifixion as a datum in the discussion. I would say that all four of the distinguishing features that Wright describes have in fact been part of the ongoing quest in various ways apparently almost since its inception. In his recent introduction to the New Testament, the late Raymond Brown notes that recent developments in historical-Jesus research (he does not refer to a 'third quest') are distinguished by two tendencies. One of these, 'the most conservative one', he says, is focused upon 'the study of christology', rather than being research into the historical Jesus; the other is the Jesus Seminar, with its sceptical and (what he perhaps mistakenly calls) a priori approach (he also treats a number of individual scholars as well, for their particular contributions to recent Jesus research).[63] In other words,

62. See S.E. Porter, review of *The Interpretation of the New Testament 1861–1986*, by Neill and Wright, in *JETS* 35 (1992), pp. 546-47.

63. See R.E. Brown, *An Introduction to the New Testament* (ABRL; New York: Doubleday, 1997), pp. 818-30, in an appendix to his volume (quotation p. 819). The individual scholars he cites as reflecting these trends (and who might be considered part of the so-called 'third quest') include Sanders, *Jesus and Judaism* (noted above by Wright); and *idem*, *Historical Figure of Jesus*; G. Theissen, *Der Schatten des Galiläers: Historische Jesusforschung in erzählender Form* (Munich: Chr. Kaiser Verlag, 1986; ET *The Shadow of the Galilean: The Quest of the Historical Jesus in Narrative Form* [trans. J. Bowden; Philadelphia: Fortress Press, 1987]); R.A. Horsley, *Jesus and the Spiral of Violence* (San Francisco: HarperSanFrancisco, 1987); *idem*, *Sociology and the Jesus Movement* (New York: Crossroad, 1989); E. Schüssler Fiorenza, *Jesus: Miriam's Child and Sophia's Prophet* (New York: Continuum, 1994); and J.P. Meier, *A Marginal Jew: Rethinking the Historical Jesus* (3 vols.; ABRL; New York: Doubleday, 1991–). Other works that would probably fall within the ambit of the 'third quest' (as well as perhaps Brown's strictures) not yet mentioned in this chapter include J.H. Charlesworth, *Jesus within Judaism: New Light from Exciting Archaeological Discoveries* (ABRL; New York: Doubleday, 1988) (cf. his 'The Historical Jesus in Light of Writings Contemporaneous with Him', *ANRW* 2.25.1, pp. 451-76); P. Stuhlmacher, *Jesus von Nazareth—Christus des Glaubens* (Stuttgart: Calwer Verlag, 1988; ET *Jesus of Nazareth—Christ of Faith* [trans. S.S. Schatzmann; Peabody, MA: Hendrickson, 1993]); I.M. Zeitlin, *Jesus and the Judaism of his Time* (Cambridge: Polity Press, 1988); H.C. Kee, *What Can We Know about Jesus?* (Understanding Jesus Today; Cambridge: Cambridge University Press, 1990); M. de Jonge, *Jesus, the Servant-Messiah* (New Haven: Yale University Press, 1991); *idem*, *God's Final Envoy: Early Christology and Jesus'*

Brown sees greater continuity, with some admitted developments, between today's kind of questing after the historical Jesus and the previous questing. For him, there is no need to posit a 'third quest', especially since much of the recent research, according to him, is not what he would see as historical-Jesus research anyway.

3. *Conclusion*

On the basis of the sketch of historical-Jesus research offered above, and confirmed by what Wright and Brown have presented (summarized briefly in section 2, above), there is little substantive basis for designating a new epoch in historical-Jesus research. The quest that is said by some to have begun in the 1980s (inconsistently elongated by Wright to the 1960s) seems to be merely a continuation of that said by some to have begun in the 1950s—with some fine-tunings and adjustments in terms of how much credence is given to parts of the body of evidence, and who is included in the discussion. Thus, in a particularly noteworthy example, Eduard Schweizer can write one life of Jesus during the so-called 'new' or 'second quest', and write another book on Jesus during the supposed 'third quest' in which he uses essentially the same criteria as he used before.[64] As Stein states, 'The same historical-critical method remains foundational for many of the researchers' involved in the so-called 'third quest'.[65] What's more important to note, in anticipation of what will be presented in Chapter 2, below, is that this historical method goes even further back, at least to the time of the so-called

Own View of his Mission (SHJ; Grand Rapids: Eerdmans, 1998); B. Witherington, III, *The Christology of Jesus* (Minneapolis: Fortress Press, 1991); B. Chilton, *The Temple of Jesus: His Sacrificial Program within a Cultural History of Sacrifice* (University Park: Pennsylvania State University Press, 1992); G. Vermes, *The Religion of Jesus the Jew* (Minneapolis: Fortress Press, 1993); W.E. Phipps, *The Wisdom and Wit of Rabbi Jesus* (Louisville, KY: Westminster/John Knox Press, 1993); E. Schweizer, *Jesus: The Parable of God. What Do We Really Know about Jesus?* (Alison Park, PA: Pickwick, 1994; Edinburgh: T. & T. Clark, 1997); Evans, *Jesus and his Contemporaries*; B. Chilton and C.A. Evans, *Jesus in Context: Temple, Purity, and Restoration* (AGJU, 39; Leiden: E.J. Brill, 1997); Chilton and Evans (eds.), *Authenticating the Words of Jesus, passim*; Chilton and Evans (eds.), *Authenticating the Activities of Jesus, passim*; among many others.

64. Cf. Schweizer, *Jesus*, esp. pp. 10-11, where he invokes the criterion of dissimilarity; and *Jesus: The Parable of God*, esp. pp. 20-23, where he briefly describes a number of criteria.

65. Stein, *Jesus the Messiah*, p. 13.

'no-quest' period, if not earlier to the time of the 'old' or 'first quest'. One cannot help but question the advisability of referring to anything other than a single multi-faceted quest of the historical Jesus, with various modifications and adjustments in approach, some of them perhaps influenced by method and others perhaps by personality or nationality. There is, to my mind, no clear way to characterize a given epoch in a singular and uniform way, and there is certainly no clearly discernible or definable break between epochs that anyone can turn to, as Wright's shifting boundaries between the so-called 'second' and 'third quests' so well illustrate.

As a specific case in point, with regard to the topic of this monograph, incisive discussion of the criteria used to assess the authenticity of any of the words or actions of Jesus—something that one would have thought crucial to the more buoyantly optimistic recent agenda—is lacking.[66] As will be shown in Chapter 2, these criteria were primarily developed in the early to middle parts of this century, as part of the rise of

---

66. Some scholars wish to abandon the term 'criterion', replacing it with 'index'. See Meyer, *Aims of Jesus*, p. 86; McKnight, *Interpreting the Synoptic Gospels*, pp. 66-69; cf. also R. Riesner, *Jesus als Lehrer: Eine Untersuchung zum Ursprung der Evangelien-Überlieferung* (WUNT, 2.7; Tübingen: Mohr Siebeck, 1981; 4th edn, 1994), pp. 86-87, who sees 'criterion' as addressing absolute questions regarding whether something is actual, while 'index' appreciates the influence of various factors that might push a judgment in one direction or another. Riesner also raises the question of what is meant by the term 'authenticity' (*Echtheit*), and realizes that it involves degrees, rather than absolutes. I am sympathetic with this attempt to use a more modest term than 'criteria', since 'index' more fully conveys that probabilities, not certainties, are being discussed. However, I retain the traditional terminology, because it is not entirely clear that criteria is not the right word for what many scholars are attempting, that is, they are arguing for a greater degree of certainty than such criteria (analysed below) can provide. I attempt to use the language of probability whenever possible and appropriate, nevertheless, recognizing that much more work needs to be done on the logical, historical, theological and linguistic dimensions of this topic. For initial attempts in some of these areas, see A. Gibson, *Biblical Semantic Logic: A Preliminary Analysis* (Oxford: Basil Blackwell, 1981); S.C. Goetz and C.L. Blomberg, 'The Burden of Proof', *JSNT* 11 (1981), pp. 39-63; L.T. Johnson, *The Real Jesus: The Misguided Quest for the Historical Jesus and the Truth of the Traditional Gospels* (San Francisco: HarperCollins, 1996); Schwarz, *Christology*, pp. 75-336; A.R. Cross, 'Historical Methodology and New Testament Study', *Themelios* 22.3 (1997), pp. 28-51; and now J.D. Crossan, L.T. Johnson and W.H. Kelber, *The Jesus Controversy: Perspectives in Conflict* (Harrisburg, PA: Trinity Press International, 1999).

form criticism, and continued even with the advent of redaction criticism.[67] In the light of the discussion of this chapter, over whether historical-Jesus research has entered a new era, one could reasonably expect to be able to find some definitive statements regarding these criteria in terms of the supposed newest quest. However, Wright does not mention them at all in his earlier work that surveys recent developments in New Testament research, and in his later work on the historical Jesus he seems consciously to abandon them. Instead of what he calls the 'old' and 'so-called' criterion of dissimilarity (see below and Chapter 2, for definition of this criterion), which he says can only be applied with caution,[68] he substitutes what appears to be the exact opposite criterion (a criterion of similarity/continuity?), in which Jesus is the central figure that unifies Judaism and the early Church.[69] Brown mentions criteria only to say that scholars are 'divided about the real value of the criteria for discerning the historical Jesus'. He then also gives the example of the criterion of dissimilarity, which he defines as eliminating as authentic any saying or event that can be derived from Judaism or early Christianity. This criterion leaves what he calls a 'monstrosity: a Jesus who never said, thought, or did anything that other Jews said, thought, or did, and a Jesus who had no connection or relationship to what his followers said, thought, or did in reference to him after he died'.[70] If these statements and characterizations are accurate (see Chapter 2, however, for a moderating analysis), it is not surprising that utilization of the same criteria that originated with the rise of form criticism during the so-called 'no quest', but that then were developed further during the so-called 'new quest' and the rise of redaction criticism, gave little hope for authenticating new data for discussion in a newly self-conscious historical approach, such as the 'new quest' was seeking to be. Nevertheless, these criteria are the ones that are still

67. W.G. Doty, 'The Discipline and Literature of New Testament Form Criticism', *ATR* 51 (1969), pp. 257-321, esp. p. 315: 'The whole movement which has just been the focus of attention in biblical studies, the movement James M. Robinson entitled "The New Quest of the Historical Jesus", comes directly out of the form-critical method'.

68. Wright, *Jesus and the Victory of God*, p. 86. One cannot help but note that without an explicit formulation by Wright of what a criterion is, there is bound to be some equivocation in his rejection of one and substitution of another.

69. Wright, *Jesus and the Victory of God*, pp. 125-31, esp. p. 128. Cf. *idem*, *The New Testament and the People of God* (London: SPCK, 1992), pp. 81-120.

70. Brown, *Introduction*, p. 827.

being used even during the so-called 'third quest', as will be shown in Chapters 2 and 3.

Despite these discouraging features, however, there has been a re-examination of the criteria for authenticity in certain circles over the last 10 to 15 years. These circles seem to be English-speaking ones for the most part, with the important caveat that some of the most significant very recent work has been by several German scholars.[71] With recent reassessment of the criteria for authenticity, and the new criteria that have emerged, one can perhaps now hear scholars stating that we are poised to enter a 'new' (even a 'third') 'quest' for the historical Jesus. This assumes, however, that the new criteria are genuinely innovative and lead to new insights, rather than simply recapitulating the previous results and methods. As Gerd Theissen states, 'The altered presuppositions of the "third quest" [note my reservations above, however] require a reformulation of method',[72] especially, one might think, in the area of criteria for authenticity. My purpose in the rest of this

71. See Chapter 3, below, for analysis of these recent attempts. The major figures include Meier, *Marginal Jew*, I, pp. 167-95; and G. Theissen, 'Historical Scepticism and the Criteria of Jesus Research *or* My Attempt to Leap across Lessing's Yawning Gulf', *SJT* 49 (1996), pp. 147-76; G. Theissen and A. Merz, *Der historische Jesus: Ein Lehrbuch* (Göttingen: Vandenhoeck & Ruprecht, 1996; ET *The Historical Jesus: A Comprehensive Guide* [trans. J. Bowden; London: SCM Press; Minneapolis: Fortress Press, 1998]), esp. pp. 115-18; Theissen and Winter, *Die Kriterienfrage in der Jesusforschung*, esp. pp. 175-232. See also R.S. Barbour, *Traditio-Historical Criticism of the Gospels* (Studies in Creative Criticism, 4; London: SPCK, 1972); E. Schillebeeckx, *Jezus, het verhaal van een levende* (Bloemendaal: Nelissen, 1974; ET *Jesus: An Experiment in Christology* [trans. H. Hoskins; New York: Seabury, 1979]), pp. 81-100; R.H. Stein, 'The "Criteria" for Authenticity', in R.T. France and D. Wenham (eds.), *Gospel Perspectives: Studies of History and Tradition in the Four Gospels*, I (Sheffield: JSOT Press, 1980), pp. 225-63; D. Polkow, 'Method and Criteria for Historical Jesus Research', in K.H. Richards (ed.), *Society of Biblical Literature 1987 Seminar Papers* (SBLSP, 26; Atlanta: Scholars Press, 1987), pp. 336-56; C.A. Evans, 'Authenticity Criteria in Life of Jesus Research', *CSR* 19 (1989), pp. 6-31; refined and updated in *idem, Jesus and his Contemporaries*, pp. 13-26; *idem, Life of Jesus Research*, pp. 127-46, with bibliography; *idem*, 'Life of Jesus', in S.E. Porter (ed.), *Handbook to Exegesis of the New Testament* (NTTS, 25; Leiden: E.J. Brill, 1997), pp. 427-75, esp. pp. 441-46.

72. Theissen and Merz, *The Historical Jesus*, p. 116, on the basis of comments in what is now published in Theissen and Winter, *Die Kriterienfrage in der Jesusforschung*, pp. 28-174.

monograph is, within the established framework of historical-Jesus re-search as recounted above in this chapter, first, to trace briefly the devel-opment of the criteria for authenticity in Chapter 2; secondly, to discuss several recent innovations regarding the criteria, and their attempt at a shift in emphasis, in Chapter 3; and, thirdly, to suggest and define three new criteria that logically grow out of these recent developments in Chapters 4–6. Only once we have reached the end of Part 2, with its discussion of the three new criteria, will be be able to determine whether we have truly entered a new era in historical-Jesus research.

Table 1. *Timeline of the Quest for the Historical Jesus*

The following table lays out much of the information presented above in a chronological fashion. The first column lists in chronological order a selection of the major
authors who have written important works on the historical Jesus, with a date usually for their major or first contribution listed. The second column lists the defining
scholars who are often cited as marking the turning points in the various so-called
quests of the historical Jesus, with the date of this contribution listed. The third
column provides the labels and dates of these supposed quests and non-quests.
Other scholars will want to add other contributors (or subtract some) from this list.
It is meant to be descriptive and hence illustrative, not definitive.

Scholar	Turning Point	'Quest'
H.S. Reimarus (1778)	H.S. Reimarus (1778)	'Old' or 'First Quest'
J.G. Herder (1796)		(1778–1906)
H.E.G. Paulus (1828)		
D.F. Strauss (1835–36)		
E. Renan (1863)		
A. Edersheim (1883)		
M. Kähler (1882)		
B. Weiss (1888)		
J. Weiss (1892)		
A. Harnack (1900)		
A. Schweitzer (1901)		
W. Wrede (1901)		
W. Sanday (1899)		
W. Bousset (1904)		
	A. Schweitzer (1906)	'No Quest' (1906–1953)
A.T. Robertson (1908)		
H.F. Soden (1909)		
T.R. Glover (1917)		
A. Schlatter (1921)		
A.C. Headlam (1923)		
J. Klausner (1925)		
R. Bultmann (1926)		
M.-J. Lagrange (1928)		
K.L. Schmidt (1929)		
G. Bell and A. Deissmann (1930)		
T.W. Manson (1931)		
F.C. Burkitt (1932)		
M. Goguel (1932)		
C.H. Dodd (1932)		

Scholar	Turning Point	'Quest'
A. Loisy (1933)		
R.H. Lightfoot (1935)		
J. Jeremias (1935)		
M. Dibelius (1939)		
G. Ogg (1940)		
C.J. Cadoux (1941)		
W. Manson (1943)		
H. Daniel-Rops (1945)		
F.-M. Braun (1947)		
G.S. Duncan (1947)		
A.M. Hunter (1950)		
V. Taylor (1950)		
E.J. Goodspeed (1950)		
	E. Käsemann (1953)	'New' or 'Second Quest'
N. Dahl (1955)		(1953–88?)
G. Bornkamm (1956)		
W. Grundmann (1956)		
H.A. Guy (1957)		
E. Stauffer (1957)		
H. Zahrnt (1960)		
H.G. Wood (1960)		
M. Enslin (1961)		
B. Gerhardsson (1961)		
J. Knox (1962)		
E.C. Colwell (1963)		
J.A. Baird (1963)		
H. Anderson (1964)		
O. Betz (1965)		
W. Neil (1965)		
N. Perrin (1967)		
C.K. Barrett (1967)		
D. Flusser (1968)		
J. Reumann (1968)		
E. Schweizer (1968)		
H.K. McArthur (1969)		
H. Braun (1969)		
H. Riesenfeld (1970)		
H.C. Kee (1970)		
L.E. Keck (1971)		
E. Trocmé (1972)		
S. Schulz (1972)		
G. Vermes (1973)		
G. Aulén (1973)		

Scholar	Turning Point	'Quest'
C.L. Mitton (1973)		
E. Schillebeeckx (1974)		
G.N. Stanton (1974)		
W. Kasper (1974)		
L. Goppelt (1975)		
I.H. Marshall (1977)		
R.H. Stein (1978)		
B.F. Meyer (1979)		
J. Riches (1980)		
H. Carpenter (1980)		
R. Riesner (1981)		
J. Marsh (1981)		
A.E. Harvey (1982)		
G. O'Collins (1983)		
B. Chilton (1984)		
E.P. Sanders (1985)		
J.H. Charlesworth (1988)	N.T. Wright (1988)	'Third Quest' (1988?–)
P. Stuhlmacher (1988)		
I.M. Zeitlin (1988)		
J.S. Bowden (1988)		
G. Theissen (1986)		
J.P. Meier (1991)		
M. De Jonge (1991)		
J.D. Crossan (1992)		
M.J. Borg (1984)		
W.E. Phipps (1993)		
M. Bockmuehl (1994)		
S. Byrskog (1994)		
J. Beker (1995)		
C.A. Evans (1995)		
B. Witherington (1995)		
N.T. Wright (1996)		
L.T. Johnson (1996)		
P. Pokorný (1998)		
H. Schwarz (1998)		

Chapter 2

HISTORICAL DEVELOPMENT OF THE CRITERIA FOR AUTHENTICITY
AND THE RISE OF FORM (AND REDACTION) CRITICISM

1. *Introduction*

In this chapter, I turn to a historically based discussion of development
of the criteria for authenticity in historical-Jesus research.[1] Here I wish

1.   Few discussions of the criteria for authenticity place that discussion in a
historical context. For those who come close, see E. Schillebeeckx, *Jezus, het ver-*
haal van een levende (Bloemendaal: Nelissen, 1974; ET *Jesus: An Experiment in*
Christology [New York: Seabury, 1979]), pp. 62-100, with useful bibliography on
pp. 88-90; F. Lentzen-Deis, 'Kriterien für die historische Beurteilung der Jesusüberlieferung in den Evangelien', in K. Kertelge (ed.), *Rückfrage nach Jesus: Zur Meth-*
odik und Bedeutung der Frage nach dem historischen Jesus (QD, 63; Freiburg:
Herder, 1974), pp. 78-117, esp. pp. 81-93; M.E. Boring, 'The Historical-Critical
Method's "Criteria of Authenticity": The Beatitudes in Q and Thomas as a Test
Case', *Semeia* 44 (1988), pp. 9-44, esp. pp. 9-12, but who actually treats the criteria
in what he says has become a traditional order (p. 12 n. 8); and G. Theissen and
D. Winter, *Die Kriterienfrage in der Jesusforschung: Vom Differenzkriterium zum*
Plausibilitätskriterium (NTOA, 34; Freiburg: Universitätsverlag; Göttingen: Van-
denhoeck & Ruprecht, 1997), esp. pp. 1-174. Cf. H.W.E. Turner, *Historicity and the*
Gospels: A Sketch of Historical Method and its Application to the Gospels (London:
Mowbrays, 1963), pp. 58-108. For synoptic rather than historical discussions of the
criteria, see W.O. Walker, 'The Quest for the Historical Jesus: A Discussion of
Methodology', *ATR* 51 (1969), pp. 38-56; N.J. McEleney, 'Authenticating Criteria
and Mark 7:1-23', *CBQ* 34 (1972), pp. 431-60; R.S. Barbour, *Traditio-Historical*
Criticism of the Gospels (Studies in Creative Criticism, 4; London: SPCK, 1972); F.
Mussner, 'Methodologie der Frage nach dem historischen Jesus', in Kertelge (ed.),
Rückfrage nach Jesus, pp. 118-47; repr. in F. Mussner, *Jesus von Nazareth im*
Umfeld Israels und der Urkirche: Gesammelte Aufsätze (ed. M. Theobald; WUNT,
111; Tübingen: Mohr Siebeck, 1999), pp. 13-42; R.H. Stein, 'The "Criteria" for
Authenticity', in R.T. France and D. Wenham (eds.), *Gospel Perspectives: Studies*
of History and Tradition in the Four Gospels, I (Sheffield: JSOT Press, 1980), pp.
225-63; R. Riesner, *Jesus als Lehrer: Eine Untersuchung zum Ursprung der*

simply to trace the basic outline of the narrative, but even this brief narrative may be more complex than some realize. As mentioned above in Chapter 1, the rise of New Testament form criticism especially in Germany of the 1920s,[2] within the course of the further and ongoing devel-

---

Evangelien-Überlieferung (WUNT, 2.7; Tübingen: Mohr Siebeck, 1981; 4th edn, 1994), pp. 87-96; D. Polkow, 'Method and Criteria for Historical Jesus Research', in K.H. Richards (ed.), *Society of Biblical Literature 1987 Seminar Papers* (SBLSP, 26; Atlanta: Scholars Press, 1987), pp. 336-56; S. McKnight, *Interpreting the Synoptic Gospels* (Guides to New Testament Exegesis; Grand Rapids: Baker Book House, 1988), pp. 59-69; J.P. Meier, *A Marginal Jew: Rethinking the Historical Jesus* (3 vols.; ABRL; New York: Doubleday, 1991–), I, pp. 167-95, with useful bibliography on pp. 186-87 n. 7; C.A. Evans, *Life of Jesus Research: An Annotated Bibliography* (NTTS, 24; Leiden: E.J. Brill, rev. edn, 1996), pp. 127-46; *idem, Jesus and his Contemporaries: Comparative Studies* (AGJU, 25; Leiden: E.J. Brill, 1995), pp. 13-26 (these reflect his earlier article, 'Authenticity Criteria in Life of Jesus Research', *CSR* 19 [1989], pp. 6-31); *idem*, 'Life of Jesus', in S.E. Porter (ed.), *Handbook to Exegesis of the New Testament* (NTTS, 25; Leiden: E.J. Brill, 1997), pp. 427-75, esp. pp. 441-46. See also the handy chronologically arranged collection of secondary literature up to the 1960s in H.K. McArthur (ed.), *In Search of the Historical Jesus* (New York: Charles Scribner's Sons, 1969).

    2.   The classic works of form criticism include K.L. Schmidt, *Der Rahmen der Geschichte Jesu: Literarkritische Untersuchungen zur ältesten Jesusüberlieferung* (Berlin: Trowitzsch, 1919); M. Dibelius, *Die Formgeschichte des Evangeliums* (Tübingen: Mohr Siebeck, 1919; 2nd edn, 1933; 6th edn, ed. G. Bornkamm, 1971; ET *From Tradition to Gospel* [trans. B. Woolf; London: Ivor Nicholson & Watson, 1934]); *idem, Gospel Criticism and Christology* (London: Ivor Nicholson & Watson, 1935); R. Bultmann, *Die Geschichte der synoptischen Tradition* (FRLANT, 29; Göttingen: Vandenhoeck & Ruprecht, 1921; 2nd edn, 1931; 6th edn, 1957; ET *History of the Synoptic Tradition* [trans. J. Marsh; Oxford: Basil Blackwell, 1963; 2nd edn, 1968]); *idem*, 'The New Approach to the Synoptic Problem', *JR* 6 (1926), pp. 337-62; repr. in S. Ogden (ed.), *Existence and Faith: Shorter Writings of Rudolf Bultmann* (New York: Meridian, 1960; London: Hodder & Stoughton, 1961), pp. 35-54; and V. Taylor, *The Formation of the Gospel Tradition* (London: Macmillan, 1933; 2nd edn, 1935). Early and important summaries of the method are W.K.L. Clarke, *New Testament Problems: Essays—Reviews—Interpretations* (London: SPCK, 1929), pp. 18-30; E.B. Redlich, *Form Criticism: Its Value and Limitations* (Studies in Theology; London: Gerald Duckworth, 1939). It must not be overlooked that there were a number of important works that anticipated form criticism of the Gospels. They include W. Wrede, *Das Messiasgeheimnis in den Evangelien: Zugleich ein Beitrag zum Verständnis des Markusevangeliums* (Göttingen: Vandenhoeck & Ruprecht, 1901; ET *The Messianic Secret* [trans. J.C.G. Greig; Cambridge: J. Clarke, 1971]); J. Wellhausen, *Das Evangelium Marci* (Berlin: G. Reimer, 1903); *idem, Das Evangelium Matthaei* (Berlin: G. Reimer, 1904); *idem, Das Evangelium*

opment of post-Enlightenment higher criticism,[3] took place in conjunction with the development of supposed criteria regarding authenticity of
the Jesus tradition. As will be noted further below, this is not to deny
that there were antecedent criteria suggested, dating all the way back to
the Enlightenment, and before, but the most important and sustained
discussion of the criteria seems to have coincided with the development
of form criticism. This growth is also often linked to the so-called 'no-
quest' period in historical-Jesus research. As a result, the criteria to a
large extent reflect the modes of thought that were typical of those who
developed form criticism, one of the most important and enduring critical methods to be utilized in New Testament studies. This link between
form criticism and historical-Jesus research is perfectly understandable.
As a result of the scepticism engendered in some circles by those typically identified as part of the 'no quest' period (and who were at the
heart of developing form criticism), the burden was placed upon those
who wished to distinguish tradition and its development within the early
Church from the purported authentic words and actions of Jesus. A number of tenets came to be identified with form criticism, as it developed
and continued to be utilized.[4] For example, form criticism was concerned with the definition and study of literary forms or types apart

Lucae (Berlin: G. Reimer, 1904); and E. Norden, *Agnostos Theos: Untersuchungen
zur Formengeschichte religiöser Rede* (Stuttgart: Teubner, 1913; repr. Darmstadt:
Wissenschaftliche Buchgesellschaft, 1956), esp. pp. 277-308.

3.   This is not the place to discuss the entire rise and development of historical
criticism. For a brief and informative guide, see E. Krentz, *The Historical-Critical
Method* (GBS; Philadelphia: Fortress Press, 1975). For brief overviews of the his-
torical development of form criticism, see W.G. Kümmel, *Das Neue Testament:
Geschichte der Erforschung seiner Probleme* (Munich: Alber, 1958; rev. edn, 1970;
ET *The New Testament: The History of the Investigation of its Problems* [trans.
S.M. Gilmour and H.C. Kee; Nashville: Abingdon Press, 1972]), esp. pp. 325-40;
E.V. McKnight, *What is Form Criticism?* (GBS; Philadelphia: Fortress Press,
1969), esp. pp. 57-78; W.G. Doty, 'The Discipline and Literature of New Testa-
ment Form Criticism', *ATR* 51 (1969), pp. 257-321, esp. pp. 260-85 for bibliog-
raphy, and pp. 285-319 for discussion; N. Perrin, *What is Redaction Criticism?*
(GBS; Philadelphia: Fortress Press; London: SCM Press, 1970), pp. 13-21; and E.E.
Ellis, 'The Historical Jesus and the Gospels', in J. Ådna, S.J. Hafemann and
O. Hofius (eds.), *Evangelium Schriftauslegung Kirche: Festschrift für Peter Stuhlmacher zum 65. Geburtstag* (Göttingen: Vandenhoeck & Ruprecht, 1997), pp. 94-
106.

from their context as now found in the Gospels. This was in an effort to recover their pre-Gospel use in the life of the early Church, and, to a lesser extent, their possible setting in the life of Jesus. Form criticism emphasized that the early Church had a formative influence upon the

4.   Overviews and assessments of form criticism in terms of its categories and major tenets abound. Among the many, especially since Doty's article ('Discipline and Literature'), see K. Koch, *Was ist Formgeschichte? Neue Wege der Bibelexegese* (Neukirchen–Vluyn: Neukirchener Verlag, 1964; 2nd edn, 1967; ET *The Growth of the Biblical Tradition: The Form-Critical Method* [trans. S.M. Cupitt; New York: Charles Scribner's Sons, 1969); H. Zimmermann, *Neutestamentliche Methodenlehre: Darstellung der historisch-kritischen Methode* (Stuttgart: Katholische Bibelwerk, 1967; 2nd edn, 1968), esp. pp. 129-76; G.N. Stanton, 'Form Criticism Revisited', in M.D. Hooker and C. Hickling (eds.), *What about the New Testament? Essays in Honour of Christopher Evans* (London: SCM Press, 1975), pp. 13-27; E.E. Ellis, 'New Directions in Form Criticism', in G. Strecker (ed.), *Jesus Christus in Historie und Theologie* (Festschrift H. Conzelmann; Tübingen: Mohr Siebeck, 1975), pp. 299-315; repr. in E.E. Ellis, *Prophecy and Hermeneutic in Early Christianity* (WUNT, 18; Tübingen: Mohr Siebeck, 1978; repr. Grand Rapids: Eerdmans, 1980), pp. 237-53; *idem*, 'Gospels Criticism: A Perspective on the State of the Art', in P. Stuhlmacher (ed.), *The Gospel and the Gospels* (Grand Rapids: Eerdmans, 1991), pp. 26-52, esp. pp. 37-41 (originally published in P. Stuhlmacher [ed.], *Das Evangelium und die Evangelien* [WUNT, 28; Tübingen: Mohr Siebeck, 1983]), pp. 27-54; S.H. Travis, 'Form Criticism', in I.H. Marshall (ed.), *New Testament Interpretation: Essays on Principles and Methods* (Exeter: Paternoster Press; Grand Rapids: Eerdmans, 1977), pp. 153-64; R.F. Collins, *Introduction to the New Testament* (Garden City, NY: Doubleday, 1983), pp. 156-95; H. Conzelmann and A. Lindemann, *Arbeitsbuch zum Neuen Testament* (Tübingen: Mohr Siebeck, 8th edn, 1985; ET *Interpreting the New Testament: An Introduction to the Principles and Methods of New Testament Exegesis* [trans. S.S. Schatzmann; Peabody, MA: Hendrickson, 1988]), pp. 59-82; R.H. Stein, *The Synoptic Problem: An Introduction* (Grand Rapids: Baker Book House, 1987), pp. 161-228; C.L. Blomberg, *The Historical Reliability of the Gospels* (Leicester: Inter-Varsity Press, 1987), pp. 20-35; C.M. Tuckett, *Reading the New Testament: Methods of Interpretation* (London: SPCK, 1987), pp. 95-115; McKnight, *Interpreting the Synoptic Gospels*, pp. 71-82; E.V. McKnight, 'Form and Redaction Criticism', in E.J. Epp and G.W. MacRae (eds.), *The New Testament and its Modern Interpreters* (The Bible and its Modern Interpreters; Atlanta: Scholars Press, 1989), pp. 149-74, esp. pp. 150-53; E.P. Sanders and M. Davies, *Studying the Synoptic Gospels* (London: SCM Press; Philadelphia: Trinity Press International, 1989), pp. 123-97, who also include a historical survey on pp. 123-37; D.L. Bock, 'Form Criticism', in D.A. Black and D.S. Dockery (eds.), *New Testament Criticism and Interpretation* (Grand Rapids: Zondervan, 1991), pp. 175-96; N.T. Wright, *The New Testament and the People of God* (London: SPCK, 1992), pp. 418-35; B. Chilton, 'Traditio-Historical Criticism and

formulation and development of tradition about Jesus, and that any given pericope had to be considered in terms of its literary form and the placement and use of that form within the early Church.[5] Redaction criticism then came into its own in the 1950s[6] as a natural extension of

Study of Jesus', in J.B. Green (ed.), *Hearing the New Testament: Strategies for Interpretation* (Grand Rapids: Eerdmans; Carlisle: Paternoster Press, 1995), pp. 37-60, esp. pp. 39-42; and C.A. Evans, 'Source, Form and Redacton Criticism: The "Traditional" Methods of Synoptic Interpretation', in S.E. Porter and D. Tombs (eds.), *Approaches to New Testament Study* (JSNTSup, 120; Sheffield: JSOT Press, 1995), pp. 17-45, esp. pp. 27-32; *idem*, 'Life of Jesus', pp. 433-37. Despite the criticism of such people as H. Palmer, *The Logic of Gospel Criticism: An Account of the Methods and Arguments Used by Textual, Documentary, Source, and Form Critics of the New Testament* (London: Macmillan; New York: St Martin's, 1968), esp. pp. 175-94; E. Güttgemanns, *Offene Fragen zur Formgeschichte des Evangeliums: Eine methodologische Skizze der Grundlagenproblematik der Form- und Redaktionsgeschichte* (BEvT, 54; Munich: Chr. Kaiser Verlag, 1970; 2nd edn, 1971; ET *Candid Questions Concerning Gospel Form Criticism: A Methodological Sketch of the Fundamental Problematics of Form and Redaction Criticism* [trans. W.G. Doty; Pittsburgh: Pickwick Press, 1979]); K. Berger, *Exegese des Neuen Testaments: Neue Wege vom Text zur Auslegung* (UTb, 658; Heidelberg: Quelle & Meyer, 1977); *idem*, 'Hellenistische Gattungen im Neuen Testament', *ANRW* 2.25.2, pp. 1031-1432; *idem*, *Einführung in die Formgeschichte* (UTb, 1444; Tübingen: Franke, 1987); G. Theissen, *Urchristliche Wundergeschichten: Ein Beitrag zur formgeschichtlichen Erforschung der synoptischen Evangelien* (SNT, 8; Gütersloh: Gerd Mohn, 1974; ET *The Miracle Stories of Early Christian Tradition* [trans. F. McDonagh; SNTW; Edinburgh: T. & T. Clark; Philadelphia: Fortress Press, 1983]), esp. pp. 1-27, form criticism still seems to be alive and well, despite acknowledgment of its weaknesses and its need for modifications (see McKnight, 'Form and Redaction Criticism', pp. 166-67).

5. See Sanders and Davies, *Studying the Synoptic Gospels*, p. 123.

6. The major works often cited as marking the instigation of redaction criticism include G. Bornkamm, 'Die Sturmstillung im Matthäusevangelium', *Wort und Dienst: Jahrbuch der Theologischen Schule Bethel* NS 1 (1948), pp. 49-54; repr. in G. Bornkamm, G. Barth and H.J. Held, *Überlieferung und Auslegung im Matthäusevangelium* (Neukirchen–Vluyn: Neukirchener Verlag, 1960; ET *Tradition and Interpretation in Matthew* [trans. P. Scott; NTL; London: SCM Press; Philadelphia: Westminster Press, 1963]), pp. 52-57, along with another article by Bornkamm ('Enderwartung und Kirche im Matthäusevangelium', in W.D. Davies and D. Daube [eds.], *The Background of the New Testament and its Eschatology: Studies in Honour of C.H. Dodd* [Cambridge: Cambridge University Press, 1954], pp. 222-60) and the 1955 and 1957 dissertations of his students, Barth and Held; H. Conzelmann, *Die Mitte der Zeit: Studien zur Theologie des Lukas* (BHT, 17; Tübingen: Mohr Siebeck, 1953; 2nd edn, 1957; 4th edn, 1962; ET *The Theology of St Luke*

form criticism[7]—with emphasis upon the individual Gospel writers as interpreters and shapers of tradition.[8] This new criticism (often linked with the so-called 'new' or 'second quest') did not significantly alter the development of the criteria for authenticity, except perhaps to see them become even more firmly entrenched. Many of the same scholars

[trans. G. Buswell; New York: Harper & Brothers; London: Faber & Faber, 1960]); W. Marxsen, *Der Evangelist Markus: Studien zur Redaktionsgeschichte des Evangeliums* (FRLANT, 67; Göttingen: Vandenhoeck & Ruprecht, 1956; 2nd edn, 1959; ET *Mark the Evangelist: Studies on the Redaction History of the Gospel* [trans. J. Boyce *et al.*; Nashville: Abingdon Press, 1969]); and E. Haenchen, *Der Weg Jesu: Eine Erklärung des Markus-Evangeliums und der kanonischen Parallelen* (Berlin: Alfred Töpelmann, 1966; Berlin: W. de Gruyter, 2nd edn, 1968). Precursors of redaction criticism are often seen in Wrede, *Messianic Secret*; R.H. Lightfoot, *History and Interpretation in the Gospels* (London: Hodder & Stoughton; New York: Harper, 1935); *idem, Locality and Doctrine in the Gospels* (London: Hodder & Stoughton, 1938); *idem, The Gospel Message of St Mark* (Oxford: Clarendon Press, 1950); N.B. Stonehouse, *The Witness of Matthew and Mark to Christ* (London: Tyndale Press, 1944; repr. Grand Rapids: Eerdmans, 1958); A.M. Farrer, *A Study in St Mark* (London: Dacre Press, 1951); *idem, St Matthew and St Mark* (London: Dacre Press, 1954); and J.M. Robinson, *The Problem of History in Mark* (SBT, 21; London: SCM Press, 1957).

7.   The final section of Bultmann's *History of the Synoptic Tradition* is entitled 'Die Redaktion des Erzählungsstoffes und die Komposition der Evangelien' (German pp. 362-92; English pp. 337-67). Sanders and Davies (*Studying the Synoptic Gospels*, pp. 201-202) see this section as inspiring Bultmann's pupils in their development of redaction criticism.

8.   For discussion and assessment of redaction criticism, among many sources (here not noting those that simply apply redaction criticism), see H. Flender, *Heil und Geschichte in der Theologie des Lukas* (BEvT, 41; Munich: Chr. Kaiser Verlag, 1965; ET *St Luke: Theologian of Redemptive History* [trans. R.H. and I. Fuller; London: SPCK, 1967]); Zimmermann, *Neutestamentliche Methodenlehre*, pp. 214-30; J. Rohde, *Die redaktionsgeschichtliche Methode: Einführung und Sichtung des Forschungestandes* (Hamburg: Furche Verlag, 1966; rev. edn, 1968; ET *Rediscovering the Teaching of the Evangelists* [trans. D.M. Barton; NTL; London: SCM Press, 1968]); R.H. Stein, 'What Is *Redaktionsgeschichte*?', *JBL* 88 (1969), pp. 45-56; *idem, Synoptic Problem*, pp. 231-72; Perrin, *Redaction Criticism*, esp. pp. 25-39; I.H. Marshall, *Luke: Historian and Theologian* (Exeter: Paternoster Press, 1970); M.D. Hooker, 'In his Own Image?', in Hooker and Hickling (eds.), *What about the New Testament?*, pp. 28-44; S.S. Smalley, 'Redaction Criticism', in Marshall (ed.), *New Testament Interpretation*, pp. 181-95; Collins, *Introduction to the New Testament*, pp. 196-230; D.A. Carson, 'Redaction Criticism: On the Legitimacy and Illegitimacy of a Literary Tool', in D.A. Carson and J.D. Woodbridge (eds.), *Scripture and Truth* (Grand Rapids: Zondervan, 1983), pp. 119-42; Blomberg, *Historical*

who were involved in development of form and redaction criticism were also those involved in development and refinement of the criteria for authenticity, although others were involved as well. In the light of this climate (see the Excursus, below, for a graphic display of the development of the major criteria for authenticity in relation to form and redaction criticism, and the so-called 'quests' for the historical Jesus), I turn now to a historically based discussion of the development of the criteria for authenticity. In this study, I have selected those criteria that seem to have been the most important in historical-Jesus research, and trace the development of each from a roughly chronological standpoint.

2. *The Criteria for Authenticity and their Development*

In this section, I will treat the major criteria often utilized and discussed in various other works on the historical Jesus. The number treated is a necessarily limited selection from the vast variety suggested and treated by other scholars. In his treatment of the topic, Polkow examines five previous treatments of the criteria for authenticity, and compiles a master list of 25 such criteria. He then formulates various combinations of these criteria, in an attempt to arrive at a manageable group for discussion.[9] Evans characterizes Polkow's treatment as 'finely nuanced', but

Reliability of the Gospels, pp. 35-43; Tuckett, *Reading the New Testament*, pp. 116-35; McKnight, *Interpreting the Synoptic Gospels*, pp. 83-95; McKnight, 'Form and Redaction Criticism', pp. 153-64; Sanders and Davies, *Studying the Synoptic Gospels*, pp. 201-98; G.R. Osborne, 'Redaction Criticism', in Black and Dockery (eds.), *New Testament Criticism and Interpretation*, pp. 199-224; G.P. Corrington, 'Redaction Criticism', in S.R. Haynes and S.L. McKenzie (eds.), *To Each its Own Meaning: An Introduction to Biblical Criticisms and their Application* (Louisville, KY: Westminster/John Knox Press, 1993), pp. 87-99; J.R. Donahue, 'Redaction Criticism: Has the *Hauptstrasse* Become a *Sackgasse*?', in E.S. Malbon and E.V. McKnight (eds.), *The New Literary Criticism and the New Testament* (JSNTSup, 109; Sheffield: JSOT Press, 1994), pp. 27-57; Evans, 'Source, Form and Redaction Criticism', pp. 33-37; *idem*, 'Life of Jesus', pp. 437-41. Several of these assessments see more modern methods developing out of redaction criticism, such as various types of literary criticism. On this, see especially S.D. Moore, *Literary Criticism and the Gospels: The Theoretical Challenge* (New Haven: Yale University Press, 1989), esp. pp. 56-58.

9.   Polkow, 'Method and Criteria', pp. 338, 342. Polkow analyses the work of Walker, 'Quest for the Historical Jesus'; McEleney, 'Authenticating Criteria'; Stein, ' "Criteria" for Authenticity'; J. Breech, *The Silence of Jesus: The Authentic Voice of the Authentic Man* (Philadelphia: Fortress Press, 1980), pp. 9, 22-26, 66-85; and

then goes on to elucidate this statement by (rightly) saying that it is 'at times "hair-splitting"'.[10] As Polkow's own study shows by his attempt to lump together various criteria, there simply are not that many criteria, and one soon realizes that the same criterion is frequently called by several different names, depending upon the scholar who is using and labelling it. Rather than attempt such a dissection, here I trace the historical development of the major criteria for authenticity that have entered into and endured in the discussion of the historical Jesus, and offer a brief critique of each one. The notes in this chapter should provide enough documentation for those wishing to pursue both the proponents and the criticisms in more detail.

a. *Criterion of Double Dissimilarity*

As noted above in defining form criticism, the development of the form-critical framework soon meant that any tradition that could be shown to go back to the early Church was surely open to question regarding its authenticity as originating with Jesus and his first followers; likewise, if the early Church could not be relied upon, neither could the Jewish context of early Christianity to provide genuinely authentic Jesus material. As a result, the criterion of dissimilarity, or, better, double dissimilarity,[11] as it was originally and has usually been formulated, was developed and began to be utilized. At least, that is how the criterion is typically described with regard to its origins and utilization. This criterion has a long and enduring history, at least from the rise of form criticism through to the current reign of redaction criticism.[12] As might be expected in the light of the development of form criticism, one of the early and (what has become) most important formulations of this criterion

Boring, 'Criteria of Authenticity'. Cf. F.G. Downing, *The Church and Jesus: A Study in History, Philosophy and Theology* (SBT, 10; London: SCM Press, 1968), pp. 93-131, who also includes a very large number (counting them is made difficult by the fact that they are not clearly differentiated as to whether they are all criteria), but does not attempt to coordinate them.

10. Evans, *Jesus and his Contemporaries*, p. 13 n. 34.

11. Schillebeeckx (*Jesus*, p. 92) calls it the 'principle of dual irreducibility'; he generally endorses it within its limits (noted below).

12. A lengthy history of this criterion, which goes all the way back to Renaissance humanism in their discussion and proceeds to the present, is to be found in Theissen and Winter, *Die Kriterienfrage in der Jesusforschung*, pp. 28-174; cf. pp. 270-316, where they provide excerpts from those who have formulated and commented upon the criterion of dissimilarity, from 1521 to 1995.

came from Rudolf Bultmann in his *History of the Synoptic Tradition*. However, the following casual formulation of this criterion is made only incidentally regarding similitudes: 'We can only count on possessing a genuine similitude of Jesus where, on the one hand, expression is given to the contrast between Jewish morality and piety and the distinctive eschatological temper which characterized the preaching of Jesus; and where on the other hand we find no specifically Christian features'.[13] Elsewhere in the same book, Bultmann admits that some of Jesus' statements resembled Jewish wisdom.[14] This latter statement would appear to be in direct contradiction with the statement regarding similitudes, and would thus apparently call into question whether he meant for his statement regarding similitudes to have any general application beyond the immediate context in which the formulation was made, that is, as the concluding statement to the section on similitudes and similar forms. In the light of what has happened in the development of the criteria for authenticity, however, such a question is now strictly academic. The reality is that what began as a casual and qualified statement by Bultmann

13. Bultmann, *Synoptic Tradition*, p. 205. C.J. den Heyer (*Wie is Jezus? Balans van 150 jaar onderzoek naar Jesus* [Zoetermeer, The Netherlands: Uitgeverij Meinema, 1996; ET *Jesus Matters: 150 Years of Research* (trans. J. Bowden: London: SCM Press, 1996)], pp. 132-33, 188) uses this statement to represent what he calls a 'minimal' approach to criteria. Bultmann was not the first to think in terms of something like this criterion, however, as Boring ('Criteria of Authenticity', p. 17) makes clear, but Bultmann has undoubtedly been the most influential. For earlier formulations, see W. Heitmüller, *Jesus* (Tübingen: J.C.B. Mohr, 1913), pp. 34-35 (to whom Bultmann dedicated his *Synoptic Tradition*); and P.W. Schmiedel, 'Gospels', in T.K. Cheyne and J.S. Black (eds.), *Encyclopaedia Biblica: A Critical Dictionary of the Literary, Political and Religious History, the Archaeology, Geography and Natural History of the Bible* (4 vols.; London: A. & C. Black, 1899–1907), II, cols. 1761-898, esp. cols. 1847, and 1881-83, where he defines his nine 'foundation-pillars for a truly scientific Life of Jesus' (col. 1881), which were unlikely to have been created by the post-Easter Church (about Jesus in general: Mk 10.17-18; Mt. 12.31-32; Mk 3.21; Mk 13.32; Mk 15.34 = Mt. 27.46; on the miracles of Jesus: Mk 8.12 = Mt. 12.38 = Lk. 11.29; Mk 6.5-6; Mk 8.14-21; Mt. 11.5 = Lk. 7.22). Cf. also his P.W. Schmiedel, *Das vierte Evangelium gegenüber den drei ersten* (Tübingen: J.C.B. Mohr, 1906; ET *The Johannine Writings* [trans. M.A. Canney; London: A. & C. Black, 1908]), pp. 25-30. See F.F. Bruce, *Tradition Old and New* (Exeter: Paternoster Press, 1970), p. 48.
14. Bultmann, *Synoptic Tradition*, pp. 101-108.

with regard to only one literary form-critical type, the similitude,[15] was nevertheless soon made into a more absolute criterion by others who utilized it.

In his so-called clarion call to re-open investigation of the historical Jesus, Ernst Käsemann actually goes further than Bultmann in the way in which he stringently formulates this criterion of dissimilarity:

> We can only sketch in a few bold strokes the embarrassment of critical research. It lies in this; while the historical credibility of the Synoptic tradition has become doubtful all along the line, yet at the same time we are still short of one essential requisite for the identification of the authentic Jesus material, namely, a conspectus of the very earliest stage of primitive Christian history; and also there is an almost complete lack of satisfactory and water-tight criteria for this material. In only one case do we have more or less ground under our feet; *when there are no grounds either for deriving a tradition from Judaism or for ascribing it to primitive Christianity...*[16]

This statement is an important part of Käsemann's outlining of an appropriate method for a return to historical-Jesus research. The statement appears to be anything but optimistic about the possibility of a quest for the historical Jesus—apart from this lone double-edged criterion of difference. Thus, this major criterion was at first incidentally formulated by Bultmann as part of his development of form criticism, and during the period of supposedly highest scepticism in Jesus research (the so-called 'no-quest' period). It was in fact fully integrated into the quest

15. Boring ('Criteria of Authenticity', p. 17) provides an alternative translation of Bultmann's statement regarding similitudes, emphasizing that Bultmann was speaking in terms of probabilities, not laying down an absolute and exclusive principle. However, the German seems more absolute in its formulation: 'Wo der Gegensatz zur jüdischen Moral und Frömmigkeit und die spezifisch eschatologische Stimmung, die das Charakteristikum der Verkündigung Jesu bilden, zum Ausdruck kommt, und wo sich andrerseits keine spezifisch christlichen Züge finden, darf man am ehesten urteilen, ein echtes Gleichnis Jesu zu besitzen' (Bultmann, *Synoptische Tradition*, p. 222).

16. E. Käsemann, 'Das Problem des historischen Jesus', *ZTK* 51 (1954), pp. 125-53 (repr. in *idem, Exegetische Versuche und Besinnungen,* I [Göttingen: Vandenhoeck & Ruprecht, 2nd edn, 1960], pp. 187-214); ET 'The Problem of the Historical Jesus', in *idem, Essays on New Testament Themes* (trans. W.J. Montague; SBT, 41; London: SCM Press, 1964; Philadelphia: Fortress Press, 1982), pp. 15-47 (36-37) (italics mine). See also O. Cullmann, *Heil als Geschichte: Heilsgeschichtliche Existenz im Neuen Testament* (Tübingen: Mohr Siebeck, 1965; ET *Salvation in History* [NTL; trans. S.G. Sowers; London: SCM Press, 1967]), p. 189.

through Käsemann's highly sceptical extension and clear solidification of it, coincidental with the inauguration of the so-called 'new' or 'second quest'. Käsemann as much as admits to the limitations imposed by this criterion when he states, regarding his attempt at analysis of Jesus, 'in so doing we must realize beforehand that we shall not, from this angle of vision, gain any clear view of the connecting link between Jesus, his Palestinian environment and his later community'.[17]

For many recent interpreters, however, the essential formulation of the criterion of double dissimilarity is to be found in Norman Perrin's now classic work on redaction criticism. Perrin's formulation appears to reflect the decisive orientation of Käsemann, since he clearly begins from the presumption of inauthenticity: 'material may be ascribed to Jesus only if it can be shown to be distinctive of him, which usually will mean dissimilar to known tendencies in Judaism before him or the church after him'.[18] This represents a significant shift, certainly from Bultmann, in both its widespread and encompassing applicability and its negativity. In other words, the only authentic Jesus material is that which meets both parts of this criterion. Nevertheless, no less a scholar than Martin Hengel uses this very criterion of double dissimilarity in his important study of Jesus as a charismatic leader, when he attempts to establish the authenticity of Mt. 8.22, 'let the dead bury the dead'. According to Hengel, the saying 'is in fact hardly one that can stem from the tradition either of the Jewish or of the later community'.[19] This is as clear an affirmation of the use of the principle as I have found.

Despite how firmly entrenched it appears to be, there have been several noteworthy points of reconsideration of this criterion. The first

17. Käsemann, 'Problem of the Historical Jesus', p. 37.

18. Perrin, *Redaction Criticism*, p. 71; cf. *idem, Rediscovering the Teaching of Jesus* (NTL; London: SCM Press; New York: Harper & Row, 1967), pp. 39-43, for what has become a classic formulation of the criteria, especially by a redaction critic. See also H. Zahrnt, *Es begann mit Jesus von Nazareth: Die Frage nach dem historischen Jesus* (Stuttgart: Kreuz, 1960; ET *The Historical Jesus* [trans. J.S. Bowden; London: Collins; New York: Harper & Row, 1963]), p. 107; Turner, *Historicity and the Gospels*, pp. 73-75; D.L. Mealand, 'The Dissimilarity Test', *SJT* 31 (1978), pp. 41-50; Walker, 'Quest for the Historical Jesus', pp. 46-47; McEleney, 'Authenticating Criteria', pp. 440-42; Sanders and Davies, *Studying the Synoptic Gospels*, pp. 304-23 (who divide the criterion into its two parts).

19. M. Hengel, *Nachfolge und Charisma* (Berlin: W. de Gruyter, 1968; ET *The Charismatic Leader and his Followers* [trans. J.C.G. Greig; Edinburgh: T. & T. Clark, 1981; repr. 1996]), p. 5 (the translation is admittedly awkward).

is that it has been argued that this criterion cannot be used in a negative way to delimit the authentic Jesus material, as tempting a possibility as that might at first seem to be. That is, critics say, if a saying does not meet this criterion, the saying is not thereby proven to be inauthentic, since it is impossible to prove a negative such as this. This procedure only shows that this criterion cannot be used to argue for the saying's authenticity.[20] A further criticism is that this criterion, by its very nature and formulation, cannot address questions of the specific words of Jesus, but only the content of his teaching in comparison with that of Judaism and the early Church.[21] Another point is that this criterion depends upon a highly and, in fact, exhaustive detailed knowledge of both Judaism and the early Church. This is a knowledge that scholarship arguably still does not possess to the degree that is required to make sure pronouncements using this criterion.[22] One needs only to compare how much more is now known of Judaism contemporary with Jesus after discovery and publication of the Dead Sea Scrolls than was known before to appreciate the strength of this criticism.[23] The major reconsideration of

20. See, e.g., R.H. Fuller, *A Critical Introduction to the New Testament* (London: Gerald Duckworth, 1966), pp. 96-97, an excellent brief summary of the criteria; C.F.D. Moule, *The Phenomenon of the New Testament* (London: SCM Press, 1967), pp. 70-72; R.T. France, 'The Authenticity of the Sayings of Jesus', in C. Brown (ed.), *History, Criticism and Faith* (Downers Grove, IL: InterVarsity Press, 1977), pp. 101-43, esp. pp. 110-14, in direct response to Perrin.

21. D. Lührmann, 'Die Frage nach Kriterien für ursprüngliche Jesusworte: Eine Problemskizze', in J. Dupont (ed.), *Jésus aux origines de la christologie* (BETL, 40; Gembloux: Duculot, 1975; Leuven: Leuven University Press/Peeters, 2nd edn, 1989), pp. 59-72, esp. pp. 62-65.

22. Barbour, *Traditio-Historical Criticism*, p. 7.

23. As mere samples of recent work on Judaism, see R.A. Kraft and G.W.E. Nickelsburg (eds.), *Early Judaism and its Modern Interpreters* (The Bible and its Modern Interpreters; Atlanta: Scholars Press; Philadelphia: Fortress Press, 1986); G. Boccaccini, *Middle Judaism: Jewish Thought 300 B.C.E. to 200 C.E.* (Minneapolis: Fortress Press, 1991); E.P. Sanders, *Judaism: Practice and Belief 63 BCE–66 CE* (London: SCM Press; Philadelphia: Trinity Press International, 1992); J.D.G. Dunn, 'Jesus and Factionalism in Early Judaism', in J.H. Charlesworth and L.L. Johns (eds.), *Hillel and Jesus: Comparative Studies of Two Major Religious Leaders* (Minneapolis: Fortress Press, 1997), pp. 156-75. G.N. Stanton ('Jesus of Nazareth: A Magician and a False Prophet who Deceived God's People?', in J.B. Green and M. Turner [eds.], *Jesus of Nazareth: Lord and Christ. Essays on the Historical Jesus and New Testament Christology* [Grand Rapids: Eerdmans; Carlisle: Paternoster Press, 1994], pp. 164-80, esp. pp. 164-65) states how little is known of

this criterion, in some circles, however, has been in terms of the re-newed acceptance and affirmation of Jesus' Jewish background.[24] This recognition of his Jewish background has led to a revision of the crite-rion's double dissimilarity to a singular dissimilarity with developments in the early Church. It *may* be true that this double criterion arrives at a 'critically assured *minimum*' of authentic Jesus tradition (at least, so the claim goes),[25] but it is thought by many scholars to be odd that Jesus, himself a Jew, should be said to be speaking authentically only when he does not reflect his genuine and authentic background.[26] As a result, a number of scholars have endorsed the single dissimilarity criterion of difference from developments in the early Church. As noted above, Bultmann himself left this form of the criterion open as a possibility, with his recognition of similarities between Jesus' teaching and Jewish wisdom. However, it subsequently was solidified by other scholars into its double form, especially by those identified with the so-called 'new' or 'second quest'. Ben Meyer is apparently one of the earliest to have

the first-century sabbath observance, noting that Reimarus's and Strauss's positions on this issue still define the terms of the debate.

24. See Theissen and Winter, *Die Kriterienfrage in der Jesusforschung*, p. 6.

25. See N. Dahl, 'Der historische Jesus als geschichtswissenschaftliches und theologisches Problem', *KD* 1 (1955), pp. 104-32; ET 'The Problem of the Histori-cal Jesus', in C.E. Braaten and R.A. Harrisville (eds.), *Kerygma and History: A Symposium on the Theology of Rudolf Bultmann* (Nashville: Abingdon Press, 1962), pp. 138-71; repr. in N.A. Dahl, *The Crucified Messiah and Other Essays* (Min-neapolis: Augsburg, 1974), pp. 48-89, 173-74 (71), who attempts to come to terms with this criterion through the 'cross-section method' (p. 68)—see under multiple attestation, below (responded to by F. Mussner, 'Der "historische" Jesus', *TTZ* 69 [1960], pp. 321-37; repr. in Mussner, *Jesus von Nazareth*, pp. 43-61, esp. pp. 53-55). Cf. Boring, 'Criteria of Authenticity', p. 21. See also H.K. McArthur, 'The Burden of Proof in Historical Jesus Research', *ExpTim* 82 (1970–71), pp. 116-19, esp. p. 117; and M.D. Hooker, 'Christology and Methodology', *NTS* 17 (1970), pp. 480-87; *idem*, 'On Using the Wrong Tool', *Theology* 75 (1972), pp. 570-81, who from the first to the second article grows in her scepticism regarding the use of the cri-terion of dissimilarity, as well as that of coherence.

26. There is the further difficulty of what it would be like for a person such as Jesus to use language that was uniquely his, and unknown to his contemporaries and followers. It is possible that he would not have been understood in any capac-ity. The result of such analysis is that the authentic Jesus becomes the incompre-hensible Jesus. This criticism is raised by Barbour, *Traditio-Historical Criticism*, p. 8, prompted by a comment by D. Daube, *The New Testament and Rabbinic Judaism* (London: Athlone Press, 1956), p. 388, regarding Jesus' use of *amen*.

clearly argued that this criterion, especially in its double form, errs in its excess, by asking too much of the criterion, especially in its relation to Judaism.[27] This criterion has been further and more rigorously criticized recently by Tom Holmén, who has shown through examination of Mt. 5.33-37 (prohibition of oaths), Mt. 5.38-48 = Lk. 6.27-36 (command to love one's enemy), and Mk 7.15 (on defilement), both that there are logical problems with the double dissimilarity criterion, and that the dissimilarity from Judaism criterion of itself does not add anything to the search for authenticity. In fact, he argues that it in principle has 'nothing to do with the question of authenticity'.[28]

The result of this brief survey and assessment of the criterion of double dissimilarity, however, is that the criterion of dissimilarity from developments in the early Church remains essentially intact.[29] Similarly —and this is perhaps the more important point—the general concept in which recognizable dissimilarities between Gospel traditions pointing to distinctive discontinuities are not easily explained by a single continuous tradition, but require the positing of an earlier and potentially authentic source, also remains intact. As a result, this criterion in this type of formulation is still widely used in historical-Jesus research.[30]

27. B.F. Meyer, *The Aims of Jesus* (London: SCM Press, 1979), p. 86. See also B. Chilton, *A Galilean Rabbi and his Bible: Jesus' Use of the Interpreted Scripture of his Time* (GNS, 8; Wilmington, DE: Michael Glazier, 1984), pp. 86-87; E.P. Sanders, *Jesus and Judaism* (London: SCM Press; Philadelphia: Fortress Press, 1985), pp. 16-17; and J.H. Charlesworth, *Jesus within Judaism: New Light from Exciting Archaeological Discoveries* (ABRL; New York: Doubleday, 1989), pp. 5-6. It must be granted, however, that some of the characterization of this criterion is in terms of a stereotyped absolute not endorsed or followed by those who actually employ it.

28. T. Holmén, 'Doubts about Double Dissimilarity: Restructuring the Main Criterion of Jesus-of-History Research', in B. Chilton and C.A. Evans (eds.), *Authenticating the Words of Jesus* (NTTS, 28.1; Leiden: E.J. Brill, 1998), pp. 47-80. A lengthier and more detailed critique of this criterion is now to be found in Theissen and Winter, *Die Kriterienfrage in der Jesusforschung*, pp. 175-232, which book will be examined in Chapter 3, below, in conjunction with Theissen's new criterion of historical plausibility, since that is the context in which the critique is offered.

29. Note, however, J.D.G. Dunn's incisive comments on this criterion in terms of the Church. He notes that we do have evidence of how the early Church faithfully handled Jesus traditions in the Synoptic material ('Can the Third Quest Hope to Succeed?', in B. Chilton and C.A. Evans [eds.], *Authenticating the Activities of Jesus* [NTTS, 28.2; Leiden: E.J. Brill, 1998], pp. 31-48, esp. p. 40).

30. Besides those advocates noted above, as a small selection of those who dis-

b. *Criterion of Least Distinctiveness*

Many of the other criteria for authenticity seem to have been developed in terms of dimensions of the form-critical agenda. This involved positioning the various traditions regarding Jesus in terms of their similarities to and differences from their backgrounds (either Jewish or in the early Church), and placing the burden of proof upon those who wished to establish the authenticity of a given saying or action. One criterion that seems to have entered the discussion almost from the outset of development of form criticism is the criterion of least distinctiveness. For example, Martin Dibelius and Bultmann, followed by Vincent Taylor—several of the major early conceptualizers and advocates of form criticism—were also apparently among the earliest proponents of this criterion. They seem to have meant by this criterion that one begins by identifying a literary type or form (crucial to form criticism itself), and delimiting its particular 'laws' of style, such as the use of pronouncements by Jesus, a particular structure surrounding an account of a miracle of Jesus, or the like. One can then distinguish an original from a secondary tradition by noting the changes in the form. In particular, these changes include the additions and stylistic developments that are typical of secondary traditions.[31] In an important article, which seems to emphasize this criterion as central to the form-critical task, Bultmann states, 'Whenever narratives pass from mouth to mouth the central point of the narrative and general structure are well preserved; but in the

---

cuss this criterion, see S. Westerholm, *Jesus and Scribal Authority* (ConBNT, 10; Lund: C.W.K. Gleerup, 1978), pp. 6-7; Stein, '"Criteria" for Authenticity', p. 243; Riesner, *Jesus als Lehrer*, pp. 89-91; M.J. Borg, *Jesus a New Vision: Spirit, Culture, and the Life of Discipleship* (San Francisco: HarperSanFrancisco, 1987), p. 101; Sanders, *Jesus and Judaism*, pp. 16-18; Meier, *Marginal Jew*, I, pp. 171-74; Evans, *Life of Jesus Research*, pp. 136-38; *idem, Jesus and his Contemporaries*, pp. 19-21. Cf., however, D.R. Catchpole, 'Tradition History', in Marshall (ed.), *New Testament Interpretation*, pp. 165-80, esp. pp. 174-76.

31. Dibelius, *From Tradition to Gospel*, pp. 6-7; Bultmann, *Synoptic Tradition*, p. 6; Taylor, *Formation of the Gospel Tradition*, pp. 26-27. This criterion functions similarly in many ways to the apparently opposite criterion of vividness of narration, in which concrete and lively details have often been interpreted as indicators of eyewitness reporting. See Meier, *Marginal Jew*, I, pp. 180-82, who notes that Taylor (*The Gospel According to St Mark* [London: Macmillan; New York: St Martin's, 2nd edn, 1966], pp. 135-49) used this criterion. Meier categorizes it as one of his dubious criteria (see Chapter 3, below, for discussion of 'dubious' criteria).

incidental details changes take place, for imagination paints such details with increasing distinctiveness'.[32] The changes typically cited include traditions becoming longer and more detailed, the elimination of Semitisms (see below on the criterion of Semitic language phenomena), the use of direct discourse, and conflation and hence growth of traditions.[33] For example, Lk. 3.7-18 might be cited as an example where many of these features are present, such as direct discourse, later Christian additions (e.g. 'with the Holy Spirit' in v. 16), and the combination of Q material with other traditions.[34]

This criterion has been critically addressed in two major ways. One is the increasing realization that any general patterns for the transmission of traditions in ancient oral cultures is far more complex than the early form critics seemed to think. In other words, the kinds and degrees of change are far more convoluted, rather than being linear and always progressing from simple to complex structures, as the form critics posited.[35] This has been shown especially clearly through extensive recent research on epic poetry, both ancient and modern.[36] The second form of criticism has directly addressed the patterns of change observable in the Gospel material itself. The most decisive work in this regard has been done by E.P. Sanders. In his *Tendencies of the Synoptic Tradition*, a phenomenal work for the industry alone that it represents, to say nothing of the significance of its results, Sanders assesses the various 'laws' of change proposed by form critics in Gospels research. Sanders takes each of the supposed tendencies in turn—increasing length, increasing detail, diminishing Semitisms, utilization of direct discourse, and the tendency to conflation—and examines the evidence from the post-canonical tradition and the Synoptic Gospels. As he concisely states in his conclusions,

32. Bultmann, 'New Approach to the Synoptic Problem', pp. 41-42. See also Walker, 'Quest for the Historical Jesus', pp. 44-46; McEleney, 'Authenticating Criteria', pp. 436-37; Stein, ' "Criteria" for Authenticity', pp. 238-40.

33. See Boring, 'Criteria of Authenticity', p. 16.

34. This example is used, and explained, by Collins, *Introduction to the New Testament*, pp. 189-92.

35. C.L. Blomberg, 'Historical Criticism of the New Testament', in D.S. Dockery, K.A. Mathews and R.B. Sloan (eds.), *Foundations for Biblical Interpretation* (Nashville: Broadman & Holman, 1994), pp. 414-33, esp. pp. 421-22.

36. See G.S. Kirk, *Homer and the Epic* (Cambridge: Cambridge University Press, 1965), esp. pp. 1-32; and A.B. Lord, *Epic Singers and Oral Tradition* (Myth and Poetics; Ithaca, NY: Cornell University Press, 1991), esp. pp. 19-22.

there are no hard and fast laws of the development of the Synoptic tradition. On all counts the tradition developed in opposite directions. It became both longer and shorter, both more and less detailed, and both more and less Semitic. Even the tendency to use direct discourse for indirect, which was uniform in the post-canonical material which we studied, was not uniform in the Synoptics themselves. For this reason, *dogmatic statements that a certain characteristic proves a certain passage to be earlier than another are never justified.*[37]

In support of his case, he marshals a wealth of statistical information that merits further examination.[38] Since it faces nearly insuperable difficulties in the light of Sanders's research, this criterion of least distinctiveness is not nearly so widely used as it once was in historical-Jesus research.

c. *Criterion of Coherence or Consistency*
Another criterion that developed similarly to those above is what has been called the criterion of coherence or consistency.[39] This criterion

---

37. E.P. Sanders, *The Tendencies of the Synoptic Tradition* (SNTSMS, 9; Cambridge: Cambridge University Press, 1969), *passim*, quotation p. 272 (emphasis his); cf. also G. Theissen, *Lokalkolorit und Zeitgeschichte in den Evangelien: Ein Beitrag zur Geschichte der synoptischen Tradition* (NTOA, 8; Göttingen: Vandenhoeck & Ruprecht, 1989; ET *The Gospels in Context: Social and Political History in the Synoptic Tradition* [trans. L.M. Maloney; Edinburgh: T. & T. Clark, 1992]), esp. p. 5.

38. Sanders (*Tendencies of the Synoptic Tradition*, p. 7) also notes the relation of his findings to the question of the solution of the Synoptic problem. He notes that much work in defence of Markan priority is based upon challengeable assumptions of form criticism. See also L.R. Keylock, 'Bultmann's Law of Increasing Distinctness', in G.F. Hawthorne (ed.), *Current Issues in Biblical and Patristic Interpretation* (Festschrift M.C. Tenney; Grand Rapids: Eerdmans, 1975), pp. 193-210, who is critical of Sanders's method, but in general agrees with his results.

39. It might well be argued that coherence and consistency are two very different concepts, since two or more things may cohere without necessarily being consistent. Things may also cohere without necessarily being historical, such as a well-constructed novel (Turner, *Historicity and the Gospels*, p. 68). See also E.D. Hirsch, Jr, *Validity in Interpretation* (New Haven: Yale University Press, 1967), esp. p. 236, who establishes criteria for establishing a probable reading of a text: legitimacy, correspondence, generic appropriateness, and plausibility or coherence, the last of which 'gives significance to all the rest'. Thus, coherence is seen to be something different from consistency. Nevertheless, this is how the terms appear to be used in the discussion of the criteria for authenticity, and they will be used here. There is

states that material that coheres or is consistent with previously established authentic material should also be regarded as authentic. This
criterion apparently stems from Bultmann and his form-critical work on
the logia of Jesus, especially in terms of Jesus' eschatological perspective, since this is one of the few widely agreed upon points around
which authentic Jesus material could be said to cohere.[40] In the light of
the importance of eschatology in historical-Jesus research, it is not surprising that this criterion was further developed by such parables scholars as C.H. Dodd and Joachim Jeremias,[41] and has continued to be

also a linguistic distinction made in discourse analysis between coherence and
cohesion: 'cohesion is a property of the text, and...coherence is a facet of the
reader's evaluation of a text. In other words, cohesion is objective, capable in principle of automatic recognition, while coherence is subjective and judgements concerning it may vary from reader to reader' (M. Hoey, *Patterns of Lexis in Text*
[Describing English Language; Oxford: Oxford University Press, 1991], p. 12; on
coherence, see D. Nunan, *Introducing Discourse Analysis* [Penguin English Applied
Linguistics; Harmondsworth: Penguin Books, 1993], pp. 59-64). A concept similar
to cohesion is described by W. Iser, *Der Akt des Lesens: Theorie ästhetischer
Wirkung* (Munich: Fink, 1976; ET *The Act of Reading: A Theory of Aesthetic Response* [trans. D.H. Wilson; Baltimore: The Johns Hopkins University Press, 1978]),
p. 15, who speaks of the value of a work being measured by 'the harmony of its
elements'. A welcome attempt to integrate literary conceptions into authenticity
criteria (and for whom I am grateful for reminding me of the work of Hirsch and
Iser) is the excellent book by A.P. Winton, *The Proverbs of Jesus: Issues of History
and Rhetoric* (JSNTSup, 35; Sheffield: JSOT Press, 1990), esp. pp. 109-125, but
where he makes an important distinction regarding the 'mythology of coherence'.
He sees it as 'indispensible to historical study, but when applied to the reported
speech of an individual, it seems inevitably to distort' (p. 120). Cf. G. Theissen,
'Historical Scepticism and the Criteria of Jesus Research *or* My Attempt to Leap
across Lessing's Yawning Gulf', *SJT* 49 (1996), pp. 147-76, esp. p. 56 n. 10, who
notes that concepts of coherence change, on the basis of time. See also discussion
of the criterion of Semitic language phenomena, below, where coherence is also
used. Cohesion will be further discussed in Chapter 6, below, when discourse analysis is introduced.

40. Bultmann, *Synoptic Tradition*, p. 105; cf. *idem*, *Theologie des Neuen Testaments* (Tübingen: Mohr Siebeck, 1948; 7th edn, ed. D. Merk, 1977; ET *Theology of
the New Testament* [2 vols.; trans. K. Grobel; London: SCM Press; New York:
Charles Scribner's Sons, 1951, 1955]), I, pp. 4-11.

41. C.H. Dodd, *The Parables of the Kingdom* (London: Nisbet, 1935; New
York: Charles Scribner's Sons, rev. edn, 1961), esp. p. 1; J. Jeremias, *Die Gleichnisse Jesu* (Zürich: Zwingli-Verlag, 1947; Göttingen: Vandenhoeck & Ruprecht,
10th edn, 1984; ET *The Parables of Jesus* [trans. S.H. Hooke; London: SCM Press,

utilized by, among others, Perrin and Charles Carlston.[42] One can see the apparent logic of this criterion and how it might be utilized, especially in parable study, where the eschatological dimension has also figured large in research. For example, Carlston begins with Jesus' eschatologically based call for repentance as 'authentic', so that an authentic parable, such as the parable of the prodigal son (Lk. 15.11-32), will cohere with this position and the conditions during Jesus' ministry.[43] In some circles, there has been much optimistic use of this criterion, because it holds out the promise of expanding the body of authentic Jesus material by establishing coherence with that material already adjudged to be authentic on the basis of other criteria.

This criterion is not nearly as well regarded as others, however, and this attitude is fairly easy to understand on the basis of how the criterion is formulated and what it assumes. Morna Hooker has pointed out how much interpretive subjectivity is involved in such a criterion, especially when it comes to defining and utilizing such nebulous and potentially subjective concepts as coherence.[44] Furthermore, this criterion must, at least in part, assume its very conclusions. That is, it must first—by some other criterion—establish what is authentic before being able to test coherence or consistency.[45] In other words, this is not a primary criterion by which one can attempt to discover authentic Jesus material, but only a secondary criterion by which one can build upon that material which has been established through other means. As has been noted so far in the course of investigating the criteria for authenticity, it is not entirely clear whether there is a fundamental criterion that will allow the establishment of unassailable material for comparison, since each of them

3rd edn, 1972]), p. 11; *idem, Neutestamentliche Theologie. I. Die Verkündigung Jesu* (Gütersloh: Gerd Mohn, 1971; ET *New Testament Theology. I. The Proclamation of Jesus* [trans. J. Bowden; NTL; London: SCM Press; New York: Charles Scribner's Sons, 1971]), p. 30.

42. Perrin, *Redaction Criticism*, p. 71; *idem, Rediscovering the Teaching of Jesus*, p. 43; C.E. Carlston, 'A *Positive* Criterion of Authenticity?', *BR* 7 (1962), pp. 33-44. See also Walker, 'Quest for the Historical Jesus', pp. 49-50; McEleney, 'Authenticating Criteria', pp. 443-44; Stein, '"Criteria" for Authenticity', pp. 250-51.

43. Carlston, '*Positive* Criterion of Authenticity?', p. 34.

44. Hooker, 'Christology and Methodology', pp. 482-83; *idem*, 'Using the Wrong Tool', pp. 576-77.

45. Theissen and Winter, *Die Kriterienfrage in der Jesusforschung*, pp. 17-19.

seems subject to valid criticism.[46] There is the further problem of the reliance of this criterion on such concepts as Jesus as an eschatological prophet. This appears to be more of an agreed assumption that grew out of discussion at the turn of the century, as noted in Chapter 1, rather than a datum that has emerged on the basis of rigorous criteria. At best, this criterion can add to what has already been determined as authentic, but only if one can first establish this authentic tradition. At worst, one is left with disagreements regarding the extents of determining legitimate coherence, since in the largest sense, one could argue, everything in the Gospel accounts already coheres at least enough to render a plausible narrative.

d. *Criterion of Multiple Attestation or Cross-Section Method*
Several other criteria were first developed in English-language Gospel scholarship. Rather than taking the negative and minimalistic approach that characterizes several of the criteria discussed above (e.g. double dissimilarity), these criteria began with a more optimistic view of recovering authentic tradition, seeking to find authenticity in tradition that was multiply attested.[47] It is also noteworthy that even though this criterion of multiple attestation, or the cross-section method, was first developed outside the parameters of German scholarship and before form criticism had been fully articulated, it was later completely integrated into this critical sphere, and many of its utilizers were influential in form-critical and later redaction-critical research. The multiply attested tradition of this criterion was first defined in terms of comparing independently attested traditions, such as Mark, Q, M (material unique to Matthew), or L (material unique to Luke), which is what is meant by taking a cross-section of the tradition. Later, in the light of further form-critical research, this criterion was also defined in terms of multiple literary forms (for example, sayings found in two or more forms within the tradition, such as parables, miracle stories, etc.). The history of each form of this criterion is worth recounting briefly.

46. See R.E. Brown, *An Introduction to the New Testament* (ABRL; New York: Doubleday, 1997), p. 827; cf. Riesner, *Jesus als Lehrer*, pp. 86-87; Theissen and Winter, *Die Kriterienfrage in der Jesusforschung*, p. 201. Many others could also be cited who make similar criticisms.
47. This is treated as two separate criteria in, e.g., Stein, ' "Criteria" for Authenticity', pp. 229-33; Boring, 'Criteria of Authenticity', pp. 12-14.

The first criterion, of multiple attestation of independent traditions, was first developed by F.C. Burkitt,[48] many years before he wrote his work on the life of Jesus.[49] His description of his process of discovery gives insight into the development of this pre-form critical criterion. As he states,

> We need, therefore, a kind of starting-point for the consideration of our Lord's doctrine, some external test that will give us a general assurance that the Saying we have before us is really from Him, and is not the half-conscious product of one school of His followers. Where shall we find such a test?
>
> It appeared to me that the starting-point we require may be found in those Sayings which have a real double attestation. The main documents out of which the Synoptic Gospels are compiled are (1) the Gospel of Mark, and (2) the lost common origin of the non-Marcan portions of Matthew and Luke, *i.e.* the source called Q. Where Q and Mark appear to report the same saying, we have the nearest approach that we can hope to get to the common tradition of the earliest Christian society about our Lord's words. What we glean in this way will indicate the general impression His teaching made upon His disciples.[50]

As a result, Burkitt claimed to identify 31 independently attested sayings found in Mark and Q. This theory was then extended with development in Synoptic Gospel studies of the four-source hypothesis, adding independent traditions M and L.[51] This criterion has found further en-

---

48. F.C. Burkitt, *The Gospel History and its Transmission* (Edinburgh: T. & T. Clark, 1906; 3rd edn, 1911), esp. pp. 147-68. Some of those who have adopted this criterion include: T.W. Manson, *The Teaching of Jesus: Studies of its Form and Content* (Cambridge: Cambridge University Press, 1931; 2nd edn, 1935), pp. 10-11; Dodd, *Parables*, pp. 26-27; J. Jeremias, 'Kennzeichen der ipsissima vox Jesu', in *Synoptische Studien: Alfred Wikenhauser zum siebzigsten Geburtstag am 22. Februar 1953 dargebracht von Freunden, Kollegen und Schulern* (Munich: Zink, 1954), pp. 86-93; ET 'Characteristics of the *Ipsissima Vox Jesu*', in *idem*, *The Prayers of Jesus* (SBT, 2.6; London: SCM Press, 1967), pp. 108-115; Dahl, 'Problem of the Historical Jesus', p. 68; H.K. McArthur, 'Basic Issues, A Survey of Recent Gospel Research', in *idem* (ed.), *In Search of the Historical Jesus*, pp. 139-44, esp. pp. 139-40, who thinks it is the most valuable of the criteria; Walker, 'Quest for the Historical Jesus', pp. 41-42; McEleney, 'Authenticating Criteria', pp. 433-35; Stein, '"Criteria" for Authenticity', pp. 229-32; Meier, *Marginal Jew*, I, pp. 174-75.

49. F.C. Burkitt, *Jesus Christ: An Historical Outline* (London: Blackie, 1932).

50. Burkitt, *Gospel History*, p. 147.

51. See B.H. Streeter, *The Four Gospels: A Study of Origins* (London: Macmil-

hancement, at least in some scholars' eyes, by inclusion of the Gospel of John and/or agrapha of Jesus,[52] and by integration of other textual discoveries made throughout this century, including the *Gospel of Thomas* and other apocryphal gospel sources, such as the *Gospel of*

lan, 1926), esp. pp. 223-70; cf. *idem*, 'St Mark's Knowledge and Use of Q', and 'The Literary Evolution of the Gospels', in W. Sanday (ed.), *Studies in the Synoptic Problem* (Oxford: Clarendon Press, 1911), pp. 165-83, 209-27 respectively. Streeter has been followed by many scholars since, so that his is the predominant (but far from the consensus) position on the Gospel sources. This certainly is not the place to debate Synoptic origins, but several important works should be mentioned. In defence of the position of Markan priority, among many works, see G.M. Styler, 'The Priority of Mark', in C.F.D. Moule, *The Birth of the New Testament* (BNTC; London: A. & C. Black, 3rd edn, 1981; HNTC; New York: Harper & Row, 1982), pp. 285-316. Defences of Q abound in recent research. See, e.g., J.S. Kloppenborg, *The Formation of Q: Trajectories in Ancient Christian Wisdom Collections* (Studies in Antiquity and Christianity; Philadelphia: Fortress Press, 1987); R.A. Piper (ed.), *The Gospel behind the Gospels: Current Studies on Q* (NovTSup, 75; Leiden: E.J. Brill, 1995); C.M. Tuckett, *Q and the History of Early Christianity: Studies on Q* (Edinburgh: T. & T. Clark, 1996); and P. Vassiliadis, ΛΟΓΟΙ ΙΗΣΟΥ: *Studies in Q* (University of South Florida International Studies in Formative Christianity and Judaism; Atlanta: Scholars Press, 1999).

52. McEleney, 'Authenticating Criteria', p. 434; Stein, ' "Criteria" for Authenticity', p. 230; cf. R.P. Martin, 'The New Quest of the Historical Jesus', in C.F.H. Henry (ed.), *Jesus of Nazareth: Saviour and Lord* (London: Tyndale Press, 1966), pp. 23-45, esp. pp. 43-44. The history of the discussion of the agrapha is an intriguing one. This history can be traced in the following sources, among others: J.H. Ropes, 'Agrapha', in J. Hastings (ed.), *A Dictionary of the Bible* (5 vols.; Edinburgh: T. & T. Clark, 1898–1904), V, pp. 343-52; A. Resch, *Agrapha: Aussercanonische Schriftfragmenta* (TU, 15.3–4; Leipzig: J.C. Hinrichs, 2nd edn, 1906); B. Jackson, *Twenty-Five Agrapha or Extra-Canonical Sayings of our Lord* (London: SPCK, 1900); M.R. James, *The Apocryphal New Testament* (Oxford: Clarendon Press, 1924), pp. 33-37; R. Dunkerley, *The Unwritten Gospel: Ana and Agrapha of Jesus* (London: George Allen & Unwin, 1925), *passim*; J. Jeremias, *Unbekannte Jesusworte* (Gütersloh: C. Bertelsmann, 2nd edn, 1951; Gütersloh: Gerd Mohn, 3rd edn, 1963; ET *Unknown Sayings of Jesus* [trans. R.H. Fuller; London: SPCK, 1957; 2nd edn, 1964]); cf. *idem*, 'Isolated Sayings of the Lord', in E. Hennecke and W. Schneemelcher (eds.), *Neutestamentliche Apokryphen* (2 vols.; Tübingen: Mohr Siebeck, 1959; ET *New Testament Apocrypha* [trans. R.McL. Wilson; London: Lutterworth; Philadelphia: Westminster Press, 1963]), I, pp. 85-90; O. Hofius, ' "Unknown Sayings of Jesus" ', in Stuhlmacher (ed.), *Gospel and the Gospels*, pp. 336-60 (originally ' "Unbekannte Jesusworte" ', in Stuhlmacher [ed.], *Das Evangelium und die Evangelien*, pp. 355-82); W.D. Stoker, *Extracanonical Sayings of Jesus* (SBLRBS, 18; Atlanta: Scholars Press, 1989); Meier, *Marginal*

Peter, etc.[53] An example that illustrates the use of multiple sources is Jesus' statement on divorce, found in three independent traditions: (1) Mk 10.2-12 = Mt. 19.3-12; (2) Q (Mt. 5.32 = Lk. 16.18); and (3) 1 Cor. 7.10-11.[54]

The second and related form of this criterion, multiple forms, was developed by Dodd. He claimed that material found in two or more forms of the Jesus tradition (such as aphorisms, parables, poetical sayings, dialogues, miracle stories, etc.) is early and may also have represented early, authentic tradition. Dodd finds, for example, multiple forms attesting to such things as Jesus' teaching on the kingdom of God, thus establishing the authenticity of this tradition that Jesus was proclaiming a realized kingdom (e.g. Mt. 5.17; 9.37-38; 13.16-17; Mk 2.18-20; 4.26-29; Lk. 11.14-22; Jn 4.35).[55] This form of the criterion, though

---

Jew, I, pp. 112-41; J.K. Elliott, *The Apocryphal New Testament* (Oxford: Clarendon Press, 1993), pp. 26-30. See the study of the issues in J.H. Charlesworth and C.A. Evans, 'Jesus in the Agrapha and Apocryphal Gospels', in Chilton and Evans (eds.), *Studying the Historical Jesus*, pp. 479-533, esp. pp. 483-91.

53. The widespread use of apocryphal gospels in research on Jesus distinguishes the Jesus Seminar. The literature on this topic is growing immensely, and will not be surveyed here. See R.J. Miller (ed.), *The Complete Gospels: Annotated Scholars Version* (Sonoma, CA: Polebridge Press, 1992; 2nd edn, 1994; San Francisco: HarperSanFrancisco, 3rd edn, 1994). In support of the use of these sources for historical-Jesus research, see D.R. Cartlidge and D.L. Dungan, *Documents for the Study of the Gospels* (Philadelphia: Fortress Press; London: Collins, 1980); J.M. Robinson, 'The Study of the Historical Jesus after Nag Hammadi', *Semeia* 44 (1988), pp. 45-55; H. Koester, *Ancient Christian Gospels: Their History and Development* (Philadelphia: Trinity Press International; London: SCM Press, 1990); J.D. Crossan, *The Historical Jesus: The Life of a Mediterranean Jewish Peasant* (San Francisco: HarperSanFrancisco, 1992), pp. 434-43; a method criticized by Evans, *Jesus and his Contemporaries*, pp. 16-17. See the study of the issues in selected essays in D. Wenham (ed.), *Gospel Perspectives: The Jesus Tradition outside the Gospels*, V (Sheffield: JSOT Press, 1985); F. Neirynck, 'The Apocryphal Gospels and the Gospel of Mark', in J.-M. Sevrin (ed.), *The New Testament in Early Christianity* (BETL, 86; Leuven: Leuven University Press/Peeters, 1989), pp. 123-75; repr. in F. Neirynck, *Evangelica II: 1982–1991 Collected Essays* (BETL, 99; Leuven: Leuven University Press/Peeters, 1991), pp. 715-72; and Charlesworth and Evans, 'Agrapha and Apocryphal Gospels', pp. 491-532.

54. Cited in McEleney, 'Authenticating Criteria', p. 433.

55. Dodd, *Parables*, pp. 26-29; *idem, History and the Gospel* (London: Nisbet, 1938), pp. 91-102, a method he attributes to E. Hoskyns and N. Davey, *The Riddle of the New Testament* (London: Faber & Faber, 1931), pp. 162-207.

used by some scholars,[56] has been relatively neglected compared to some of the other criteria.[57]

This criterion in both of its forms, however, has been, where not rejected, at least highly qualified. The reasons for this are several. One is that this criterion, despite its attention to either recognized sources (Mark, Q, M, L) or various literary forms (aphorisms, parables, etc.), fails to provide a criterion that determines specific words of Jesus. Like many of the criteria in historical-Jesus research, it is apparently better at establishing general motifs in the teaching of Jesus,[58] as Burkitt admitted at the outset. This limitation is especially clear when the criterion examines individual literary forms, where the argument is made that authentic material is reflected in the fact that Jesus spoke about a certain subject in various ways. As in the example above, Dodd thought that he had proved the authenticity of Jesus' teaching of a realized kingdom of God, but he could not go so far as to argue for the specific wording that Jesus would have used to proclaim this kingdom, only that he did so. A further criticism of Dodd in his approach has been that he is not always clear what constitutes a literary form that is brought into his analysis.[59] In conjunction with this, the criticism has also been made that this criterion judges whether one can use particular sources in historical-Jesus research (since they have parallel material), but does not evaluate the reliability of the sources themselves.[60] Further, the point has been raised that multiply attested tradition points to an earlier stage in the tradition, but it does not necessarily indicate authenticity, which

---

56. Some of those who support this criterion include J.M. Robinson, 'The Formal Structure of Jesus' Message', in W. Klassen and G.F. Snyder (eds.), *Current Issues in New Testament Interpretation: Essays in Honor of Otto A. Piper* (London: SCM Press; New York: Harper & Row, 1962), pp. 91-110, 273-84, esp. pp. 96-97; E. Trocmé, *Jésus de Nazareth vu par les témoins de sa vie* (Neuchâtel: Delachaux & Niestlé, 1972; ET *Jesus and his Contemporaries* [trans. R.A. Wilson; London: SCM Press, 1973]), *passim*; Walker, 'Quest for the Historical Jesus', pp. 42-43; McEleney, 'Authenticating Criteria', pp. 435-36; Meyer, *Aims of Jesus*, p. 87.

57. See Stein, ' "Criteria" for Authenticity', pp. 232-33.

58. Perrin, *Rediscovering the Teaching of Jesus*, pp. 45-47; cf. Evans, *Jesus and his Contemporaries*, pp. 15-18.

59. McEleney, 'Authenticating Criteria', p. 435, citing from Dodd's *History and the Gospel* his use of the pericope of the woman caught in adultery (Jn 7.53–8.11) (p. 93), the saying in Lk. 10.18 (p. 96), and the incident with the Samaritan woman (Jn 4.15) (p. 99).

60. Theissen and Winter, *Die Kriterienfrage in der Jesusforschung*, p. 12.

must then be determined through other criteria.[61] This criterion, especially the form that analyses sources, also assumes a particular solution
to the Synoptic problem (Markan priority), and the relation of these
sources. Some scholars would today not accept this once more widely
held solution, and as a result a number of alternatives continue to be
promoted and developed. Some scholars wish to dispense with Q as one
of the Gospel sources,[62] others advocate revival of what has been called
the Griesbach hypothesis (Matthaean priority),[63] and still others offer

61. Fuller, *Critical Introduction*, pp. 97-98.
62. Some of those who wish to 'dispense' with Q, thus eliminating one of the
major independent traditions include A.M. Farrer, 'On Dispensing with Q', in D.E.
Nineham (ed.), *Studies in the Gospels: Essays in Memory of R.H. Lightfoot*
(Oxford: Basil Blackwell, 1957), pp. 55-88; *idem, A Study in St Mark*; *idem, St
Matthew and St Mark*; M.D. Goulder, *Luke—A New Paradigm* (2 vols.; JSNTSup,
20; Sheffield: JSOT Press, 1989) (on Goulder, see M.S. Goodacre, *Goulder and the
Gospels: An Examination of a New Paradigm* [JSNTSup, 133; Sheffield: Sheffield
Academic Press, 1996]).
63. For some of those who wish to revive what is known as the Griesbach hypothesis, see W.R. Farmer, 'An Historical Essay on the Humanity of Jesus Christ',
in W.R. Farmer, C.F.D. Moule and R.R. Niebuhr (eds.), *Christian History and Interpretation: Studies Presented to John Knox* (Cambridge: Cambridge University Press,
1967), pp. 101-26, who links the historical-Jesus issues to his source view of the
Gospels; *idem, The Synoptic Problem: A Critical Analysis* (New York: Macmillan;
London: Collier-Macmillan, 1964); *idem, The Gospel of Jesus: The Pastoral Relevance of the Synoptic Problem* (Louisville, KY: Westminster/ John Knox Press,
1994); W.R. Farmer (ed.), *New Synoptic Studies: The Cambridge Gospel Conference and Beyond* (Macon, GA: Mercer University Press, 1983); B. Orchard and
H. Riley, *The Order of the Synoptics: Why Three Synoptic Gospels?* (Macon, GA:
Mercer University Press, 1987); cf. H.-H. Stoldt, *Geschichte und Kritik der Markushypothese* (Göttingen: Vandenhoeck & Ruprecht, 1977; ET *History and Criticism
of the Marcan Hypothesis* [trans. D.L. Niewyk; SNTW; Macon, GA: Mercer
University Press; Edinburgh: T. & T. Clark, 1980]). Two important assessments of
the Griesbach hypothesis are C.M. Tuckett, *The Revival of the Griesbach Hypothesis: An Analysis and Appraisal* (SNTSMS, 44; Cambridge: Cambridge University
Press, 1983), and S.E. Johnson, *The Griesbach Hypothesis and Redaction Criticism*
(SBLMS, 41; Atlanta: Scholars Press, 1991), and the methodological issues raised
by F.G. Downing, 'Compositional Conventions and the Synoptic Problem', *JBL*
107 (1988), pp. 69-85. These opinions have generated a number of colloquia on
their differing perspectives: e.g. see B. Corley (ed.), *Colloquy on New Testament
Studies: A Time for Reappraisal and Fresh Approaches* (Macon, GA: Mercer University Press, 1983), pp. 29-194; C.M. Tuckett (ed.), *Synoptic Studies: The Ampleforth Conferences of 1982 and 1983* (JSNTSup, 7; Sheffield: JSOT Press, 1984);

alternative competing hypotheses to account for Gospel origins,[64] among other possible solutions. One can see that if any of the alternatives to Markan priority and the two- and four-source hypotheses proves correct, this criterion for authenticity would have serious difficulties being

D.L. Dungan (ed.), *The Interrelations of the Gospels* (BETL, 95; Leuven: Leuven University Press/Peeters, 1990). For a collection of some of the major statements in the debate, see A.J. Bellinzoni, Jr (ed.), *The Two-Source Hypothesis: A Critical Appraisal* (Macon, GA: Mercer University Press, 1985).

64. There have been other theories of Gospel independence as well, such as J.M. Rist, *On the Independence of Matthew and Mark* (SNTSMS, 32; Cambridge: Cambridge University Press, 1978). At one time lectionary hypotheses were also fashionable: see P. Carrington, *The Primitive Christian Calendar: A Study in the Making of the Marcan Gospel* (Cambridge: Cambridge University Press, 1952); cf. *idem*, *According to Mark: A Running Commentary on the Oldest Gospel* (Cambridge: Cambridge University Press, 1960); M.D. Goulder, *The Evangelists' Calendar: A Lectionary Explanation of the Development of Scripture* (London: SPCK, 1978). These theories have not generally caught on. See the critiques in C.H. Dodd, 'The Primitive Catechism and the Sayings of Jesus', in A.J.B. Higgins (ed.), *New Testament Essays: Studies in Memory of Thomas Walter Manson 1893–1958* (Manchester: Manchester University Press, 1959), pp. 106-18 (repr. in C.H. Dodd, *More New Testament Studies* [Grand Rapids: Eerdmans, 1968], pp. 11-29); L.L. Morris, *The New Testament and the Jewish Lectionaries* (London: Tyndale Press, 1964); *idem*, 'The Gospels and the Jewish Lectionaries', in R.T. France and D. Wenham (eds.), *Gospel Perspectives: Studies in Midrash and Historiography*, III (Sheffield: JSOT Press, 1983), pp. 129-56. Related to this discussion are various theories of Gospel transmission that rely upon Jewish practice of the time: see H. Riesenfeld, 'The Gospel Tradition and its Beginnings', in K. Aland (ed.), *Studia Evangelica* (TU, 73; Berlin: Akademie-Verlag, 1958); repr. with other essays in H. Riesenfeld, *The Gospel Tradition* (trans. E.M. Rowley and R.A. Kraft; Philadelphia: Fortress Press; Oxford: Basil Blackwell, 1970), pp. 1-29; B. Gerhardsson, *Memory and Manuscript: Oral Tradition and Written Transmission in Rabbinic Judaism and Early Christianity* (ASNU, 22; trans. E.J. Sharpe; Lund: C.W.K. Gleerup, 1961); *idem*, *Tradition and Transmission in Early Christianity* (ConBNT, 20; trans. E.J. Sharpe; Lund: C.W.K. Gleerup, 1964); both of Gerhardsson's volumes are republished, with a new 'Preface' (Biblical Resource Series; Grand Rapids: Eerdmans; Livonia, MI: Dove Booksellers, 1998), pp. ix-xxii, where he responds to his critics; *idem*, 'Der Weg der Evangelientradition', in Stuhlmacher (ed.), *Evangelium und die Evangelien*, pp. 79-102; Riesner, *Jesus als Lehrer*, pp. 97-498; *idem*, 'Jüdische Elementarbildung und Evangelienüberlieferung', in France and Wenham (eds.), *Gospel Perspectives*, I, pp. 209-23; *idem*, 'Jesus as Preacher and Teacher', in H. Wansbrough (ed.), *Jesus and the Oral Gospel Tradition* (JSNTSup, 64; Sheffield: JSOT Press, 1991), pp. 185-210; and S. Byrskog, *Jesus the Only Teacher: Didactic Authority and Transmission in Ancient Israel,*

sustained in its present form. In other words, a competing hypothesis for the origin of the Gospels leaves this criterion without an adequate foundational assumption for those advocating such a hypothesis in order to use it, and no foundation if the model of Synoptic relations were to be significantly altered.

e. *Criterion of Semitic Language Phenomena*
A last criterion to mention here, more because of its longevity than its explanatory power, is that of Semitic (Aramaic) language phenomena and/or Palestinian environmental features. The first sub-section refers to particular grammatical features in the Greek of the New Testament that are thought to be directly traceable to a Semitic, and most likely, Aramaic origin. The second refers to various environmental features of Palestine that are mentioned, often inadvertently, in the Gospels and are said to point to origin of the tradition in Palestine.[65] These environmental features would include reference to various practices, customs, geographical features, or beliefs that are thought to have been characteristic of first-century Palestine. The idea is that many of these would probably have only been known to or by someone who had firsthand acquaintance with that environment. The presumption with each of these sub-

---

Ancient Judaism and the Matthean Community (ConBNT, 24; Stockholm: Almqvist & Wiksell, 1994). For an assessment of this perspective, see W.D. Davies, 'Reflections on a Scandinavian Approach to "The Gospel Tradition" ', in *Neotestamentica et Patristica: Eine Freudesgabe, Herrn Professor Dr Oscar Cullmann zu seinem 60. Geburtstag überreicht* (NovTSup, 6; Leiden: E.J. Brill, 1962), pp. 14-34 (repr. in W.D. Davies, *The Setting of the Sermon on the Mount* [Cambridge: Cambridge University Press, 1964], pp. 464-80); Sanders, *Tendencies of the Synoptic Tradition*, pp. 26-29, 294-96; P.H. Davids, 'The Gospels and Jewish Tradition: Twenty Years after Gerhardsson', in France and Wenham (eds.), *Gospel Perspectives*, I, pp. 75-99. Related is the theory of oral transmission of B.F. Westcott, *An Introduction to the Study of the Gospels* (London: Macmillan, 1851; 8th edn, 1895), pp. 165-212, developed by B. Chilton, *Profiles of a Rabbi: Synoptic Opportunities in Reading about Jesus* (BJS, 177; Atlanta: Scholars Press, 1989), esp. pp. 3-45. A very recent study of the Synoptic problem is D.L. Dungan, *A History of the Synoptic Problem: The Canon, the Text, the Composition, and the Interpretation of the Gospels* (ABRL; New York: Doubleday, 1999).

65. See, e.g., J. Jeremias, *Die Gleichnisse Jesu* (Zürich: Zwingli-Verlag, 1947; Göttingen: Vandenhoeck & Ruprecht, 10th edn, 1984; ET *The Parables of Jesus* [trans. S.H. Hooke; London: SCM Press, 3rd edn, 1972]), esp. pp. 48-66; and the recent work by Theissen, *Lokalkolorit und Zeitgeschichte in den Evangelien*; ET *The Gospels in Context*.

sections is that a larger number of Semitic or Palestinian environmental features in a given passage is more likely to indicate authentic tradition regarding Jesus, because he spoke a Semitic language (Aramaic, and possibly Hebrew) and lived in Palestine. These features are treated as separate items in several discussions of criteria, but are placed together in others.[66] I place them together here for the purposes of categorization, while concentrating almost exclusively on the discussion of language. This issue of language is often intertwined with two other questions— one regarding the nature of the Greek of the New Testament, and the other the larger topic of the languages of Palestine, including not only Aramaic and Greek, but Hebrew and even Latin.[67] These issues will only be touched upon here as they impinge upon the issue of the use of Semitic languages as a criterion for authenticity in historical-Jesus research (a more detailed discussion of some of these issues is to be found in Chapter 4).

Discussion of the Aramaic features of the language of Jesus as found in the Gospels goes back to the seventeenth century, at least, with heightened discussion beginning in the eighteenth century and proceeding more or less continuously to the present. In terms of Jesus research of the last 100 years, major proponents of the theory that one can retrovert to Jesus' original Aramaic through translational difficulties in Greek, such as A. Meyer and Dalman,[68] were early on thoroughly as-

66. Those who separate them include Stein, '"Criteria" for Authenticity', pp. 233-38; Boring, 'Criteria of Authenticity', pp. 14-16; Meier, *Marginal Jew*, I, pp. 178-80; among others. Those who conflate them include Fuller, *Critical Introduction*, pp. 95, 97; Schillebeeckx, *Jesus*, pp. 98-99; Evans, *Jesus and his Contemporaries*, pp. 22-23; among others. Cf. Polkow, 'Method and Criteria', pp. 352-55, who divides even further, between Palestinian context and style.

67. On both the issue of the nature of the Greek of the New Testament and the larger issue of the languages of Palestine, see S.E. Porter, 'Introduction: The Greek of the New Testament as a Disputed Area of Research', in *idem* (ed.), *The Language of the New Testament: Classic Essays* (JSNTSup, 60; Sheffield: JSOT Press, 1991), pp. 11-38, where fuller bibliography can be found, and the rest of the volume's essays by proponents of various hypotheses. For a recent summary, see L. Rydbeck, 'The Language of the New Testament', *TynBul* 49.2 (1998), pp. 361-68.

68. A. Meyer, *Jesu Muttersprache: Das galiläische Aramäisch in seiner Bedeutung für die Erklärung der Reden Jesu und der Evangelien überhaupt* (Freiburg: Mohr Siebeck, 1896); G. Dalman, *Grammatik des jüdisch-palästinischen Aramäisch* (Leipzig: J.C. Hinrichs, 1894; 2nd edn, 1905; repr. Darmstadt: Wissenschaftliche Buchgesellschaft, 1960); *idem*, *Die Worte Jesu: Mit Berücksichtigung des*

sessed by Schweitzer.[69] Since then, others who have made a significant contribution by addressing the question of the Aramaic features of the language in which Jesus may have spoken[70] include such scholars as: C.F. Burney, who chronicled the poetic features of Jesus' language, seeing them as reflecting Semitic poetry;[71] Charles Torrey, who posited that translational difficulties revealed not flaws but the translators' attempts to maintain the sense of the original;[72] and Jeremias, who in building

nachkanonischen jüdischen Schrifttums und der aramäistischen Sprache erörtert (Leipzig: J.C. Hinrichs, 1898; rev. edn, 1930; ET *The Words of Jesus: Considered in the Light of Post-Biblical Jewish Writings and the Aramaic Language* [trans. D.M. Kay; Edinburgh: T. & T. Clark, 1909]); *idem, Jesus–Jeschua: Die drei Sprachen Jesu, Jesus in der Synagoge, auf dem Berge beim Passahmahl, am Kreuz* (Leipzig: J.C. Hinrichs, 1922; ET *Jesus–Jeshua: Studies in the Gospels* [trans. P.P. Levertoff; London: SPCK, 1929]).

69. A. Schweitzer, *Von Reimarus zu Wrede: Eine Geschichte der Leben-Jesu-Forschung* (Tübingen: Mohr Siebeck, 1906; 2nd edn, 1910; 6th edn, 1951; ET *The Quest of the Historical Jesus: A Critical Study of its Progress from Reimarus to Wrede* [trans. W. Montgomery; London: A. & C. Black, 1910]), pp. 270-93, who chronicles the debate to that time.

70. I use 'may' because there has been debate over the dialect of Aramaic that Jesus spoke, so some of the features often cited may not apply to that dialect. For a summary of this discussion, see L.T. Stuckenbruck, 'An Approach to the New Testament through Aramaic Sources: The Recent Methodological Debate', *JSP* 8 (1991), pp. 3-29. After recounting the history of discussion over the last 100 years, he shows that three major positions have been advanced: those following Dalman and his advocacy of a form of Aramaic related to the Targum Onqelos (*Words of Jesus*, p. 82), those following P.E. Kahle and his advocacy of the Aramaic of the Cairo Geniza and Qumran Aramaic (*The Cairo Geniza* [Oxford: Basil Blackwell, 2nd edn, 1959], esp. pp. 195-200), and those following J.A. Fitzmyer and his endorsement of Palestinian Aramaic of the Roman period, including that of Qumran and of other documents ('The Study of the Aramaic Background of the New Testament', 'The Phases of the Aramaic Language', and 'The Contribution of Qumran Aramaic to the Study of the New Testament', all in his *A Wandering Aramean: Collected Aramaic Essays* [SBLMS, 25; Missoula, MT: Scholars Press, 1979], pp. 1-27, 57-84 and 85-113; repr. in *The Semitic Background of the New Testament* [Biblical Resource Series; Grand Rapids: Eerdmans; Livonia, MI: Dove Booksellers, 1997], with corrections). For collections of such Aramaic texts, see J.A. Fitzmyer and D.J. Harrington, *A Manual of Palestinian Aramaic Texts* (Biblica et Orientalia, 34; Rome: Biblical Institute Press, 1978); K. Beyer, *Die aramäische Texte vom Toten Meer* (Göttingen: Vandenhoeck & Ruprecht, 1984).

71. C.F. Burney, *The Poetry of Our Lord* (Oxford: Clarendon Press, 1925); cf. his *The Aramaic Origin of the Fourth Gospel* (Oxford: Clarendon Press, 1922).

72. C.C. Torrey, 'The Translations Made from the Original Aramaic Gospels',

upon Burney's research was perhaps the first to make widespread use of Semitic or Aramaic criteria in establishing authentic sayings of Jesus, as evidenced especially in his *Parables of Jesus* and his *The Eucharistic Words of Jesus*, and later in his *New Testament Theology*.[73] Since Jeremias, invoking Semitic criteria has been widespread, and is to be found in numerous commentaries, as well as in the work of other such scholars as T.W. Manson, Matthew Black, Fitzmyer, Dunn, Chilton, Evans, and now Maurice Casey, among many others right up to the present.[74]

There have been several important trends in this discussion that are worth noting in the light of the topic of this monograph. One is that many of the early disputants, such as Dalman, discussed Aramaic in terms of the surrounding Greek milieu.[75] Although recognition of the

in D.G. Lyon and G.F. Moore (eds.), *Studies in the History of Religions* (Festschrift C.H. Toy; New York: Macmillan, 1912), pp. 269-317; *idem, Our Translated Gospels: Some of the Evidence* (Cambridge, MA: Harvard University Press, 1916); *idem, The Four Gospels: A New Translation* (New Haven: Yale University Press, 1958).

73. Jeremias, *Parables of Jesus*, pp. 25-26; *idem, Die Abendmahlsworte Jesu* (Göttingen: Vandenhoeck & Ruprecht, 1935; 4th edn, 1967; ET *The Eucharistic Words of Jesus* [London: SCM Press, 1966]); *idem,* 'Characteristics of the *Ipsissima Vox Jesu*', pp. 108-15; *idem, New Testament Theology*, esp. pp. 3-37. Cf. also Dodd, *History and the Gospel*, pp. 89-90.

74. Manson, *Teaching of Jesus*, pp. 45-86; *idem, The Sayings of Jesus* (London: SCM Press, 1937); M. Black, *An Aramaic Approach to the Gospels and Acts* (Oxford: Clarendon Press, 1946; 2nd edn, 1954; 3rd edn, 1967; repr. with 'Introduction: An Aramaic Approach Thirty Years Later', by C.A. Evans, pp. v-xxv; Peabody, MA: Hendrickson, 1998); J.A. Fitzmyer, 'Methodology in the Study of the Aramaic Substratum of Jesus' Sayings in the New Testament', in Dupont (ed.), *Jésus aux origines de la christologie*, pp. 73-102; rev. in his *A Wandering Aramean*, pp. 1-27; J.D.G. Dunn, *The Evidence for Jesus: The Impact of Scholarship on our Understanding of How Christianity Began* (London: SCM Press, 1985), p. 3; Chilton, *Galilean Rabbi and his Bible*, esp. pp. 57-147; C.A. Evans, 'Life of Jesus', in Porter (ed.), *Handbook to Exegesis*, pp. 427-75, esp. pp. 447-55; M. Casey, *Aramaic Sources of Mark's Gospel* (SNTSMS, 102; Cambridge: Cambridge University Press, 1998); *idem,* 'An Aramaic Approach to the Synoptic Gospels', *ExpTim* 110.7 (1999), pp. 275-78. It is institutionalized as a part of the history of New Testament scholarship in A.M. Hunter, *Interpreting the New Testament 1900–1950* (London: SCM Press, 1951), pp. 26-33. See also Walker, 'Quest for the Historical Jesus', pp. 43-44; McEleney, 'Authenticating Criteria', pp. 438-40; Stein, ' "Criteria" for Authenticity', pp. 236-38.

75. One feature to notice is the changing opinion of J. Wellhausen on the rela-

multilingual environment of Palestine has remained important for some scholars engaged in such discussion (such as Fitzmyer, who treats the four possible languages of Palestine—Greek, Aramaic, Hebrew and Latin),[76] the later tendency has been to bifurcate discussion. The concentration since the rise of form and later redaction criticism has been on Jesus as a Semitic (Aramaic) language user. This has been almost to the exclusion in some circles of acknowledgment of even the possibility of Jesus as a Greek language user. It is only recently that discussion of Jesus' possible use of Greek has been seriously re-introduced, with much resistance to such a proposal in some circles.[77] A more recent trend has been the development of more explicit criteria by which one can determine Semitic features in the Greek of the Gospels. Discussion throughout most of the twentieth century was to varying degrees concentrated on perceived oddities in the Greek of the New Testament or what were contended to be mistranslations;[78] however, much of this

---

tionship between the Aramaic and Greek backgrounds of the New Testament, from the first to the second editions of his *Einleitung in die drei erste Evangelien* (Berlin: G. Reimer, 1905; 2nd edn, 1911), (1st edn) pp. 7-43, (2nd edn) pp. 7-32, placing more stress in the latter on the Gospels in their relation to the Koine than he had before.

76. See J.A. Fitzmyer, 'The Languages of Palestine in the First Century AD', *CBQ* 32 (1970), pp. 501-31; repr. with revisions and additions in Porter (ed.), *Language of the New Testament*, pp. 126-62.

77. Recent work that has attempted to re-open the discussion includes Meier, *Marginal Jew*, I, pp. 255-68; S.E. Porter, 'Jesus and the Use of Greek in Galilee', in Chilton and Evans (eds.), *Studying the Historical Jesus*, pp. 123-54; *idem*, 'Did Jesus Ever Teach in Greek?', *TynBul* 44.2 (1993), pp. 199-235; repr. in *idem*, *Studies in the Greek New Testament: Theory and Practice* (SBG, 6; New York: Peter Lang, 1996), pp. 139-71. The response has been varied, as discussion in this and subsequent chapters shows.

78. Besides those already mentioned above, such as A. Meyer, Wellhausen, Dalman, Burney, Torrey, Black and Fitzmyer, others who give serious attention to translation as an indicator of Aramaic background, and related factors, include E. Nestle, *Philologica Sacra: Bemerkungen über die Urgestalt der Evangelien und Apostelgeschichte* (Berlin: Reuther & Reichard, 1896); F. Blass, *Philology of the Gospels* (London: Macmillan, 1898); M. Wilcox, 'Jesus in the Light of his Jewish Environment', *ANRW* 2.25.1, pp. 131-95; *idem*, 'Semitisms in the New Testament', *ANRW* 2.25.2, pp. 978-1029; *idem*, 'The Aramaic Background of the New Testament', in D.R.G. Beattie and M.J. McNamara (eds.), *The Aramaic Bible: Targums in their Historical Context* (JSOTSup, 166; Sheffield: JSOT Press, 1994), pp. 362-78; F. Zimmermann, *The Aramaic Origin of the Four Gospels* (New York: Ktav,

examination has neglected a number of crucial linguistic factors regarding translation between Greek and Aramaic. Lincoln Hurst has argued that these factors include the failure to appreciate the polysemous nature of words within languages.[79] Thus, there is often, if not usually, no iconicity between lexical items in two different languages. Hence one-for-one translation (or retroversion from Greek to Aramaic), so often relied upon in studies of the Aramaic background of the New Testament, is rendered a near impossibility. The factor of diachronic linguistic development (that is, how a language changes over time) is also not often taken into account in such discussions. This results in inappropriate comparisons of languages from differing time periods, and failing to note the possibility of various types of diachronic linguistic change. There is the further problem of failure to appreciate the various ways and means by which translations are made, and their varying purposes. In fact, translation theory has been one area in which there has been much recent development, much of it surprisingly almost completely ignored by biblical scholars, who are nevertheless often involved in translation.[80] Even such an advocate of the Aramaic source hypothesis

1979), esp. pp. 3-23; and G. Schwarz, *'Und Jesu Sprach': Untersuchungen zur aramäischen Urgestalt der Worte Jesu* (BWANT, 118; Stuttgart: W. Kohlhammer, 2nd edn, 1987). This viewpoint is also reflected in a number of commentaries.

79. See L.D. Hurst, 'The Neglected Role of Semantics in the Search for the Aramaic Words of Jesus', *JSNT* 28 (1986), pp. 63-80; repr. in C.A. Evans and S.E. Porter (eds.), *The Historical Jesus: A Sheffield Reader* (BibSem, 33; Sheffield: Sheffield Academic Press, 1995), pp. 219-36. Hurst also realizes the importance of various linguistic levels or styles and the potential of semantic field theory. As a result, he offers a translation model based upon the theory of Eugene A. Nida (e.g. Nida and C.R. Taber, *The Theory and Practice of Translation* [Helps for Translators; Leiden: E.J. Brill, 1969]). Other work in translation theory reflecting this perspective includes: E.A. Nida, *Toward a Science of Translating with Special Reference to Principles and Procedures Involved in Bible Translating* (Leiden: E.J. Brill, 1964); E.A. Nida, *Language Structure and Translation: Essays by Eugene A. Nida* (ed. A.S. Dil; Stanford: Stanford University Press, 1975); J. De Waard and E.A. Nida, *From One Language to Another: Functional Equivalence in Bible Translating* (Nashville: Nelson, 1986); P.C. Stine (ed.), *Issues in Bible Translation* (UBSMS, 3; London: United Bible Societies, 1988); P.A. Soukup and R. Hodgson (eds.), *From One Medium to Another: Basic Issues for Communicating the Scriptures in New Media* (New York: American Bible Society; Kansas City: Sheed & Ward, 1997); among others.

80. For a sample of recent work in translation theory, much of which recognizes the importance of translating in terms of an entire discourse, see D. Crystal, 'Some

as Matthew Black recognizes the limitations of the method. He admits that only in the words of Jesus can translation from Aramaic be considered, but that even in the parables of Jesus, long considered as providing the basis of authentic material (see above, and Chapters 5 and 6, below), 'it cannot, I think, be sufficiently emphasized that in the majority of the longer connected parables, for example in Q, the "translation" is not literal but literary; in other words, it is doubtful if it can be justly described as translation at all in some cases, even where the evidence points to the existence and use of an Aramaic source'.[81] The failure to be able to show that what are considered the earliest texts in the Synoptic tradition, such as the Lord's prayer, the sermon on the mount, or Q, are translations from Aramaic originals has prompted Hans Dieter Betz to conclude that 'For simple historical reasons, the Aramaic hypothesis is presently in trouble'.[82]

More recent discussion has attempted to salvage this criterion and to be more explicit in this regard. There have been two recent developments along these lines worth noting. The first is that of Casey. Casey's major argument is that the Aramaic of the Dead Sea Scrolls, including that of targums, now provides sufficient evidence for the kind of Aramaic in use in Palestine in the first century to be able to reconstruct underlying Aramaic substrata at several places in Mark's Gospel (9.11-13; 2.23–3.6; 10.35-45; 14.12-26). Many will undoubtedly welcome the confidence with which Casey speaks of performing this task of retro-

Current Trends in Translation Theory', *The Bible Translator* 27 (1976), pp. 322-29; S. Bassnett, *Translation Studies* (New Accents; London: Routledge, rev. edn, 1991 [1980]); B. Hatim and I. Mason, *Discourse and the Translator* (LSLS; London: Longman, 1990); R.T. Bell, *Translation and Translating: Theory and Practice* (Applied Linguistics and Language Study; London: Longman, 1991); P. Newmark, *About Translation* (Multilingual Matters, 74; Clevedon: Multilingual Matters, 1991); L. Venuti (ed.), *Rethinking Translation: Discourse, Subjectivity, Ideology* (London: Routledge, 1992); P. Zlateva (ed.), *Translation as Social Action: Russian and Bulgarian Perspectives* (Translation Studies; London: Routledge, 1993); B. Hatim and I. Mason, *The Translator as Communicator* (London: Routledge, 1997); S. Bassnett and H. Trivedi (eds.), *Post-Colonial Translation: Theory and Practice* (Translation Studies; London: Routledge, 1999).

81. Black, *Aramaic Approach*, p. 274.

82. H.D. Betz, 'Wellhausen's Dictum "Jesus was not a Christian, but a Jew" in Light of Present Scholarship', *ST* 45 (1991), pp. 83-110; repr. in *idem, Antike und Christentum: Gesammelte Aufsätze IV* (Tübingen: Mohr Siebeck, 1998), pp. 1-31 (13).

version. However, there are a number of problems with his theory and method. Casey recognizes that translational issues must be considered, but even though he includes Hurst's important article in his bibliography, he does not use it in discussing matters of translation.[83] His discussion is essentially confined to citing a number of examples of the types of changes that occur in the receptor language when translation is performed. These examples are drawn from a range of theoretical sources but without serious attention to translational theory. In defining his method of approach, Casey claims that before the discovery of the Aramaic Scrolls the two best works on the Aramaic hypothesis were those of A. Meyer and M. Black.[84] Nevertheless, he recognizes the shortcomings of Black's method, especially in terms of the limited Aramaic evidence available to him—a fault Casey attempts to correct by using the Dead Sea Scrolls, among other sources.[85] Even so, the amount of Galilean Aramaic available for his reconstruction is admittedly quite small. Thus, it comes as somewhat of a surprise, as well as a disappointment, when Casey introduces his seven-part method, which looks much like the criteria used by Meyer and Black much earlier in the twentieth century: 'We select for this purpose passages which show some signs of having been translated literally', beginning with passages with purported mistakes in the Greek.[86] The next step is to 'begin the detailed work of *making up* a possible Aramaic substratum', using the Aramaic texts of the Dead Sea Scrolls.[87] The rest of his procedural steps are essentially confined to refining this reconstructed Aramaic text from what he calls a first-century Jewish perspective.[88] This procedure begs many important questions, several of which are addressed further in Chapter 4, below. In terms of verification, how does one recognize a mistranslation into Greek, how does one check the Aramaic reconstruction, how does one assess idiomatic features of this Aramaic, and, perhaps most importantly, how does one have any confidence that working back from such a fragile first step can result in anything but a tissue of fragile speculation? For Casey, the first-century Jewish perspective is

83. Casey, *Aramaic Sources*, pp. 93-106.
84. Casey, *Aramaic Sources*, p. 253.
85. Casey, *Aramaic Sources*, pp. 29-33. For a summary of such criticism of Black, see Evans, 'Introduction', to Black, *Aramaic Approach*, pp. vi-ix.
86. Casey, *Aramaic Sources*, p. 107.
87. Casey, *Aramaic Sources*, p. 108 (italics mine).
88. Casey, *Aramaic Sources*, pp. 109-10.

an Aramaic-speaking one, a perspective that I will attempt to refine in Chapter 4. However, when Casey actually undertakes to examine specific passages, it looks as if he departs from even his own tenuous and questionable procedures. At the outset of three out of four of his chapters utilizing his method, he begins with his Aramaic reconstruction, and then attempts to justify it throughout the rest of the chapter, apparently the reverse of the method he proposes. It appears that not much has advanced in use of the Aramaic hypothesis in the last 100 years, at least in so far as the approach of Casey is concerned. In fact, in several ways, Casey's method appears to have left behind the careful and relatively cautious method of many of his predecessors, including Black.

A second approach also relies upon the targums, but is much more modest in its claims and goals. Chilton has argued for two criteria for determining whether the words of Jesus reflect a Semitic (Aramaic targums) source: what he calls dictional and thematic coherence.[89] As he states regarding what is meant by dictional coherence, this means 'a substantive verbal similarity,[90] not only in respect of a few words'. However, as he notes, 'naturally we are only concerned with cases in which Jesus' sayings contain dictional elements which are peculiar to the Targum', and in particular those that contain dominical references to Isaiah. As to thematic coherence, as Chilton admits, 'the judgment of thematic similarity is rather more subjective than the observation of verbal agreement'. Regarding his findings, Chilton is quite modest in his claims: 'The evidence permits only of the conclusion that some interpretative traditions, later incorporated in the Targum [of Isaiah], had a formative influence on the wording of some of the sayings of Jesus'.[91] In the light of the admitted limitations of Chilton's method in terms of scope (it is confined to places where there is possible coherence of the words of Jesus with the targums, leaving any other sayings of Jesus outside of consideration) and acknowledged subjectivity, it is interesting to note that Evans has attempted to expand Chilton's criteria to

89. Chilton, *Galilean Rabbi and his Bible*, pp. 70-71, 90-137.

90. Whether the word coherence is the right term for what is being advocated here is arguable, certainly in the light of Chilton's own definition. Coherence would seem to imply the factor of intelligibility, whereas here he is simply referring to verbal similarity, which in itself says nothing of intelligibility. This merits further discussion.

91. Chilton, *Galilean Rabbi and his Bible*, p. 70 for all quotations above.

include a third criterion of exegetical coherence.[92] Evans defines this as a further refinement of thematic coherence, in which there are 'points of agreement between Jesus' or the evangelist's understanding of a passage and the way it is understood by the meturgeman—the Aramaic translator/interpreter. The agreement lies not so much in theme but in a particular point of interpretation' of Scripture.[93] Again, obvious limitations of this third criterion involve what is meant by points of agreement and its confinement to places where Scripture is being interpreted.

Despite the above criticisms as well as recent developments, there is still divided opinion on the strength of the Semitic language criterion. Evans, as might be expected from his attempt to extend Chilton's criterion of coherence, wishes to maintain it as providing confirmation and support for other criteria,[94] but Meier categorizes it as a dubious or secondary criterion.[95] Meier's reasoning is that the criterion, as used by Jeremias to the present, does nothing more than place the tradition in Palestine and possibly in the Aramaic-speaking church, but it cannot be any more specific than this.[96] Even Chilton tacitly admits to such a generalized use of the criterion when he states that 'the citations of the Targum to Isaiah in the New Testament record of Jesus' words make better sense as traditional elements in the dominical sayings than as redactional innovations'.[97] Further, to claim that a saying of Jesus has a

---

92. C.A. Evans, *Word and Glory: On the Exegetical and Theological Background of John's Prologue* (JSNTSup, 89; Sheffield: JSOT Press, 1993), pp. 18-27; *idem*, ' "Do This and You Will Live": Targumic Coherence in Luke 10:25-28', in B. Chilton and C.A. Evans, *Jesus in Context: Temple, Purity, and Restoration* (AGJU, 39; Leiden: E.J. Brill, 1997), pp. 377-93, esp. pp. 378-81; and *idem*, 'From Gospel to Gospel: The Function of Isaiah in the New Testament', in C.C. Broyles and C.A. Evans (eds.), *Writing and Reading the Scroll of Isaiah: Studies of an Interpretive Tradition* (2 vols.; VTSup, 70.1–2; Formation and Interpretation of Old Testament Literature, 1; Leiden: E.J. Brill, 1997), II, pp. 651-91, esp. pp. 667-74. The third criterion, exegetical coherence, is only specifically mentioned by name in Evans, 'From Gospel to Gospel', II, p. 670; *idem*, 'Introduction', to Black, *Aramaic Approach*, pp. xii-xiii, xv-xvii. Evans gives examples of all three of the criteria.
93. Evans, 'Introduction', to Black, *Aramaic Approach*, p. xii.
94. Evans, *Jesus and his Contemporaries*, p. 23.
95. Meier, *Marginal Jew*, I, pp. 179-80; also Schillebeeckx, *Jesus*, pp. 98-99. See also Sanders and Davies, *Studying the Synoptic Gospels*, pp. 333-34.
96. See Sanders, *Tendencies of the Synoptic Tradition*, pp. 297-300.
97. Chilton, *Galilean Rabbi and his Bible*, pp. 89-90.

distinctive Aramaic character to it that coheres with what Jesus would have said already implies that one has a clear idea of what Jesus said. As already noted above, Sanders has shown that there are no general rules by which one can determine whether Semitisms increase or decrease in the development of tradition, making it difficult to use retroversion as a means of establishing early tradition.[98] The proposals of Chilton and Evans might be seen as a way forward in this discussion, and in certain ways they are, because of their breaking free of dependence upon highly debatable judgments regarding translation and retroversion. However, here is another sense in which their proposals subordinate this form of the Semitic hypothesis to a subsidiary role, focused upon a rather narrow part of the tradition. This criterion is also now clearly dependent upon the criterion of coherence, with all of its shortcomings. These shortcomings include: the inability to establish the earliness and reliability of the targumic traditions as providing the bedrock material with which the Jesus tradition may or may not cohere,[99] problems related to conceptual transference between languages, and the problem that coherence implies more than simply correlation, but an abstract idealization that is inappropriate for judging a report of the thoughts and words of a given individual.[100] A last objection is that the linguistic environment of Palestine was far more complex than this scenario seems to assume. That is, this criterion seems to assume that the early Church, including Jesus, was almost exclusively Aramaic speaking, and that environment alone is the possible source of parallels.

---

98. Sanders, *Tendencies of the Synoptic Tradition*, pp. 190-255.

99. Chilton (*Galilean Rabbi and his Bible*, pp. 40-48; cf. *idem*, *The Glory of Israel: The Theology and Provenience of the Isaiah Targum* [JSOTSup, 23; Sheffield: JSOT Press, 1982]) admits that the targumic material is actually later than the material in the New Testament, but his hypothesis depends upon being able to determine which strands are as early as the time of Jesus. Of course, if one is to use a criterion of coherence to determine this, that is, the early targumic material is similar to Jesus material (or other purportedly early material), then one runs the risk of creating a circular argument, in which one is using the Jesus material and the targumic material to 'prove' each other's earliness and presumed authenticity. See also S. Kaufman, 'On Methodology in the Study of the Targums and their Chronology', *JSNT* 23 (1985), pp. 117-24; *idem*, 'Dating the Language of the Palestinian Targums and their Use in the Study of First Century CE Texts', in Beattie and McNamara (eds.), *The Aramaic Bible*, pp. 118-41.

100. See Winton, *Proverbs of Jesus*, pp. 119-21.

3. *Conclusion*

Much more could be, and has been, said about the rise of form criticism and redaction criticism and the development of the criteria for authenticity. The above criteria are those that have figured most prominently in a wide range of discussion, from early in the twentieth century to recent research. Rather than treat each criterion in a synchronic fashion, as is the case in the vast majority of recent treatments of this subject, I have opted for a diachronic approach. This diachronic analysis has allowed the development of the criteria to be placed within the conceptual framework of the rise especially of form criticism (but also in relation to redaction criticism), and with regard to the various proponents of these positions.

A number of further observations can be made about this development. The first is the surprising amount of continuity in the development of these criteria. This continuity is seen in a number of ways. One is to observe the proponents of the various criteria in terms of the kind of approach taken to the quest for the historical Jesus noted in Chapter 1, above. There does not seem to be an appreciable difference in their approaches. In other words, one might take a more conservative or traditional approach to the possibility of recovering authentic material about Jesus, such as does Dodd, or take a more progressive approach that disparages such a quest, as does Bultmann, and yet still be actively involved in developing and modifying the criteria for authenticity. Likewise, there does not appear to be a significant difference regarding the 'period' of quest that is involved and the approach one takes to criteria. The classic example must surely be the development of the criterion of double dissimilarity, noted above. A casual statement by Bultmann regarding one form of Gospel literature, the similitude, perhaps not even reflecting Bultmann's own priorities regarding criteria (see his stronger dependence upon the criterion of least distinctiveness), becomes a much stronger and more rigidly defined statement in Käsemann, which is further strengthened by Perrin. This correlates with the kinds of comments observed in the previous chapter, where, almost regardless of the approach one takes to the quest or the 'period' in which one writes, there is often difficulty in distinguishing the process and the results found from one discussion of Jesus to another. Thus Dibelius, a contemporary of Bultmann, can write during the so-called 'second' quest a life that is much more similar to that of Bornkamm; and a number of scholars during both periods can proclaim their scepticism that there are the materials to write any life of Jesus, while many others are doing that very thing. As Doty rightly says in conjunction with the analysis above, 'it must be noted that no one of the so-called New Questers proceeded without a firm training in form critical discipline, nor would any of them deny its continuing importance'.[101] The same appears to be the case for many in the supposed 'third quest' as well, even with the rise of redaction criticism. In any event, there is a tremendous continuity with regard to the criteria, despite the quest or critical mode in fashion.

A further observation is that the criteria seem to reflect the presuppositions of the time to a large extent. For example, the criterion of double dissimilarity clearly emerges from the assumptions at the outset of the development of form criticism, with its emphasis upon the formative role of the early Church regarding dominical tradition. This results in a criterion that, from the outset, is suspicious of any saying of Jesus that seems to reflect what that early Church may have thought and said. Similarly, the nineteenth-century romanticized view of Jesus as a Jewish peasant is to be found in the emphasis placed upon the criterion of the Semitic or Aramaic phenomena in the Gospels, even after new evidence regarding the use of Greek was entered into the scholarly debate.

Finally, one can comment with regards to the nature of the criticism of these criteria. On the one hand, there is certainly a commendable emphasis by a number of scholars upon developing these criteria, taking the earlier comments of such scholars as Bultmann and attempting to shape them into useful tools for historical-Jesus research. Although a number of other criteria have been discussed in certain circles, the ones selected above are the ones that keep returning for further refinement and discussion in the secondary literature. On the other hand, there is currently a surprisingly small amount of stringent internal criticism of these criteria. The range of the criticism seems to exist fairly strictly within the parameters of what are the agreed grounds for discussion. Subsequent chapters in this monograph attempt to break this deadlock first by offering an analysis of several recent proposals, and then in Part 2 by introducing three new criteria for consideration.

---

101. Doty, 'Discipline and Literature', p. 316. See also D.G.A. Calvert, 'An Examination of the Criteria for Distinguishing the Authentic Words of Jesus', *NTS* 18 (1971–72), pp. 209-19, esp. p. 219.

Table 2. *The Rise of the Criteria and the Development of Form and Redaction Criticism in 'Quests' for the Historical Jesus*

This table lays out in chronological order the approximate dates for instigation and initial development of the major criteria for authenticity discussed above, as well as several supposedly new criteria discussed in Chapter 3, below. Alongside these are the dates of the major initial developments of form and redaction criticism, and the dates of the supposed 'quests' for the historical Jesus.

Criteria	Criticism	'Quest'
Preliminary Criteria	Higher Criticism (Post-Enlightenment)	'Old' or 'First Quest' (1778–1906)
Criterion of Multiple Attestation/ Cross-Section Method (1906–)		'No Quest' (1906–1953)
Criterion of Double Dissimilarity (1913–)		
Criterion of Least Distinctiveness (1919–)	Form Criticism (1919–21)	
Criterion of Coherence/ Consistency (1921–)		
Criterion of Semitic Language Phenomena (1925–)		
	Redaction Criticism (1948–56)	
Criterion of Embarrassment (1953–)		'New' or 'Second Quest' (1953–88?)
Criterion of Rejection and Execution (1985–)		
		'Third Quest' (1988?–)
Criterion of Historical Plausibility (1997–)		

Chapter 3

RECENT DEVELOPMENTS IN THE CRITERIA FOR AUTHENTICITY

1. *Introduction*

The previous two chapters have discussed two major topics—first, the history of historical-Jesus research and, secondly, the major contours in discussion of the criteria for authenticity throughout their development and well into what some have (and I suggest incorrectly) called the 'second' and 'third quests' of the historical Jesus. However, within the last 10 to 15 years or so, there has been renewed discussion of the criteria in some circles. This renewed discussion is not simply in terms of analysing and re-analysing the traditional criteria, which is what so much of the work of the last 50 years has been, but in terms of introducing new criteria, elevating some of the older ones, and demoting still others. There have been two recent treatments that I wish to examine here, the first because of the apparent influence its proponent has had on a number of other recent historical-Jesus scholars, and the second because of its advocate's attempt to shift the focus of discussion and debate. I will summarize the arguments marshalled by the proponents of these renewed discussions, and then draw out what I see as their significance for further historical-Jesus research. As I have argued in Chapter 1, if there were to be a genuine 'third quest' of the historical Jesus, it would need to involve a thorough and complete re-assessment of the criteria for authenticity. The two major assessments that I have in mind here are the following: that by John Meier in the first volume of his monumental study of the historical Jesus, *A Marginal Jew*,[1] and that by Gerd Theissen, who, along with Annette Merz and Dagmar Winter, has focused upon critical assessment of the criterion of dissimilarity as im-

---

1. J.P. Meier, *A Marginal Jew: Rethinking the Historical Jesus* (3 vols.; ABRL; New York: Doubleday, 1991–), I, pp. 167-95.

petus for introducing a new criterion of historical plausibility.[2] There are, to be sure, other attempts at developing new criteria for authenticity, but I will analyse these two (see the excursus at the end of Chapter 2, above, for inclusion of these recent efforts in a graphic display of the history of the criteria for authenticity).[3]

2. John Meier's Primary and Secondary Criteria for Authenticity

What many consider the most important re-assessment of the criteria for authenticity that has taken place during the period hailed as the

2.   G. Theissen, 'Historical Scepticism and the Criteria of Jesus Research *or My Attempt to Leap across Lessing's Yawning Gulf'*, *SJT* 49 (1996), pp. 147-76; G. Theissen and D. Winter, *Die Kriterienfrage in der Jesusforschung: Vom Differenzkriterium zum Plausibilitätskriterium* (NTOA, 34; Freiburg: Universitätsverlag; Göttingen: Vandenhoeck & Ruprecht, 1997); G. Theissen and A. Merz, *Der historische Jesus: Ein Lehrbuch* (Göttingen: Vandenhoeck & Ruprecht, 1996; ET *The Historical Jesus: A Comprehensive Guide* [trans. J. Bowden; London: SCM Press; Minneapolis: Fortress Press, 1998]), esp. pp. 115-18. Cf. the useful review in J. Roloff, 'G. Theissen and D. Winter, The Question of Criteria in Jesus Research: From Dissimilarity to Plausibility', *Review of Theological Literature* 1 (1999), pp. 54-58.

3.   M.E. Boring ('The Historical-Critical Method's "Criteria of Authenticity": The Beatitudes in Q and Thomas as a Test Case', *Semeia* 44 [1988], pp. 9-44, here pp. 14-15) refers to Vernon K. Robbins's 'Pragmatic Relations as a Criterion for Authentic Sayings', *Forum* 1.3 (1985), pp. 35-63, as providing a new criterion for linguistic discussion, but he does not include it in his own praxis. It does not seem to have caught on in other circles either. Evans does not cite it in his recent bibliography, C.A. Evans, *Life of Jesus Research: An Annotated Bibliography* (NTTS, 24; Leiden: E.J. Brill, rev. edn, 1996). There are reasons for scepticism regarding Robbins's approach. The first is that he admits that it brings together many of the traditional criteria, along with some other hermeneutical stances (p. 37). A second is that he relies upon the category of syllogism, thus requiring that he engage in a major interpretive exercise to formulate the syllogism that he then analyses for authenticity. A third is that Robbins appears to rely upon a particular view of early Christianity, emphasizing the personal over the spiritual fields of discourse, and the personal being closest to authentic when it emphasizes the state of hunger, weeping, abuse and oppression (heavy shades of the nineteenth-century romanticism). A fourth is that Robbins in fact relies quite heavily upon the criterion of least to growing distinctiveness, already analysed in Chapter 2, above. Finally, Robbins's criterion describes what are called fields of discourse, that is, specific types of subject matter, but does not provide a means of adjudicating the actual words of Jesus. He continues in a similar vein in V.K. Robbins, *The Tapestry of Early Christian Discourse: Rhetoric, Society and Ideology* (London: Routledge, 1996).

'third quest' appeared in the first volume of Meier's *A Marginal Jew*, his massive (and ongoing) re-examination of most dimensions of the life of Jesus. It is fitting that at the outset of his projected three-volume study he lays out what he considers the criteria by which one can determine what words or actions come from Jesus. This assessment has been followed by a number of scholars, and has recently been heralded by several other 'third-quest' scholars as the most rigorous treatment of the criteria to date.[4]

For Meier, there are two sets of criteria: primary criteria, and secondary or dubious criteria.[5] The primary criteria include: the criterion of discontinuity, the criterion of multiple attestation, the criterion of coherence (these three criteria discussed in Chapter 2, above), and two others not so far discussed, the criterion of embarrassment and the criterion of rejection and execution.[6] He demotes to the position of secondary or dubious criteria the criterion of traces of Aramaic, the criterion of Palestinian environment (both discussed in Chapter 2, above, under the same heading), the criterion of vividness of narration, the criterion of the tendencies of the developing Synoptic tradition (discussed

4.   Several scholars who have essentially followed Meier include E. Schweizer, *Jesus: The Parable of God. What Do We Really Know about Jesus?* (Alison Park, PA: Pickwick, 1994; Edinburgh: T. & T. Clark, 1997), pp. 20-21; C.A. Evans, *Jesus and his Contemporaries: Comparative Studies* (AGJU, 25; Leiden: E.J. Brill, 1995), pp. 13-26, who calls Meier's the best treatment; *idem, Life of Jesus Research*, pp. 127-46; *idem*, 'Life of Jesus', in S.E. Porter (ed.), *Handbook to Exegesis of the New Testament* (NTTS, 25; Leiden: E.J. Brill, 1997), pp. 427-66, esp. pp. 441-46; and S. McKnight, 'Public Declaration or Final Judgment? Matthew 10:26-27 = Luke 12:2-3 as a Case of Creative Redaction', in B. Chilton and C.A. Evans (eds.), *Authenticating the Words of Jesus* (NTTS, 28.1; Leiden· E.J. Brill, 1998), pp. 363-83, esp. p. 378, who does similarly.

5.   Meier, *Marginal Jew*, I, pp. 167-95. However, one must note that Meier's treatment is in many respects foreshadowed by several other scholars, including E. Schillebeeckx (*Jezus, het verhaal van een levende* [Bloemendaal: Nelissen, 1974; ET *Jesus: An Experiment in Christology* [trans. H. Hoskins; New York: Seabury, 1979], pp. 88-100), who divides the criteria into valid and invalid criteria; and D. Polkow, 'Method and Criteria for Historical Jesus Research', in K.H. Richards (ed.), *Society of Biblical Literature 1987 Seminar Papers* (SBLSP, 26; Atlanta: Scholars Press, 1987), pp. 336-56, esp. p. 342. Polkow's treatment also falls roughly within the period of the so-called 'third quest', but has perhaps drawn a few too many fine distinctions, especially over the labels of various criteria (see Evans, *Jesus and his Contemporaries*, p. 13 n. 34).

6.   Meier, *Marginal Jew*, I, pp. 168-77.

in Chapter 2 in relation to the criterion of least distinctiveness, but also see below), and the criterion of historical presumption.[7] Even though his differentiating of the two categories of criteria is not unique to him, Meier has drawn attention to the importance of distinguishing between those criteria that he believes are more and less useful for historical-Jesus research on the basis of their logic and application. Since several of the primary criteria advocated by Meier have already been discussed in Chapter 2, these will not be discussed further here. Instead, I wish to examine what Meier says about the criteria of embarrassment and of rejection and execution. Along with his distinguishing primary and secondary criteria, these two further criteria, which are not as essentially a part of the history of discussion of the criteria for authenticity as those treated in Chapter 2, give Meier's treatment a different kind of emphasis than the work of many previous scholars. His criteria have a much more positive or maximal cast to them.[8]

a. *The Criterion of Embarrassment (or Movement against the Redactional Tendency)*
The criterion of embarrassment, as Meier and others call it, has been known by a number of different names,[9] and has had several different

7. Meier, *Marginal Jew*, I, pp. 178-83. Cf. Polkow, 'Method and Criteria', p. 342, who designates preliminary (discounting redaction, discounting tradition), primary (dissimilarity, coherence, multiple attestation), and secondary (Palestinian context, style, scholarly consensus) criteria.

8. See C.J. den Heyer, *Wie is Jezus? Balans van 150 jaar onderzoek naar Jesus* (Zoetermeer, The Netherlands: Uitgeverij Meinema, 1996; ET *Jesus Matters: 150 Years of Research* [trans. J. Bowden: London: SCM Press, 1996]), pp. 132-33, for the language of minimal and maximal criteria.

9. See Polkow, 'Method and Criteria', p. 341, who cites such criteria as dissimilarity, modification, execution, embarrassment, incongruity, theological divergency and hermeneutic potential as all 'basically variations on an old and familiar theme'. This is probably spreading the net a bit too wide, but see below. Meier (*Marginal Jew*, I, p. 168) attributes the term criterion of 'embarrassment' to Schillebeeckx, but gives no specific reference (it is presumably *Jesus*, pp. 91-92, although Schillebeeckx does not use the term 'embarrassment' here in the English version). This criterion perhaps had its earliest formulation by P.W. Schmiedel, 'Gospels', in T.K. Cheyne and J.S. Black (eds.), *Encyclopaedia Biblica: A Critical Dictionary of the Literary, Political and Religious History, the Archaeology, Geography and Natural History of the Bible* (4 vols.; London: A. & C. Black, 1899–1907), II, cols. 1761-898, esp. cols. 1881-83, according to I.H. Marshall, *I Believe in the Historical Jesus* (Grand Rapids: Eerdmans, 1977), pp. 205-206, 213. Meier (*Marginal Jew*, I,

modifications upon it. Despite these various incarnations, it has not been nearly as prevalent in discussion of the criteria as have some others, until its recent rejuvenation by Meier and a few other historical-Jesus scholars.[10] As this criterion has come to be known and to function, it does not go back to the rise of form criticism. It is usually seen to originate with the so-called 'new' or 'second quest' for the historical Jesus, in particular in the formulation by Ernst Käsemann in his 1953 lecture on the historical Jesus. In that lecture, in an almost casual added comment (already cited in part in Chapter 2, above), he says that 'In only one case do we have more or less safe ground under our feet; when there are no grounds either for deriving a tradition from Judaism or for ascribing it to primitive Christianity [this is the criterion of double dissimilarity, discussed in Chapter 2, above], and *especially when Jewish Christianity has mitigated or modified the received tradition, as having found it too bold for its taste*'.[11]

This statement has been developed in two major, yet distinctly different directions, depending upon whether one places emphasis upon the redaction of the tradition or the relation of the Church to the tradition.[12] One of the two formulations speaks of the criterion of divergent patterns from the redaction. As Calvert says, 'the inclusion of material which does not especially serve [the Gospel writer's] purpose may well be taken as a testimony to the authenticity of that material, or at least to the inclusion of it in the tradition of the Church in such a clear and con-

---

p. 187 n. 9) notes that this criterion is also known as 'modification' or 'tendencies of the developing Synoptic tradition'. He claims to take what is best from that criterion in his criterion of embarrassment, since he categorizes 'tendencies of the developing Synoptic tradition' as a secondary criterion. For the criterion of modification, he cites W.O. Walker, 'The Quest for the Historical Jesus: A Discussion of Methodology', *ATR* 51 (1969), pp. 38-56, esp. p. 48; and Boring, 'Criteria of Authenticity', p. 21.

10. See Polkow, 'Method and Criteria', p. 338.

11. E. Käsemann, 'Das Problem des historischen Jesus', *ZTK* 51 (1954), pp. 125-53 (repr. in *idem, Exegetische Versuche und Besinnungen*, I [Göttingen: Vandenhoeck & Ruprecht, 1960], pp. 187-214); ET 'The Problem of the Historical Jesus', in *idem, Essays on New Testament Themes* (trans. W.J. Montague; SBT, 41; London: SCM Press, 1964; Philadelphia: Fortress Press, 1982), pp. 15-47 (37) (italics mine).

12. See R.H. Stein, 'The "Criteria" for Authenticity', in R.T. France and D. Wenham (eds.), *Gospel Perspectives: Studies of History and Tradition in the Four Gospels*, I (Sheffield: JSOT Press, 1980), pp. 225-63, esp. pp. 245-48; Evans, *Life of Jesus Research*, pp. 134-36; *idem, Jesus and his Contemporaries*, pp. 18-19.

sistent way that the evangelist was loath to omit it'.[13] In this formulation of the criterion, 'authenticity is supported when the tradition cannot
easily be explained as the creation of a given evangelist or his community'.[14] The emphasis is upon testing the tradition against the specific
redactional tendencies of the Gospel writer. This formulation is much
closer to the traditional criterion of developing tendencies of the Synoptic tradition. Meier dismisses this criterion as 'highly questionable'
on the basis of the work of E.P. Sanders, who has shown that 'the whole
attempt to formulate laws of the developing Synoptic tradition and then
to apply them to the earlier oral tradition is dubious'.[15] However, there
is a second, and arguably more useful, formulation of the criterion,

13. D.G.A. Calvert, 'An Examination of the Criteria for Distinguishing the Authentic Words of Jesus', *NTS* 18 (1971–72), pp. 209-19 (219); cf. C.F.D. Moule,
The Phenomenon of the New Testament (London: SCM Press, 1967), pp. 56-76;
R.N. Longenecker, 'Literary Criteria in Life of Jesus Research: An Evaluation and
Proposal', in G.F. Hawthorne (ed.), *Current Issues in Biblical and Patristic Interpretation* (Festschrift M.C. Tenney; Grand Rapids: Eerdmans, 1975), pp. 217-29,
esp. pp. 225-29 (although some of the sources he cites are of questionable relevance); Stein, ' "Criteria" for Authenticity', p. 248. This criterion has been utilized
by those of the so-called Scandinavian school of Jesus research, who have studied
the principles of transmission of the tradition in terms of Jesus' Jewish background.
See H. Riesenfeld, *The Gospel Tradition* (trans. E.M. Rowley and R.A. Kraft;
Philadelphia: Fortress Press; Oxford: Basil Blackwell, 1970), p. 72; B. Gerhardsson, *Memory and Manuscript: Oral Tradition and Written Transmission in Rabbinic Judaism and Early Christianity* (ASNU, 22; trans. E.J. Sharpe; Lund: C.W.K.
Gleerup, 1961), esp. pp. 193-261; *idem*, *Tradition and Transmission in Early
Christianity* (ConBNT, 20; trans. E.J. Sharpe; Lund: C.W.K. Gleerup, 1964), esp.
pp. 37-40 (both of Gerhardsson's volumes repr. in Biblical Resource Series; Grand
Rapids: Eerdmans; Livonia, MI: Dove Booksellers, 1998); R. Riesner, *Jesus als
Lehrer: Eine Untersuchung zum Ursprung der Evangelien-Überlieferung* (WUNT,
2.7; Tübingen: Mohr Siebeck, 1981; 4th edn, 1994), pp. 97-498, on the Jesus tradition and its transmission; *idem*, 'Jüdische Elementarbildung und Evangelienüberlieferung', in France and Wenham (eds.), *Gospel Perspectives*, I, pp. 209-23, esp.
pp. 209-11; *idem*, 'Jesus as Preacher and Teacher', in H. Wansbrough (ed.), *Jesus
and the Oral Gospel Tradition* (JSNTSup, 64; Sheffield: JSOT Press, 1991), pp.
185-210, esp. pp. 195-96, 203-208; and S. Byrskog, *Jesus the Only Teacher:
Didactic Authority and Transmission in Ancient Israel, Ancient Judaism and the
Matthean Community* (ConBNT, 24; Stockholm: Almqvist & Wiksell, 1994), esp.
pp. 309-98.

14. Evans, *Jesus and his Contemporaries*, p. 18 n. 46.

15. Meier, *Marginal Jew*, I, p. 182, citing E.P. Sanders, *The Tendencies of the
Synoptic Tradition* (SNTSMS, 9; Cambridge: Cambridge University Press, 1969).

which some have called the criterion of embarrassment, contradiction or modification by Jewish Christianity. According to this criterion, 'authenticity is supported when the tradition cannot easily be explained as the creation of the Church in general'.[16] According to Meier, tradition that would have embarrassed or created some difficulty for the early Church, but that has been left in at the risk of embarrassment, even if it has been toned down, is presumably authentic. He cites as examples the baptism of Jesus by John, and Jesus' statement in Mk 13.32 that he does not know the day or hour of the end.[17]

Meier and others also recognize limitations to this criterion, however. These include the fact that such clear-cut cases of embarrassment as those noted just above are few in the Gospels, and, perhaps more importantly for historical-Jesus research, not sufficient to get anything close to a full, complete or even representative picture of Jesus.[18] It would indeed be an odd portrait of Jesus, if all that he is recorded as doing or saying were things embarrassing to the early Church. Another limitation of this criterion is that determining what might have been embarrassing to the early Church is also very difficult. This is due especially to the lack of detailed evidence for the thought of the early Church, apart from that found in the New Testament. An example that Meier gives is Jesus' supposed words of dereliction on the cross, Ps. 22.1. Meier argues that these were not words of dereliction at all, even though many in the early Church, including the authors of Luke's and John's Gospels, may have taken them in that way.[19] Meier also recognizes that this criterion of embarrassment must also be used in conjunction with others, although he does not expand on what he means by that statement.[20] As we have seen in Chapter 2, however, a similar statement could be made for virtually every one of the criteria for authenticity. Virtually every one of the criteria that still seems to have validity has the limitation that

16. Evans, *Jesus and his Contemporaries*, p. 18 n. 46. See also N. Perrin, *Rediscovering the Teaching of Jesus* (NTL; London: SCM Press; New York: Harper & Row, 1967), p. 39; Walker, 'Quest for the Historical Jesus', pp. 48-49; N.J. McEleney, 'Authenticating Criteria and Mark 7:1-23', *CBQ* 34 (1972), pp. 431-60, esp. pp. 442-43; Stein, '"Criteria" for Authenticity', p. 246; B.F. Meyer, *The Aims of Jesus* (London: SCM Press, 1979), p. 86.

17. Meier, *Marginal Jew*, I, p. 169.

18. Meier, *Marginal Jew*, I, p. 170.

19. Meier, *Marginal Jew*, I, p. 170. Cf. T.E. Schmidt, 'Cry of Dereliction or Cry of Judgment? Mark 15:34', *BBR* 4 (1994), pp. 145-53.

20. Meier, *Marginal Jew*, I, p. 171.

there is a perceivable gap between what the criterion seems to establish and what can be grounded in the life of Jesus, so that a given criterion cannot provide an absolute bedrock for grounding the traditions of the historical Jesus, but is in some way dependent upon other criteria used in conjunction. One cannot help but note that this may well create a vicious circular argument, in which various criteria, each one in itself insufficient to establish the reliability or authenticity of the Jesus tradition, are used to support other criteria.[21] Lastly, a criticism that Meier does not note, but that Polkow does, is that in some ways—despite Meier's efforts to avoid such a similarity by taking a more positive view towards the tradition—this criterion is a specific form of the criterion of double dissimilarity.[22] In other words, the point of embarrassment is reached when what Jesus is saying or doing does not fit with what the early Church, its authors, or even Jews of the time would have recognized as 'acceptable' behaviour or words for the eschatological prophet. Thus, this criterion may not be as fundamental or well grounded as Meier has suggested.

b. *The Criterion of Rejection and Execution*

The second criterion of Meier that merits discussion here is that of rejection and execution,[23] or, according to Evans's terminology, historical coherence.[24] For both Meier and Evans, this is the most important of all of the criteria in historical-Jesus research. Like the criterion of

---

21. This is not the only area of New Testament studies that utilizes such argumentation, in which the sum of a number of inconclusive arguments is asserted to be decisive. It is often found in discussions of authorship of the Pauline letters as well. Nevertheless, because it is widespread does not make it a stronger argument.

22. Polkow, 'Method and Criteria', p. 341.

23. Meier, *Marginal Jew*, I, p. 177, with reference to Schilleebeeckx, *Jesus*, p. 97. Anticipating him also is Walker, 'Quest of the Historical Jesus', p. 55; A.P. Winton, *The Proverbs of Jesus: Issues of History and Rhetoric* (JSNTSup, 35; Sheffield: JSOT Press, 1990), esp. p. 123.

24. Evans, *Jesus and his Contemporaries*, pp. 13-15. It must be noted that Evans's criterion of historical coherence is not simply to be equated with the criterion of coherence or consistency often cited in historical-Jesus research, since his use of it implies motivation for historical correlations (see discussion in Chapter 2, above). As noted in Chapter 2, if this is the proper term for it, the traditional criterion of coherence must rely on other criteria, to build up a core of authentic Jesus tradition. See Meier, *Marginal Jew*, I, pp. 176-77, who places it in the category of secondary criteria.

embarrassment, however, it too has not figured largely in the history of scholarly discussion of the criteria. Again, tracing its history and development depends upon which other criteria one thinks it is most closely related to.[25] Evans looks to E.P. Sanders's discussion of the actions of Jesus, in which authentic tradition regarding Jesus' actions must explain why Jesus attracted sufficient attention from authorities so that he was finally executed.[26] Hence, Evans gives this criterion priority, since he too wishes to begin with what he considers to be essential facts about Jesus as the backbone of historical-Jesus research, against which other actions and the sayings can be judged.[27] As a starting point in this quest, Evans agrees with Sanders's eight 'almost indisputable' facts regarding Jesus, give or take a couple.[28] Meier, on the other hand, does not see

25. Polkow ('Method and Criteria', p. 341) places execution under the criterion of dissimilarity, along with modification, embarrassment, incongruity, theological divergency and hermeneutic potential. Here he is clearly too broad in his categorization. He also sees the criterion of execution as the result of the data gathered by other criteria, such as dissimilarity, modification, embarrassment, incongruity and hermeneutic potential (p. 340).

26. Evans, *Jesus and his Contemporaries*, p. 13, citing E.P. Sanders, *Jesus and Judaism* (London: SCM Press; Philadelphia: Fortress Press, 1985), p. 7.

27. Evans, *Jesus and his Contemporaries*, p. 14. Evans notes that the original contexts of Jesus' sayings are now lost, and there are no reliable extra-canonical sources for finding them, as there are reliable extra-biblical sources regarding a number of facts regarding the world in which Jesus acted.

28. Evans, *Jesus and his Contemporaries*, p. 15, citing Sanders, *Jesus and Judaism*, p. 11. The eight facts of Sanders cited by Evans are that (1) Jesus was baptized by John the Baptist, (2) he was a Galilean who preached and healed, (3) he called disciples and spoke of twelve of them, (4) he confined his activity to Israel, (5) he engaged in a controversy about the Temple, (6) he was crucified outside Jerusalem by the Roman authorities, (7) his followers continued as an identifiable movement after his death, and (8) some Jews persecuted some members of this new movement. To these Evans adds that Jesus was probably viewed as a prophet by the populace, he often spoke of the kingdom of God, he criticized the ruling priests as part of his Temple controversy, and he was crucified as 'king of the Jews' by the Romans. See also now C.A. Evans, 'Authenticating the Activities of Jesus', in B. Chilton and C.A. Evans (eds.), *Authenticating the Activities of Jesus* (NTTS, 28.2; Leiden: E.J. Brill, 1998), pp. 3-29, esp. pp. 3-5, where he expands his list on the basis of subsequent work by Sanders (*The Historical Figure of Jesus* [London: Allen Lane/Penguin, 1993], esp. pp. 10-11) and N.T. Wright (*Jesus and the Victory of God* [Minneapolis: Fortress Press, 1996], esp. pp. 147-48), noting the summaries found in M.A. Powell, *Jesus as a Figure in History: How Modern Historians View*

this criterion as having priority, but instead being 'notably different from the [other authentic] criteria'.[29] Its difference lies in the fact that it does not speak directly to whether Jesus actually said or did anything specifically. Instead, according to Meier, it points interpreters to the 'historical fact that Jesus met a violent end at the hands of Jewish and Roman officials and then asks us what historical words and deeds of Jesus can explain his trial and crucifixion...'[30]

It seems clear to me that this criterion of rejection and execution is being used in two very different, and arguably incompatible, ways by Evans and Meier. Evans treats it as the fundamental criterion for historical-Jesus research, and uses it in a very specific and precise way—he assumes the fact of Jesus' execution at the hands of the Jewish and Roman authorities, builds this fact into a network of what he would see as coherent facts, and argues that any specific action or word of Jesus that is coherent with this historical scenario is potentially authentic. Meier treats this criterion as an unspecific stipulation, not useful for adjudicating individual actions and words but as a means of drawing attention to Jesus' violent death, and actions compatible with this. It is not clear to me whether those on either side of this difference of definition and utilization realize the fundamental antipathy that has been created.[31] It may well be that such categorical distinctions are incompatible, at least as they are currently being defined. The point that Meier and Evans both seem to be noting, however, is that this criterion moves away from the criterion of dissimilarity. It clearly enshrines a principle of similarity (and what they call coherence), once one can agree on certain common basic facts (even if these may have to be established by going outside of the Gospels, to the surrounding historical milieu).

the Man from Galilee (Louisville, KY: Westminster/John Knox Press, 1998), pp. 117, 154-55.

29. Meier, *Marginal Jew*, I, p. 177.

30. Meier, *Marginal Jew*, I, p. 177.

31. I note again the major difficulties with defining the concept of coherence (see Chapter 2, above). By invocation of this concept, one could well maintain that everything in the Gospels is authentic, since the Gospels themselves form arguably coherent narratives—at least that is how they have often been interpreted. See also M.D. Hooker, 'Christology and Methodology', *NTS* 17 (1970), pp. 480-87, esp. pp. 482-83; *idem*, 'On Using the Wrong Tool', *Theology* 75 (1972), pp. 570-81, esp. pp. 576-77, who discusses the subjective and problematic nature of the concept of coherence.

This brief discussion of Meier's two further criteria—especially that of rejection and execution with its emphasis upon making connections as a means of establishing authentic Jesus tradition—provides a suitable transition to the work of Theissen.

3. *Gerd Theissen and the Criterion of Historical Plausibility*

The change from the view of Polkow, who places the criterion of execution in the category of a criterion of dissimilarity,[32] to that of Meier and Evans, who place it in the category of a positive criterion,[33] represents what appears to be a major shift in perspective in a relatively small period of time. The challenge of this potential shift in perspective regarding the criteria for authenticity has recently been taken up by Theissen. In his first publication on the issue, Theissen addressed the question of Lessing's ditch. He argued that there was a means of traversing the ditch—it was not by leaping across but by jumping in and swimming across, using a set of four criteria based upon the traditional ones.[34] This proposal has been further developed in monograph form encouraged by and in conjunction with the work of his student, Winter. This has resulted in a major assessment of the criterion of dissimilarity and the proposal for a new criterion of historical plausibility.[35] This proposal has been popularized by Theissen and Merz in a German and English-translated handbook on the historical Jesus for students.[36] The theoretical discussion of the criteria is apparently primarily the work of Theissen, since he is primarily responsible for sections 1, 3 and 4 of the volume with Winter. Section 1 offers an assessment of previous criteria and section 3 develops the criterion of historical plausibility.[37] I wish to con-

---

32. Polkow, 'Method and Criteria', p. 341.

33. Meier, *Marginal Jew*, I, p. 177; Evans, *Jesus and his Contemporaries*, pp. 13-15.

34. Theissen, 'Historical Scepticism', esp. p. 153, for a graphic display of his 'lifebelt' of criteria.

35. Theissen and Winter, *Die Kriterienfrage in der Jesusforschung*, esp. pp. 175-232. I will utilize primarily this volume, since this represents Theissen's fullest statement, although I will also utilize the article and the student handbook, which provide useful summaries of various dimensions of Theissen's work.

36. Theissen and Merz, *The Historical Jesus*, pp. 115-18.

37. Theissen and Winter, *Die Kriterienfrage in der Jesusforschung*, pp. ix-x. However, Theissen admits in 'Historical Scepticism', p. 152, that many of the ideas come from Winter's dissertation, which is the basis of section 2 of the monograph.

centrate upon his criterion of historical plausibility, since it offers an attempt at a new step forward in the discussion of the criteria for authenticity in historical-Jesus research. However, in order to discuss his new criterion of plausibility, it will be necessary to place Theissen's proposal in the context of the critique he offers of the other criteria.

a. *The Major Criteria in Historical-Jesus Research*

As a prelude to his introduction of a new criterion, Theissen briefly surveys and offers a critique of what he sees as the three major criteria: source-based theories of multiple attestation, dissimilarity, and coherence. His criticisms of them are telling (as noted in Chapter 2, above). For example, he argues that the criterion of multiple attestation is not a real criterion, since, as was also noted in Chapter 2, it can only be used in conjunction with other criteria. The sources can be evaluated as to whether they can be brought to bear with each other to authenticate words or actions, but the criterion itself does not reveal whether these sources are reliable—that must be determined by the other criteria.[38] Likewise, the criterion of coherence is also dependent upon other criteria to establish the authentic tradition against which the material being evaluated is tested. In fact, according to Theissen, the criterion of coherence is based on the criterion of dissimilarity.[39]

As a result of this assessment, Theissen notes that the criterion of dissimilarity is in fact the only real criterion used in historical-Jesus research.[40] However, again as noted above, the criterion of dissimilarity is not really a single criterion, but what Theissen calls essentially two different criteria. One criterion relates to the dissimilarity between Jesus and the later Church, and the other relates to the dissimilarity between Jesus and Jewish thought.[41] Nevertheless, in Theissen's mind, both of these criteria that make up the criterion of dissimilarity result from

---

38. Theissen and Winter, *Die Kriterienfrage in der Jesusforschung*, pp. 12-16; Theissen and Merz, *The Historical Jesus*, p. 115.

39. Theissen and Winter, *Die Kriterienfrage in der Jesusforschung*, pp. 17-19; Theissen and Merz, *The Historical Jesus*, p. 115.

40. Further evidence for this distinction can be found even in the way that the criteria are categorized, such as by Calvert, 'Distinguishing the Authentic Words of Jesus', p. 211; Polkow, 'Method and Criteria', esp. p. 342.

41. Theissen and Winter, *Die Kriterienfrage in der Jesusforschung*, pp. 19-23; Theissen and Merz, *The Historical Jesus*, p. 115; Theissen, 'Historical Scepticism', pp. 159-62.

theological and historical motives.[42] The criterion regarding Jesus and the later Church is, in his words, 'dogmatics disguised'.[43] By this he means that the agenda of eighteenth- and nineteenth-century Life-of-Jesus research—emphasizing the differences between Jesus and the documents of the Church—is preserved in this criterion, even though that quest itself is no longer followed. The criterion regarding Jesus and Jewish thought, again reflecting traditional ecclesiastical positions, suppresses or underestimates Jesus' connection with Judaism, which, according to Theissen, has resulted in the emergence of an anti-Jewish portrait of Jesus. There is the further difficulty, so Theissen maintains, that the criterion of dissimilarity is not workable, since 'negative historical generalizations can hardly be verified, as we do not know all the sources, but have only a random selection'.[44] There is the further difficulty that 'it is almost impossible to establish complete originality',[45] especially for a human being, which this criterion seems to demand. As a result, Theissen says that he rejects the criteria for research into the historical Jesus, calling them 'one-sided'. He boldly concludes: 'There are no reliable criteria for separating authentic from inauthentic Jesus tradition. Neither the criterion of difference or [*sic*] the criterion of coherence can fulfil this task.'[46]

As noted above, Theissen's description is perhaps a better description of much German use of the criterion of double dissimilarity than it is of some later modified forms of the criterion, which recognize that Jesus must be seen as firmly placed within his Jewish context.[47] The revision of this criterion began with Käsemann and has continued to the present, as Theissen himself recognizes.[48] Nevertheless, Theissen's overall point of criticism, as noted above, appears to be valid that the criterion argues

42. Theissen and Winter, *Die Kriterienfrage in der Jesusforschung*, pp. 23-26.

43. Theissen and Merz, *The Historical Jesus*, p. 115; cf. Theissen and Winter, *Die Kriterienfrage in der Jesusforschung*, p. 23.

44. Theissen and Merz, *The Historical Jesus*, p. 115; cf. Theissen and Winter, *Die Kriterienfrage in der Jesusforschung*, p. 23.

45. Theissen and Merz, *The Historical Jesus*, p. 115; cf. Theissen and Winter, *Die Kriterienfrage in der Jesusforschung*, p. 25.

46. Theissen and Merz, *The Historical Jesus*, p. 115.

47. A recent exponent of this position is T. Holmén, 'Doubts about Double Dissimilarity: Restructuring the Main Criterion of Jesus-of-History Research', in Chilton and Evans (eds.), *Authenticating the Words of Jesus*, pp. 47-80.

48. Theissen and Winter, *Die Kriterienfrage in der Jesusforschung*, pp. 6, 24-25, 175; Theissen and Merz, *The Historical Jesus*, p. 116.

for a unique minimum and tends to equate this with the limits of authenticity. His dismissal of these three traditional criteria, including the central criterion of dissimilarity, leads Theissen to offer his new proposal.

b. *The Criterion of Historical Plausibility*
In response to the elimination of the standard criteria, including the criterion of double dissimilarity, Theissen posits a new criterion, which he calls the criterion of historical plausibility.[49] Like the criterion of double dissimilarity, this criterion is also two-sided: in terms of Jesus' relation to Judaism one speaks of a plausibility of context, and in terms of Jesus' relation to Christianity one speaks of a plausibility of consequence.[50] What authenticity means for Theissen is determined in terms of probabilities. This important methodological point regarding probability, rather than the kind of disjunction emphasized by the criterion of double dissimilarity, is discussed in some detail by Theissen.[51] Rejecting Ranke's idea that one can know history 'as it actually happened' (*wie es eigentlich gewesen*), Theissen emphasizes that one must assess plausible scenarios. That is, one creates a complex picture of Jesus, which cannot be rejected apart from creating a more plausible scenario.[52] This is one of the most important insights, it seems to me, that

49. This criterion is not really new to Theissen, as is made clear by examining McEleney, 'Authenticating Criteria', pp. 445-48, who defines the 'criterion of historical presumption', citing others that he claims have a similar perspective. This criterion is rejected by Meier, *Marginal Jew*, I, p. 183, as a secondary or dubious criterion.

50. Theissen and Winter, *Die Kriterienfrage in der Jesusforschung*, p. 175.

51. Theissen and Winter, *Die Kriterienfrage in der Jesusforschung*, pp. 194-214. It is noteworthy how little theoretical discussion there is to draw upon from New Testament scholars, however. One of the few sources of substance is J.K. Riches and A. Millar, 'Conceptual Change in the Synoptic Tradition', in A.E. Harvey (ed.), *Alternative Approaches to New Testament Study* (London: SPCK, 1985), pp. 37-60.

52. Theissen and Winter, *Die Kriterienfrage in der Jesusforschung*, pp. 206, 207. Theissen draws here on I. Lakatos, 'Falsification and the Methodology of Scientific Research Programmes', in I. Lakatos and A. Musgrave (eds.), *Criticism and the Growth of Knowledge: Proceedings of the International Colloquium in the Philosophy of Science, London, 1965, Volume 4* (Cambridge: Cambridge University Press, 1970), pp. 91-196, esp. p. 119: 'Contrary to naive falsificationism, *no experiment, experimental report, observation statement or well-corroborated low-level falsifying hypothesis alone can lead to falsification. There is no falsification before the emergence of a better theory*' (italics in the original).

Theissen develops in his book, and is worth considering for any similar attempt at explanation of data.

In order to create this kind of a complex picture of Jesus, under the umbrella of his criterion of plausibility with its two manifestations, Theissen posits the use of other sub-criteria.[53] He begins with the criterion of plausibility of consequence in Christianity. This plausibility of consequence is posited as a criterion to replace that of the criterion of dissimilarity from the early Church. There are two sub-criteria invoked at this point—resistance to the redactional tendency and source coherence. These may at first seem to be in opposition. Theissen does not see it this way, however, arguing that 'Coherence and opposition to the tendency are complementary criteria for the plausibility of historical influence'.[54] Resistance or opposition to the tendency refers to elements of the tradition that go against its general trend of development within the early Church. This sub-criterion is virtually identical to that of resistance to the redactional tendency, already discussed above (with the same attendant shortcomings). Two potential problems with this sub-criterion are raised and addressed by Theissen.[55] One is that of places where there are parts of the tradition that seem to be at odds with the general picture of Jesus. He believes that these too can be evaluated in a positive light. As he states, 'For some inconsistencies are historical relics which have been preserved despite powerful tendencies to revere Jesus (e.g. his baptism by John, his conflict with his family, the charge of being in league with the devil, the betrayal and flight of the disciples, the crucifixion)'.[56] The second is the recognition that there was an inherent plurality to early Christianity, which resulted in different developments.[57]

The second sub-criterion of the criterion of plausibility of consequence in Christianity is that of source coherence. Theissen believes

53. Note how these criteria have developed from what Theissen describes in 'Historical Scepticism', esp. pp. 156-62, 166-70.

54. Theissen and Merz, *The Historical Jesus*, p. 116.

55. Theissen and Winter, *Die Kriterienfrage in der Jesusforschung*, pp. 178-80.

56. Theissen and Merz, *The Historical Jesus*, p. 117. In Theissen and Winter, *Die Kriterienfrage in der Jesusforschung*, p. 178, reference is made to W. Marxsen, *Anfangsprobleme der Christologie* (Gütersloh: Gerd Mohn, 1960; ET *The Beginnings of Christology: A Study in its Problems* [Facet Books, Biblical Series, 22; Philadelphia: Fortress Press, 1969; 2nd edn, 1979]), p. 15 (German); and Schillebeeckx, *Jesus*, p. 81.

57. Theissen and Winter, *Die Kriterienfrage in der Jesusforschung*, p. 179.

that, if sources independent of each other reveal the same things, there is a chance we are dealing with authentic tradition. The reasoning is that, if there are multiple independent sources attesting to the same tradition, the tradition itself must be older than its sources and may well reflect the influence of Jesus. Theissen goes on to break down this criterion into three further sub-parts. Theissen wishes to distinguish between a correspondence in content and genuine multiple attestation. As he states, 'two clearly different sayings can fit together well in terms of content, but each may only be attested once. Multiple attestations of substantial motifs and subjects in independent streams of tradition (in Q, Mark, Matt.[S], Luke[S], Thomas and John) are therefore an important criterion.'[58] Thus, he re-introduces what is known as the cross-section argument (*Querschnittsbeweis*).[59] He further re-introduces the sub-criterion of multiple attestation in differing literary forms,[60] in which tradition in different literary forms and genres may have been influenced by the historical Jesus. The third sub-criterion is that of multiple attestation of the same tradition, but in variant forms independent of each other. Thus, Theissen concludes regarding this criterion of plausibility of historical development that it makes use of three traditional criteria: dissimilarity,

58. Theissen and Merz, *The Historical Jesus*, p. 116. Matt.[S] and Luke[S] represent Matthew's and Luke's special material, usually referred to as M and L.

59. Theissen and Winter, *Die Kriterienfrage in der Jesusforschung*, p. 181, where reference is made to N.A. Dahl, 'Der historische Jesus als geschichts-wissenschaftliches und theologisches Problem', *KD* 1 (1955), pp. 104-32, here p. 117; ET 'The Problem of the Historical Jesus', in C.E. Braaten and R.A. Harrisville (eds.), *Kerygma and History: A Symposium on the Theology of Rudolf Bultmann* (Nashville: Abingdon Press, 1962), pp. 138-71; repr. in N.A. Dahl, *The Crucified Messiah and Other Essays* (Minneapolis: Augsburg, 1974), pp. 48-89, 173-74, here p. 68; G. Schille, 'Ein neuer Zugang zu Jesus? Das traditionsgeschichtliche Kriterium', *Zeichen der Zeit* 40 (1986), pp. 247-53, here p. 250; F. Mussner, 'Methodologie der Frage nach dem historischen Jesus', in K. Kertelge (ed.), *Rückfrage nach Jesus* (QD, 63; Freiburg: Herder, 1974), pp. 118-47, here pp. 134-35; repr. in F. Mussner, *Jesus von Nazareth im Umfeld Israels und der Urkirche* (ed. M. Theobald; WUNT, 111; Tübingen: Mohr Siebeck, 1999), pp. 13-42, here pp. 29-30. Theissen and Merz (*The Historical Jesus*, p. 116) make reference to H. Schürmann, 'Kritische Jesuserkenntnis: Zur kritischen Handhabung des "Unähnlichkeitskriteriums"', in *idem*, *Jesus—Gestalt und Geheimnis: Gesammelte Beiträge* (Paderborn: Bonifatius, 1994), pp. 420-34, here p. 425.

60. Theissen and Winter, *Die Kriterienfrage in der Jesusforschung*, pp. 181-82, where reference is made to C.H. Dodd, *History and the Gospel* (London: Nisbet, 1938), pp. 91-102.

coherence and multiple attestation, although for each he attempts to define and utilize them in a positive rather than a negative way. This criterion has apparently been further refined and expanded in Theissen's handbook, where he expands what is meant by tradition to include motifs and subject-matter, as well as traditions. He is able, through this expansion, to include actions and sayings in his discussion, whereas in his monograph he tends to deal with sayings when he is dealing with source coherence.[61]

The second plank of Theissen's two-part criterion of historical plausibility consists of the criterion of plausibility of historical context in relation to Judaism of the time of Jesus. This criterion also consists of two sub-criteria. The first sub-criterion is that of conformity to context, and the second is that of contextual individuality. Again, as in his discussion of the first plank, what appears at first thought to be a contradiction in formulation is necesssary, in Theissen's mind, to establish his criterion. The first sub-criterion, that of conformity to context, is formulated by him in this way: 'the better a tradition suits its concrete Jewish Palestinian and Galilean context the more its claim to authenticity'.[62] Here it is not difficult for him to marshal a number of examples, including those related to sabbath, purity and the Temple. He concludes by stating that 'fundamentally each historical portrait is only understandable in the context of its own world'.[63] This appears to be a formulation in direct conflict with the traditional criterion of double dissimilarity, with its differentiation between Jesus and Judaism. However, the second sub-criterion is introduced by Theissen to deal with the issue of individuality. This sub-criterion is that of contextual individualism, in which individual characteristics of Jesus are introduced.[64] These include such things as how he compares with other charismatics of his age, indicators of his specialness such as his use of *amen*, and the fact

61. Theissen and Merz, *The Historical Jesus*, p. 117, where reference is made to E. Fuchs, 'The Quest of the Historical Jesus (1956)', in *idem, Studies of the Historical Jesus* (trans. A. Scobie; SBT, 42; London: SCM Press, 1964), pp. 11-31, here p. 21; first published as 'Die Frage nach dem historischen Jesus', *ZTK* 53 (1956), pp. 210-29; repr. in *idem, Zur Frage nach dem historischen Jesus* (Tübingen: Mohr Siebeck, 1960), pp. 143-67, here pp. 154-55.

62. Theissen and Winter, *Die Kriterienfrage in der Jesusforschung*, p. 183; cf. Theissen, 'Historical Scepticism', pp. 166-68.

63. Theissen and Winter, *Die Kriterienfrage in der Jesusforschung*, p. 186.

64. Theissen and Winter, *Die Kriterienfrage in der Jesusforschung*, pp. 186-91; cf. Theissen, 'Historical Scepticism', pp. 168-70.

that his individual complexity cannot derive from a single tradition. Even when Jesus looks to be different from this environment, this difference, Theissen believes, must be demonstrable as growing plausibly from the context. This is where the individuality and uniqueness of Jesus come from. This difference does not consist of his complete originality, but of the way he stands out from his environment.

Theissen thus draws his discussion together by claiming that overall historical plausibility is the result of the joining together of consequential and contextual plausibility, and of the uniqueness of the historical figure of Jesus. By this, he seems to mean that behind this profile of the unique features of Jesus—which are established through contrast with his context by means of his breaking away from direct causality—is his Jewishness. Theissen provides a small chart that attempts to show that Judaism developed through the historical context of Jesus into Christianity, but that this was not a single stream of development.[65]

In conclusion, Theissen believes that historical-Jesus research should not be oriented to theological goals.[66] Similarly, the goal is not to reconstruct individual sayings, but rather to take what is known to create a complex portrait of the person of Jesus himself. To do this, one must weigh probabilities, and it is here that the criteria must play their roles. To summarize, Theissen notes that the criterion of Jewish contextual plausibility has two aspects. The first is that what Jesus has done and said must be consonant with Judaism of the first half of the first century in Galilee, and the second that what Jesus has done and said must be recognizable as those actions and words of an individual reflecting the Judaism of that time. Likewise, the criterion of consequent historical plausibility has two aspects as well. The first is that the ways in which the Jesus tradition differs from the early Christian sources, as it is part of the developing tradition, can lay claim in different ways to historical plausibility. The second is that the coherence of individual elements of independent, different traditions, sources and literary forms within the Jesus tradition can also create historical plausibility.[67] Theissen displays this schema in a chart that illustrates four partial criteria that con-

---

65. Theissen and Winter, *Die Kriterienfrage in der Jesusforschung*, p. 192.
66. Theissen and Winter, *Die Kriterienfrage in der Jesusforschung*, p. 215, where reference is made to Sanders, *Jesus and Judaism*, pp. 333-34.
67. Theissen and Winter, *Die Kriterienfrage in der Jesusforschung*, p. 216.

stitute the criterion of plausibility. The plausibility of context and plausibility of influence interact with the factors of both coherence/agreement and incoherence/disagreement to create four sub-criteria: source coherence, adverse tendencies, context correspondence and contextual individuality.[68]

Theissen is to be highly commended for attempting to shift the criteria for authenticity from what he sees as the overly negative and minimalistic criterion of double dissimilarity to one that takes a more positive view of the tradition in its multifariousness. He has also raised several important questions of method, regarding how one weighs evidence and creates models for analysis of data. When one looks more closely at his programme for historical-Jesus research, however, one sees that there is a shift in emphasis rather than a genuine shift in method. Several notes of reservation must be noted in this regard. The first is Theissen's continued fundamental reliance upon the traditional criteria. The same criticisms that have been marshalled regarding these in Chapter 2 and above, as well as Theissen's own criticisms of them, would still seem to have significant force. For example, it is unclear why the criterion of multiple attestation, which has been criticized for only being able to evaluate the sources and not their reliability, in this new framework becomes more trustworthy. Similarly, the criterion of coherence is used somewhat ambiguously by Theissen. In some respects, this criterion appears to be a rejuvenation of the traditional criterion of coherence, criticized in Chapter 2 for relying upon previously established tradition. This shortcoming is not overcome by Theissen's positing it as a sub-criterion. In other respects, however, this new criterion of coherence appears to be similar to the criterion of historical coherence as developed above by Evans, although Theissen does not directly link the use of the criterion with such key events as the execution of Jesus. Much of Theissen's reaction against the criterion of dissimilarity is against the double form, which, as noted in Chapter 2, has already come under serious attack. Nevertheless, he ends up preserving the criterion of double dissimilarity, even if it is in a modified form.

This leads to a second criticism, with regard to how Theissen uses both coherence and dissimilarity. In his discussion, it is difficult to see when it is appropriate to invoke one, and when the other, without leading to unreconcilable conflict in determining whether the tradition is reli-

---

68. Theissen and Winter, *Die Kriterienfrage in der Jesusforschung*, p. 217; cf. Theissen and Merz, *The Historical Jesus*, p. 118.

able or authentic. Theissen regularly invokes the concept of plausibility, and in many ways he is on firm ground for doing so in the light of recent discussion of scientific method. However, he leaves the discussion unclear exactly what plausibility means in this context, and, perhaps more importantly, how plausibility works in relation to judging both coherent and dissimilar traditions.

A final criticism is with regard to Theissen's concept of a complex portrait of Jesus. This seems to be a realistic and necessary distinction to make in the sense that the Jesus of history was undoubtedly a much more complex figure than a simple analysis of individual sayings or parts of sayings could reveal. However, if this complex portrait is based upon the criteria noted above, then it will remain within the limitations that Theissen wishes to escape. In Theissen's conclusion, the criterion of historical plausibility is used as a means of mediating for the other criteria, but it is these criteria that have been used to adjudicate the tradition. In other words, one must establish authentic sayings apart from the criterion of plausibility (that is, on the basis of the traditional criteria) in order to use this supposed new criterion. This makes the criterion a potentially useful guide, but somewhat redundant and not free from the errors of its sub-criteria, including still that of dissimilarity. The final result is that it is clear that the criterion of dissimilarity has persisted in historical-Jesus research, and that other criteria, even that of historical plausibility, have yet to alter the fundamental shape of the criteria significantly.[69]

4. *Conclusion*

An examination of the history of discussion of the criteria for authenticity, and of two important recent attempts to re-assess these criteria, shows that despite several significant, and useful, efforts to re-evaluate the criteria, there are a number of consistent and persistent conclusions that keep emerging. One is the fundamental importance of the criterion of dissimilarity for historical-Jesus research. Another is the significance given to building an interpretive structure around this criterion. The overall tendency of use of the criteria in the history of historical-Jesus research has been a recent shift in emphasis from the more minimalistic conclusions drawn from form (and redaction) criticism to a more pos-

---

69. See Holmén, 'Doubts about Double Dissimilarity', pp. 73-74 n. 106.

itive analysis appreciating Jesus' Jewish background and strongly emphasizing historical coherence with this factor when assessing his words
and actions. However, the criterion of dissimilarity still persists in recent
historical-Jesus research, in at least two forms. One is simply as a major
criterion still invoked and utilized in the discussion, as is evidenced even
in the work of Theissen analysed above. Another is as a focal point for
other criteria. Although not to the same extent in Theissen, in the work
of others, including that of Meier, the criterion of dissimilarity still
stands as an important criterion for historical-Jesus research. Alongside
it, scholars have introduced other criteria, including several that purportedly have a more positive orientation to the tradition, such as that of
historical coherence. How these criteria now work together, a question
that Theissen explicitly addresses but that Meier does not, is still left
unresolved. In other words, the criteria for authenticity have essentially
moved along a consistent trajectory of continuous development. There
have been several new ideas introduced into the discussion, but few
major methodological shifts from this singular orientation. The rest of
this volume is dedicated to introducing three new criteria in an attempt
to see if such a shift can at least begin to be made.

Part II

NEW PROPOSALS

Chapter 4

THE CRITERION OF GREEK LANGUAGE AND ITS CONTEXT

1. *Introduction*

The revisionist spirit has come to the fore in recent work on the criteria for authenticity, especially as seen in the recent work of Meier and Theissen discussed in Chapter 3, above. Despite these and several other major efforts, the criteria remain much the same. Thus, I would like to suggest that other criteria can and should be entered into the discussion. I have tried to be fair in my criticism of the criteria that have been developed in historical-Jesus research over most of this century. However, the end result has been, in my estimation, negative in many respects. One of the possible, and perhaps in many ways most logical and necessary, results would be to abandon the search for criteria altogether and to re-evaluate the way in which historical-Jesus research is conducted. I have sympathy for those who argue in this way. However, before the entire enterprise is finally abandoned, perhaps it is worth introducing several more criteria that may break the deadlock we have noted above. As an attempt in this regard, I wish to introduce three new criteria for authenticity focused around the Greek language: the criterion of Greek language and its context (this chapter), the criterion of Greek textual variance (Chapter 5), and the criterion of discourse features (Chapter 6). What distinguishes these criteria is their attention to matters of Greek language and sound linguistic methodology. These will be explained as they are introduced and utilized in this and subsequent chapters, but without detailed reference to the findings of scholars using other criteria regarding these same passages. My desire is for these new criteria to be established on their own grounds, without prejudging the results or depending too much upon other criteria that might call into question or jeopardize their findings. The ensuing proposals are designed to take us further than the most recent discussion, but not necessarily to suggest final solutions. The results are tentative and meant to be suggestive of areas of further historical-Jesus research.

2. *Aramaic and Greek as the Languages of Jesus: Recent Discussion*

One of the traditional criteria for authenticity has been that of Semitic (Aramaic) language phenomena and Palestinian environment, as introduced and analysed in Chapter 2. As a result of the heavy emphasis of the supposed 'third quest' of the historical Jesus on the Jewishness of Jesus, it might seem that this criterion would come back into strong favour. In some ways, as noted in Chapter 2, there is an ongoing struggle regarding this criterion, with Meier placing it in the category of those of dubious value, and Evans wishing to retain it for its supportive function.[1] Holmén's recent discussion of the criterion of double dissimilarity suggests that Meier is perhaps rejecting the criterion of Semitic language phenomena, at least in part, because of his rejection of the criterion of double dissimilarity itself. This is even though he accepts the criterion of discontinuity, a revised form of the criterion of dissimilarity.[2] With renewed emphasis upon the Jewishness of Jesus, Meier's position might seem to be in tension with rejection of the criterion of Semitic language phenomena. Nevertheless, both Evans and Meier agree that this criterion cannot establish authenticity, but can be, at best, only supportive of other criteria.

I believe, however, that there are other linguistic criteria that can be used in attempting to authenticate the words (and actions) of Jesus, and that these can draw upon the use of the Greek language and its context (for my response to recent arguments against such a position, and material assumed in the discussion within the body of this chapter, see the Excursus at the end of this chapter). This criterion has three stages to its utilization. The criterion first examines an episode's participants and their backgrounds, then analyses the context and theme of discussion, and concludes with determination of whether the episode has a claim to recording the Greek words of Jesus. This criterion begins, however,

---

1.   J.P. Meier, *A Marginal Jew: Rethinking the Historical Jesus* (3 vols.; ABRL; New York: Doubleday, 1991–), I, pp. 179-80; C.A. Evans, *Jesus and his Contemporaries: Comparative Studies* (AGJU, 25; Leiden: E.J. Brill, 1995), p. 23.

2.   T. Holmén, 'Doubts about Double Dissimilarity: Restructuring the Main Criterion of Jesus-of-History Research', in B. Chilton and C.A. Evans (eds.), *Authenticating the Words of Jesus* (NTTS, 28.1; Leiden: E.J. Brill, 1998), pp. 47-80, esp. pp. 74-80.

with informed re-examination in linguistic terms of what one means by Jesus' Jewishness. This kind of investigation is not usually undertaken in detail by those invoking this Jewish background for Jesus.[3] For example, even Theissen in his desire to introduce the criterion of historical plausibility, with continuity seen between Jesus and his Jewish background, does not go into requisite detail on what this Jewishness means.[4] One of the major reasons for continued use of the Semitic (Aramaic) language and Palestinian environment criterion, and one that made it useful to the criterion of dissimilarity, was that Jesus was, following this criterion, seen to be dissimilar from the traditions of the early Church. The early Church clearly was a Greek-speaking church, as evidenced, so the sub-text of this theory goes, by the fact that the writings of the New Testament are all in Greek, and the early Church fathers all wrote in Greek, as well (e.g. *Didache, Epistle of Barnabas, Shepherd of Hermas, 1 Clement, Epistle to Diognetus*, Ignatius, Polycarp).[5] The result is a disjunction that goes back at least to the early part of the twentieth century, as noted in Chapter 2. This situation was probably encouraged

---

3.   For example, in his survey of the state of research, B.B. Scott does not treat the linguistic issues ('From Reimarus to Crossan: Stages in a Quest', *CR* 2 [1994], pp. 253-80, esp. pp. 258-72).

4.   G. Theissen and D. Winter, *Die Kriterienfrage in der Jesusforschung: Vom Differenzkriterium zum Plausibilitätskriterium* (NTOA, 34; Freiburg: Universitätsverlag; Göttingen: Vandenhoeck & Ruprecht, 1997); G. Theissen and A. Merz, *Der historische Jesus: Ein Lehrbuch* (Göttingen: Vandenhoeck & Ruprecht, 1996; ET *The Historical Jesus: A Comprehensive Guide* [trans. J. Bowden; London: SCM Press, 1998]), esp. pp. 115-18. One of the few to do so is W.S. Vorster, *Speaking of Jesus: Essays on Biblical Language, Gospel Narrative and the Historical Jesus* (NovTSup, 92; ed. J.E. Botha; Leiden: E.J. Brill, 1999), pp. 285-99, esp. p. 288 (revised from *Hervormde Teologiese Studies* 47.1 [1991], pp. 121-35).

5.   I resist the urge to enter here into discussion of the reasons for the early separation between Christianity and Judaism. An examination of both ancient and modern views of this question, with our own proposal for the reasons for an early separation, are found in S.E. Porter and B.W.R. Pearson, 'Why the Split? Christians and Jews by the Fourth Century', *JGRChJ* 1 (2000), forthcoming. An examination of the perspectives of Christians, Jews and Romans in the ancient world on this topic is found in Porter and Pearson, 'Ancient Understandings of the Christian–Jewish Split', in S.E. Porter and B.W.R. Pearson (eds.), *Christian–Jewish Relations through the Centuries* (JSNTSup, 192; RILP, 6; Sheffield: Sheffield Academic Press, forthcoming 2000). On language issues, see A. Vögtle, 'Die griechische Sprache und ihre Bedeutung für die Geschichte des Urchristentums', in H. Gundert (ed.), *Der Lebenswert des Griechischen* (Karlsruhe: Badenia, 1973), pp. 77-93.

by the untimely deaths of several strong advocates[6] of seeing the Greek of the New Testament in the context of the then recently discovered papyri and similar texts.[7] This disjunction between the supposed Aramaic-speaking early Church located in Palestine and the next generation

6.   With the deaths of such scholars as the lesser known but very important Albert Thumb in 1915, James Hope Moulton in 1917, and Adolf Deissmann in 1937, the field was left to Semitic-language advocates, who promoted the disjunction between the supposed Aramaic-speaking early Church and the Greek-speaking Christians of the next generation (see M. Reiser, *Syntax und Stil des Markusevangeliums im Licht der hellenistischen Volksliteratur* [WUNT, 2.11; Tübingen: Mohr Siebeck, 1984], p. 2). Deissmann was one of the first to realize fully the relevance of the papyri for study of the vocabulary of the Greek of the New Testament, noted in his *Bibelstudien* (Marburg: Elwert, 1895) and *Neue Bibelstudien* (Marburg: Elwert, 1897), translated together as *Bible Studies* (trans. A. Grieve; Edinburgh: T. & T. Clark, 1901), and 'Hellenistisches Griechisch', in A. Hauck (ed.), *Realencyklopädie für protestantische Theologie und Kirche*, VII (Leipzig: J.C. Hinrichs, 3rd edn, 1899), pp. 627-39 (ET in S.E. Porter [ed.], *The Language of the New Testament: Classic Essays* [JSNTSup, 60; Sheffield: JSOT Press, 1991], pp. 39-59), and developed in *Licht vom Osten* (Tübingen: Mohr Siebeck, 1908; 4th edn, 1923; ET *Light from the Ancient East* [trans. L.R.M. Strachan; London: Hodder & Stoughton, 1910; 4th edn, 1927]) and *Philology of the Greek Bible: Its Present and Future* (trans. L.R.M. Strachan; London: Hodder & Stoughton, 1908). Moulton was one of the first to appreciate the relevance of the papyri for study of the syntax of the Greek of the New Testament, noted in his 'Grammatical Notes from the Papyri', *Classical Review* 15 (1901), pp. 31-39, 434-42; 18 (1904), pp. 106-12, 151-55; developed in his 'Notes from the Papyri', *Expositor* Sixth Series 3 (1901), pp. 271-82; 7 (1903), pp. 104-21; 8 (1903), pp. 423-39; 'Characteristics of New Testament Greek', *Expositor* Sixth Series 9 (1904), pp. 67-75, 215-25, 310-20, 359-68, 461-72; 10 (1904), pp. 24-34, 168-74, 276-83, 353-64, 440-50; and *Prolegomena*, to *A Grammar of New Testament Greek* (Edinburgh: T. & T. Clark, 1906; 3rd edn, 1908); and summarized in his *The Science of Language and the Study of the New Testament* (Inaugural Lecture; Manchester: Manchester University Press, 1906) and 'New Testament Greek in the Light of Modern Discovery', in H.B. Swete (ed.), *Essays on Some Biblical Questions of the Day: By Members of the University of Cambridge* (London: Macmillan, 1909), pp. 461-505 (repr. in Porter [ed.], *Language of the New Testament*, pp. 60-97); among other works. Moulton and G. Milligan also produced *The Vocabulary of the Greek Testament Illustrated from the Papyri and Other Non-Literary Sources* (London: Hodder & Stoughton, 1914–29) (which included much information previously published in *Expositor*). Both Deissmann (*Bible Studies*, pp. 63-85; *Light from the Ancient East*, pp. 1-145; *Philology*, pp. 39-65) and Moulton (*Prolegomena*, pp. 4-8; 'New Testament Greek'; *Science*) recognized the multilingual context in which the New Testament was written. Thumb did important work on the Greek dialects, and the history of Greek, including the Koine, in such works

of Greek-speaking Christians in the greater Mediterranean world has persisted in New Testament scholarship. This is despite a significant body of scholarship throughout the century that has resisted such a simplistic bifurcation.[8]

as *Handbuch der griechischen Dialekte* (Indogermanische Bibliothek; Heidelberg: Winter, 1909); *Die griechische Sprache im Zeitalter des Hellenismus: Beiträge zur Geschichte und Beurteilung der KOINH* (Strassburg: Trübner, 1901). These and other works by these three scholars and others are discussed in S.E. Porter, 'Introduction: The Greek of the New Testament as a Disputed Area of Research', in *idem* (ed.), *Language of the New Testament*, pp. 11-38, esp. pp. 12-17; repr. with corrections and additions in *idem*, *Studies in the Greek New Testament: Theory and Practice* (SBG, 6; New York: Peter Lang, 1996), pp. 75-99, esp. pp. 76-80. See also F.-M. Abel, *Grammaire du grec biblique: Suivie d'un choix de papyrus* (EB; Paris: J. Gabalda, 1927).

7. One must not think, however, that it was only with discovery of the papyri that the view that the Greek of the New Testament reflected the Greek of the Graeco-Roman world was first proposed. The papyrologists had been anticipated by almost 50 years by E. Masson in the preface to his translation of Winer's grammar ('Translator's Prolegomena', to G.B. Winer, *A Grammar of the New Testament Diction* [trans. E. Masson; Edinburgh: T. & T. Clark, 1859; 6th edn, 1866], pp. i-x, esp. pp. iii-viii; noted in J.R. Harris, 'The So-Called Biblical Greek', *ExpTim* 25 [1913], pp. 54-55), and by J.B. Lightfoot in lectures delivered in 1863 (recounted in Moulton, *Prolegomena*, p. 242).

8. A number of scholars early in the century supported Deissmann and Moulton's perspective, a viewpoint recently revived with some vigour. Early advocates include: H.St.J. Thackeray, *A Grammar of the Old Testament in Greek According to the Septuagint* (Cambridge: Cambridge University Press, 1909); L. Radermacher, *Neutestamentliche Grammatik: Das Griechisch des Neuen Testaments im Zusammenhang mit der Volkssprache* (HNT, 1; Tübingen: Mohr Siebeck, 1911; 2nd edn, 1925); A.T. Robertson, *A Grammar of the Greek New Testament in the Light of Historical Research* (New York: Hodder & Stoughton, 1914; Nashville: Broadman, 4th edn, 1934); G. Milligan, *The New Testament Documents: Their Origin and Early History* (London: Macmillan, 1913), pp. 35-80; *idem*, 'The Grammar of the Greek New Testament', *ExpTim* 31 (1919–20), pp. 420-24; *idem*, *Here and There among the Papyri* (London: Hodder & Stoughton, 1922); H.G. Meecham, *Light from Ancient Letters: Private Correspondence in the Non-Literary Papyri of Oxyrhynchus of the First Four Centuries, and its Bearing on New Testament Language and Thought* (London: Allen & Unwin, 1923); E.J. Goodspeed, 'The Original Language of the New Testament', in *idem*, *New Chapters in New Testament Study* (New York: Macmillan, 1937), pp. 127-68; E.C. Colwell, *The Greek of the Fourth Gospel: A Study of its Aramaisms in the Light of Hellenistic Greek* (Chicago: University of Chicago Press, 1931); *idem*, 'The Greek Language', in G. Buttrick (ed.), *The Interpreter's Dictionary of the Bible*, II (Nashville: Abingdon Press, 1962), pp. 479-87.

The linguistic picture of the early Church, however, is certainly far more complex than has often been appreciated in recent research and writing. In Roman Palestine of the first century CE, Jesus, as well as many of his closest followers, who also came from Galilee, was probably multilingual. He spoke Aramaic to be sure, and Greek to be almost as sure, and possibly even Hebrew.[9] (There is no significant evidence of

More recent advocates include: H. Koester, *Introduction to the New Testament.* I. *History, Culture, and Religion of the Hellenistic Age* (Philadelphia: Fortress Press, 1982), pp. 103-113; M. Silva, 'Bilingualism and the Character of Palestinian Greek', *Bib* 61 (1980), pp. 198-219 (repr. in Porter [ed.], *Language of the New Testament*, pp. 205-226); S.E. Porter, *Verbal Aspect in the Greek of the New Testament, with Reference to Tense and Mood* (SBG, 1; New York: Peter Lang, 1989), pp. 111-61. This does not include such extra-biblical Greek scholars as P.W. Costas, *An Outline of the History of the Greek Language, with Particular Emphasis on the Koine and the Subsequent Periods* (Chicago: Ukrainian Society of Sciences of America, 1936; repr. Chicago: Ares, 1979), esp. pp. 27-71; R. Browning, *Medieval and Modern Greek* (Cambridge: Cambridge University Press, 2nd edn, 1983), pp. 19-52; L. Rydbeck, *Fachprosa, vermeintliche Volkssprache und Neues Testament: Zur Beurteilung der sprachlichen Niveauunterschiede im nachklassischen Griechisch* (Uppsala: University of Uppsala; Stockholm: Almqvist & Wiksell, 1967), esp. pp. 187-99 (ET in Porter [ed.], *Language of the New Testament*, pp. 191-204); G.H.R. Horsley, 'Divergent Views on the Nature of the Greek of the Bible', *Bib* 65 (1984), pp. 393-403; *idem*, *New Documents Illustrating Early Christianity*. V. *Linguistic Essays* (New South Wales, Australia: Macquarie University, 1989), esp. pp. 23-26; and G. Horrocks, *Greek: A History of the Language and its Speakers* (LLL; London: Longman, 1997), esp. pp. 92-95.

9. Major advocates of the use of Hebrew in first-century Palestine, a subject of considerable debate that lies outside the scope of this volume, include M.H. Segal, 'Mishnaic Hebrew and its Relation to Biblical Hebrew and to Aramaic', *JQR* 20 (1908), pp. 670-700, 734-37; *idem*, *A Grammar of Mishnaic Hebrew* (Oxford: Clarendon Press, 1927), pp. 5-19; W. Chomsky, 'What Was the Jewish Vernacular during the Second Commonwealth?', *JQR* 42 (1951–52), pp. 193-212; H. Birkeland, *The Language of Jesus* (Avhandlinger utgitt av Det Norske Videnskaps-Akademi I. II. Historish-Filosofisk Klasse I; Oslo: Dybwad, 1954), esp. pp. 1-40; E.Y. Kutscher, 'Hebrew Language: Mishnaic', *EncJud*, XVI, cols. 1592-93; *idem*, *A History of the Hebrew Language* (ed. R. Kutscher; Leiden: E.J. Brill, 1982), pp. 15-20; G.A. Rendsburg, 'The Galilean Background of Mishnaic Hebrew', in L.I. Levine (ed.), *The Galilee in Late Antiquity* (New York: Jewish Theological Seminary of America; Cambridge, MA: Harvard University Press, 1992), pp. 225-40; and M. Hadas-Lebel, *Histoire de la langue hébraïque: Des origines à l'époque de la Mishna* (Paris: Peeters, 1995). Advocates among biblical scholars of at least the possibility of Jesus' use of Hebrew include: T.W. Manson, *The Teaching of Jesus: Studies of its Form and Content* (Cambridge: Cambridge University Press, 1931;

Jesus' ability to speak Latin, the 'official' language of the empire.)[10] In discussing multilingualism, it is often useful to differentiate levels of linguistic competence. This factor is closely linked to the issue of literacy. According to recent estimates, probably only 20 to 30 per cent of the males in a given Hellenistic city, at the most, would have been able to read *and* write (perhaps a higher percentage could read some). There was probably a much lower percentage among those in the rural areas. Literacy in the ancient world was directly related to levels of education, access to which was primarily focused on the city, and tended to favour males, especially those with economic resources.[11] Multilingualism is

2nd edn, 1935), pp. 45-50; J.M. Grintz, 'Hebrew as the Spoken and Written Language in the Last Days of the Second Temple', *JBL* 79 (1960), pp. 32-47; J.A. Emerton, 'Did Jesus Speak Hebrew?', *JTS* NS 12 (1961), pp. 189-202; *idem*, 'The Problem of Vernacular Hebrew in the First Century AD and the Language of Jesus', *JTS* NS 24 (1973), pp. 1-23; R.H. Gundry, 'The Language Milieu of First-Century Palestine: Its Bearing on the Authenticity of the Gospel Tradition', *JBL* 83 (1964), pp. 404-408; J. Barr, 'Which Language Did Jesus Speak?—Some Remarks of a Semitist', *BJRL* 53 (1970), pp. 9-29; *idem*, 'Hebrew, Aramaic and Greek in the Hellenistic Age', in W.D. Davies and L. Finkelstein (eds.), *The Cambridge History of Judaism*. II. *The Hellenistic Age* (Cambridge: Cambridge University Press, 1989), pp. 79-114, esp. p. 113; C. Rabin, 'Hebrew and Aramaic in the First Century', in S. Safrai and M. Stern (eds.), *The Jewish People in the First Century* (CRINT, 1.2; Assen: Van Gorcum; Philadelphia: Fortress Press, 1976), pp. 1007-1039; M.O. Wise, 'Languages of Palestine', in J.B. Green, S. McKnight and I.H. Marshall (eds.), *Dictionary of Jesus and the Gospels* (Downers Grove, IL: InterVarsity Press, 1992), pp. 434-44, esp. pp. 435-37, 441.

10. On the use of Latin, see J.A. Fitzmyer, 'The Languages of Palestine in the First Century AD', *CBQ* 32 (1970), pp. 501-31; repr. with corrections and additions in Porter (ed.), *Language of the New Testament*, pp. 126-62, esp. pp. 129-33; and A. Millard, 'Latin in First-Century Palestine', in Z. Zevit, S. Gitin and M. Sokoloff (eds.), *Solving Riddles and Untying Knots: Biblical, Epigraphic, and Semitic Studies in Honor of Jonas C. Greenfield* (Winona Lake, IN: Eisenbrauns, 1995), pp. 451-58.

11. W.V. Harris, *Ancient Literacy* (Cambridge, MA: Harvard University Press, 1989), esp. pp. 116-46 on the Hellenistic era (see p. 141 for the statistics cited above). Harris uses a range of evidence, including papyri, noting that inscriptions, the traditional source, cannot always be relied upon because of the role that social status and related factors played in their construction and the ability to read them (pp. 221-22). Not all would agree with Harris's statistics, but virtually all are agreed that the ancient world was predominantly, though certainly far from exclusively, an oral culture. See P.J. Achtemeier, '*Omne verbum sonat*: The New Testament and the Oral Environment of Late Western Antiquity', *JBL* 109 (1990), pp. 3-27; F.D.

also a complex subject, for which there are many fuzzy boundaries to the categories.[12] One way of characterizing multilingualism is in terms of diachronic categories, such as first language versus second or acquired languages. There are often difficulties surrounding the age of acquisition and possible attrition of the first language.[13] Another way is to describe one's multilingual ability in synchronic terms. Here one distinguishes between active or productive and passive or receptive multilingualism, while realizing that the scale is a cline or continuum, rather than a disjunction. Active multilingualism involves the ability to understand and to express oneself in a language, whereas passive multilingualism involves being able to understand but not to express oneself in a language.[14] There are also numerous sociolinguistic issues connected with when and how one switches from one language to another (code

Gilliard, 'More Silent Reading in Antiquity: *Non Omne Verbum Sonabat*', *JBL* 112 (1993), pp. 689-94; and C.W. Davis, *Oral Biblical Criticism: The Influence of the Principles of Orality on the Literary Structure of Paul's Epistle to the Philippians* (JSNTSup, 172; Sheffield: Sheffield Academic Press, 1999), pp. 11-28. A critique of some recent theories of orality is offered by L.W. Hurtado, 'Greco-Roman Textuality and the Gospel of Mark: A Critical Assessment of Werner Kelber's *The Oral and the Written Gospel*', *BBR* 7 (1997), pp. 91-106.

12. For a brief summary, see B. Spolsky, 'Bilingualism', in F.J. Newmeyer (ed.), *Linguistics: The Cambridge Survey*. IV. *Language: The Socio-Cultural Context* (Cambridge: Cambridge University Press, 1988), pp. 100-18; and representative statements by J.A. Fishman, G. Sankoff, R.F. Salisbury, N. Denison and A.P. Sorensen, Jr, in J.B. Pride and J. Holmes (eds.), *Sociolinguistics* (Harmondsworth: Penguin Books, 1972), pp. 13-93.

13. On these issues, see P. Fletcher and M. Garman (eds.), *Language Acquisition: Studies in First Language Development* (Cambridge: Cambridge University Press, 2nd edn, 1986); W. Klein, *Second Language Acquisition* (CTL; Cambridge: Cambridge University Press, 1986); L. Loveday, *The Sociolinguistics of Learning and Using a Non-Native Language* (Oxford: Pergamon Press, 1982); H.W. Seliger and R.M. Vago (eds.), *First Language Attrition* (Cambridge: Cambridge University Press, 1991); K. Hyltenstam and L.K. Obler (eds.), *Bilingualism across the Lifespan: Aspects of Acquisition, Maturity, and Loss* (Cambridge: Cambridge University Press, 1989).

14. See H. Baetens Beardsmore, *Bilingualism: Basic Principles* (Multilingual Matters, 1; Clevedon: Multilingual Matters, 1982; 2nd edn, 1986), esp. pp. 1-42, for useful definitions of a range of categories in bilingualism; cf. also F. Grosjean, *Life with Two Languages: An Introduction to Bilingualism* (Cambridge, MA: Harvard University Press, 1982); J.F. Hamers and M.H.A. Blanc, *Bilingualité et bilinguisme* (Brussels: Pierre Mardaga, 1983; ET *Bilinguality and Bilingualism* [Cambridge: Cambridge University Press, 1989]).

switching),[15] and how languages are important for group formation, identity, and acceptance.[16]

According to the description above, Jesus would probably be best described as productively multilingual in Greek and Aramaic, and possibly Hebrew, though only Aramaic would have been his first language, and Greek and Hebrew being second or acquired languages.[17] If Hebrew were mostly confined to use in liturgical contexts (although it may have extended beyond this use in certain circles), it may have been that Jesus was only passively multilingual in Hebrew. He may also have been passively multilingual in Latin, although if he had any knowledge of Latin at all it is likely that it was confined to recognition of a few common words. This depiction reflects the linguistic realities of the Mediterranean world of Roman times, including that of the eastern Mediterranean, and is supported by widespread and significant literary, epigraphic

15. Code switching, a very important topic in sociolinguistics, especially when multilingualism is involved, is discussed in W. Downes, *Language and Society* (London: Fontana, 1984), pp. 65-71; R. Wardhaugh, *An Introduction to Sociolinguistics* (Oxford: Basil Blackwell, 1986; 2nd edn, 1992), pp. 103-16; J. Holmes, *An Introduction to Sociolinguistics* (London: Longman, 1992), pp. 41-53, with useful examples; S. Romaine, *Language in Society: An Introduction to Sociolinguistics* (Oxford: Oxford University Press, 1994), pp. 55-64. In biblical studies, it is discussed in J.M. Watt, *Code-Switching in Luke and Acts* (Berkeley Insights in Linguistics and Semiotics, 31; New York: Peter Lang, 1997); cf. S.E. Porter (ed.), *Diglossia and Other Topics in New Testament Greek* (JSNTSup, 193; SNTG, 6; Sheffield: Sheffield Academic Press, forthcoming 2000), Part 1.

16. See D. Sharp, *Language in Bilingual Communities* (EILS; London: Edward Arnold, 1973).

17. Studies on bilingualism with regard to Greek and the New Testament include Silva, 'Bilingualism and the Character of Palestinian Greek', pp. 23-26; Porter, *Verbal Aspect*, pp. 154-56, with extensive references to secondary literature. We have no way of knowing whether Jesus could read or write Greek or Aramaic. Meier (*Marginal Jew*, I, pp. 268-78) thinks that Jesus was literate in Semitic languages. Jesus' multilingualism was very different from that of Paul, who clearly was a first-language speaker of Greek and literate in it. His point in Phil. 3.5 seems to be that he *also* spoke a Semitic language—probably Aramaic as a first language, as well as Hebrew acquired in Pharisaical training. On this passage, see M. Hengel, 'Der vorchristliche Paulus', in M. Hengel and U. Heckel (eds.), *Paulus und das antike Judentum* (WUNT, 58; Tübingen: Mohr Siebeck, 1991), pp. 177-291; ET *The Pre-Christian Paul* (with R. Deines; trans. J. Bowden; London: SCM Press; Philadelphia: Trinity Press International, 1991), esp. pp. 34-37. On Paul's linguistic ability, see U. Wilamowitz-Moellendorff, *Die griechische Literatur des Altertums* (Stuttgart: Teubner, 3rd edn, 1912; repr. 1995), pp. 232-33.

and other evidence. As a result of the conquests of Alexander III ('the Great'), and the rule of the Hellenistic kings (the Diadochi and their successors), the Graeco-Roman world was one in which Greek became the language of trade, commerce and communication among the now joined (if not always united) people groups.[18] In other words, Greek was the *lingua franca*[19] for the eastern Mediterranean, displacing Aramaic.[20]

18. Important and linguistically informed histories of Greek, including its development into the Graeco-Roman period, are to be found in Thumb, *Die griechische Sprache*, esp. pp. 161-201; A. Meillet, *Aperçu d'une histoire de la langue grecque* (Paris: Hachette, 3rd edn, 1930), esp. pp. 245-54; Costas, *Outline of the History of the Greek Language*, esp. pp. 27-71; E. Schwyzer, *Griechische Grammatik* (2 vols.; Munich: Beck, 1939, 1950), I, pp. 16-31; A. Debrunner, *Geschichte der griechischen Sprache*. II. *Grundfragen und Grundzüge des nachklassischen Griechisch* (ed. A. Scherer; Sammlung Göschen, 114/114a; Berlin: W. de Gruyter, 2nd edn, 1969); Browning, *Medieval and Modern Greek*, pp. 19-52; *idem*, 'Von der Koine bis zu den Anfängen des modernen Griechisch', in H.-G. Nesselrath (ed.), *Einleitung in die griechische Philologie* (Stuttgart: Teubner, 1997), pp. 156-68; J. Humbert, *Histoire de la langue grecque* (Que sais-je?, 1483; Paris: Presses Universitaires de France, 1972); G. Thomson, *The Greek Language* (Cambridge: Heffer, 1972), pp. 31-37; L.R. Palmer, *The Greek Language* (London: Faber & Faber, 1980), pp. 3-198; A. López Eire, 'Del ático a la *koiné*', *Emerita* 49 (1981), pp. 377-92; Horrocks, *Greek*, esp. pp. 3-127, the last undoubtedly now being the best work on the subject. Several useful collections of essays on the subject are C. Brixhe (ed.), *La koiné grecque antique* (3 vols.; TMEA, 10, 14, 17; Nancy: Presses Universitaires de Nancy, 1993–98). Specific treatments of the dialects and phonology are not mentioned here, but the subject merits examination. For a summary of the issues applied to New Testament studies, see S.E. Porter, 'The Greek Language of the New Testament', in *idem* (ed.), *Handbook to Exegesis of the New Testament* (NTTS, 25; Leiden: E.J. Brill, 1997), pp. 99-130, esp. pp. 99-104; and L. Rydbeck, 'The Language of the New Testament', *TynBul* 49.2 (1998), pp. 361-68.

19. A *lingua franca* is a common variety of language used for commercial and other functional purposes, where a language is needed to facilitate communication between people who often do not share the same first language, and hence where some will be non-native speakers of it. See R.A. Hudson, *Sociolinguistics* (CTL; Cambridge: Cambridge University Press, 2nd edn, 1996), p. 7; Holmes, *Introduction to Sociolinguistics*, pp. 85-89.

20. Of course, even with the sudden onslaught of Alexander, the linguistic shift from Aramaic to Greek did not occur overnight. The transition was a gradual one throughout the Hellenistic period, in many ways working from the top socio-economic levels down. But, as the evidence indicates, the transformation eventually was effected, so that Greek became the *lingua franca*. On the movement of Hellenism in the east, see the collection of essays in A. Kuhrt and S. Sherwin-White (eds.), *Hellenism in the East* (London: Gerald Duckworth, 1987).

As Barr points out, Greek came to encompass 'a wider world, in fact, than that which Aramaic had made accessible under the Persians'.[21] The Hellenistic conquerors brought with them and imposed not only their language, but also their culture and various social and political institutions, which served as a major unifying factor for this Hellenistic world.[22] Later, the Romans preserved and extended much of this culture. The imposed their administrative structure upon a territory in which Greek still remained and was extended as the *lingua franca* with even more and more people speaking it as a first language,[23] but also within which there were various local languages that were to varying degrees still used.[24] Palestine appears to be one of these types of linguistic regions.[25] Besides the use of Greek as the *lingua franca*, there was con-

21. Barr, 'Hebrew, Aramaic and Greek', p. 101.

22. On Alexander and his legacy, see C.B. Welles, *Alexander and the Hellenistic World* (Toronto: Hakkert, 1970); M. Cary, *The Legacy of Alexander: A History of the Greek World from 323 to 146 B.C.* (New York: Dial, 1932); W. Tarn and G.T. Griffith, *Hellenistic Civilisation* (London: Edward Arnold, 1927; 3rd edn, 1952).

23. On the coming of the Romans, especially in the east, see M. Cary, *A History of Rome down to the Reign of Constantine* (London: Macmillan, 1935; 2nd edn, 1954); A.H.M. Jones, *Cities of the Eastern Roman Provinces* (Oxford: Clarendon Press, 1937); *idem, The Greek City from Alexander to Justinian* (Oxford: Clarendon Press, 1940); M. Rostovtzeff, *Social and Economic History of the Roman Empire* (2 vols.; Oxford: Clarendon Press, 1926; 2nd edn rev. P.M. Fraser, 1957); E.J. Owens, *The City in the Greek and Roman World* (London: Routledge, 1991).

24. There have been a number of interesting studies of the relation of Greek to particular regions and indigenous languages (on Semitisms in Greek, see below). As a sample, besides sections in volumes mentioned above, see Thumb, *Die griechische Sprache*, pp. 167-69; C. Brixhe, *Essai sur le Grec Anatolien: Au début de notre ère* (TMEA, 1; Nancy: Presses Universitaires de Nancy, 1984); E. Gibson, *The 'Christians for Christians' Inscriptions of Phrygia* (HTS, 32; Atlanta: Scholars Press, 1978); cf. R. MacMullen, 'Provincial Languages in the Roman Empire', *AJP* 87 (1966); repr. in *idem, Changes in the Roman Empire: Essays in the Ordinary* (New Haven: Yale University Press, 1990), pp. 32-40, 282-86. On such issues, see C.J. Hemer, 'Reflections on the Nature of New Testament Greek Vocabulary', *TynBul* 38 (1987), pp. 65-92, esp. pp. 68-75.

25. The largest body of such Greek linguistic information comes from the papyri of Egypt. It has been argued by some that the Greek of the Egyptian papyri was influenced by various other languages, including Semitic languages, and therefore is not an accurate representation of Hellenistic Greek. This has been argued by, e.g., L.-Th. Lefort, 'Pour une grammaire des LXX', *Muséon* 41 (1928), pp. 152-60; J. Vergote, 'Grec biblique', in *DBSup*, III, cols. 1353-60; and especially F. Gignac,

tinued use of Aramaic, the language of the Jews since their exile in the sixth century BCE (Aramaic was the *lingua franca* of the Babylonian and later Persian worlds of their times),[26] and possibly even of Hebrew in some circles for religious or liturgical purposes.[27] This type of

'The Language of the Non-Literary Papyri', in D.H. Samuel (ed.), *Proceedings of the Twelfth International Congress of Papyrology* (Toronto: Hakkert, 1970), pp. 139-52; *idem, A Grammar of the Greek Papyri of the Roman and Byzantine Periods* (2 vols.; Milan: Cisalpino, 1976, 1981), I, pp. 46-48; *idem*, 'The Papyri and the Greek Language', *Yale Classical Studies* 28 (1985), pp. 155-65, esp. pp. 157-58. This theory has been ably refuted by S.-T. Teodorsson, who claims that no other kind of Greek has ever been found in Egypt, indicating that there was no previous 'pure' Greek, no evidence of the kind of creolization process argued for above, and no evidence of this Greek being considered as in any way departing from the acceptable norms of Hellenistic Greek. See his *The Phonology of Ptolemaic Koine* (Gothenburg: Acta Universitatis Gothoburgensis, 1977), pp. 25-35; cf. *idem*, 'Phonological Variation in Classical Attic and the Development of Koine', *Glotta* 57 (1979), pp. 61-75; S.G. Kapsomenos, 'Das Griechische in Ägypten', *Museum Helveticum* 10 (1953), pp. 248-63; P. Muysken, 'Are Creoles a Special Type of Language?', in F.J. Newmeyer (ed.), *Linguistics: The Cambridge Survey. II. Linguistic Theory: Extensions and Implications* (Cambridge: Cambridge University Press, 1988), pp. 285-301. This analysis of the linguistic situation of Egypt can perhaps be confirmed also through the exchange of papyri between Egypt and Palestine attested in the Zenon archive (V. Tcherikover, 'Palestine under the Ptolemies [A Contribution to the Study of the Zenon Papyri]', *Mizraim* 4–5 [1937], pp. 9-90; C. Orrieux, *Les papyrus de Zenon: L'horizon d'un grec en Egypte au IIIe siècle avant J.C.* [Paris: Macula, 1983]), and the Greek papyri that have now been found outside of Egypt (see H.M. Cotton, W.E.H. Cockle and F.G.B. Millar, 'The Papyrology of the Roman Near East: A Survey', *JRS* 85 [1995], pp. 214-35), all with recognizably similar grammatical structure (on the grammar of the papyri of Palestine and environs, see N. Lewis, *The Documents from the Bar Kokhba Period in the Cave of Letters: Greek Papyri* [Jerusalem: Israel Exploration Society, Hebrew University of Jerusalem, Shrine of the Book, 1989], pp. 13-19; although Lewis's work on Semitisms needs to be re-assessed, as noted in S.E. Porter, 'The Greek Papyri of the Judaean Desert and the World of the Roman East', in S.E. Porter and C.A. Evans [eds.], *The Scrolls and the Scriptures: Qumran Fifty Years After* [JSPSup, 26; RILP, 3; Sheffield: Sheffield Academic Press, 1997], pp. 293-311, esp. p. 304 n. 53).

26. See Wise, 'Languages of Palestine', p. 437.

27. For brief introductions to the history of the Jews, see A.R.C. Leaney, *The Jewish and Christian World 200 B.C. to A.D. 200* (Cambridge: Cambridge University Press, 1984); P. Schäfer, *The History of the Jews in Antiquity: The Jews of Palestine from Alexander the Great to the Arab Conquest* (Luxembourg: Harwood, 1995); J.H. Hayes and S.R. Mandell, *The Jewish People in Classical Antiquity from Alexander to Bar Kochba* (Louisville: Westminster/John Knox Press, 1998).

linguistic scenario is accurate for Jews as well as for other people groups distributed throughout the Graeco-Roman world (at least three out of four Jews lived outside of Palestine).[28]

28. See W.A. Meeks, *The First Urban Christians* (New Haven: Yale University Press, 1983), p. 34. It is worth noting that, on the basis of Jewish settlement patterns, the vast majority of Jews of the ancient Graeco-Roman world were Greek-speaking as their first language, regardless of whether they also acquired the ability to speak Aramaic or Hebrew. See V. Tcherikover, *Hellenistic Civilization and the Jews* (trans. S. Applebaum; 1959; repr. New York: Atheneum, 1975), p. 347: 'the Jews outside Palestine spoke, wrote, and generally thought in Greek', citing a variety of evidence in support, including Philo, *Conf. Ling.* 129, who refers to Greek as 'our language' (pp. 524-25); J.N. Sevenster, *Do You Know Greek? How Much Greek Could the First Jewish Christians Have Known?* (NovTSup, 19; Leiden: E.J. Brill, 1968), pp. 77-96; E.C. Polomé, 'The Linguistic Situation in the Western Provinces of the Roman Empire', *ANRW* 2.29.2, pp. 509-53, esp. p. 515; and P. Wexler, 'Recovering the Dialects and Sociology of Judeo-Greek in Non-Hellenic Europe', in J.A. Fishman (ed.), *Readings in the Sociology of Jewish Languages* (Contributions to the Sociology of Jewish Languages, 1; Leiden: E.J. Brill, 1985), pp. 227-40, esp. p. 227, where he notes that 'The Jews became the carriers of Greek language and culture in diverse parts of the world'; contra Watt, *Code-Switching in Luke and Acts*, p. 5; cf. B. Bar-Kochva, *Pseudo-Hecataeus, 'On the Jews': Legitimizing the Jewish Diaspora* (Berkeley: University of California Press, 1996). The development of the Septuagint is one of the key pieces of evidence in this regard, parts of which have now, of course, been found in Palestine as well. Besides the Minor Prophets scroll (E. Tov [ed.], *The Greek Minor Prophets Scroll* [DJD, 8; Oxford: Clarendon Press, 1990]), note also 4QLXXLev^a, 4QLXXLev^b, 4QLXXNum, 4QLXXDeut, 7QLXXExod and 7QEpistJer, besides a number of other Greek documents in Cave 7, the identification of which remains highly problematic. See S.E. Porter, 'Why so Many Holes in the Papyrological Evidence for the Greek New Testament?', in K. van Kampen and S. McKendrick (eds.), *The Bible as Book: The Transmission of the Greek Text* (London: British Library Publications; Grand Haven, MI: Scriptorium, forthcoming 2000). On modern theories of the origin of the Septuagint, see S. Jellicoe, *The Septuagint and Modern Study* (Oxford: Clarendon Press, 1968), pp. 59-73, who notes the consensus view that the Greek translation of the Law was made to 'meet the needs of the Egyptian Jewish communities who could no longer understand Hebrew' (p. 59); M. Müller, *The First Bible of the Church: A Plea for the Septuagint* (JSOTSup, 206; Copenhagen International Seminar, 1; Sheffield: Sheffield Academic Press, 1996), pp. 36-41. However, the translators may not have always understood what they were translating, indicating some of the linguistic barriers of the time: see E. Tov, 'Did the Septuagint Translators Always Understand their Hebrew Text?', in A. Pietersma and C. Cox (eds.), *De Septuaginta: Studies in Honour of John William Wevers on his Sixty-Fifth Birthday* (Ontario: Benben, 1984), pp. 53-70; cf. J. Barr, *The Typology of Literalism in*

This is not the place to cite in detail the extensive evidence now available to illustrate the use of Aramaic in Palestine, or, and more importantly here, the use of Greek in Palestine, and by Jews. Nor is it the place to raise the related question of Semitisms and Semitic influence on the Greek of the New Testament.[29] It is perhaps sufficient here merely to mention the kinds of evidence available to establish the use of these languages. The use of Aramaic rests upon the fact that the language of the Jews upon their return by the Persians from exile is found not only in the Aramaic portions of the biblical writings of Daniel and Ezra, but also in the Aramaic words in the New Testament[30] and in a variety of extra-biblical texts written in Aramaic, such as *1 Enoch*. Aramaic is also found in a large amount of inscriptional, ossuary, epistolary, papyrological and literary evidence, especially that from Qumran and other Judaean Desert sites such as Murabba'at, Masada and Nahal Hever, and evidenced in the targums and later rabbinic literature. Much of this

---

Ancient Biblical Translations (Nachrichten der Akademie der Wissenschaften in Göttingen I. Philologisch-Historische Klasse. Mitteilungen des Septuaginta-Unternehmens, 15; Göttingen: Vandenhoeck & Ruprecht, 1979). The ancient tradition (*Ep. Arist.* 32, 39, 46, 47–50) has 72 Palestinian Jewish elders performing the translation. This may simply be ancient Jewish apologetic for the translation, but it also probably reflects linguistic realities regarding linguistic competence. On the *Letter of Aristeas*, see Jellicoe, *Septuagint and Modern Study*, pp. 39-58.

29. The question of Semitisms in the Greek of the New Testament has been debated for years, often unproductively because of a failure to distinguish linguistic issues clearly (see Chapter 2, above). See Silva, 'Bilingualism and the Character of Palestinian Greek', pp. 205-27; Porter, *Verbal Aspect*, pp. 111-61, where a distinction is made between levels of Semitic influence: (1) direct translation, (2) intervention, when a form that cannot reasonably be formed or paralleled in Greek is attributable to the influence of a Semitic construction, and (3) enhancement, when a rarely used construction paralleled in Greek has its frequency of occurrence greatly increased due to association with a Semitic language (p. 118). Only the second, intervention, should be counted as a Semitism in the New Testament. On language contact, see the classic study by U. Weinreich, *Languages in Contact: Findings and Problems* (Publications of the Linguistic Circle of New York, 1; New York: Linguistic Circle of New York, 1953).

30. For example, the use of such words as *amen, rabbi, abba*, and other words in such places as Mk 5.41; 7.34; 15.34 = Mt. 27.46. J. Jeremias (*Neutestamentliche Theologie*. I. *Die Verkündigung Jesu* [Gütersloh: Gerd Mohn, 1971; ET *New Testament Theology*. I. *The Proclamation of Jesus* (NTL; trans. J. Bowden; London: SCM Press; New York: Charles Scribner's Sons, 1971)], pp. 4-6) counts a total of 26 Aramaic words in all used in the Gospels.

evidence has only come to light in the last 60 or so years.[31] Often overlooked, however, is the fact that there is a similar kind and probably an even larger quantity of evidence for the use of Greek in Roman Palestine, including Galilee. The arguments for the use of Greek in Palestine are based upon the role of Greek as the *lingua franca* of the Roman empire, the specific Hellenized linguistic and cultural character of lower Galilee surrounded by the cities of the Decapolis, and the linguistic fact that the New Testament has been transmitted in Greek from its earliest documents. There is also a range of inscriptional evidence (e.g. Jewish funerary inscriptions), numerous Greek papyri, and significant literary evidence, including Jewish books being written in or translated into Greek in Palestine.[32] From this range of evidence

31. Surveys and selections of this evidence may be found in J.A. Fitzmyer and D.J. Harrington, *A Manual of Palestinian Aramaic Texts* (Biblica et Orientalia, 34; Rome: Biblical Institute Press, 1978); K. Beyer, *Die aramäische Texte vom Toten Meer* (Göttingen: Vandenhoeck & Ruprecht, 1984); Fitzmyer, 'Languages of Palestine', pp. 147-58; *idem*, 'The Contribution of Qumran Aramaic to the Study of the New Testament', *NTS* 20 (1973–74), pp. 383-407; repr. in *idem, A Wandering Aramean: Collected Aramaic Essays* (Missoula, MT: Scholars Press, 1979), pp. 85-113 (repr. in *The Semitic Background of the New Testament* [Biblical Resource Series; Grand Rapids: Eerdmans; Livonia, MI: Dove Booksellers, 1997], with corrections); E. Schürer, *The History of the Jewish People in the Age of Jesus Christ* (3 vols.; rev. G. Vermes, F. Millar and M. Black; Edinburgh: T. & T. Clark, 1973–87), II, pp. 20-26; and E.M. Meyers and J.F. Strange, *Archaeology, the Rabbis and Early Christianity* (London: SCM Press, 1981), pp. 73-78.

32. Surveys and selections of this evidence may be found in P. Benoit, J.T. Milik and R. de Vaux (eds.), *Les grottes de Murabba'at* (DJD, 2; Oxford: Clarendon Press, 1961), nos. 89-155 (pp. 212-67), 164 (pp. 275-77); Sevenster, *Do You Know Greek?*; M. Hengel, *Judentum und Hellenismus: Studien zu ihrer Begegnung unter besonderer Berücksichtigung Palästinas bis zur Mitte des 2.Jh.s v. Chr.* (WUNT, 10; Tübingen: Mohr Siebeck, 1969; 2nd edn, 1973; ET *Judaism and Hellenism: Studies in their Encounter in Palestine during the Early Hellenistic Period* [2 vols.; trans. J. Bowden; London: SCM Press; Philadelphia: Fortress Press, 1974]), I, pp. 58-106; *idem* with C. Markschies, 'Zum Problem der "Hellenisierung" Judäas im 1. Jahrhundert nach Christus'; ET *The 'Hellenization' of Judaea in the First Century after Christ* (trans. J. Bowden; London: SCM Press; Philadelphia: Trinity Press International, 1989), esp. pp. 7-18; Fitzmyer, 'Languages of Palestine', pp. 134-47; B.Z. Wacholder, *Eupolemus: A Study of Judaeo-Greek Literature* (Cincinnati: Hebrew Union College, Jewish Institute of Religion, 1974), esp. pp. 259-306; Meyers and Strange, *Archaeology*, pp. 78-88; Lewis, *Documents from the Bar Kokhba Period*; Schürer, *History of the Jewish People*, II, pp. 29-80 (although he is sceptical regarding the use of Greek), III.1, pp. 517-21, 528-31; P.W. van der Horst,

the logical conclusion can be drawn that in fact a sizeable number of Jews in Palestine used Greek.[33]

3. *The Criterion of Greek Language and its Context*

With the discussion above and that to be found in the Excursus of this chapter as a foundation, I here attempt to define and exemplify a criterion of Greek language and its context to be used in historical-Jesus research. In dealing with questions of language, the approach of Chilton and Evans and the emphasis of Theissen upon probability provide, I think, serious improvements over other methods. Chilton and Evans

Ancient Jewish Epitaphs: An Introductory Survey of a Millennium of Jewish Funerary Epigraphy (300 BCE–700 CE) (Contributions to Biblical Exegesis and Theology, 2; Kampen: Kok Pharos, 1991); G.E. Sterling, 'Recluse or Representative? Philo and Greek-Speaking Judaism beyond Alexandria', in E.H. Lovering, Jr (ed.), *Society of Biblical Literature 1995 Seminar Papers* (SBLSP, 34; Atlanta: Scholars Press, 1995), pp. 595-616; H.M. Cotton and A. Yardeni (eds.), *Aramaic, Hebrew and Greek Documentary Texts from Nahal Hever and Other Sites* (DJD, 27; Oxford: Clarendon Press, 1997), pp. 133-279.

33. Further attestation includes Acts 6.1, which makes a linguistic distinction between Jews in Jerusalem who spoke Aramaic and those who spoke Greek. Apparently, before the third century CE, terms such as Ἑλληνισταί and Ἑβραῖοι were virtually exclusively linguistic terms referring to language competence. In the Acts context, distinguishing those outside Palestine as Greek speakers would not have been necessary, but assumed, but apparently there was a significant part of the Jewish population that spoke mostly Greek even of those resident in Jerusalem. This view was proposed by C.F.D. Moule ('Once More, Who were the Hellenists?', *ExpTim* 70 [1958–59], pp. 100-102), further endorsed by Fitzmyer ('Languages of Palestine', p. 144), Hengel (*Judaism and Hellenism*, I, pp. 2, 58; 'Zwischen Jesus und Paulus', *ZTK* 72 [1975], pp. 151-206; ET in *idem, Between Jesus and Paul: Studies in the Earliest History of Christianity* [trans. J. Bowden; Philadelphia: Fortress Press, 1983], pp. 1-29, esp. pp. 8-9 with notes; with Markschies, 'Hellenization' of Judaea, pp. 7-8 with notes; with Deines, *Pre-Christian Paul*, pp. 54-55) and C.C. Hill (*Hellenists and Hebrews: Reappraising Division within the Earliest Church* [Minneapolis: Fortress Press, 1992], pp. 22-24), and most recently supported by H.A. Brehm ('The Meaning of Ἑλληνιστής in Acts in Light of a Diachronic Analysis of ἑλληνίζειν', in S.E. Porter and D.A. Carson [eds.], *Discourse Analysis and Other Topics in Biblical Greek* [JSNTSup, 113; Sheffield: JSOT Press, 1995], pp. 180-99). See also M. Hengel, 'Jerusalem als jüdische *und* hellenistische Stadt', in B. Funck (ed.), *Hellenismus: Beiträge zur Erforschung von Akkulturation und politischer Ordnung in den Staaten des hellenistischen Zeitalters* (Tübingen: Mohr Siebeck, 1996), pp. 269-306.

helpfully differentiate dimensions of comparison,[34] and Theissen emphasizes how probability theory requires that a scenario found to be inadequate (such as the Aramaic hypothesis) must be replaced by a more plausible hypothesis.[35] In terms of developing a linguistic criterion regarding the Greek language, units for analysis—whether these involve activities of Jesus or words of Jesus, or both—are here examined in the light of the multilingual and hence multifarious cultural contexts of the Gospels (as defined above)[36] to see whether units of analysis display plausible correlation between the participants and their language or actions. It is considered established on the basis of the above discussion and the Excursus of this chapter that Jesus *could* have spoken Greek— the question is whether he *did* on a given occasion. The purpose of this Greek-language criterion is to determine if there are definable and characteristic features of various episodes that point to a Greek-language based unity between the participants, the events depicted, and concepts discussed. That is, on the basis of the events depicted and words record-

34. B. Chilton, *A Galilean Rabbi and his Bible: Jesus' Use of the Interpreted Scripture of his Time* (GNS, 8; Wilmington, DE: Michael Glazier, 1984), pp. 70-71, 90-137; C.A. Evans, *Word and Glory: On the Exegetical and Theological Background of John's Prologue* (JSNTSup, 89; Sheffield: JSOT Press, 1993), pp. 18-27; *idem*, ' "Do This and You Will Live": Targumic Coherence in Luke 10:25-28', in B. Chilton and C.A. Evans, *Jesus in Context: Temple, Purity, and Restoration* (AGJU, 39; Leiden: E.J. Brill, 1997), pp. 377-93; *idem*, 'From Gospel to Gospel: The Function of Isaiah in the New Testament', in C.C. Broyles and C.A. Evans (eds.), *Writing and Reading the Scroll of Isaiah: Studies of an Interpretive Tradition* (2 vols.; VTSup, 70.1–2; Formation and Interpretation of Old Testament Literature, 1; Leiden: E.J. Brill, 1997), II, pp. 651-91, esp. pp. 667-74; *idem*, 'Introduction', pp. xii-xiii, xv-xvii, in M. Black, *An Aramaic Approach to the Gospels and Acts* (Oxford: Clarendon Press, 1946; 2nd edn, 1954; 3rd edn, 1967; repr. with 'Introduction: An Aramaic Approach Thirty Years Later,' by C.A. Evans, pp. v-xxv; Peabody, MA: Hendrickson, 1998).

35. Theissen and Winter, *Die Kriterienfrage in der Jesusforschung*, pp. 206-209. For an attempt to distinguish levels of probability in historical-Jesus research, see E.P. Sanders and M. Davies, *Studying the Synoptic Gospels* (London: SCM Press; Philadelphia: Trinity Press International, 1989), esp. pp. 312, 313.

36. See H.D. Betz, 'Wellhausen's Dictum "Jesus was not a Christian, but a Jew" in Light of Present Scholarship', *ST* 45 (1991), pp. 83-110; repr. in *idem*, *Antike und Christentum: Gesammelte Aufsätze IV* (Tübingen: Mohr Siebeck, 1998), pp. 1-31, here p. 13. I avoid using the term *Sitz im Leben* in describing this criterion, since that term already has numerous misleading connotations from its use in form criticism.

ed by the participants, the question is asked whether the probability would be greater that Greek would have been the language of communication used between Jesus and his conversation partners, or not.[37] This Greek linguistic criterion seems to work best in terms of beginning with the actions and moving to the words of Jesus, and proceeds through the three phases noted above.

Three caveats must be registered, however, regarding this criterion, and the others discussed in subsequent chapters as well. The first is that these criteria are developed as independently of the traditional criteria for authenticity as is possible. This is not necessarily because of the problems with these criteria (as noted in Chapters 2 and 3), but so as to develop these new language-based criteria on their own terms. The traditional criteria will only be introduced as a means of reinforcing the findings of these Greek-language criteria, but the strength of the results is dependent upon these new criteria and their interrelationships in the first instance. The second caveat is that there is a conscious restraint from the consultation of a wide range of secondary literature on the passages discussed in this and the following chapters, especially literature that addresses issues of authenticity with regard to the Jesus tradition. The reason for this restraint is that I am attempting to develop these criteria with as little outside influence and interference from other criteria as possible, especially as such influences might be masked in discussion of other issues in the secondary literature. The third caveat is with regard to what is meant by authenticity. The use of this term could raise a number of excruciating problems of definition. It will suffice to say that I use the term as it has been used in previous historical-Jesus research, as noted in Chapters 1–3 above—that is, as indicating an earlier tradition that has definable hallmarks that indicate that it might well

---

37. This is not the place to debate some of the issues connected with theories of scientific discovery and model building. Some of those writers who have influenced my thinking in this area (without all agreeing at every point) are I. Lakatos, 'Falsification and the Methodology of Scientific Research Programmes', in I. Lakatos and A. Musgrave (eds.), *Criticism and the Growth of Knowledge: Proceedings of the International Colloquium in the Philosophy of Science, London, 1965, Volume 4* (Cambridge: Cambridge University Press, 1970), pp. 91-196, esp. pp. 118-22; T. Kuhn, *The Structure of Scientific Revolutions* (International Encyclopedia of Unified Science; Chicago: University of Chicago Press, 1962; 2nd edn, 1970), esp. pp. 66-76, 111-35; and K.R. Popper, *Conjectures and Refutations: The Growth of Scientific Knowledge* (London: Routledge & Kegan Paul, 1963; 4th edn, 1972), esp. pp. 3-30, 33-65.

have originated with Jesus, or at least it comes as close to this as we can reasonably find using the means at our disposal.[38] In other words, the criteria indicate episodes where the probability is that the material could have originated with Jesus, but without necessarily hoping for or achieving absolute certainty. This definition will not satisfy all involved in the debate, but is as far as criteria of this sort seem so far to be able to progress.

a. *Participants and their Background*
In determining whether in a given instance Jesus may have spoken Greek, and whether a particular Gospel records Jesus' words on that occasion, one must first note the participants in the dialogue. Then one must determine, on the basis of their particular background and region of origin, the level of probability that Greek would have been the linguistic medium for those involved in the incident. In other words, in a given context one must determine the likelihood of whether Jesus would have spoken Greek, by determining the probability of his conversation partners speaking Greek.[39] The range of linguistic competence in Greek runs the gamut from their incapacity (in a relatively small percentage of instances)[40] to their being able to speak only Greek, with all points of

38. See E.P. Sanders, *Jesus and Judaism* (London: SCM Press; Philadelphia: Fortress Press, 1985), p. 357 n. 30: 'The word "authenticity" is used as a convenient short term. An "authentic" saying is one which we have good reason to believe is as close to something that Jesus said as we can hope for.'

39. This formulation attempts to come to terms with the requirements laid down by Betz, 'Wellhausen's Dictum', esp. p. 16. See the Excursus, below.

40. It is often stated that those in a rural context of the eastern Mediterranean, in particular Palestine, would have only known their native language, such as Aramaic for Jews (see Schürer, *History of the Jewish People*, II, p. 74; R.A. Horsley, *Archaeology, History and Society in Galilee: The Social Context of Jesus and the Rabbis* [Valley Forge, PA: Trinity Press International, 1996], pp. 170-71; among many others). The evidence, however, is that even where native languages persisted, Greek was known, even if those in rural contexts did not fully adapt to Hellenistic culture. For example, the Roman empire and influence had already extended eastward to the border of Parthia by the beginning of the Imperial period, and continued to extend eastward. See F. Millar, *The Roman Near East 31 BC–AD 337* (Cambridge, MA: Harvard University Press, 1993), pp. 437-88. An excellent example of the nature of this influence is the bilingual Asoka inscription (250 BCE), from northern India (the easternmost Greek inscription ever found), edited and discussed most recently in L. Rydbeck, 'ΕΥΣΕΒΕΙΑΝ ΕΔΕΙΞΕΝ ΤΟΙΣ ΑΝΘΡΩΠΟΙΣ', in T. Fornberg and D. Hellholm (eds.), *Texts and Contexts: Biblical Texts in their Textual and Situ-*

probability in between. If it can be determined that Jesus' listeners would have been barely able to speak Greek, it is less likely that the conversation took place in Greek than if they would have been expected to speak in Greek.

In Jerusalem, what I consider to be a conservative estimate by Martin Hengel is that 10-15 per cent of the Jews who lived there spoke Greek as their first language.[41] As a result, it is less likely that in a given instance Jesus would have spoken Greek to Jews from Jerusalem, and more likely that he would have spoken Aramaic. With Jews from outside of Palestine and from areas of high probability regarding the speaking of Greek, even if now in Jerusalem, it is very likely that Jesus would have spoken with them in Greek. A possible instance of this situation might be recorded in Mk 12.13-17 = Mt. 22.16-22 = Lk. 20.20-26, where Jesus is speaking with Pharisees and Herodians in Jerusalem (Luke does

---

ational Contexts. Essays in Honor of Lars Hartmen (Oslo: Scandinavian University Press, 1995), pp. 592-96. From a slightly later period is Dura-Europos. See G.D. Kilpatrick, 'Dura-Europos: The Parchments and the Papyri', *GRBS* 5 (1964), pp. 215-25. See also B. Lifshitz, 'L'hellénisation des Juifs de Palestine: A propos des inscriptions de Besara (Beth-Shearim)', *RB* 72 (1965), pp. 520-38, esp. p. 523 ('Or précisément, cet aspect des inscriptions et surtout des épitaphes gréco-juives montre que la langue grecque était parlée par un nombre considérable de Juifs habitant les bourgades et les villages, et non pas seulement par les citadins ou les gens éduqués') and p. 538 ('La langue grecque et la culture hellénique avaient pénétré dans toutes les communautés juives de l'Orient grec'); Palmer, *Greek Language*, pp. 175-76; Horrocks, *Greek*, pp. 63-64; and the evidence in Sevenster, *Do You Know Greek?*, pp. 96-175. Confusion of language and culture is a problem in Jones, *The Greek City*, pp. 289-95; recognized and corrected in D. Mendels, *The Rise and Fall of Jewish Nationalism: Jewish and Christian Ethnicity in Ancient Palestine* (ABRL; New York: Doubleday, 1992; repr. Grand Rapids: Eerdmans, 1997), p. 22; cf. E.S. Gruen, *Heritage and Hellenism: The Reinvention of Jewish Tradition* (Berkeley: University of California Press, 1998), who notes that the use of Greek did not mean cultural subordination. Instead he believes that the Jews appropriated Greek culture. Here is the final paragraph of his book: 'The world of Greek culture was not an alien one to Hellenistic Jews. They thrived within it and they made its conventions their own. They engaged in Hellenic discourse but addressed their message to fellow Jews. Their free adaptation of the Scriptures, imaginative fictions, and light-hearted recreations of Hellenistic history gave readers pride in Jewish heritage and amusement in its novel reformulation' (p. 297).

41. Hengel with Deines, *Pre-Christian Paul*, p. 55; cf. Hengel with Markschies, *'Hellenization' of Judaea*, p. 10, where the figure of 10-20 per cent is used.

not specify who Jesus' conversational partners are).[42] Like Paul, the Pharisees here may have included Jews from outside Palestine (note that Jews from outside of Palestine predominantly spoke Greek, many if not most of them probably exclusively).[43] However, this would not necessarily be required for them to speak Greek.[44] The Herodians were probably supporters or followers of (or from the household of) the Herods, here during Antipas's time, and may well have spoken only Greek, as did the Romanized Herods.[45]

---

42. G. Dalman, *Jesus–Jeschua: Die drei Sprachen Jesu, Jesus in der Synagogue, auf dem Berge beim Passahmahl, am Kreuz* (Leipzig: J.C. Hinrichs, 1922; ET *Jesus–Jeshua: Studies in the Gospels* [trans. P.P. Levertoff; London: SPCK, 1929]), p. 2; W.E. Bundy, *Jesus and the First Three Gospels: An Introduction to the Synoptic Tradition* (Cambridge, MA: Harvard University Press, 1955), pp. 439-41; F.F. Bruce, 'Render to Caesar', in E. Bammel and C.F.D. Moule (eds.), *Jesus and the Politics of his Day* (Cambridge: Cambridge University Press, 1984), pp. 249-63, where the relation of the passage to P. Egerton 2 and *Gos. Thom.* 100 is discussed. Vincent Taylor speculates that the involvement of the Herodians 'may indicate that the story belongs to the Galilean period' (*The Gospel According to St Mark* [London: Macmillan, 1959], p. 478), but that speculation is unnecessary in the light of the differentiations made here.

43. As noted above, the strength of Paul's claim in Phil. 3.5 is that he was a Jew from outside of Palestine who could also speak a Semitic language. See T. Rajak, *Josephus: The Historian and his Society* (London: Gerald Duckworth, 1983; Philadelphia: Fortress Press, 1984), p. 53, who says that in the first century CE the two obvious sources of Greek speech in Jerusalem were the Herodian court and Diaspora Jews, and that these to some extent overlapped.

44. See Hengel with Markschies, *'Hellenization' of Judaea*, p. 37, citing B.Z. Wacholder, *Nicolaus of Damascus* (Berkeley: University of California Press, 1962), p. 48: 'Certainly the leading Pharisees studied Greek, even when they attempted to discourage its dissemination among the people'.

45. Although Herod the Great's specific education is unknown (Kokkinos thinks he was taught Greek at Marisa or Ascalon), he seems to have mastered Greek, and demanded Greek culture and *paideia* to surround him. Not only did he mint only Greek coins (eliminating the bilingual coins of his predecessors, the Hasmoneans), but he had inscriptions written that referred to himself as a 'lover of Romans' and 'lover of Caesar' (IG III, nos. 550, 551), and was instructed in philosophy and rhetoric by Nicolaus of Damascus (F. Jacoby, *Die Fragmente der greichischen Historiker* [3 vols. and 16 parts; Leiden: E.J. Brill, 1954–69], IIa, no. 90, frag. 135 [p. 422]), the former tutor of the children of Cleopatra and Antony (see Schürer, *History of the Jewish People*, I, pp. 28-34). Herod wrote his own memoirs (Josephus, *Ant.* 174), probably in Greek. He also ensured that his children and grandchildren received a Roman education (Josephus, *Ant.* 15.342-43; 16.6, 203, 242-43; 17.20-

Among Roman officials, Aramaic was virtually unknown (as were almost all native languages of the Roman territories among Romans).[46] Thus, if a conversation took place between Jesus and a Roman official, it is highly likely that they would have spoken in Greek.[47] There may be two examples to include here: one is Jesus' conversation with the centurion (ἑκατόνταρχος) in Capernaum in Galilee about an ill servant (παῖς), recorded in Mt. 8.5-13.[48] Luke 7.1-10 and Jn 4.46-54, however,

---

21, 52-53, 94; 18.143; 19.360), which would have meant an education in the Greek language, so that they were said to be 'thoroughly conversant with Hellenic culture' (Josephus, *Life* 359 [LCL]). Herod and his family also promoted Hellenistic culture (*paideia*), architecture and sport, among other things. On the Hellenistic dimension of Herod, as well as his children, see M. Grant, *Herod the Great* (London: Weidenfeld & Nicolson, 1971), pp. 115-21; H. Hoehner, *Herod Antipas* (SNTSMS, 17; Cambridge: Cambridge University Press, 1972), pp. 5-17 (cf. pp. 18-19); Rajak, *Josephus*, pp. 53-55; Hengel with Markschies, *'Hellenization' of Judaea*, pp. 32-39; N. Kokkinos, *The Herodian Dynasty: Origins, Role in Society and Eclipse* (JSPSup, 30; Sheffield: Sheffield Academic Press, 1998), esp. pp. 122-27. On Greek in Roman education, see H.I. Marrou, *Histoire de l'education dans l'antiquité* (Paris: Seuil, 3rd edn, 1948; ET *A History of Education in Antiquity* [trans. G. Lamb; London: Sheed & Ward, 1956]), pp. 255-73. On the Herodians, and the uncertainty regarding who they were, and when they existed, see L.L. Grabbe, *Judaism from Cyrus to Hadrian* (Minneapolis: Augsburg Fortress, 1992; London: SCM Press, 1994), pp. 501-502; W.L. Knox, *The Sources of the Synoptic Gospels. I. St Mark* (ed. H. Chadwick; Cambridge: Cambridge University Press, 1953), pp. 9-10; Hoehner, *Herod Antipas*, pp. 331-39, who notes the Herodians' antipathy to the Pharisees and possible relation to the Sadducees; P. Richardson, *Herod: King of the Jews and Friend of the Romans* (Columbia: University of South Carolina Press, 1996), pp. 259-60, who believes that the Herodians originated with Herod the Great; and M. Casey, *Aramaic Sources of Mark's Gospel* (SNTSMS, 102; Cambridge: Cambridge University Press, 1998), pp. 186-89. Cf. R.H. Gundry, *Matthew: A Commentary on his Literary and Theological Art* (Grand Rapids: Eerdmans, 1982), p. 442; and W.D. Davies and D.C. Allison, Jr, *A Critical and Exegetical Commentary on the Gospel According to Saint Matthew* (3 vols.; ICC; Edinburgh: T. & T. Clark, 1988–97), III, p. 212 n. 19, who list alternative views.

46. See Marrou, *History of Education*, p. 256.

47. The question of an interpreter must always be taken into account. This is addressed below, in the Excursus.

48. S.E. Porter, 'Did Jesus Ever Teach in Greek?', *TynBul* 44.2 (1993), pp. 199-235, esp. pp. 228-29; *idem*, 'Jesus and the Use of Greek in Galilee', in B. Chilton and C.A. Evans (eds.), *Studying the Historical Jesus: Evaluations of the State of Current Research* (NTTS, 19; Leiden: E.J. Brill, 1994), pp. 123-54, esp. pp. 151-52; *idem*, *Studies in the Greek New Testament*, pp. 165-66. On the meaning of ἑκατόνταρχος, see the discussion in E.-J. Vledder, *Conflict in the Miracle Stories: A*

have significant variations in what are usually considered parallel accounts of the same episode. Luke 7.3 has 'elders of the Jews' coming as emissaries to Jesus, and Jn 4.46 refers to a βασιλικός in Cana of Galilee who has an ill son. The significant differences in the Johannine passage may well indicate a tradition independent of that of the Synoptics that should be given consideration.[49] The βασιλικός, like the ἑκατόνταρχος, is either a commander of a troop of soldiers serving under Herod Antipas, who had non-Jewish Roman auxiliary troops under his command, or even a Roman officer—in any event, he was almost assuredly not Jewish.[50] Regarding the Matthaean and Lukan accounts, there are several common features to them. They both retain Jesus' commendation of the ἑκατόνταρχος as a man demonstrating faith not found in Israel, and they see him as a Gentile,[51] and presumably a Greek

Socio-Exegetical Study of Matthew 8 and 9 (JSNTSup, 152; Sheffield: Sheffield Academic Press, 1996), p. 179 n. 46.

49. See R. Bultmann, *Das Evangelium des Johannes* (MeyerK; Göttingen: Vandenhoeck & Ruprecht, 1947; 2nd edn, 1964, supplement 1966; ET *The Gospel of John: A Commentary* [trans. G.R. Beasley-Murray; Oxford: Basil Blackwell, 1971]), p. 204. There has been much scepticism regarding the use of Johannine tradition in historical-Jesus research. Much of this, though certainly not all, has been related to the symbolic character of some language of the Fourth Gospel. This factor must be taken into account, but does not seem to be of relevance to the examples from John's Gospel cited in this study, except as noted below. To some extent, however, the criteria being developed here attempt to move beyond facile generalizations about the differences between the Synoptic Gospels and John by introducing sociolinguistically based criteria. On the literary character of John's Gospel, see R.A. Culpepper, *Anatomy of the Fourth Gospel: A Study in Literary Design* (Philadelphia: Fortress Press, 1983), esp. pp. 180-98. The case for independence of the Johannine tradition is made by C.H. Dodd, *Historical Tradition in the Fourth Gospel* (Cambridge: Cambridge University Press, 1963), pp. 188-95; and summarized in terms of Synoptic relations in D.L. Bock, *Luke* (2 vols.; Baker Exegetical Commentary on the New Testament, 3A, B; Grand Rapids: Baker Book House, 1994, 1996), I, pp. 630-33. See Chapter 5, below, on the history of discussion of the independence of Johannine tradition, when discussing Jn 18.29-38 in relation to the Synoptic accounts.

50. On the ἑκατόνταρχος and βασιλικός, see A.H. Mead, 'The βασιλικός in John 4.46-53', *JSNT* 23 (1985), pp. 69-72 (repr. in C.A. Evans and S.E. Porter [eds.], *New Testament Backgrounds: A Sheffield Reader* [BibSem, 43; Sheffield: Sheffield Academic Press, 1997], pp. 203-206); cf. Schürer, *History of the Jewish People*, I, pp. 362-67.

51. Davies and Allison, *Matthew*, II, p. 19. According to Vledder (*Conflict in the Miracle Stories*, pp. 180-81), the sense of the episode comes from the centurion being a Gentile in a Jewish societal context.

speaker, rather than an Aramaic speaker. Commentators are divided on which version is primary, but there is reason to think that Matthew's is, with the centurion coming directly to Jesus.[52] This reasoning includes the fact that in Matthew, the most 'Jewish' of the Gospels,[53] the retention of the direct communication with a Gentile is more unusual than Jesus communicating with Jews. In the Lukan account, however, the intermediaries give an independent testimony to the Gentile's humility, integrity and hence faith.[54] The other incident of Jesus speaking with a Roman official involves Jesus' trial before the prefect Pilate in Jerusalem, recorded in Mk 15.2-5 = Mt. 27.11-14 = Lk. 23.2-4 = Jn 18.29-38.[55] There is no interpreter mentioned in the account, which is exactly

52. See R.A.J. Gagnon, 'The Shape of Matthew's Q Text of the Centurion at Capernaum: Did it Mention Delegations?', *NTS* 40 (1994), pp. 133-42.

53. See R.T. France, *Matthew—Evangelist and Teacher* (Exeter: Paternoster Press, 1989), pp. 108-19.

54. See R.P. Martin, 'The Pericope of the Healing of the "Centurion's" Servant/ Son (Matt 8:5-13 par. Luke 7:1-10): Some Exegetical Notes', in R.A. Guelich (ed.), *Unity and Diversity in New Testament Theology: Essays in Honor of George E. Ladd* (Grand Rapids: Eerdmans, 1978), pp. 14-22, here pp. 17-18; R.A.J. Gagnon, 'Statistical Analysis and the Case of the Double Delegation in Luke 7:3-7a', *CBQ* 55 (1993), pp. 709-31; *idem*, 'Luke's Motives for Redaction in the Account of the Double Delegation in Luke 7:1-10', *NovT* 36 (1994), pp. 122-45; D.R. Catchpole, 'The Centurion's Faith and its Function in Q', in F. Van Segbroeck, C.M. Tuckett, G. Van Belle and J. Verheyden (eds.), *The Four Gospels 1992: Festschrift Frans Neirynck* (3 vols.; BETL, 100; Leuven: Leuven University Press/Peeters, 1992), I, pp. 517-40, esp. pp. 528-32; repr. in D.R. Catchpole, *The Quest for Q* (Edinburgh: T. & T. Clark, 1993), pp. 280-308, esp. pp. 293-98; and the earlier study, A. Harnack, *Sprüche und Reden Jesu: Die zweite Quelle des Matthäus und Lukas* (BENT, 2; Leipzig: J.C. Hinrichs, 1907; ET *The Sayings of Jesus: The Second Source of St Matthew and St Luke* [trans. J.R. Wilkinson; CThL; London: Williams & Norgate; New York: Putnam's Sons 1908]), pp. 74-77.

55. Porter, 'Did Jesus Ever Teach in Greek?', pp. 224-26; *idem*, 'Jesus and the Use of Greek', pp. 152-53; *idem*, *Studies in the Greek New Testament*, pp. 162-63; cf. A. Roberts, *Greek: The Language of Christ and his Apostles* (London: Longmans, Green, 1888), p. 165; Dalman, *Jesus–Jeshua*, p. 6; Manson, *Teaching of Jesus*, p. 46; Birkeland, *Language of Jesus*, p. 17; Sevenster, *Do You Know Greek?*, p. 26; Betz, 'Wellhausen's Dictum', p. 15; among others. Cf. A.N. Sherwin-White, *Roman Society and Roman Law in the New Testament* (Sarum Lectures, 1960–61; Oxford: Clarendon Press, 1963), pp. 24-27, for an analysis of Pilate's interrogation of Jesus in terms of what might have been expected from a Roman official at the time. On Pilate, see H.K. Bond, *Pontius Pilate in History and Interpretation* (SNTSMS, 100; Cambridge: Cambridge University Press, 1998), esp. pp. 105-16.

what one might have expected in a juridical context with a Roman provincial authority (see discussion in the Excursus, below). From what has been said above regarding linguistic competence, there is the further plausibility that the Jewish leaders, including those of the Sanhedrin, would have been able to speak Greek, especially since they had regular and frequent contact with the Roman administration.[56]

In other regions of Palestine, the probability of Jesus speaking Greek would have varied. For example, along the coast of Palestine and in Galilee (as noted above), especially in the surrounding cities of the Decapolis, the use of Greek would have been relatively high, even among Jews, and certainly among non-Jews and Roman officials. Examples of Jesus probably speaking Greek in such a context are three. One is Jesus' conversation, in the region of Tyre in Mk 7.25-30,[57] or Tyre and Sidon in Mt. 15.21-28, with a woman who has a sick daughter.[58] In Mk 7.26, she is emphatically called a ἑλληνίς, a συροφοινίκισσα τῷ γένει.[59] In Mt. 15.22, she is called a χαναναία. The Syrophoenicians (as distinguished from other Phoenician groups) can probably be identified with what are traditionally called the Canaanites, and hence these are parallel accounts involving a Gentile woman.[60] Nevertheless, the differences as

56. Even one as sceptical of our knowledge of who spoke Greek in Palestine as Horsley concedes that the upper class of Jews, of whom many of the Sanhedrin would have been members, would have done so (*Archaeology*, p. 229). The pace of the trial narrative, in which conversation is held between combinations of four parties—Pilate, Jesus, the Jewish leaders, and the crowd—also mitigates against an interpreter (or would it require several interpreters?) being involved. See Roberts, *Greek*, pp. 161-62.

57. Many early manuscripts read 'Tyre and Sidon', including ℵ A B *f*1, 13 Majority text. This may be assimilation to Mk 7.31 and Mt. 15.21, however. See G. Dalman, *Orte und Wege Jesu* (Leipzig: J.C. Hinrichs, 3rd edn, 1924; ET *Sacred Sites and Ways: Studies in the Topography of the Gospels* [trans. P.P. Levertoff; London: SPCK, 1935]), pp. 198-200.

58. Porter, 'Did Jesus Ever Teach in Greek?', pp. 226-27; *idem*, 'Jesus and the Use of Greek', pp. 149-50; *idem, Studies in the Greek New Testament*, p. 164. Bundy (*Jesus and the First Three Gospels*, p. 278) notes that the 'majority of critics have accepted [Jesus'] journey [north to Tyre] as historical'.

59. See R.H. Gundry, *Mark: A Commentary on his Apology for the Cross* (Grand Rapids: Eerdmans, 1993), pp. 379-80; D. Rhoads, 'Jesus and the Syrophoenician Woman in Mark', *JAAR* 62 (1994), pp. 343-75, esp. p. 351.

60. See H.B. Swete, *The Gospel According to Mark* (London: Macmillan, 1898), p. 156-57; C.S. Mann, *Mark* (AB, 27; Garden City, NY: Doubleday, 1986), pp. 320; R. Guelich, *Mark 1–8:26* (WBC, 34A; Dallas: Word Books, 1989), p. 385; G. Sch-

noted above probably also indicate that these accounts are from independent sources (see Chapter 5, for further discussion of the independence of the accounts).[61] What had once been an indigenously Semitic-
speaking area had long been under significant Hellenistic influence and
antagonistic to the Jews (see Josephus, *Apion* 1.69-72). The area evidenced widespread use of Greek, eradicating virtually all signs of the
indigenous language.[62] The account in Mark's Gospel, referring to her
as a Greek woman, makes it clear so that the reader knows that the
woman was a Greek-speaker despite her birth; otherwise the reference
is unnecessary and gratuitous.[63]

The second example is the approach near Bethany of 'certain Greeks'
(ἕλληνές τινες) to Philip, who went to Andrew, with requests for Jesus,
recorded in Jn 12.20-28.[64] The use of ἕλληνες here almost certainly
refers to Greek-speaking Gentiles (rather than Greeks themselves; cf.
Acts 6.1).[65] Though near Bethany, those approaching were probably

warz, 'ΣΥΡΟΦΟΙΝΙΚΙΣΣΑ—ΧΑΝΑΝΑΙΑ (Markus 7.26/Matthäus 15.22)', *NTS* 30 (1984), pp. 626-28.

61. Taylor, *Mark*, p. 347; Davies and Allison, *Matthew*, II, pp. 542-43.
62. Millar, *Roman Near East*, pp. 264-95.
63. G. Theissen, 'Lokal- und Sozialkolorit in der Geschichte von der syro-phönischen Frau (Mk 7:24-30)', *ZNW* 75 (1984), pp. 202-25; repr. in *idem, Lokal-kolorit und Zeitgeschichte in den Evangelien: Ein Beitrag zur Geschichte der synoptischen Tradition* (NTOA, 8; Göttingen: Vandenhoeck & Ruprecht, 1989; ET *The Gospels in Context: Social and Political History in the Synoptic Tradition* [trans. L.M. Maloney; Edinburgh: T. & T. Clark, 1992]), pp. 61-80, esp. pp. 66-70: 'We can presume at least that the Syrophoenician woman knew Greek, but probably also that she was thoroughly integrated in Greek culture' (p. 69); F. Dufton, 'The Syro-phoenician Woman and her Dogs', *ExpTim* 100 (1988–89), p. 417; Gundry, *Mark*, p. 375; D.A. Hagner, *Matthew* (2 vols.; WBC, 33A, B; Dallas: Word Books, 1993, 1995), I, p. 441: 'almost certainly the conversation between her and Jesus would have been held in Greek'.
64. Porter, 'Did Jesus Ever Teach in Greek?', pp. 227-28; *idem*, 'Jesus and the Use of Greek', pp. 150-51; *idem, Studies in the Greek New Testament*, pp. 164-65. It is unclear that Jesus actually spoke with the Greeks, but if they did, Greek would apparently have been the language they used.
65. C.K. Barrett, *The Gospel According to St John* (London: SPCK; Philadel-phia: Westminster, 2nd edn, 1978 [1955]), p. 421; contra J.A.T. Robinson, 'The Destination and Purpose of St John's Gospel', *NTS* 6 (1960), pp. 117-31, here p. 120 (repr. in J.A.T. Robinson, *Twelve New Testament Studies* [SBT, 34; London: SCM Press, 1962], pp. 107-25, here p. 111), who thinks they are Greek-speaking Jews;

from a Greek-speaking area such as the Decapolis. This makes sense in the light of their approaching Philip and Andrew, two disciples who had Greek names, and who (along with Peter, apparently; cf. Jn 1.44) were from Bethsaida in Gaulinitis. Gaulinitis was not technically in Galilee, but close enough so that it was quite possibly referred to as being in Galilee, especially after 66–70 CE.[66] Among Jesus' disciples, not only Andrew and Philip had Greek names, but the names of Simon, Bartholomew and Thaddaeus may well have derived from Greek or gone easily into Greek.[67] This scenario of Greek speaking is consonant also with the fact that several of Jesus' disciples were fishermen, which would have required that they conduct much of their business of selling fish in Greek.[68] The account does not say whether Jesus actually spoke to these Greeks. Dalman thought that these Greek-speakers went to the disciples because Jesus was not identified with the Greek-speaking Jews, not necessarily because Jesus could not speak Greek.[69] The narrative itself gives no indication why the Greeks did not approach Jesus directly. The reasons could have been related to Jesus' perceived status, since Jesus' response gives no indication that he could not communicate with them.[70] The people involved in such a conversation all had the indicative background and origins for such a conversation to have taken place in Greek.

The third example for consideration in this category is Jesus' conversation with the Samaritan woman in Jn 4.4-26.[71] Samaria had been a

---

D.A. Carson, *The Gospel According to John* (Leicester: Inter-Varsity Press; Grand Rapids: Eerdmans, 1991), pp. 435-36.

66. See Barrett, *John*, p. 421; cf. Carson, *John*, p. 436.

67. See Hengel with Markschies, *'Hellenization' of Judaea*, pp. 16-17; *idem* with Deines, *Pre-Christian Paul*, pp. 55-56. Mark 3.16 and Lk. 6.14 say that Simon was given the Greek name Peter (πέτρος), but Jn 1.42 says that Jesus gave him the name Cephas.

68. See J.A.L. Lee, 'Some Features of the Speech of Jesus in Mark's Gospel', *NovT* 27 (1985), pp. 1-36, esp. p. 6.

69. Dalman, *Jesus–Jeshua*, p. 5. Cf. Bultmann, *John*, p. 423, who 'spiritualizes' the episode.

70. Sevenster, *Do You Know Greek?*, pp. 25-26; Roberts, *Greek*, pp. 157-59. Most scholars are sceptical that Jesus spoke with the Greeks, however. See L.L. Morris, *The Gospel According to John* (NICNT; Grand Rapids: Eerdmans, 1971), p. 592; although R.E. Brown, *The Gospel According to John* (2 vols.; AB, 29, 29A; Garden City, NY: Doubleday, 1966, 1970), I, pp. 466-67, is open to it.

71. Roberts, *Greek*, pp. 145-47.

multilingual area since the third century BCE, with Greek used especially for the purposes of a *lingua franca*, that is, for economic and
administrative, rather than religious, purposes.[72]

Of course, there is the possibility that a conversation of Jesus may
have occurred outside the person's place of origin. In such instances,
identification of the person (by name and other instructive factors) may
well give indications of the linguistic context. In the light of the Greek
names of many of Jesus' disciples, including Peter, and their origins
near Galilee,[73] it is also plausible that Jesus' conversation with them in
or around one of the ancient highly Hellenized cities of the north, Caesarea Philippi,[74] occurred in Greek, as recorded in Mk 8.27-30 = Mt.
16.13-20 = Lk. 9.18-21 (Luke does not mention the location).[75] Caesarea Philippi, earlier known as Panias because of the grotto dedicated
to Pan, had been rebuilt both by Herod the Great and especially by
Philip. It was predominantly a non-Jewish city (Josephus, *Life* 13),

72. Hengel with Markschies, *'Hellenization' of Judaea*, p. 8; cf. Millar, *Roman Near East*, p. 341. This is not to say that Greek was not used in this region for reli-gious purposes, however. The Isis and Serapis cult flourished there until it was replaced by the cult of Kore in Roman times. SEG VIII no. 95 has a dedicatory inscription to Serapis and Isis (201 BCE) and SEG VIII no. 96 has a list of priests of Zeus Olympius (second century BCE). *NewDocs* 1 (1976), no. 68 has a third- or fourth-century CE inscription to Kore, with a history of the religious environment given there.

73. Dalman, *Jesus–Jeshua*, p. 5; Hengel with Markschies, *'Hellenization' of Judaea*, pp. 16-17; *idem* with Deines, *Pre-Christian Paul*, pp. 55-56.

74. See Dalman, *Sacred Sites and Ways*, pp. 202-204; Tcherikover, *Hellenistic Civilization*, p. 101; Schürer, *History of the Jewish People*, I, pp. 169-71; Hengel with Markschies, *'Hellenization' of Judaea*, pp. 14-15; *NewDocs* 1 (1976), no. 67, for the bilingual (Greek and Aramaic) inscription to the God in Dan; and R.C. Gregg and D. Urman, *Jews, Pagans, and Christians in the Golan Heights: Greek and Other Inscriptions of the Roman and Byzantine Eras* (South Florida Studies in the History of Judaism, 140; Atlanta: Scholars Press, 1996), pp. 280-83, for the latest archaeological findings.

75. Porter, 'Did Jesus Ever Teach in Greek?', pp. 229-35; *idem, Studies in the Greek New Testament*, pp. 166-71; G.R. Selby, *Jesus, Aramaic and Greek* (Don-caster: Brynmill Press, 1989), p. 54. Taylor (*Mark*, p. 374) notes that the place should be taken seriously, since Mark rarely gives place names. It is possible that this episode continues in Mk 8.31-33 = Mt. 16.21-23 = Lk. 9.22, but both Mark and Matthew possibly indicate a break in the narrative (καὶ ἤρξατο and ἀπὸ τότε ἤρξατο). Luke continues the account simply with a participle (εἰπών), but he has not given any indication of location at the beginning of the episode.

where Titus and Vespasian rested during the Jewish War. For mid-level officials, such as local Jewish tax collectors, there is a fairly equal weighting on either side whether Jesus would have spoken Greek or Aramaic. For example, whether Jesus spoke to Levi/Matthew in Greek or Aramaic would probably have depended on a number of other contextual factors, such as their location near Capernaum in Galilee, as seen in Mk 2.13-14 = Mt. 9.9 = Lk. 5.27-28[76] (see below). This is because conversation in either language was probably possible.

This first phase of this criterion attempts to establish on the basis of the linguistic background and origin of Jesus' conversational partners whether it is plausible that they and Jesus spoke Greek. In some instances, which might be suggestive for the use of Greek, we know too little about Jesus' disputants. For example, in Mk 5.1-20 = Lk. 8.26-39 = Mt. 8.28-34, Jesus speaks with the demon-possessed man in either Gerasa or Gadara, both in the eastern part of the Decapolis. Both cities were thoroughly Hellenized,[77] but we know next to nothing about the demon-possessed man (or those with whom he may have spoken: Mk 5.17 = Mt. 8.34 = Lk. 8.36-37). The linguistic situation can get even more complex. For example, if there was a mixed audience, in which language did Jesus speak? In Mk 3.8 = Mt. 4.25 = Lk. 6.17, a mixed crowd is gathered,[78] but Jesus specifically addresses his disciples in Mt. 5.1.[79] One simply cannot tell what language or languages might have been used. There may even have been code-switching in such an incident. Nevertheless, this framework establishes the broad parameters in which determination of the probabilities of whether Jesus spoke Greek on a particular occasion must be made. The result of this survey is that there are eight episodes in the Gospels that might well indicate on the basis of the participants and their origins that Greek was spoken when they conversed with Jesus.

76. See Bundy, *Jesus and the First Three Gospels*, pp. 142-43, who notes the lack of connectedness of this episode; cf. Schürer, *History of the Jewish People*, I, p. 374.

77. See Schürer, *History of the Jewish People*, II, pp. 149-55, 132-36.

78. See A.W. Argyle, 'Did Jesus Speak Greek?', *ExpTim* 67 (1955–56), pp. 92-93, esp. p. 93.

79. Among other examples, Roberts (*Greek*, pp. 145-57) argues that the Sermon on the Mount (cf. also Lk. 6) was originally spoken in Greek. Whereas one could possibly compare the sermonic traditions in Matthew and Luke, the context of participants does not clearly point in that direction.

b. *Context and Theme of Discussion*

The second phase of this criterion enters into the equation the context and theme of discussion. Not only is the probability of the participants being able to speak Greek necessary, but the context and theme of their discussion must fit within this linguistic scenario as well. Context of discussion includes a variety of public and personal factors (including issues of theology, politics, etc.). Intimate conversations between Jesus and, for example, a Jewish woman from Jerusalem about purity laws might well be presumed to be in Aramaic. But a conversation with a Samaritan woman, who was at the least sceptical about a Jew speaking with her at all (Jn 4.4-26),[80] could easily have treated mundane issues, such as the drawing of water, in Greek (even if these mundane issues were given symbolic value by either Jesus or the Gospel author, and understood that way by the Gospel's readers).[81] It is, therefore, entirely plausible that Jesus' discussion with the Syrophoenician or Canaanite Gentile woman in Tyre (or Sidon) would be in Greek (Mk 7.25-30 = Mt. 15.21-28). The same would seem to hold for Jesus' discussion with 'certain Greeks' (Jn 12.20-28), if indeed he actually spoke to them. A public discussion with a Roman official about Roman law also might well be presumed to be in Greek. Similarly, a discussion with a centurion in Capernaum about his personal affairs would probably be in Greek (Mt. 8.5-13), as would a discussion with a commander in Cana (Jn 4.46-54). In a more formal context, Jesus' interrogation by Pilate over whether he was the king of the Jews, a political question for the Roman official over Jesus' guilt or innocence in Roman law,[82] would probably have been in Greek as well (Mk 15.2-5 = Mt. 27.11-14 = Lk. 23.2-4 = Jn 18.29-38). A discussion with a Jew about Roman law might also be in Greek. This is due to the nature of the topic, in which there are limitations on technical vocabulary in Aramaic for discussion, as well as the topic being one linked with the Romans rather than Judaism.[83]

---

80. Brown, *John*, I, pp. 175-76, on the attitude of the woman.

81. Barrett, *John*, p. 228.

82. So virtually all commentators, often citing the *titulus* in support. For recent discussion, see J.B. Green, *The Death of Jesus: Tradition and Interpretation in the Passion Narrative* (WUNT, 2.33; Tübingen: Mohr Siebeck, 1988), p. 288; W. Wiefel, *Das Evangelium nach Matthäus* (THKNT; Berlin: Evangelische Verlagsanstalt, 1998), p. 472.

83. The number of Greek loanwords that appear in Aramaic (discussed above)

The most difficulty in determining the language used for discussion is caused by theological content. Since so much of Jesus' teaching seems to relate to the Old Testament, it would seem logical to think that this teaching, especially to a Jewish audience, would be in Aramaic. However, the fact that the vast majority of quotations of the Old Testament in the Gospels, including those reportedly uttered by Jesus, follow the Septuagint must be noted at this point.[84] In the light of the widespread use of Greek in Palestine even by Jews, as well as the use of Greek by Jews from outside of Palestine, and the evidence for the use of the Greek version of the Jewish Scriptures even in Palestine (all noted above), it is not so easy to dismiss the use of the Septuagint by Jesus as simply the result of the Gospel writers or later redaction. Many Jews, even of Palestine, may well have known their Scriptures only or predominantly in Greek (especially those who only knew Greek).[85] Hence, Jesus' discussion with his disciples in Caesarea Philippi over a range of theological matters might also have taken place in Greek (Mk 8.27-30 = Mt. 16.13-20 = Lk. 9.18-21). In the light of Jesus' discussion with the Pharisees and Herodians taking place over the picture and the inscription on a Roman coin, it is likely that this discussion involved the use of Greek as well (Mk 12.13-17 = Mt. 22.16-22 = Lk. 20.20-26).[86] The possibility of Jesus speaking with Levi/Matthew[87] in Greek in the region of Galilee is also possible, but the language is confined to only two words,

attests to the apparent belief by Aramaic language users that their vocabulary was in need of additional words to suit their communicative purposes. Cf. Barr, 'Hebrew, Aramaic and Greek', p. 86 on Hebrew in this regard.

84. For recent discussion, with implications for Synoptic source criticism, see D.S. New, *Old Testament Quotations in the Synoptic Gospels, and the Two-Document Hypothesis* (SBLSCS, 37; Atlanta: Scholars Press, 1993), p. 123.

85. See Millar, *Roman Near East*, p. 352.

86. It is unclear whether the coin had Greek or Latin writing on it. For Greek, see Dalman, *Jesus–Jeshua*, p. 2 and n. 6; for Latin, the more likely choice, see H.St.J. Hart, 'The Coin of "Render unto Caesar..." (A Note on Some Aspects of Mark 12:13-17; Matt. 22:15-22; Luke 20:20-26)', in Bammel and Moule (eds.), *Jesus and the Politics of his Day*, pp. 241-48, with photographs on p. 246; followed by Davies and Allison, *Matthew*, III, p. 216. The language of the coin does not affect the analysis offered here, due to the nature of the use of Greek as the *lingua franca* of the eastern Mediterranean of the Roman empire, and the use of Latin primarily for official matters (including most coinage) and by the army.

87. On the equation of Matthew and Levi, see Hagner, *Matthew*, I, pp. 237-38.

rendering the specific content in relation to the context fairly minimal (Mk 2.13-14 = Mt. 9.9 = Lk. 5.27-28).

This phase of this criterion is concerned to establish a plausible thematic linkage between the subject matter of Jesus' conversation and the use of Greek to express such themes. Further, the appropriateness of such a discussion taking place in Greek must be seen to exist between the context of discussion and the theme. The eight episodes noted above seem to fulfil this dimension of the criterion as well, in that their subject matter is suitable to a context in which Greek was used as the linguistic medium for the discussion.

c. *Determination of the Words of Jesus*
The third phase of this criterion actually attempts to determine whether the Greek words that Jesus is recorded as using have any claim to authenticity. The discussion over Semitisms (Aramaisms), especially the question of translation from Aramaic into Greek and back, has shown how unreliable such a criterion is. This is so much so that one often cannot determine whether any particular Greek wording or phrases, even those that are awkward in Greek (and may well reflect Semitic interference),[88] had their origins in Aramaic. At this point, this new criterion for authenticity is reinforced if several of the traditional criteria discussed in Chapters 2 and 3, above, are also seen to be relevant. These would include the criterion of multiple independent traditions (see Chapter 5, below, on textual variance), as well as if what is preserved in the words falls within the purview of the criteria of embarrassment (it is unlikely that the Church created statements by Jesus or depicted him in actions that were an embarrassment to it, or that went against the

---

88. In one episode, in which Jesus is reported to be in the Decapolis, he heals a man by using the word *ephphatha* (Mk 7.31-37, esp. v. 34; not recorded in Mt. 15.29-31). One wonders if the word *ephphatha*, either Aramaic or Hebrew, is mentioned specifically here because the author realized that the reader (or hearer) would not have expected the use of a Semitic language in this Greek-speaking context. Of course, we do not know anything about the deaf man, and his use of language. On *ephphatha*, see the summary of discussion in Guelich, *Mark 1–8:26*, pp. 395-96, with bibliography on pp. 389-90. A similar episode might be found in Mk 5.21-43, esp. v. 41, where Jesus utters *talitha koum* (not found in Mt. 9.25 or Lk. 8.54). One might object that this occurs in the house of a synagogue ruler named Jairus. However, there were Greek-speaking synagogues (note the Theodotus inscription, below), and this one is located in Galilee, which at least raises the possibility of the linguistic situation being more complex than first glance would indicate.

redactional tendency), of dissimilarity (the single dissimilarity criterion allows for statements that do not reflect the beliefs of the early Church to be authentic), and of execution (Jesus may well have said things in Greek that contributed to his execution by the Romans). However, this use of other criteria is not a necessity. If one can show that the linguistic situation—in the light of its participants, their origins, the context of discussion and the theme—warrants the use of Greek, one can legitimately argue for the probability that this conversation of Jesus took place in Greek.

With regard to the eight episodes in which Greek might have been used, in seven of them words of Jesus are recorded (the exception is Jn 12.20-28), although not in all of the Gospel accounts. These passages include the following:

1. Mt. 8.5-13 = Jn 4.46-54: Jesus' conversation with the centurion or commander (but the Johannine account diverges in terms of wording)
2. Jn 4.4-26: Jesus' conversation with the Samaritan woman[89]
3. Mk 2.13-14 = Mt. 9.9 = Lk. 5.27-28: Jesus' calling of Levi/Matthew
4. Mk 7.25-30 = Mt. 15.21-28: Jesus' conversation with the Syrophoenician or Canaanite woman
5. Mk 12.13-17 = Mt. 22.16-22 = Lk. 20.20-26: Jesus' conversation with the Pharisees and Herodians over the Roman coin of Caesar
6. Mk 8.27-30 = Mt. 16.13-20 = Lk. 9.18-21: Jesus' conversation with his disciples at Caesarea Philippi
7. Mk 15.2-5 = Mt. 27.11-14 = Lk. 23.2-4 = Jn 18.29-38: Jesus' trial before Pilate.

A feature to note in virtually all of these episodes is that the words of Jesus are often very short and to the point. This feature perhaps shows resistance by redactors to expatiate upon Jesus' teaching in these Greek-language contexts. One can also note that, in certain of the episodes, the words of Jesus common to two or more sources are confined to a few short verses. One notes the following instances of Jesus' words in five of the episodes noted above: Jesus' calling of Levi/Matthew con-

---

89. There may be an instance of code-switching from Greek to Aramaic when the disciples appear, as part of a strategy by the disciples to distinguish themselves from a Samaritan woman. See Watt, *Code-Switching in Luke and Acts*, pp. 35-51.

sists of two overlapping words in Mk 2.14 = Mt. 9.9 = Lk. 5.27; Jesus' conversation with the centurion is confined to Mt. 8.7, 13, with Johannine-sounding language in Jn 4.48; Jesus' conversation with the Gentile woman in Mk 7.27, 29 = Mt. 15.26, 28 is confined to two verses; Jesus' conversation with the Pharisees and Herodians over the coin is found in Mk 12.15, 16, 17 = Mt. 22.19, 20, 21 = Lk. 20.24, 25; and Jesus' trial before Pilate has only a single verse with the words of Jesus in the Synoptic Gospels: Mk 15.2 = Mt. 27.11 = Lk. 23.3 (= Jn 18.37, with John's account having a greater number of words recorded—see Chapter 5, below). The other two episodes have a mix of shorter and longer statements. Jesus' conversation with his disciples at Caesarea Philippi has short statements in Mk 8.27, 29 and Lk. 9.18, 19, and both short statements and an extended statement in Mt. 16.13, 15, 17-19. Jesus' conversation with the Samaritan woman in Jn 4.4-26 also has a mix of shorter (vv. 7, 16, 26) and longer (vv. 10, 13-14, 17-18, 21-24) statements.

In the next chapter, a further criterion will be introduced and applied to these episodes in order to be more precise regarding passages that may contain authentic words of Jesus in Greek. However, in support of the above analysis, traditional criteria can be invoked at this point, including especially that of historical plausibility in terms of the linguistic context. In each of these episodes, a case has been made that it is historically plausible on the linguistic and contextual bases established above to argue that Jesus spoke in Greek. In that sense, all seven of these episodes are seen to be historically plausible as authentic to the Jesus tradition, at least in so far as the conversation taking place in Greek is concerned.

One is not confined to using only this criterion, however. In the light of the other traditional criteria, one could argue that, as a minimum, there is reasonably high probability of authenticity in Greek for the short statements by Jesus in the following four episodes. (1) The first is Jesus' conversation with his disciples at Caesarea Philippi. As noted above, this conversation takes place between Jesus and his disciples, several of whom had Greek names and many of whom came from Galilee, a region of relatively high Hellenistic influence, in the vicinity of a highly hellenized city of the north. Their topic of conversation is of a theological sort, with Jesus asking his disciples τίνα με λέγουσιν οἱ ἄνθρωποι εἶναι; (Mk 8.27 = Mt. 16.13 = Lk. 9.18, essentially the same wording in each Gospel—see Chapter 5, for further discussion), and then essentially repeating the question (Mk 8.29 = Mt. 16.15 = Lk. 9.20).

160   *The Criteria for Authenticity in Historical-Jesus Research*

The disciples give various answers to the first question, and in response to the second Peter affirms that Jesus is the Christ, at which point he tells them to tell no one. It is only in Matthew's Gospel that Peter's confession elicits a lengthier response by Jesus that is cited in the Gospel:

> μακάριος εἶ, Σίμων Βαριωνᾶ, ὅτι σὰρξ καὶ αἷμα οὐκ ἀπεκάλυψέν σοι ἀλλ᾽ ὁ πατήρ μου ὁ ἐν τοῖς οὐρανοῖς. κἀγὼ δέ σοι λέγω ὅτι σὺ εἶ Πέτρος, καὶ ἐπὶ ταύτῃ τῇ πέτρᾳ οἰκοδομήσω μου τὴν ἐκκλησίαν καὶ πύλαι ᾅδου οὐ κατισχύσουσιν αὐτῆς. δώσω σοι τὰς κλεῖδας τῆς βασιλείας τῶν οὐρανῶν, καὶ ὃ ἐὰν δήσῃς ἐπὶ τῆς γῆς ἔσται δεδεμένον ἐν τοῖς οὐρανοῖς, καὶ ὃ ἐὰν λύσῃς ἐπὶ τῆς γῆς ἔσται λελυμένον ἐν τοῖς οὐρανοῖς (Mt. 16.17-19).

The traditional criteria that support the probability of authenticity on the basis of the criterion of Greek language and its context are several. One of these is multiple attestation, with Matthew having a good chance of priority, and hence independence, at least in Mt. 16.17-19. The arguments for Matthaean independence in 16.17-19 include, among several others, the wordplay revolving around the giving of Peter's name, the use of the word ἐκκλησία, language regarding heaven and Hades (plus other Semitic wording and phrasing), and possibly the implications of the use of the perfect passive periphrastic construction and the language of binding and loosing.[90] A further traditional criterion is that of embarrassment or of moving against the redactional tendency. This criterion can be divided into its two potentially complementary dimensions at this point. The point of embarrassment includes the closing command of the episode to tell no one that he is the Christ. The movement against the redactional tendency, in terms of Matthaean independence, includes (as already noted above) the introduction of a number of words or grammatical features not characteristic of Matthew, such as the word ἐκκλη-

---

90. See Porter, 'Did Jesus Ever Teach in Greek?', p. 230; cf. *idem*, 'Vague Verbs, Periphrastics, and Matthew 16:19', *FN* 1 (1988), pp. 154-73, esp. pp. 171-72; repr. in *idem*, *Studies in the Greek New Testament*, pp. 103-23, esp. pp. 121-23; O. Cullmann, *Petrus: Jünger—Apostel—Märtyrer* (Berlin: Evangelische Verlagsanstalt, 2nd edn, 1961; *Peter: Disciple, Apostle, Martyr: A Historical and Theological Study* [trans. F.V. Filson; London: SCM Press, 1962]), pp. 176-217 (although Mt. 16.17-19 need not have originated in a passion context: see R.H. Gundry, 'The Narrative Framework of Matthew XVI.17-19: A Critique of Professor Cullmann's Hypothesis', *NovT* 7 [1964], pp. 1-9); M. Wilcox, 'Peter and the Rock: A Fresh Look at Matthew 16:17-19', *NTS* 22 (1975), pp. 73-88; Davies and Allison, *Matthew*, II, pp. 602-43 (at least regarding vv. 17-19); Hagner, *Matthew*, II, pp. 465-66.

σία, the perfect passive periphrastic construction (cf. Mt. 18.18), and the language of binding and loosing.[91] The last traditional criterion to note is that of historical plausibility, especially in terms of the setting in the life of Jesus and his disciples. In other words, it is historically plausible that Jesus would discuss such issues as his perceived identity, as seen by others and by his closest followers, in the course of his ministry, especially before turning towards Jerusalem.[92] There are also features of the longer passage in Matthew that indicate a Jewish background (the criterion of Semitic language phenomena), but also authenticity in Greek, such as the wordplay on Peter's name, and invoking the concepts of binding and loosing.[93] This treatment illustrates how this new Greek language criterion can be used, especially in relation to the traditional criteria.

Three further episodes are worth considering as having reasonably high probability of authenticity. (2) The second episode is Jesus' trial before Pilate. The criteria of multiple attestation (see above and Chapter 5, below, for further discussion of this criterion in relation to this episode), of moving against the redactional tendency,[94] of historical plausibility, and of execution or historical consequence[95]—a noteworthily

91. On both dimensions, see the evidence and sources cited in Porter, 'Vague Verbs', pp. 168-69, 155-62; *idem, Studies in the Greek New Testament*, pp. 118-20, 104-12.

92. Whether one believes that Jesus had messianic consciousness or not, it is still historically plausible to think that he asked the question of what others thought of him. On some of the issues, see Davies and Allison, *Matthew*, II, pp. 594-601.

93. See Porter, 'Did Jesus Ever Teach in Greek?', pp. 230-31, 232-35; *idem, Studies in the Greek New Testament*, pp. 167-68, 169-71, 121-23; following B.F. Meyer, *The Aims of Jesus* (London: SCM Press, 1979), pp. 185-97; cf. also Davies and Allison, *Matthew*, II, pp. 608-15; Hagner, *Matthew*, II, pp. 465-66.

94. The criterion of movement against the redactional tendency includes the use of specific language not found elsewhere in the Gospels, as noted and discussed in Chapter 5, below.

95. From the episode, it is clear that Jesus' agreement with Pilate that he is king of the Jews (Mk 15.9, 12 follow on from a positive response in 15.2; Lk. 23.11 depends on a positive response in Lk. 23.3; and Jn 18.39 depends on a positive answer in 18.37) contributes directly to the historical consequence of his execution. Some scholars have wished either to deny or to downplay as passively affirmative Jesus' response to Pilate, but this does not seem to be the best interpretation. See J. Irmscher, 'Σὺ λέγεις (Mk. 15,2—Mt. 27,11—Lk. 23,3)', *Studii Clasice* 2 (1960), pp. 151-58, who surveys scholarly opinion; D.R. Catchpole, 'The Answer of Jesus to Caiaphas (Matt. xxvi.64)', *NTS* 17 (1970–71), pp. 213-26; and, most recently,

wide range and number of criteria—would all seem to have relevance here in support of Jesus uttering any statements he made in Greek. (3) The third episode is Jesus' conversation with the centurion or commander. The criteria of importance for establishing this probability are those of multiple attestation (see above), of embarrassment or of movement against the redactional tendency,[96] and of historical plausibility. (4) The fourth and final episode with reasonably high probability of authenticity is Jesus' conversation with the Syrophoenician or Canaanite woman. The criteria of importance here include those of multiple attestation (see above, and Chapter 5), of embarrassment or movement against the redactional tendency,[97] and of historical plausibility.

There is reasonable probability that there are authentic words of Jesus in two further passages worth noting. (1) The first episode is the conversation with the Pharisees and Herodians over Caesar's coin. Here the criteria of direct relevance are those of *possible* multiple attestation (see Chapter 5, below), of embarrassment or of movement against the redactional tendency,[98] of execution or historical consequence, and of historical plausibility. (2) The second episode is the calling of Levi. The criteria of importance here are those of embarrassment,[99] and of historical plausibility.

R.E. Brown, *The Death of the Messiah: From Gethsemane to the Grave* (2 vols.; ABRL; New York: Doubleday; London: Chapman, 1994), I, pp. 488-93, 733.

96. The criterion of embarrassment or of movement against the redactional tendency is seen in Jesus' commendation of a non-Jew for faith not seen in Israel, possibly implying Jesus' omplicity with the Romans.

97. The criterion of embarrassment or movement against the redactional tendency is seen in Jesus seemingly being bested in the conversation with the woman. See M.D. Hooker, *The Gospel According to Saint Mark* (BNTC; Peabody, MA: Hendrickson, 1991), p. 182.

98. The criterion of embarrassment or movement against the redactional tendency includes the apparent colusion of Jesus with Roman authorities and institutions, and denying Jewish institutions. See Hooker, *Mark*, p. 280; L.T. Johnson, *The Gospel of Luke* (SP, 3; Collegeville, MN: Liturgical Press, 1991), pp. 311-12, who cites the evidence from Josephus on how controversial taxation in Judaea under Quirinius was (Josephus, *Ant.* 18.1-10, 23-25; 20.102; *War* 2.117-18; 253-58).

99. The criterion of embarrassment is seen in Jesus' association with and yet apparent non-judgment of a person employed in a profession that falls between the Jewish and Roman worlds, appreciated by neither. See Vledder, *Conflict in the Miracle Stories*, pp. 204-12.

There is some probability that there are authentic words of Jesus in one further passage, Jesus' conversation with the Samaritan woman. The criteria of embarrassment or of movement against the redactional tendency,[100] and of historical plausibility are useful in this context. However, questions regarding John's Gospel and its use of highly symbolic language, as noted above, make it impossible to say more than that the scene is a probable though far from certain one in which Greek would have been used.[101] This is not to say that other episodes in the Gospels do not contain authentic Greek words of Jesus (or that other episodes might also have taken place in Greek that this criterion cannot address), only that this point cannot be argued here on the basis of this criterion, without further confirmatory support from other criteria.

4. *Conclusion*

This criterion of Greek language constitutes an important means of beginning discussion of whether the Greek words of Jesus in a passage are authentic, but it cannot on its own determine whether the words recorded are the exact words of Jesus (see Chapter 5, below, on the criterion of Greek textual variance). This, therefore, is a general criterion that delimits episodes that capture the authentic flavour of the words of Jesus, not a specific criterion that establishes the actual wording. Nevertheless, this criterion can expand the perspective for discussion of the criteria in an attempt to determine the weight of probability that Jesus spoke Greek on a given occasion, and that the words recorded were in fact something similar to those in the Gospel accounts. This criterion does not need to rely upon any of the traditional criteria, so long as the separate phases of the criterion are satisfied, to create the reasonable presumption that Jesus may have spoken in Greek on a particular occasion. However, if these same words are further supported by several of the traditional criteria, such as being recorded in multiple independent traditions or forms, there is further support for the presumption that Jesus, in fact, may well have uttered the words recorded. It is also to be noted that this criterion does not work in the negative, that is, just because

---

100. The criterion of embarrassment or of movement against the redactional tendency is seen in Jesus being depicted as being exhausted and in need of physical refreshment.

101. On the literary character of this passage, see W. Munro, 'The Pharisee and the Samaritan in John: Polar or Parallel?', *CBQ* 57 (1995), pp. 710-28.

words or actions of Jesus cannot be shown by this criterion to have originated in Greek does not mean that they did not, and certainly does not prove that the words were uttered in Aramaic. It simply shows that this criterion cannot be used to argue that the words were spoken in Greek. The corrective value of this criterion for historical-Jesus research is that we should not reject any words or episode as inauthentic, or as the creation of a later Greek-speaking Church, simply because they appear to have been spoken in Greek or were spoken in a Greek-speaking environment, or were spoken to those who appear to have been themselves Greek-speaking. The linguistic environment of Roman Palestine during the first century was much more complex, and allows for the possibility that Jesus himself may well have spoken Greek on occasion.

EXCURSUS: A RESPONSE TO MAURICE CASEY
ON THE LANGUAGES OF JESUS[102]

On the basis of the data presented above in section 2, and the use of the traditional criteria for authenticity (including multiple attestation and dissimilarity to redactional tendencies—both of these are treated in Chapters 2 and 3, above), I have previously discussed several passages where I thought that Jesus possibly spoke Greek. These passages included the following: Mk 7.25-30; Jn 12.20-28; Mt. 8.5-13 = Lk. 7.2-10; and Mt. 16.13-20 = Mk 8.27-30 = Lk. 9.18-21. From this discussion, I showed that we may well have the words of Jesus recorded in his conversation with Pilate in Mk 15.2 (= Mt. 27.11; Lk. 23.3; Jn 18.33), σὺ λέγεις 'you say'.[103] A number of major scholars in the first half of the twentieth century recognized the multilingual linguistic environment of Roman Palestine.[104] Perhaps more impor-

---

102. This Excursus, along with some earlier material in this chapter, is an expanded and developed form of an article to appear as 'Jesus and the Use of Greek: A Response to Maurice Casey', *BBR* 10 (2000).

103. This opinion has been published, in different forms, in Porter, 'Jesus and the Use of Greek', pp. 123-54; *idem*, 'Did Jesus Ever Teach in Greek?', pp. 199-235; *idem*, *Studies in the Greek New Testament*, pp. 139-71; *idem*, 'Greek Language of the New Testament', pp. 110-12; and L.M. McDonald and S.E. Porter, *Early Christianity and its Sacred Literature* (Peabody, MA: Hendrickson, forthcoming 2000), chap. 3; and is to be developed further in S.E. Porter, *The Language of Jesus and his Contemporaries* (SHJ; Grand Rapids: Eerdmans, forthcoming).

104. Besides Deissmann and Moulton, noted above, those in the first half of the century emphasizing the multilingual environment include T.K. Abbott, *Essays, Chiefly on the Original Texts of the Old and New Testaments* (London: Longmans, Green, 1891), esp. pp.

4. *The Criterion of Greek Language and its Context*   165

tantly for the topic that is being discussed here in this Excursus, however, numerous scholars in the second half of the twentieth century,[105] despite the strength of the Aramaic hypothesis, have entertained the same idea—that Roman Palestine's linguistic environment was probably multilingual (with Greek and Aramaic, if not also

129-82; Milligan, *New Testament Documents*, pp. 36-43; Dalman, *Jesus–Jeshua*, pp. 1-37; Vergote, 'Grec Biblique', cols. 1366-67; and Black, *Aramaic Approach*, p. 16.

105. In the second half of the century, among others, see Birkeland, *Language of Jesus*; M. Smith, 'Aramaic Studies and the Study of the New Testament', *JBR* 26 (1958), pp. 304-13; Emerton, 'Did Jesus Speak Hebrew?', pp. 189-202; Gundry, 'Language Milieu of First-Century Palestine', pp. 405-407; S. Lieberman, *Greek in Jewish Palestine: Studies in the Life and Manners of Jewish Palestine in the II–IV Centuries C.E.* (New York: Feldheim, 2nd edn, 1965); *idem*, 'How Much Greek in Jewish Palestine?', in A. Altmann (ed.), *Biblical and Other Studies* (Cambridge, MA: Harvard University Press, 1963), pp. 123-41; Sevenster, *Do You Know Greek?*; Barr, 'Which Language Did Jesus Speak?', pp. 9-10; Fitzmyer, 'Languages of Palestine', pp. 126-62; *idem*, 'Did Jesus Speak Greek?', *BARev* 18.5 (1992), pp. 58-77; K. Treu, 'Die Bedeutung des Griechischen für die Juden im römischen Reich', *Kairos* 15 (1973), pp. 123-44; H. Leclercq, 'Note sur le grec néo-testamentaire et la position du grec en Palestine au premier siècle', *Les études classiques* 42 (1974), pp. 243-55; P. Lapide, 'Insights from Qumran into the Languages of Jesus', *RevQ* 8 (1975), pp. 483-86; Silva, 'Bilingualism and the Character of Palestinian Greek', pp. 206-10; Rabin, 'Hebrew and Aramaic in the First Century', pp. 1007-39; G. Mussies, 'Greek in Palestine and the Diaspora', in Safrai and Stern (eds.), *The Jewish People in the First Century*, pp. 1040-64; *idem*, 'Greek as the Vehicle of Early Christianity', *NTS* 29 (1983), pp. 356-69; Hengel, *Judaism and Hellenism*; *idem*, *Between Jesus and Paul*, pp. 1-29; *idem* with Markschies, *'Hellenization' of Judaea*, esp. pp. 7-18; S. Freyne, *Galilee from Alexander the Great to Hadrian 323 BCE to 135 CE: A Study of Second Temple Judaism* (Notre Dame: University of Notre Dame Press; Wilmington, DE: Michael Glazier, 1980; repr. Edinburgh: T. & T. Clark, 1998), pp. 139-41; Meyers and Strange, *Archaeology*, pp. 73-78; R. Schmitt, 'Die Sprachverhältnisse in den östlichen Provinzen des römischen Reiches', *ANRW* 2.29.2, pp. 554-86; Rajak, *Josephus*, pp. 46-64; B. Spolsky, 'Jewish Multilingualism in the First Century: An Essay in Historical Sociolinguistics', in Fishman (ed.), *Readings in the Sociology of Jewish Languages*, pp. 35-50, esp. pp. 40-41; *idem*, 'Diglossia in Hebrew in the Late Second Temple Period', *Southwest Journal of Linguistics* 10.1 (1991), pp. 85-104, esp. p. 95; B. Reicke, *The Roots of the Synoptic Gospels* (Philadelphia: Fortress Press, 1986), p. 50; Horsley, *New Documents Illustrating Early Christianity*, pp. 6-26; Meier, *Marginal Jew*, I, pp. 255-68; Vorster, *Speaking of Jesus*, pp. 21-36 (revised from *Neot* 24.2 [1990], pp. 215-28), p. 295; H.C. Kee, 'Early Christianity in the Galilee: Reassessing the Evidence from the Gospels', in Levine (ed.), *The Galilee in Late Antiquity*, pp. 3-22, esp. pp. 20-22; J.W. Voelz, 'The Linguistic Milieu of the Early Church', *CTQ* 56.2-3 (1992), pp. 81-97; Millar, *Roman Near East*, p. 352; R.A. Horsley, *Galilee: History, Politics, People* (Valley Forge, PA: Trinity Press International, 1995), pp. 249-51; M. Adinolfi, 'L'ellenizzazione della Palestina', in M. Adinolfi and P. Kaswalder (eds.), *Entrarono a Cafarnao: Lettura interdisciplinare di Mc 1. Studi in onore di P. Virginio Ravanelli* (Studium Biblicum Franciscanum, 44; Jerusalem: Franciscan Printing Press, 1997), pp. 29-35; C.A. Evans, 'Life of Jesus', in Porter (ed.), *Handbook to Exegesis*, pp.

Hebrew), and, therefore, that Jesus may have spoken Greek at least on occasion.[106] Nevertheless, in two recent works, Maurice Casey strongly disagrees with my findings on several accounts.[107] His arguments deserve a response.

One of the first points to notice is that Casey mis-characterizes my position. Regarding the question of the language in which Jesus taught, after rightly noting that most opt for Aramaic, Casey states that 'those particularly expert in Greek or Hebrew have argued that he taught primarily in the one or the other. Recently, Professor S.E. Porter has reopened the question with a vigorous restatement of the view that Jesus taught in Greek. A regrettable feature of Professor Porter's work is that he downplays or even omits important Aramaic evidence.'[108] I explicitly reject the disjunction betwen Greek and Aramaic into which Casey tries to force me, a disjunction that seems so vital to the case that he is making in his monograph (see Chapter 2, above). The question, to my mind, is not whether Jesus taught in Aramaic *or* Greek, but whether there is evidence that he *also* taught in Greek, without necessarily downgrading the fact that he undoubtedly taught in Aramaic. In one article I state:

> Regarding the question of the languages Jesus may have known and used in his itinerant ministry, current scholarly opinion follows the conclusion of Dalman, who stated that, though Jesus may have known Hebrew, and probably spoke Greek (N.B.), he

427-75, esp. p. 447. This is not to say that there have not been those who have disputed this linguistic situation. This survey is meant to show the range of those who see a similar linguistic context, even if they do not draw the same conclusions regarding the language of Jesus that I do.

106. Those emphasizing that Jesus may have spoken Greek include Roberts, *Greek*, *passim*; *idem*, *A Short Proof that Greek was the Language of Christ* (Paisley: Alexander Gardner, 1893); S.W. Patterson, 'What Language Did Jesus Speak?', *The Classical Outlook* 23 (1946), pp. 65-67; G. Bardy, *La question des langues dans l'église ancienne* (Etudes de théologie historique, 1; Paris: Beauchesne, 1948); T. Nicklin, *Gospel Gleanings: Critical and Historical Notes on the Gospels* (London: Longmans, Green, 1950), pp. 290-300; A.W. Argyle, 'Did Jesus Speak Greek?', *ExpTim* 67 (1955–56), pp. 92-93, 383; *idem*, 'Greek among the Jews of Palestine in New Testament Times', *NTS* 20 (1974), pp. 87-89; N. Turner, *Grammatical Insights into the New Testament* (Edinburgh: T. & T. Clark, 1965), pp. 174-88; *idem*, 'The Language of the New Testament', in M. Black and H.H. Rowley (eds.), *Peake's Commentary on the Bible* (London: Nelson, 1962), pp. 659-62; among his other writings; P.E. Hughes, 'The Languages Spoken by Jesus', in R.N. Longenecker and M.C. Tenney (eds.), *New Dimensions in New Testament Study* (Grand Rapids: Zondervan, 1974), pp. 127-43; Selby, *Jesus, Aramaic and Greek, passim*; J.M. Ross, 'Jesus's Knowledge of Greek', *IBS* 12 (1990), pp. 41-47.

107. M. Casey, 'In Which Language Did Jesus Teach?', *ExpTim* 108.11 (1997), pp. 326-28 (328); the bulk of this article is repeated in his *Aramaic Sources of Mark's Gospel*, esp. pp. 65-68, 76-78; cf. *idem*, 'An Aramaic Approach to the Synoptic Gospels', *ExpTim* 110.7 (1999), pp. 275-78.

108. Casey, 'In Which Language Did Jesus Teach?', p. 326; cf. *idem*, *Aramaic Sources*, p. 63.

certainly taught in Aramaic.[109] With this conclusion long maintained, it might seem unnecessary to undertake again an investigation of this topic, except for the fact that it is still not commonly recognized just how strong the probability—even likelihood—is that Jesus not only had sufficient linguistic competence to converse with others in Greek but also even to teach in Greek during his ministry.[110]

Not only that, but along with Casey I recognize that, 'Although it was once thought by some scholars that Aramaic had entered a period of decline in the two centuries on either side of Christ's birth, in the last fifty years many important discoveries have confirmed the significant place of the Aramaic language'.[111] After recognizing some limitations to the Aramaic evidence, I conclude that 'Nevertheless, this [the Aramaic] theory has many important supporters and almost assuredly will continue to dominate scholarly discussion'.[112]

After making the above cited statements, Casey then gives evidence for the use of Aramaic, much if not most of which is listed in my articles, and summatively mentioned above. On the evidence from the Gospels, I agree again that there is evidence that Jesus taught in Aramaic, although Casey's evidence is less substantial than he seems to think. That Jesus is recorded as using Aramaic in prayer or on the cross, that Jesus gave Aramaic epithets to his inner group of disciples, and that his disciples are recorded as occasionally using Aramaic words (all examples that Casey cites) says nothing about the language in which Jesus *taught*. Of the examples he notes, only Jesus' use of 'son of man' seems germane.[113]

---

109. In a footnote, I cite Dalman, *Jesus–Jeshua*, pp. 1-37, along with others who discuss the language options.

110. Porter, 'Did Jesus Ever Teach in Greek?', pp. 199-200; *idem*, *Studies in the Greek New Testament*, pp. 139-40; cf. *idem*, 'Jesus and the Use of Greek', p. 123, for a shorter, though similar, statement, and p. 124, for much the same statement.

111. Porter, 'Did Jesus Ever Teach in Greek?', pp. 200-201; *idem*, *Studies in the Greek New Testament*, p. 140; cf. *idem*, 'Jesus and the Use of Greek', pp. 124-25. Cf. Casey, 'In Which Language Did Jesus Teach?', p. 326; *idem*, *Aramaic Sources*, esp. pp. 76-81.

112. Porter, 'Did Jesus Ever Teach in Greek?', p. 202; *idem*, *Studies in the Greek New Testament*, p. 141; cf. *idem*, 'Jesus and the Use of Greek', pp. 125-26. At this point I offer a lengthy footnote giving a number of scholars who argue for the Aramaic hypothesis and Jesus' use of the language. See Chapter 2, above, and the list of advocates above of the multilingual environment of Palestine, most of whom accept Aramaic as one of the languages.

113. Casey, 'In Which Language Did Jesus Teach?', p. 327; cf. *idem*, *Aramaic Sources*, pp. 65 and 111-21. Not all would agree even on 'son of man', despite the strong protestations of others: Ross, 'Jesus's Knowledge of Greek', pp. 43-46. Note that there are suggestive implications raised recently by C.F.D. Moule, ' "The Son of Man": Some of the Facts', *NTS* 41 (1995), pp. 277-79, with his statements regarding the idiomatic Greek nature of the Greek of ὁ υἱὸς τοῦ ἀνθρώπου. Cf. C.C. Caragounis, *The Son of Man: Vision and Interpretation* (WUNT, 38; Tübingen: Mohr Siebeck, 1986), esp. pp. 173-74. The adjectival attributive genitive pattern, of *nomen rectum* following the *nomen regens* without repetition of the article, was very common in classical Greek (H.W. Smyth, *Greek Grammar* [rev. G.M. Messing; Cambridge, MA: Harvard University Press, 1929; rev. edn,

Even regarding this Aramaic material, however, with which I am in substantial agreement, Casey has introduced several points that I must question. One is his use of the term *lingua franca*. On the basis of the Temple inscription warning Gentiles of the penalty for entry to the inner-court (found in OGIS II no. 598; SEG VIII no. 169; CIJ II no. 1400) being in Greek[114] and the inscription on the shekel trumpets being in Aramaic, and on the basis of Gamaliel purportedly writing three letters, one to Galilee, in Aramaic, Casey claims to have shown that 'Aramaic was the *lingua franca* of Israel'.[115] Several comments must be made regarding his understanding of the concept of a *lingua franca*. Casey is probably right that the Temple inscription was written primarily for Gentiles, but it may not have been written exclusively for them, since the Romans regularly had edicts and similar pronouncements written in Greek for the indigenous population. An example of this is the unilingual (although there are signs that it was translated from Latin, as might be expected) Greek decree of a Caesar forbidding the violation of sepulchres (SEG VIII no. 13).[116] This inscription most likely dates to the first century CE, and was probably erected in Nazareth in Galilee, although both points are disputed. Perhaps not a formal decree but a response by a Caesar to a question regarding these sepulchral violations, this decree would have applied as much to Jews as to anyone else. It can be reasonably assumed that it would only have had significance if those who

1956], p. 294), the Greek of the Ptolemaic papyri (E. Mayser, *Grammatik der griechischen Papyri aus der Ptolemäerzeit* [3 vols.; Berlin: W. de Gruyter, 1906–1934; 2nd edn of vol. 1, 1970], II.2, p. 143), and that of the New Testament, where it is the predominant form (F. Blass and A. Debrunner, *A Greek Grammar of the New Testament and Other Early Christian Literature* [trans. R.W. Funk; Chicago: University of Chicago Press, 1961], §271). In fact, there was an apparent increase in proportion of this attributive genitive pattern to a ratio of two times as frequent as that of the next most common one in the Ptolemaic papyri. This increase makes the idea of Semitic influence on the use of this pattern in the Greek of the New Testament difficult to sustain. See S.E. Porter, 'The Adjectival Attributive Genitive in the New Testament: A Grammatical Study', *Trinity Journal* NS 4 (1983), pp. 3-17, esp. pp. 4-5. A linguistic approach to the 'son of man' problem has recently been proposed by W. Schenk, *Das biographische Ich-Idiom 'Menschensohn' in den frühen Jesus-Biographien: Der Ausdruck, seine Codes und seine Rezeptionen in ihren Kotexten* (FRLANT, 177; Göttingen: Vandenhoeck & Ruprecht, 1997).

114. There is also the report by Josephus that the inscription was in Latin. See Josephus, *War* 5.193-94; 6.124-25, where Titus says that the Jews erected the inscription; *Ant.* 15.417; cf. *Ant.* 12.145. The inscription (of which two instances have been found) is conveniently published in Deissmann, *Light from the Ancient East*, p. 80, and J. Finegan, *The Archaeology of the New Testament: The Life of Jesus and the Beginnings of the Early Church* (Princeton, NJ: Princeton University Press, 1969), pp. 119-20, who prints both versions; cf. Schürer, *History of the Jewish People*, II, p. 222 n. 85; and P. Segal, 'The Penalty of the Warning Inscription from the Temple of Jerusalem', *IEJ* 39 (1989), pp. 79-84.

115. Casey, 'In Which Language Did Jesus Teach?', p. 326; *idem, Aramaic Sources*, p. 78; cf. p. 76.

116. For other editions, see van der Horst, *Ancient Jewish Epitaphs*, p. 159, with commentary on p. 160; Sevenster, *Do You Know Greek?*, pp. 117-18.

read it (or had it read to them) were able to understand Greek.[117] Casey's further argument that some inscriptions have survived in Aramaic proves nothing, since some—if not more—have survived in Greek as well. However, his understanding of a *lingua franca* is obviously limited. No one is disputing that Jews in Palestine often had Aramaic as a first language and communicated with each other in Aramaic.[118] At the time of the return from exile, it is true, Aramaic was the *lingua franca* of the Persian empire, and the Jews had adopted this language for the obvious reasons of enabling them to communicate and do business with their overlords. The extent of a people group, including the Jews, adopting the language of their dominators (whether this is economically, politically or culturally dominant—they often go together) is well illustrated by this point. However, by the time of the first century, the *lingua franca* was Greek, even for many Jews in Palestine, and even if they also used Aramaic to communicate with each other. I find it interesting, if not a bit perplexing, that virtually all biblical scholars will accept that the Jews adopted Aramaic, the *lingua franca* of the Persian empire, as their first language, with many if not most Jews of the eastern Mediterranean speaking it in the fourth century BCE. Many of these same scholars, however, will almost categorically reject the idea that the Jews adopted Greek, the *lingua franca* of the Graeco-Roman world, as their language, even though the social, political, cultural and, in particular, linguistic contexts were similar in so many ways, and the evidence is at least as conclusive.[119]

Further, Casey cites the fact that Josephus claims to have written his *Jewish War* first in Aramaic, but needed assistance from Greek speakers when he wrote it in Greek, as supposed evidence that 'Aramaic continued to be used in Israel for centuries'.[120] I am not disputing that Aramaic continued to be used in Palestine. These statements by Josephus, however, are not as straightforward as Casey represents them. Several issues merit brief discussion. Josephus states in *Apion* 1.50 that he had assistance with rendering *The Jewish War* into Greek, and in *War* 1.3 that he 'translated' it (cf. *Ant.* 10.218).[121] However, Josephus makes no comment on the same process taking place with regard to his *Antiquities of the Jews*. In fact, he states potentially contrary evidence. In *Ant.* 20.263-65, after admitting that his Jewish knowledge outstripped that of others, he states,

117. See Porter, 'Did Jesus Ever Teach in Greek?', p. 220; *idem*, *Studies in the Greek New Testament*, pp. 158-59; *idem*, 'Jesus and the Use of Greek', p. 145.

118. See Porter, *Verbal Aspect*, p. 155. Nevertheless, Jews from outside of Palestine almost assuredly spoke Greek probably as their first language, as noted above, so even Casey's generalization about Jews in Palestine is subject to question.

119. For a clear statement of the linguistic situation, see Vorster, *Speaking of Jesus*, p. 29.

120. Casey, 'In Which Language Did Jesus Teach?', p. 326; *idem*, *Aramaic Sources*, p. 78. That it was Hebrew instead of Aramaic is posited by Birkeland, *Language of Jesus*, pp. 13-14.

121. The word often rendered 'translate' (μεταβάλλειν) has a wide range of meanings, from simply change or transform to translate. See Rajak, *Josephus*, p. 176.

> I have also laboured strenuously to partake of the realm of Greek prose and poetry, after having gained a knowledge of Greek grammar, although the habitual use of my native tongue has prevented my attaining precision in the pronunciation. For our people do not favour those persons who have mastered the speech of many nations, or who adorn their style with smoothness of diction, because they consider that not only is such skill common to ordinary freemen but that even slaves who so choose may acquire it... Consequently, though many have laboriously undertaken this training, scarcely two or three have succeeded... (LCL).[122]

This tangled statement raises a number of questions—was it or was it not easy to learn Greek? Was it something that everyone could and did know, or was it not?[123] Fitzmyer minimizes the significance of this as evidence for the Palestinian linguistic milieu, since Josephus composed his writings in Rome.[124] However, there is probably more to be learned from this statement than some have realized. Josephus says that he went to Rome in 51 CE as an emissary (*Life* 11–13). Although some have doubted that he knew Greek,[125] it is more likely that he was selected for the trip because he could speak Greek.[126] In this respect, Josephus admits respecting the historian Justus, author of a history of the Jewish wars against Vespasian (and known only through what is said about him by Josephus), for his knowledge of Greek, acquired in the Greek educational system in Tiberias (*Life* 34–42, 336–60; cf. also 65, 88, 175–78, 186, 279, 390–93, 410). Further, it is not uncommon to find ancient authors commenting on their literary inadequacies.[127] As a result, Rajak argues that it was not that Josephus did not have a knowledge of what she calls 'the ordinary [Greek] language, spoken or written', but that Josephus had not been

---

122. As Louis Feldman reminds readers (L.H. Feldman [trans.], *Josephus Jewish Antiquities Book XX General Index* [LCL, 456; Cambridge, MA: Harvard University Press, 1965], pp. 139-40), 'there were many Jews, including rabbis, who knew the Greek language and literature well'. The classic example, perhaps, is the statement in Rabbi Simeon, son of Gamaliel I that, of his father's 1000 students at the begining of the second century, 500 studied Torah and 500 studied Greek wisdom (*t. Soṭ.* 15.8; *b. Soṭ.* 49b). Numerous loan words from Greek have been found in Jewish writings, including over 1500 in the Talmud, and Greek personal names were often found in Jewish writings. It is difficult to know how much use of Greek these factors suggest. See Schürer, *History of the Jewish People*, II, pp. 53-54, 73-74; Lieberman, *Greek in Jewish Palestine*, pp. 1-67. What is noteworthy is that despite the two Jewish revolts in Palestine, which may well have turned Jews away from Graeco-Roman culture, the evidence for Jewish loan words in Greek is apparently heaviest in the third and fourth centuries CE.

123. See Sevenster, *Do You Know Greek?*, pp. 61-76.

124. Fitzmyer, 'Languages of Palestine', p. 139.

125. See H.St.J. Thackeray, *Josephus: The Man and the Historian* (1929; repr. New York: Ktav, 1967), p. 102.

126. Barr, 'Hebrew, Aramaic and Greek', p. 113. After all, Juvenal called Rome 'a Greek town' (3.61).

127. See Rajak, *Josephus*, pp. 47-48, who cites A. Postumius Albinus, rebuked by the elder Cato for his undue modesty, according to Aulus Gellius (*N.A.* 11.8.2) and Polybius (39.12). See also Cicero, *Brut.* 81; Dionysius of Halicarnassus 1.7.2.

formally educated in the language and could not write the kind of Atticistic prose that would have been desirable in Rome. This was probably due to the aversion of some Jews of the time to this level of Greek education.[128] Thus, regarding the *Antiquities of the Jews*, Rajak believes that it may well have been possible by 80 or 90 CE (after composition of *The Jewish War*) for Josephus to write a lengthy work such as the *Antiquities of the Jews* in Greek.[129] Regarding *The Jewish War*, Rajak raises the question of whether there was in fact any resemblance between the Greek text that we have (which she contends has no Semitisms)[130] and the supposed original Aramaic version. It may be that Josephus revised an earlier draft, which has now disappeared without trace, since later Christians did not preserve the manuscript, possibly because it was of minimal value compared to the Greek version.[131] In other words, one may view these statements of Josephus in very different ways than does Casey.[132]

With regard to my arguments for the use of Greek, Casey cites one sentence in one of my footnotes as indicating my belief that Jesus did not speak Aramaic. In the midst of my presentation of the evidence for Aramaic, already noted above, I refer to the fact that the position that Jesus' primary language was Aramaic is argued by inference. In the footnote I state that 'Some may be surprised that I refer to the "inference" that Jesus spoke and taught in Aramaic. The confirmatory "proof" often marshalled that Jesus taught in Aramaic is the several quotations from Aramaic cited in the Gospels. By this reasoning it is more plausible to argue that Jesus did most of his teaching in Greek, since the Gospels are all Greek documents.'[133] Of course, taking only the last sentence out of context, and disregarding how it is used by me, one could understand the opposite of what the context of my discussion indicates. Casey makes further sweeping statements about my supposed failure to differentiate material properly. When I refer to Galilee being 'completely surrounded by hellenistic culture', he counters that 'This hellenistic culture was however Gentile, and its presence in cities such as Tyre and Scythopolis is entirely consistent with its rejection by Aramaic-speaking Jews'.[134]

128. Rajak, *Josephus*, pp. 51-52; and Wise, 'Languages of Palestine', p. 440. Cf. P. Bilde, *Flavius Josephus between Jerusalem and Rome: His Life, his Works, and their Importance* (JSPSup, 2; Sheffield: JSOT Press, 1988), p. 62.

129. Rajak, *Josephus*, p. 233.

130. This reflects the view that the one supposed Semitism in Josephus (προστιθέναι meaning 'again') has been paralleled in non-Semitic Greek. For discussion, and bibliography, see Porter, *Verbal Aspect*, pp. 119-20.

131. Rajak, *Josephus*, p. 176.

132. On the dangers of the use and abuse of Josephus in New Testament research, see S. Mason, *Josephus and the New Testament* (Peabody, MA: Hendrickson, 1992), pp. 7-34.

133. Porter, 'Did Jesus Ever Teach in Greek?', p. 201 n. 7; *idem, Studies in the Greek New Testament*, p. 141; *idem*, 'Jesus and the Use of Greek in Galilee', p. 125 n. 9. The last sentence is cited by Casey, 'In Which Language Did Jesus Teach?', p. 327; *idem, Aramaic Sources*, p. 65.

134. Casey, 'In Which Language Did Jesus Teach?', p. 327; *idem, Aramaic Sources*, p. 66.

Several points may be made here. The first is that this rejection of Hellenistic culture is not as complete as Casey would like us to suppose, since there has been a range of evidence of various types of economic, linguistic and other forms of acculturation. Perhaps the most obvious are the Jewish funerary inscriptions in Greek.[135] Casey, admitting that they date from the first to the sixth centuries, claims that I do not draw the necessary conclusion regarding *how many* Jews in first-century Capernaum spoke Greek.[136] There seems to be some confusion on Casey's part here. On the one hand, he claims that in Galilee there was rejection of Hellenistic culture. On the other hand, assuming that the use of Greek for funerary inscriptions admits of at least some acceptance of Greek culture,[137] Casey goes on to admit that such evi-

---

135. See van der Horst, *Ancient Jewish Epitaphs*, pp. 23-24: 'that Greek was indeed the predominant language of the Jews becomes even more apparent when one looks at the situation in Roman Palestine. There, too, the majority of the inscriptions are in Greek, not a vast majority to be sure, but at least more than half of them (between 55 and 60%)... It is only in Jerusalem that the number of Semitic epitaphs seems to equal approximately the number of those in Greek. Of course these data shed significant light on the much discussed problem of the hellenization of Judaism in the Hellenistic and Roman periods... If even rabbis and their families phrased their epitaphs in Greek, there is only one natural explanation for that phenomenon: Greek was the language of their daily life.' See also H.J. Leon, *The Jews of Ancient Rome* (Philadelphia: Jewish Publication Society of America, 1960; Peabody, MA: Hendrickson, rev. edn, 1995), pp. 75-92, esp. pp. 75-76. There have been questions raised regarding the linguistic competence demonstrated by the inscriptions in Palestine. Horsley (*New Documents*, p. 21) contends that the Greek epitaphs 'reveal only a rudimentary ability in written Greek', but he does not think this necessarily indicates the level of spoken Greek, which he believes was widespread at the time in Palestine. Lieberman (*Greek in Jewish Palestine*, p. 30), however, takes the rudimentary language to indicate that these inscriptions represent the language spoken by the people and not just the learned. Certainly when compared with the classical inscriptions the language appears to be poor. But as van der Horst indicates (*Ancient Jewish Epitaphs*, p. 24), as poor as the Greek is, it is no different from that of pagan non-literary sources of the time (see also Lifshitz, 'L'hellénisation des Juifs de Palestine', esp. p. 523). Also to be noted is the tomb of the 'Goliath' family, in which over half of the epitaphs are in Greek, much of the writing in better-formed letters than those of the Aramaic inscriptions (see R. Hachlili, 'The Goliath Family in Jericho: Funerary Inscriptions from a First Century A.D. Jewish Monumental Tomb', *BASOR* 235 [1979], pp. 31-65; cf. *NewDocs* 6 [1980–81], no. 23). Further, van der Horst notes that regional variation in the percentage of inscriptions in Greek (e.g. in Rome 78 per cent are in Greek but only 1 per cent are in Hebrew) seems to confirm his view that Greek was actually used by those buried with Greek epitaphs: 'One should not assume that they used Greek only on their tombstones as a kind of sacred language...for their sacred language remained Hebrew, as is witnessed by the many Greek and Latin inscriptions ending in the single Hebrew word shalom, or the expressions *shalom 'al mishkavo* or *shalom 'al Yisra'el*' (*Ancient Jewish Epitaphs*, p. 23). Barr ('Hebrew, Aramaic and Greek', pp. 102-103) cites occurrence of Greek personal names as indicative of the place of Greek.

136. Casey, 'In Which Language Did Jesus Teach?', p. 327; *idem, Aramaic Sources*, p. 66.

137. Horsley (*Archaeology*, p. 170; *idem, Galilee*, pp. 247-49) also raises the legitimate

dence exists, but criticizes me for not specifying the *number* that used Greek. Since my point is that some from that area, including possibly Jesus, used Greek, it appears that Casey has made my case for me. I am not necessarily arguing that all or even a vast majority of Jews used Greek, only that some did, as he seems to be admitting. Casey does not mention the fact that all of the funerary inscriptions at Beth She'arim (near Beth She'an/Scythopolis) from the first two centuries are in Greek.[138] Elsewhere he admits that the *lingua franca* of the eastern half of the Roman empire was Greek.[139] Surely, he does not mean to say the eastern half except Galilee or Palestine, or does he? Whatever Casey may mean, his comment is clearly out of keeping with recent research on Galilee.[140] The latest work on mobil-

question of the relation of spoken to written Greek, as found in the inscriptions, and whether the inscriptions can be taken as indicative of the language used by people. Despite these reservations, Horsley still concludes that 'much of the population of Lower Galilee must been [*sic*] able to communicate a bit in Greek' (*Galilee*, p. 249; but contra *idem*, *Archaeology*, p. 171?).

138. Meyers and Strange, *Archaeology*, p. 85. Eighty per cent of the inscriptions there from the first four centuries CE are in Greek (p. 101). One might well see a trend here that Casey misses. The inscriptions from Beth She'arim are in M. Schwabe and B. Lifshitz (eds.), *Beth She'arim. II. The Greek Inscriptions* (New Brunswick, NJ: Rutgers University Press, for the Israel Exploration Society and the Institute of Archaeology, Hebrew University, 1974), where there is further reference to other Palestinian inscriptions. Questions have been raised about whether those buried at Beth She'arim were local or from the Diaspora or whether many represented reinterment, and whether those buried included any other than simply the higher social stratum. See Sevenster, *Do You Know Greek?*, p. 145; and Horsley, *Galilee*, p. 248. The linguistic features of the inscriptions would argue against their being written only by the higher social stratum, and recent findings indicate that the site, the central cemetery for all Jews, included those from both the Diaspora and Palestine. Besides Schwabe and Lifshitz (eds.), *Beth She'arim*, pp. 201-206, see Z. Weiss, 'Social Aspects of Burial in Beth She'arim: Archeological Finds and Talmudic Sources', in Levine (ed.), *The Galilee in Late Antiquity*, pp. 357-71, esp. pp. 366-67. However, the Greek documents from Masada would tend to confirm the multilingual culture of Jews over a range of socio-economic levels at the time. See H.M. Cotton and J. Geiger, *Masada, The Y. Yadin Excavations 1963–65. II. The Latin and Greek Documents* (Jerusalem: Israel Exploration Society, 1989), esp. pp. 9-10. See also Jewish funerary inscriptions from the first or second centuries in Jerusalem (e.g. *NewDocs* 1 [1976], no. 70).

139. Casey, 'In Which Language Did Jesus Teach?', p. 328; *idem*, *Aramaic Sources*, p. 67. Casey also admits that Greek was used throughout Israel (*Aramaic Sources*, pp. 73-76).

140. Important recent studies to consider are Freyne, *Galilee*, *passim*; *idem*, 'The Geography, Politics, and Economics of Galilee and the Quest for the Historical Jesus', in Chilton and Evans (ed.), *Studying the Historical Jesus*, pp. 75-121; *idem*, 'Jesus and the Urban Culture of Galilee', in Fornberg and Hellholm (eds.), *Texts and Contexts*, pp. 597-622; E.M. Meyers, 'The Cultural Setting of Galilee: The Case of Regionalism and Early Judaism', *ANRW* 2.2.19, pp. 686-702; Levine (ed.), *The Galilee in Late Antiquity*; A. Overman, 'Recent Advances in the Archaeology of the Galilee in the Roman Period', *CR* 1 (1993), pp. 35-58; Horsley, *Archaeology*; *idem*, *Galilee*; D.A. Fiensy, 'Jesus' Socioeco-

ity and modes of transportation indicates that lower Galilee was fully participatory in the Roman world of its day, connected together by a complex trade network that allowed movement of people and goods. Even if people maintained different private beliefs, their public lives were already a part of this Roman world.[141] Responding directly to the kinds of claims that Casey makes, the archaeologist Meyers notes: 'While it is commonplace to assume that the cities of the Decapolis represented a band of gentile cities that contained the extent and spread of Jewish culture, such assumptions are quite misleading'. He goes on to note the complex interplay of Judaism with various cities of the Decapolis, and cites other research that indicates that there was 'a far greater economic exchange system at work between Jewish areas and sites and the cities of the Decapolis than previously assumed'.[142]

Regarding multilingualism, Casey rejects my view that in Palestine the prestige language was Greek. He states that

> We may imagine this view being held at the court of Herod Antipas, and in a technical sense among Aramaic-speaking Jews who used Greek for business purposes. Porter gives us no reason to believe that this was the view of chief priests, scribes, Jewish peasants, or the Jesus movement. In a sense, the prestige language was Hebrew, the language of the Torah... From another perspective, instruction in the halakhah was given to most Jews in Aramaic, into which the Torah was translated. This could be perceived as the central factor, and peasants and craftsmen might operate only among Aramaic-speaking Jews. From this perspective, politics, education and economics were run in Aramaic. Fundamentally, therefore, Jewish people could take a different view of what a prestige language was from that found in the multicultural research on which Porter depends.[143]

nomic Background', in J.H. Charlesworth and L.L. Johns (eds.), *Hillel and Jesus: Comparative Studies of Two Major Religious Leaders* (Minneapolis: Fortress Press, 1997), pp. 225-55, esp. pp. 245-54, specifically on Jesus.

141. J.F. Strange, 'First Century Galilee from Archaeology and from the Texts', in D.R. Edwards and C.T. McCollough (eds.), *Archaeology and the Galilee: Texts and Contexts in the Graeco-Roman and Byzantine Periods* (South Florida Studies in the History of Judaism, 143; Atlanta: Scholars Press, 1997), pp. 39-48, esp. p. 47; cf. also D. Edwards, 'First Century Urban/Rural Relations in Lower Galilee: Exploring the Archaeological and Literary Evidence', in D.J. Lull (ed.), *Society of Biblical Literature 1988 Seminar Papers* (SBLSP, 27; Atlanta: Scholars Press, 1988), pp. 169-82, esp. p. 171; *idem*, 'The Socio-Economic and Cultural Ethos of the Lower Galilee in the First Century: Implications for the Nascent Jesus Movement', in Levine (ed.), *The Galilee in Late Antiquity*, pp. 53-73, esp. pp. 55-60.

142. E.M. Meyers, 'Jesus and his Galilean Context', in Edwards and McCollough (eds.), *Archaeology and the Galilee*, pp. 57-66 (62).

143. Casey, 'In Which Language Did Jesus Teach?', p. 328; *idem, Aramaic Sources*, p. 66. Casey does not mention what this 'multicultural research' is, but it can surely be of no less inherent relevance than the few citations of work on multilingualism and of translation studies that he cites (*Aramaic Sources*, pp. 55, 93-106). Casey's reference to 'the Aramaic into which the Torah was translated' reflects his apparent belief in the targumic tradition already being firmly established by the time of the first century CE on the basis of fragments of what appear to be targums being found at Qumran (*Aramaic Sources*, pp. 33-

The issue of prestige languages involves consideration of a range of social, eco-nomic, linguistic and political issues, and is not nearly so straightforward a matter of personal choice as Casey seems to imply.[144] It is true that the hierarchy of lan-guages in a multilingual environment and their relation to first and second lan-guages may vary, as is the case between Egypt and Palestine.[145] Further, one may well admit that Hebrew would have been the prestige language for some, if not many, Jews in a religious or liturgical context.[146] These are not at issue here. The issue is the relation of Greek and Aramaic, and their relation to the *lingua franca*. It *may* be that there were some Jews who never had any contact with those other than Aramaic-speaking Jews and may also have only spoken Aramaic (I am doubtful, but include this for the sake of argument). Their speaking only Aramaic does not mean that their language constituted the *lingua franca*, as defined above. However, what was the situation for a number of craftsmen and others who did business with those other than Jews in Palestine? Casey admits that some might have been in that sit-uation, and even raises the question of whether Jesus would have known any Greek, since his work as a craftsman may well have taken him to the Hellenistic city of Sepphoris. However, Casey wishes to exclude the Jesus movement from those who spoke Greek.[147] On what basis? The Gospels depict a movement that travelled fairly widely and extensively within Palestine, and had numerous contacts recorded with those who were not Jewish, and not presumably Aramaic-speaking (since the prestige language situation that Casey [wrongly, I think] posits would only apply to Jews). Jews may have wished to take a view such as Casey's, but if they wished to communicate in their line of work or for any other purpose with any one other than Jews, they would have needed to know the prestige language, Greek. Jesus is de-picted in the Gospels as such a person, since he was a carpenter or craftsman (Mk

35). Besides the Targum of Job (4QtgJob), Casey only seems to cite the fragmentary 4Q156 (= Lev. 16.12-21).

144. Others who have confused the issue of prestige languages include Meier, *Marginal Jew*, I, pp. 291 n. 21, 294 n. 39; Grabbe, *Judaism from Cyrus to Hadrian*, pp. 156-58. On prestige languages, where issues of society, power and economics are all brought to bear, see E. Haugen, 'Problems of Bilingualism', *Lingua* 2 (1950), pp. 271-90, esp. p. 278; *idem*, 'Dialect, Language, Nation', *American Anthropologist* 68 (1966), pp. 922-35; repr. in Pride and Holmes (eds.), *Sociolinguistics*, pp. 97-111; Hudson, *Sociolinguistics*, pp. 31-34. The related issue of diglossia is often introduced here (referring to C. Ferguson, 'Diglossia', *Word* 15 [1959], pp. 325-40): e.g. Horsley, *Archaeology*, pp. 158-59; Watt, *Code-Switch-ing in Luke and Acts*, pp. 47-48. For a discussion of the issues, and whether the term is best applied to this linguistic situation, see the essays in Part 1 in Porter (ed.), *Diglossia and Other Topics*.

145. See Porter, *Verbal Aspect*, pp. 154-55.

146. But cf. E.M. Meyers, 'Galilean Regionalism: A Reappraisal', in W.D. Green (ed.), *Approaches to Ancient Judaism. V. Studies in Judaism and its Greco-Roman Context* (Atlanta: Scholars Press, 1985), pp. 115-31, esp. p. 121, who thinks that Aramaic may have become the 'surrogate holy language'.

147. Casey, 'In Which Language Did Jesus Teach?', p. 328; *idem, Aramaic Sources*, pp. 66, 81-82.

6.3), economically a middle level vocation.[148] From Nazareth, near Sepphoris, a thoroughly Hellenized city, a man in his work would have needed to be involved in reciprocal trade, which was widespread in that region.[149] As Kee concludes in his discussion of Jesus in Galilee, 'This means that for Jesus to have conversed with inhabitants of cities in the Galilee, and especially of cities of the Decapolis and the Phoenician region, he would have had to have known Greek, certainly at the conversational level'.[150]

The last issue that Casey raises is that of interpreters. The first instance he cites is that of Titus negotiating with those in Jerusalem. Casey questions my suggestion that it is unknown whose fault it is that Titus was not understood when he addressed the rebels, the situation requiring that Josephus speak in the 'native tongue' (Josephus, *War* 5.360-61).[151] Casey states that 'It is perfectly well known' whose deficiency it was.[152] Casey is correct that Titus was reportedly fluent in Greek (Suetonius, *Titus* 3.2).[153] That does not mean that the situation is as clear-cut as Casey contends, since even if Aramaic was 'the *lingua franca* [*sic*—see above] of Jerusalem Jews'[154] he must contend further that none of those listening had any knowledge whatsoever of Greek. Here is not the place to get involved in the recent debate over the nature of the Jewish uprising and the social composition of the rebels.[155] It is sufficient to note, however, that the major groups of rebels represented those from both rural and urban settings, priestly and non-priestly classes, and from all over Palestine (including also Idumaeans).[156] Is Casey contending that

148. See Meier, *Marginal Jew*, I, pp. 278-85.

149. See Edwards, 'First Century Urban/Rural Relations', pp. 172-76; *idem*, 'Socio-Economic and Cultural Ethos', pp. 55-60; Meier, *Marginal Jew*, I, pp. 278-85.

150. Kee, 'Early Christianity in the Galilee', p. 21. Cf. Overman, 'Archaeology of the Galilee', p. 45: 'we find now that Greek was far more pervasive and influential than we thought even a decade ago'.

151. Note that this is one of only two places in *The Jewish War* that Josephus refers to his 'native tongue' (ἡ πάτριος γλῶσσα), the other being 1.3, treated above. He also refers to the 'Hebrew' in 6.97, but it is unclear whether this is the same language. Josephus in *Antiquities of the Jews* refers to the 'tongue of the Hebrews' or 'language of the Hebrews' or uses similar types of phrases in 1.34, 36, 117, 146, 204, 258, 333; 3.252; 6.22; 7.67; 9.290; 11.148, 286, and to Hebrew in 10.8 and 11.159. See Rajak, *Josephus*, pp. 230-31.

152. Casey, 'In Which Language Did Jesus Teach?', p. 328; *idem*, *Aramaic Sources*, p. 67. But cf. Sevenster, *Do You Know Greek?*, pp. 63-65; Fitzmyer, 'Languages of Palestine', p. 138, who recognize the difficulties in interpreting the situation.

153. A number of the emperors were known for their accomplishments in Greek, even if they had to work hard to realize them. See Suetonius, *Aug.* 89; *Claud.* 42.

154. Casey, 'In Which Language Did Jesus Teach?', p. 328; *idem*, *Aramaic Sources*, p. 67.

155. See J.S. McLaren, *Turbulent Times? Josephus and Scholarship on Judaea in the First Century CE* (JSPSup, 29; Sheffield: Sheffield Academic Press, 1998), esp. pp. 122-78.

156. See D. Rhoads, *Israel in Revolution: 6–74 C.E. A Political History Based on the Writings of Josephus* (Philadelphia: Fortress Press, 1976), pp. 94-149, who discusses the

none of the Jews in Jerusalem during the siege spoke Greek? The episode gives no evidence of even a passive understanding of Greek. From the evidence, one cannot determine whether at least some in Jerusalem during the revolt spoke Greek or not. The situation was a highly politically charged one, where entering into direct communication with the Romans, even if one spoke the same language, may have been politically unwise.[157] There is also the possibility of dialectal interference, and the possibility that if Greek were being used it was being used by some for whom it was a first and others a second or acquired language.[158] A somewhat similar incident is possibly recorded in Mk 15.34, where Jesus reportedly spoke Aramaic, but was apparently misunderstood by those standing by.[159] Does this mean that the listeners did not speak or understand Aramaic (if we follow Casey's logic)? This is certainly one interpretation, but not the only one. When one considers that some of the Jewish rebels came from Galilee, where Greek was spoken, and some were linked to rebels at Masada, where Greek documents have also been found dating to

major rebels or rebel groups and their possible origins and social levels: the Zealots, the Sicarii, John of Gischala, the Idumaeans, and Simon Bar Giora. One must also not overlook the importance of such evidence as the Theodotus inscription (SEG VIII no. 244; CIJ II no. 1404), an inscription commemorating a Theodotus, son of Vettenos, a priest and head of the synagogue, the son and grandson of the head of the synagogue, who himself built a synagogue for the reading of the law and study of the commandments, found in Jerusalem and probably erected before 70 CE. The inscription is discussed and plate reproduced in Deissmann, *Light from the Ancient East*, pp. 439-41, with photograph between pp. 140-41; and discussed in Sevenster, *Do You Know Greek?*, pp. 131-33; and R. Riesner, 'Synagogues in Jerusalem', in R. Bauckham (ed.), *The Book of Acts in its First Century Setting. IV. Palestinian Setting* (Grand Rapids: Eerdmans; Exeter: Paternoster Press, 1995), pp. 179-211, esp. pp. 194-200. H.C. Kee ('The Transformation of the Synagogue after 70 C.E.', *NTS* 36 [1990], pp. 1-24, esp. pp. 7-9; 'Defining the First-Century CE Synagogue: Problems and Progress', *NTS* 41 [1995], pp. 481-500, esp. pp. 482-84) has called the dating of the Theodotus inscription into question. However, he has received virtually no support for his position. The most serious responses on this point are found in Riesner (above); E.P. Sanders, *Jewish Law from Jesus to the Mishnah: Five Studies* (London: SCM Press; Philadelphia: Trinity Press International, 1990), pp. 341-43 nn. 28, 29; K. Atkinson, 'On Further Defining the First-Century CE Synagogue: Fact or Fiction?, *NTS* 43 (1997), pp. 491-502; and P.W. van der Horst, 'Was the Synagogue a Place of Sabbath Worship before 70 CE?', in S. Fine (ed.), *Jews, Christians, and Polytheists in the Ancient Synagogue: Cultural Interaction during the Greco-Roman Period* (London: Routledge, 1999), pp. 18-43, esp. pp. 18-23. See also the Herodian inscription honouring a man named Paris who paid for a stone pavement on or around the Temple, noted in B. Isaac, 'A Donation for Herod's Temple in Jerusalem', *IEJ* 33 (1983), pp. 86-92.

157. Note that in the similar incident in Josephus, *War* 6.95, when Josephus addresses those in the city in 'Hebrew' (*War* 6.97), he positions himself so that he can be heard by all (not just John of Gischala) and earnestly appeals to them (*War* 9.97: πολλὰ προσηντιβόλει), indicating the emotional element involved in the confrontation.

158. See Hudson, *Sociolinguistics*, pp. 24-36.

159. On this topic from a linguistic perspective, see J.M. Watt, 'Of Gutturals and Galileans: The Two Slurs of Matthew 26.73', in Porter (ed.), *Diglossia and Other Topics*.

the rebellion, one cannot help but think that other factors besides linguistic competence entered into the scenario when Titus addressed the Jews in Jerusalem. The situation may well have involved conscious code-switching by the Jews in Jerusalem. In other words, the rebels intentionally reverted to their 'private' language (unknown to the Romans) and feigned inability to understand Greek in order to force the Romans to deal with them on their own terms, that is, by translating into Aramaic, something the Romans would have been loath to do. In any event, we cannot conclude from the episode, in which Titus's Greek was not understood but Josephus's 'native language' was, that no one in Jerusalem during the revolt could speak Greek.

Regarding Jesus' trial before Pilate, Casey criticizes me for not realizing that an interpreter must have been present, since the Synoptic Gospels are 'uninterested in interpreters'[160] and other documents do not mention interpreters. Casey is right that there are a number of problems regarding the Synoptic accounts of Jesus' trial, but it does not seem necessary to create more problems than there really are. For example, in Josephus interpreters are specifically mentioned in *War* 6.96, 129 and 327, indicating that at least some writers are interested in them and do mention them. I may be wrong that there was no interpreter at the trial of Jesus, but I am not alone in thinking that the scenario may be plausible as reported. The conclusion of H.I. Marrou regarding Roman officials is as follows: 'in fact Roman officials could understand Greek and speak it, and they found it better to do without interpreters,' so that, in the East, the cross-examination of witnesses, and the court proceedings generally, were carried on in Greek'.[161] To my suggestion that there is a possibility that we may have some of the actual words of Jesus recorded in the Gospels, a conclusion that seems logically to follow from the evidence that I have mentioned above, Casey says that it is a 'fundamentalist's dream', and 'ultraconservative assumptions are required to carry it through'.[162]

Is it such a 'fundamentalist's dream'? Are ultraconservative or uncritical assumptions required to conclude in this way? Scholars other than simply myself might well have something to say on these questions. As has recently been recognized by one scholar, the 'problem of the language(s) Jesus spoke has to be raised anew in the light of recent discoveries'.[163] Certainly, Aramaic is thought to have been widely

160. Casey, 'In Which Language Did Jesus Teach?', p. 328; cf. *idem, Aramaic Sources,* pp. 67, 82.

161. Marrou, *History of Education,* p. 256, citing Valerius Maximus 8.7.6 and Suetonius, *Tib.* 71. Cf. also Roberts, *Greek,* p. 165; Mussies, 'Greek in Palestine', p. 1056.

162. Casey, 'In Which Language Did Jesus Teach?', p. 328; cf. *idem, Aramaic Sources,* p. 67, where Casey changes 'ultraconservative' to 'uncritical'. Cf. however Casey's most recent comments regarding finding the authentic words of Jesus in Mt. 11.4-6 = Lk. 7.22-23: 'the process of reconstruction simply adds to the arguments for supposing that the words of Jesus are genuine, by showing that they could be spoken and transmitted in the language in which Jesus taught' ('Aramaic Approach', p. 277). Here it appears that Casey and I for the most part simply disagree on what that language might have been, rather than that the goal is a worthwhile one to pursue.

163. Betz, 'Wellhausen's Dictum', p. 11. I note that much of what Betz says clearly

used by Jesus, but 'The fact is that none of Jesus' sayings is transmitted in Aramaic'.[164] More to the point, 'The Gospel writers take it as self-evident that Jesus and his contemporaries spoke and taught in Greek. Even the author of Acts, the only New Testament author to raise the language question, does not doubt Jesus' ability or practice of speaking Greek.'[165] And, indeed, there are Aramaic loanwords and peculiar expressions in the Gospels, as well as place names and other proper names that reflect Palestinian culture. However, 'we now also know that the New Testament sources, even the older ones, are not thoroughgoing translations from the Aramaic… There is no reason, however, to assume that long stretches of texts have been translated from the Aramaic. Most of even the oldest layers of the synoptic tradition give the impression that they existed in Greek from the start.'[166] This formulation raises many questions, a few of which can be pursued here. For example, 'the situation does mean, first of all, that the question of Jesus' language(s) cannot be answered on the basis of the New Testament texts'; any estimation of Jesus' language must 'be based on the linguistic environment of Palestine, and not the New Testament'.[167] The evidence indicates that the assumption of an Aramaic background must be re-assessed, in terms of seeing Palestine as bilingual or multilingual.[168] In fact, 'There was never an early Christian community that spoke only Aramaic which was then succeeded by a Greek-speaking church'. Instead, there was a complex multilingual environment, in which 'Anyone involved in teaching would certainly have expected to be multilingual, at least to a degree'.[169]

Where does Jesus fit within this scenario? The 'evidence we now have is such that a knowledge of Greek can no longer be denied to Jesus'.[170] As a craftsman, who did business in Galilee, Jesus would have needed to be able to converse in Greek. This conclusion 'fits with the picture of the synoptic tradition, according to which Jesus has no difficulty in conversing in Greek with the centurion from Capernaum, Pilate or the Syro-Phoenician woman…'[171] Thus, the ' "roots of the 'Jewish-Christian/Hellenistic' or more precisely the Greek-speaking Jewish-Christian community in which the message of Jesus was formulated in Greek for the first time clearly extend back to the very earliest community in Jerusalem"'.[172] If it is true that the Jesus tradition, at least in significant parts from the outset, existed in Greek, the

---

resonates with what I have published. I am only sorry that I did not know of his article earlier. Casey did not apparently know of Betz's work either.

164. Betz, 'Wellhausen's Dictum', p. 12.

165. Betz, 'Wellhausen's Dictum', p. 12.

166. Betz, 'Wellhausen's Dictum', pp. 12, 13.

167. Betz, 'Wellhausen's Dictum', p. 13.

168. Betz, 'Wellhausen's Dictum', p. 14, citing Hengel with Markschies, *'Hellenization' of Judaea*, pp. 7-8.

169. Betz, 'Wellhausen's Dictum', p. 15.

170. Betz, 'Wellhausen's Dictum', p. 15.

171. Betz, 'Wellhausen's Dictum', p. 15.

172. Betz, 'Wellhausen's Dictum', p. 15, here quoting Hengel with Markschies, *'Hellenization' of Judaea*, p. 18.

'question is, rather, whether the assumption of an Aramaic *Vorlage* should not be given up altogether. It would be much more consistent with both the gospel tradition and the multilinguistic culture to assume that Greek versions of Jesus' sayings existed from the beginning.'[173]

These preceding statements, made by no less than Hans Dieter Betz, provide a suitable backdrop for continuing the discussion regarding the knowledge of Greek in Palestine by Jews, including Jesus, and the use of Greek by him and his first and subsequent followers.[174] Casey has not adequately refuted the case that has been made for the use of Greek, and a way forward would be to avoid unhelpful disjunctive thinking, and to recognize and enter fully into the scholarly discussion the factor of the complex multilingual world of first-century Palestine. This discussion provides a suitable foundation for developing a criterion for authenticity based upon Greek language (see above in this chapter).

173. Betz, 'Wellhausen's Dictum', p. 16. Betz goes on to note that 'If at that time Aramaic versions of sayings of Jesus also existed, they have not been preserved. The existence of Aramaic sayings of Jesus can be assumed, but without further evidence there is no way to either prove or disprove such an assumption' (p. 16). However, one does not need to conclude as a result that, if Jesus spoke Greek, he was a Cynic philosopher. See H.D. Betz, 'Jesus and the Cynics: Survey and Analysis of a Hypothesis', *JR* 74 (1994), pp. 453-75; repr. in *idem, Antike und Christentum*, pp. 32-56, where he is critical of the hypothesis. See now also D.E. Aune, 'Jesus and Cynics in First-Century Palestine: Some Critical Considerations', in Charlesworth and Johns (eds.), *Hillel and Jesus*, pp. 176-92.

174. Betz ('Wellhausen's Dictum', p. 16) differentiates whether Jesus taught in Greek from the question of whether he was able to speak Greek, concluding that one cannot be certain whether Jesus taught in Greek, apart from considering whether Jesus' disciples spoke Greek. At this point, he contends, the answer is unknown, but he advocates further critical questioning. I am not as non-committal as Betz is at this point, in the light of the linguistic milieu in Palestine, especially Galilee, that he outlines above.

Chapter 5

THE CRITERION OF GREEK TEXTUAL VARIANCE

1. *Introduction*

An area of noticeable neglect in recent study of the Jesus tradition is that of textual variants. In two recent articles, my colleague, Matthew Brook O'Donnell, and I have attempted to bring these back into the discussion, both for the words of Jesus and for the activities of Jesus.[1] Much of the groundwork that is laid in these two articles, especially the one on the words of Jesus, is relevant for the discussion of this monograph, and in particular for this chapter. This material summarized here to establish the context for establishment and development of this second criterion. The criterion of Greek textual variance, as will be defined below, is dependent upon broader concepts regarding textual variants in manuscripts. In essence, the methods of textual criticism, so long neglected in historical-Jesus research, suggest a method by which one can utilize the traditions themselves as found in the Gospels to develop a criterion for authenticity. Thus, it is the neglect of this dimension of textual study that must first be addressed, before the criterion can be fully implemented. This criterion will then be employed to analyse a number of select passages, already entered into discussion by the first criterion, that of Greek language and its context (see Chapter 4, above), to see if there is a basis for positing the authenticity of any of the specific words of Jesus in the Gospels.

---

1.   See S.E. Porter and M.B. O'Donnell, 'The Implications of Textual Variants for Authenticating the Words of Jesus', in B. Chilton and C.A. Evans (eds.), *Authenticating the Words of Jesus* (NTTS, 28.1; Leiden: E.J. Brill, 1998), pp. 97-133 (used in section 2, below); and S.E. Porter and M.B. O'Donnell, 'The Implications of Textual Variants for Authenticating the Activities of Jesus', in B. Chilton and C.A. Evans (eds.), *Authenticating the Activities of Jesus* (NTTS, 28.2; Leiden: E.J. Brill, 1998), pp. 121-51. Numerous new textual variants were introduced into these two articles, partly due to a computer glitch at the post-proofreading stage. See the Excursus at the end of this chapter for a list of corrections.

2. *Textual Variants and the Words of Jesus*

When various, specific passages are discussed in historical-Jesus research, such as a kingdom saying or a parable or a pronouncement of Jesus, reference is usually made to pertinent textual variants. For example, in an article on Mt. 23.39 = Lk. 15.35b, Dale Allison notes in his first footnote that there is variation in the wording in these verses, and cites manuscript evidence to which he returns later in his article;[2] and at several places in his discussion of Mk 2.1-12, G.D. Kilpatrick brings textual variants into his analysis.[3] This is to be expected and desired in exegetical work focusing upon the text of the New Testament. Almost inevitably, since they are confined to individual passages, these comments must be limited in what they say about a given variant, since the variant is not seen within any larger context, such as the patterns of variants in a certain manuscript or in a single biblical book. However, if dealing with pertinent variants in a single passage is important to doing historical-Jesus research concerned with the words of Jesus, then it would seem logical to think that exploration of the entire complex of the words of Jesus with regard to their textual variants would also be important. This study would certainly seem to have relevance for many of the traditional criteria for authenticity, specifically that of multiple attestation (is a saying, including particular words or phrases, found in more than one independent source or tradition?).[4] The criterion of multiple attestation, despite the criticisms levelled above in Chapter 2, has a much closer relation to the actual wording of a Gospel text than do others, such as historical coherence, for example. This criterion takes on added significance when multiply attested sources indicate that the words of Jesus were originally spoken in Greek (the criterion of Greek language and its context). So far as it can be determined from the pertinent secondary literature, however, this kind and degree of interest in the actual wording (variant or otherwise) of the words of Jesus is not the case among contemporary historical-Jesus scholars. Thus, before the

---

2.   D.C. Allison, Jr, 'Matthew 23.39 = Luke 13.35B as a Conditional Prophecy', *JSNT* 18 (1983), pp. 75-84; repr. in C.A. Evans and S.E. Porter (eds.), *The Historical Jesus: A Sheffield Reader* (BibSem, 33; Sheffield: Sheffield Academic Press, 1995), pp. 262-70.

3.   G.D. Kilpatrick, 'Jesus, his Family and his Disciples', *JSNT* 15 (1982), pp. 3-19; repr. in Evans and Porter (eds.), *The Historical Jesus*, pp. 13-28.

4.   See Chapter 2, above, for discussion of the criterion of multiple attestation.

two essays mentioned above were published, there was, to our knowledge, no systematic or extended study of how any given variant is to be seen within the context of all of the variants of the words of Jesus in the Gospels.[5]

One of the few works to address systematically the question of textual criticism in Jesus research is Norman Perrin's *Jesus and the Language of the Kingdom*. In it, he addresses the importance of textual criticism as the first step in the hermeneutical process, by making a statement that, I trust, most New Testament scholars would hold to be fundamental: 'we begin by establishing the text to be interpreted'.[6] In his volume, Perrin is concerned with language about the kingdom, and thus proceeds to analyse previous work in this regard. In each instance, he starts by summarizing what previous scholars have done in the area of textual criticism, before analysing their use of historical criticism, in order to get to his area of major interest, literary criticism. In the area of parable research, he notes that work on textual criticism has been done, seeing this as the best possible arena for viewing 'the problems and possibilities' of the hermeneutical approach that he is advocating. He first looks at the work of Joachim Jeremias, concluding that 'it is to Jeremias above all others that we owe our present ability to reconstruct the parables very much in the form in which Jesus told them'.[7] Whereas

---

5.   Three major sources were specifically consulted before arriving at this estimation, and were not disputed by any other evidence subsequently discovered (we would, of course, welcome discovering such a resource). These sources include the extensive study of historical-Jesus research by C.A. Evans, *Life of Jesus Research: An Annotated Bibliography* (NTTS, 24; Leiden: E.J. Brill, rev. edn, 1996); F. Neirynck *et al.*, *The Gospel of Mark: A Cumulative Bibliography 1950–1990* (BETL, 102; Leuven: Peeters/Leuven University Press, 1992), esp. pp. 628-29; and W.R. Telford, 'Major Trends and Interpretive Issues in the Study of Jesus', in B. Chilton and C.A. Evans (eds.), *Studying the Historical Jesus: Evaluations of the State of Current Research* (NTTS, 19; Leiden: E.J. Brill, 1994), pp. 33-74. Similarly, a recent collection of essays extracted from the last 20 years or so of publication of a major journal in New Testament studies, *JSNT*, confirms this picture. There are essays on topics and exegetical issues, and even a section on linguistic and stylistic aspects of Jesus' teaching, but apart from one essay, all of these essays confine themselves to a particular phrase or pericope. See Evans and Porter (eds.), *The Historical Jesus*.

6.   N. Perrin, *Jesus and the Language of the Kingdom: Symbol and Metaphor in New Testament Interpretation* (NTL; London: SCM Press; Philadelphia: Fortress Press, 1976), p. 2.

7.   Perrin, *Jesus and the Language*, p. 101, citing J. Jeremias, *The Parables of*

Jeremias was, according to Perrin, the one to whom so much is owed in this regard, the same he thinks cannot be said of subsequent interpreters. Perrin concludes that, with regard to textual criticism of the parables, the New Hermeneutic of Ernst Fuchs, Eta Linnemann and Eberhard Jüngel 'has little to offer',[8] since they simply follow the work of Jeremias, as did Robert Funk in his metaphorical interpretation,[9] and Dan Otto Via.[10] It is with the work of John Dominic Crossan, according to Perrin, that 'the most important work since Jeremias' has been done in 'establishing the text to be interpreted'.[11]

Two comments may be made about Perrin's work. The first is that, on the basis of the research that is known to me, his work on textual variants in terms of the parables and the kingdom of God is unique. For example, two recent articles on the state of research regarding the parables of Jesus and the kingdom of God in Jesus research do not even mention textual criticism as an area of concern or importance for the current study of the topic.[12] The second comment is that, even with

Jesus (New York: Charles Scribner's Sons, 2nd rev. edn, 1972), who, as seen in Chapter 1, above, wrote during the so-called 'no quest' period. Note that Perrin is also tacitly appealing to the criterion of Semitic language phenomena, since it is the basis for much of Jeremias's work on parables in terms of the teaching of Jesus (see Chapter 2, above).

8.   Perrin, *Jesus and the Language*, p. 120, citing E. Fuchs, *Studies of the Historical Jesus* (trans. A. Scobie; SBT, 42; London: SCM Press, 1964); E. Linnemann, *Jesus of the Parables* (trans. J. Sturdy; New York: Harper & Row, 1967 [= *Parables of Jesus* (London: SPCK, 1966)]); and E. Jüngel, *Paulus und Jesus* (Tübingen: Mohr Siebeck, 1962).

9.   Perrin, *Jesus and the Language*, p. 132, citing R.W. Funk, *Language, Hermeneutic, and Word of God* (New York: Harper & Row, 1966).

10.   Perrin, *Jesus and the Language*, p. 153, citing D.A. Via, Jr, *The Parables: Their Literary and Existential Dimension* (Philadelphia: Fortress Press, 1967).

11.   Perrin, *Jesus and the Language*, p. 166, citing J.D. Crossan, *In Parables: The Challenge of the Historical Jesus* (New York: Harper & Row, 1973).

12.   See C.L. Blomberg, 'The Parables of Jesus: Current Trends and Needs in Research', in Chilton and Evans (eds.), *Studying the Historical Jesus*, pp. 231-54; B. Chilton, 'The Kingdom of God in Recent Discussion', in Chilton and Evans (eds.), *Studying the Historical Jesus*, pp. 255-80. The issue of textual variants is not raised in two similar studies by Blomberg: 'New Horizons in Parable Research', *Trinity Journal* 3 (1982), pp. 3-17; 'Interpreting the Parables of Jesus: Where Are We and Where Do We Go from Here?', *CBQ* 53 (1991), pp. 50-78. Neither do textual variants feature in any significant way in any of the selected essays in the recent collection edited by Chilton: *The Kingdom of God in the Teaching of Jesus*

Perrin's concern, what he seems to mean by textual criticism is the mini-malist agenda of establishing the parameters of the extent of Jesus' words, such as whether he spoke Lk. 16.9-13 in the parable of the unjust steward, not the particular wording and its variants within the parable itself.

There are at least two major reasons why textual variants have been neglected in historical-Jesus research. The first is that some of the prin-ciples of textual criticism seem to move in the opposite direction from the criteria used to establish authentic Jesus tradition, and hence the methods may appear to be at odds. Several of the traditional criteria for authenticity, as noted above in Chapter 2, are dependent upon similari-ties—or even forms of harmonization—in traditions, such as the criteria of multiple attestation and coherence. However, one of the assumptions of much textual criticism is that later scribes are the ones who tended towards conformity of traditions and harmonized them.[13] As Epp says in a recent summary of textual criticism, 'Subtle influences such as par-allel passages, especially in the Synoptic Gospels…led scribes to con-form the texts they were producing to those more familiar parallel forms that were fixed in their minds'.[14] As a result of this and other assump-tions, Epp outlines 11 criteria of textual criticism regarding internal evi-dence, showing 'scribal habits as they functioned in the copying pro-

(Issues in Religion and Theology, 5; Philadelphia: Fortress Press; London: SPCK, 1984). It must be stated, however, that Chilton does show serious concern for the text when he studies individual pericopes in his *God in Strength: Jesus' Announce-ment of the Kingdom* (SNTU, B.1; Freistadt: Plöchl, 1979; repr. BibSem, 8; Shef-field: JSOT Press, 1987), *passim*.

13. It must also be admitted that some of the criteria of textual criticism are in conformity with several of the traditional criteria for authenticity in historical-Jesus research, including adopting the shorter or shortest reading (the assumption being that scribes tended to expand their texts—the criterion of least distinctiveness), adopting a reading that uses Semitic forms of expression (the criterion of Semitic language phenomena), and adopting a reading that does not conform with theology, ideology or the context contemporary with that of the scribe (the criterion of double dissimilarity). On the criteria, see E.J. Epp, 'Textual Criticism in the Exegesis of the New Testament, with an Excursus on Canon', in S.E. Porter (ed.), *Handbook to Exegesis of the New Testament* (NTTS, 25; Leiden: E.J. Brill, 1997), pp. 45-97, esp. pp. 62-63; cf. B.M. Metzger, *The Text of the New Testament: Its Transmission, Corruption, and Restoration* (New York: Oxford University Press, 3rd edn, 1992), pp. 197-98.

14. Epp, 'Textual Criticism in Exegesis', p. 60.

cess'.[15] Most of these text-critical criteria are based on whether a variant does or does not conform to a stated norm, with several emphasizing the difference of the authentic variant from the later harmonized tradition. These text-critical criteria include adopting the harder or hardest reading in a variant unit, since 'Scribes tend to smooth or fix rough or difficult readings'.[16] More specifically, three of these text-critical criteria address the issue of conformity to a parallel. Number 8 states: 'A variant's lack of conformity to parallel passages or to extraneous items in the context generally. Scribes tend, consciously or unconsciously, to shape the text being copied to familiar parallel passages in the Synoptic Gospels or to words or phrases just copied.'[17] Criteria 9 and 10 are similar with regard to Old Testament passages and liturgical forms and usages. In other words, there is a distinct potential for conflict between at least some of the criteria of textual criticism, which emphasize diversity in traditions as indicating textual authenticity, and several of the traditional criteria for authenticity in historical-Jesus research.

A recent study by Craig Evans may well give further insight into a potentially even more significant reason why it is that textual variants have been neglected in recent historical-Jesus research. In his recent study of issues regarding the life of Jesus in a handbook to exegesis, Evans deals ably with source, form and redaction criticism, but does not treat textual criticism. In his discussion of the practice of exegesis, however, Evans turns to linguistic aspects. He rightly states that 'Linguistic study is closely tied to several, and perhaps in some cases all, of the dimensions of Jesus research'. He also rightly notes that four languages were used in Palestine (Aramaic, Greek, Hebrew and Latin, in their order of usage among Jews), but states his judgment that Jesus' 'mother tongue was Aramaic and that he could converse in Greek, but normally did not teach in it'.[18] He then goes on to give examples of linguistic aspects of exegesis, virtually all of which reflect an Aramaic retroversion, and how knowledge of Aramaic helps to understand a partic-

15. Epp, 'Textual Criticism in Exegesis', p. 61.

16. Epp, 'Textual Criticism in Exegesis', p. 63.

17. Epp, 'Textual Criticism in Exegesis', p. 63. Of 104 variant units in Mark where the major manuscripts differ, there are only 13 instances where, in the Nestle–Aland 27th edn, a reading from a parallel passage is adopted. See Porter and O'Donnell, 'Authenticating the Words of Jesus', p. 119.

18. C.A. Evans, 'Life of Jesus', in Porter (ed.), *Handbook to Exegesis*, pp. 427-75 (447).

ular passage in the Gospels. When Evans turns to Jesus' teaching, he discusses three literary types: parables, noting how much Jesus' parables have in common with those of the rabbis; proverbs, where he begins with one that supposedly is found verbatim in the Babylonian Talmud (*b. Ber.* 8b); and prayers, where further parallels with Jewish literature are drawn.[19] In other words, if Evans is at all representative of current practice among scholars (my impression is that he pays much closer attention to the text than do most), when the linguistic dimensions of the words of Jesus are discussed among contemporary historical-Jesus scholars, the tendency is to discuss the Aramaic words of Jesus, not the Greek words. One can understand this tendency by observing Evans's analysis. If Jesus taught in Aramaic, not Greek, textual criticism of the Greek text can easily be dismissed or not even considered. Textual criticism of the Greek text would be an exercise in a form of secondary criticism, since, according to this view, textual criticism would be confined at best to the study of variants in the translated words of Jesus, that is, the concepts represented by the words in Greek, though originally delivered in Aramaic.

This position has become a widespread perspective since the rise of the Aramaic language hypothesis, treated elsewhere in this monograph (see Chapter 2, for a history of this discussion in terms of the criterion of Semitic language phenomena; and Chapter 4, in terms of the issues regarding Palestinian multilingualism). As noted in Chapter 4, early research on the relation among the languages in use in Roman Palestine recognized a complex multilingualism. However, this shifted to the clear domination of the Aramaic hypothesis, that is, that Jesus' language was primarily, if not exclusively, Aramaic. This view has persisted throughout much, if not most, subsequent historical-Jesus research. As an illustration that in many ways historical-Jesus research has not changed through its supposed several quests, one can examine comments on the relation of Aramaic to Greek. For example, during the supposed 'no-quest' period, during which in fact much English-language scholarship continued to examine the historical Jesus, T.W. Manson states this about the relation between the languages with regard to retroversion, and hence potential textual variants:

> At this point a new problem—the linguistic—arises. Up to this point we
> are dealing with Greek Gospels... But the mother-tongue of our Lord

19. Evans, 'Life of Jesus', pp. 455-60.

and the Apostles was not Greek but Galilean Aramaic, so that, even if we could push the analysis of the Greek evidence to its farthest limit, we should be left with the hazardous enterprise of retranslation in order to get back to the *ipsissima verba* of Jesus; and, at the end, we should have no certainty that anything more than an Aramaic Targum of the Greek had been produced. More than that, it may be questioned whether the result would be worth the labour involved.[20]

During the so-called 'second' and 'third quests', the Aramaic hypothesis has remained firmly entrenched, even when typifying Jesus as a Galilean peasant.[21] Thus, Funk *et al.* can state:

Accordingly, *if Jesus spoke only in Aramaic*, his original words have been lost forever. The words of Jesus recorded in the gospels are thus at best a translation from Aramaic into Greek or some other ancient tongue.[22]

In the most recent sustained effort in this regard, Maurice Casey makes a concerted effort to make it worth the labour by laying down 'a standard procedure for reconstructing Aramaic sources from the witness of our Greek Gospels',[23] which he then attempts to work out in four subsequent chapters.

One can readily understand the current neglect of attention to variants in the Greek words of Jesus in the Gospels. There has been a consistent marginalization of Greek and elevation of Aramaic, despite the fact that the evidence itself has not changed, only the ideological and methodological framework in which the evidence is treated. Some of the earliest scholars, who advocated consideration of Aramaic yet within a context in which Greek also was seen to be important (e.g. Dalman), are now marshalled as support for what amounts to an almost exclusive Aramaic hypothesis.[24] The result can only be that the Greek text of the

20. T.W. Manson, *The Teaching of Jesus: Studies of its Form and Content* (Cambridge: Cambridge University Press, 1931; 2nd edn, 1935), pp. 10-11.

21. See J.D. Crossan, *The Historical Jesus: The Life of a Mediterranean Jewish Peasant* (San Francisco: HarperSanFrancisco, 1992).

22. R.W. Funk *et al.*, *The Parables of Jesus: Red Letter Edition* (Sonoma, CA: Polebridge Press, 1988), p. 2 (my emphasis).

23. M. Casey, *Aramaic Sources of Mark's Gospel* (SNTSMS, 102; Cambridge: Cambridge University Press, 1998), p. 107. See Chapter 2, above, for an evaluation of Casey's method and results; cf. Chapter 4 Excursus.

24. Besides those scholars noted above, in Chapter 2 with regard to the criterion of Semitic language phenomena, and in Chapter 4 concerning recent proposals regarding the language of Jesus (e.g. Meyer, Nestle, Blass, Dalman, Burney, Manson, Jeremias, Torrey, Black, Bardy, Fitzmyer, Lapide, Wilcox, Chilton, Evans, Wise and

New Testament, which has the textual variants, is reduced in significance, since it is not the words of Jesus in this text that are being discussed, but the thoughts or reconstructed words of Jesus that lie behind them.

In recent discussion, however, the Aramaic hypothesis has rightly come into question among a number of scholars. As discussed especially in Chapter 2, above (see also Chapters 3 and 4), Meier has noted that it does not suffice as an adequate criterion for distinguishing the words of Jesus.[25] There are three major reasons for this. The first is that presumably others besides Jesus in the early Church also spoke Aramaic, so that even though Jesus may have said something in Aramaic, so may any number of others. Thus, even those who claim that they can retrovert into Aramaic from Greek may still be left without a basis for authenticating words of Jesus, but only Aramaic words of the early Church. The second criticism revolves around the question of retroversion itself. Whether a saying does or does not go easily into Aramaic actually says next to nothing about whether an Aramaic source lies behind a statement of Jesus in Greek. This has been adequately argued in the incisive essay by Lincoln Hurst. He demonstrates that translation is a far more complex process than often realized, and rarely relies on word for word equivalence between languages, so often used in Aramaic retroversion.[26] The third criticism, raised by Hans Dieter Betz, involves simply the lack of direct and sustained evidence for Jesus' and

Casey), other advocates of the Aramaic hypothesis regarding the language of Jesus include the following (the list must be selective in the light of the domination of this theory for the last almost 70 years): P. Joüon, 'Quelques aramaïsmes: Sous-jacent au grec des Evangiles', *RSR* 17 (1927), pp. 210-29; F. Büchsel, 'Die griechische Sprache der Juden in der Zeit der Septuaginta und des Neuen Testaments', *ZAW* 60 (1944), pp. 132-49; E. Schürer, *The History of the Jewish People in the Age of Jesus Christ* (3 vols.; rev. G. Vermes, F. Millar and M. Black; Edinburgh: T. & T. Clark, 1973–87), II, pp. 20-28; L. Feldman, 'How Much Hellenism in Jewish Palestine?', *HUCA* 57 (1986), pp. 83-111; G. Mussies, 'Languages (Greek)', *ABD* 4 (1992), pp. 195-203; L.L. Grabbe, *Judaism from Cyrus to Hadrian* (Minneapolis: Augsburg Fortress, 1992; London: SCM Press, 1994), pp. 156-58.

25. J.P. Meier, *A Marginal Jew: Rethinking the Historical Jesus* (3 vols.; ABRL; New York: Doubleday, 1991–), I, pp. 178-79.

26. L.D. Hurst, 'The Neglected Role of Semantics in the Search for the Aramaic Words of Jesus', *JSNT* 28 (1986), pp. 63-80; repr. in Evans and Porter (eds.), *The Historical Jesus*, pp. 219-36.

the early Church's use of Aramaic.[27] The Aramaic hypothesis is further threatened, of course, by the widespread and significant evidence that Jesus himself may have used Greek in some of his teaching, and almost assuredly in some conversation. It is often forgotten in recent discussion of the Aramaic hypothesis that one of its most important early advocates, Dalman himself, for example, categorically stated that:

> We have a perfect right to assume that Pilate, in putting the question to our Lord: 'Art though the King of the Jews?', did not need to use an interpreter, and that our Lord answered him in the same language: 'Thou sayest' (Mk. xv. 2 f.; Mt. xxvii. 11; Lk. xxiii. 3), even though the form of the answer emanates less from the Greek than from the Semitic idiom (cf. Mt. xxvi. 64).[28]

Thus, in the light of the weaknesses of the exclusively Aramaic hypothesis, and the strength of the Greek hypothesis as noted in Chapter 4, above, the lack of attention to textual variants in the Greek Jesus tradition is a serious shortcoming. The more it is realized that Jesus may have spoken Greek, the more important becomes direct attention to his reputed words—and their textual variants. More to the point for this chapter is the role that textual variants might play in developing a criterion for authenticity of these Greek words of Jesus.

3. *The Criterion of Greek Textual Variance and the Greek Words of Jesus*

Once the criterion of Greek language is introduced, it becomes important to determine not only whether Jesus may have said something like such a statement (see the criterion of Greek language and its context, in Chapter 4, above), but whether he possibly said the very words recorded. There is value for historical-Jesus research in being able to assess the authenticity of the tenor of the words of Jesus (the so-called *ipsissima vox*), obviously since this is the level on which the vast majority of research has functioned for most of this century. However, it would seem that if the criteria for authenticity are able to provide a more

27. H.D. Betz, 'Wellhausen's Dictum "Jesus was not a Christian, but a Jew" in Light of Present Scholarship', *ST* 45 (1991), pp. 83-110; repr. in *idem, Antike und Christentum: Gesammelte Aufsätze IV* (Tübingen: Mohr Siebeck, 1998), pp. 1-31.

28. G. Dalman, *Jesus–Jeshua: Die drei Sprachen Jesu, Jesus in der Synagogue, auf dem Berge beim Passahmahl, am Kreuz* (Leipzig: J.C. Hinrichs, 1922; ET *Jesus–Jeshua: Studies in the Gospels* [trans. P.P. Levertoff; London: SPCK, 1929]), p. 6.

precise tool, such that even the so-called *ipsissima verba* could be assessed, then this level of analysis must be pursued as well.[29] In order to do that, assessment of the stability of the tradition is vital to such analysis. The criterion of Greek textual variance, a modification of attention to textual variants, while it has value for the actions of Jesus, is more relevant for determining whether the Gospels record authentic words in the Jesus tradition (as that terminology is used in historical-Jesus research). So much of the discussion regarding authenticating the actions and words of Jesus has revolved around establishing whether Jesus may have said or done something that approximates what is being discussed. In such a context, variation of wording, even of an important word, regarding an action or utterance of Jesus may not alter the general picture, especially if one is convinced that the original words uttered by Jesus were in Aramaic. However, such a variant in the Greek words of Jesus has far greater consequences, if Jesus himself could have uttered them in Greek. Within a context where it is deemed probable that Jesus spoke Greek, this criterion includes what is normally called textual criticism. However, it extends the concept to include textual variance, that is, variations in wording between traditions. This criterion posits that, where there are two or more independent traditions with similar wording, the level of variation is greater the further one is removed from the common source. Conversely, the less variation points to stability and probable preservation of the tradition, and hence the possibility that the source is authentic to Jesus. It is, of course, only logical to assume that the common source of two independent traditions is earlier than either of them, and, in terms of the Jesus tradition in the Gospels, has a reasonable claim to authenticity.

The criterion of Greek textual variance as defined above requires multiple traditions or multiple forms, which can be shown to be indepen-

---

29. See J.K. Riches, 'The Actual Words of Jesus', *ABD* 3 (1992), pp. 802-804, esp. p. 802: 'The actual words of Jesus—or *ipsissima verba*—refers to the words which Jesus actually spoke. This should be distinguished from the *ipsissima vox* (the very voice), a term which can be applied to sayings which give the sense but not the exact linguistic form of his actual utterances. In this sense, with a very few exceptions (words like *abba, ephphatha*) we simply do not have such *ipsissima verba* of Jesus. He spoke, in all probability, in Aramaic and the NT is written in Greek... Thus the Greek sayings attributed to Jesus in the gospels can at best give the sense of what he said, not the actual form of words.' The intention of this chapter is, of course, to move to what Riches states is desirable, attempting to overcome the limitations he cites.

dent, but that have wording that is similar. The major limitations of the criterion of multiple traditions or multiple forms—its failure to be able to return to the original wording, but only deal with motifs (the major shortcoming); the limitation on the usability of the sources; and even its dependence on the Markan hypothesis—are for the most part overcome by its utilization in a Greek language context, where translation or retroversion is not a part of the interpretive or analytical process. Translation or retroversion forces there to be a shift from the language of the Gospel to a hypothetical source or tradition, trying to capture the *ipsissima vox* of Jesus, but more likely confined, at best, to a conceptual correlation. This new criterion of Greek textual variance builds upon—indeed, perhaps it is better to say transforms—the criterion of multiple attestation into a useful tool within the Greek language context, by allowing the use of multiple traditions or forms without the limitation of a particular source hypothesis and without the creation of an artificial linguistic barrier. If the criterion of Greek language is fulfilled (as argued in Chapter 4, above—or argued for the particular traditions on other grounds),[30] the sources of the traditions being discussed are seen to be independent, and the specific wording of these independent traditions corresponds to each other, there is a strong probability that these specific words are authentic to the Jesus tradition, as that concept is defined in historical-Jesus research. However, there may be both textual variants and textual variance among the differing accounts, which affects the level of confidence regarding the authenticity of the saying.

With regard to the passages that have been examined in Chapter 4, there are four that qualify for further examination in the light of the criterion of textual variance:[31]

30. I attempt to treat this criterion of textual variance as a separate criterion in its own right, so however one arrives at the point of consideration of the Greek wording is another matter than this criterion addresses.

31. The episode of the calling of Levi/Matthew (Mk 2.13-14 = Mt. 9.9 = Lk. 5.27-28), even though it has two words in common in the Synoptic accounts, is not considered here, because the traditions do not seem to be independent. See W.E. Bundy, *Jesus and the First Three Gospels: An Introduction to the Synoptic Tradition* (Cambridge, MA: Harvard University Press, 1955), pp. 142-44. The episode of Jesus' conversation with the centurion or commander (Mt. 8.5-13 = Jn 4.46-54) does not have common wording in the words of Jesus, regardless of what one might think of the independence of the traditions. The episode of Jesus' conversation with the Samaritan woman (Jn 4.4-26) has only a single source.

1. Mk 7.25-30 = Mt. 15.21-28: Jesus' conversation with the Syrophoenician or Canaanite woman
2. Mk 12.13-17 = Mt. 22.16-22 = Lk. 20.20-26: Jesus' conversation with the Pharisees and Herodians over the Roman coin of Caesar
3. Mk 8.27-30 = Mt. 16.13-20 = Lk. 9.18-21: Jesus' conversation with his disciples at Caesarea Philippi
4. Mk 15.2-5 = Mt. 27.11-14 = Lk. 23.2-4 = Jn 18.29-38: Jesus' trial before Pilate.

There are two independent, yet related, stages to the utilization of this criterion. As a first step in the process of testing these Greek words of Jesus according to this criterion, any text-critical issues must be resolved, so that one is comparing decided texts with each other.[32] It is at this point that much previous historical-Jesus research has overlooked variants that might well affect a given pericope. This situation is worth

32. Major works on the principles of New Testament textual criticism include B.F. Westcott and F.J.A. Hort, *The New Testament in the Original Greek*. II. *Introduction, Appendix* (Cambridge: Macmillan, 1881; repr. Peabody, MA: Hendrickson, 1988); E. Nestle, *Einführung in das griechische Neue Testament* (Göttingen: Vandenhoeck & Ruprecht, 2nd edn, 1899; ET *Introduction to the Textual Criticism of the Greek New Testament* [trans. W. Edie; TTL; London: Williams & Norgate, 1901]); A.T. Robertson, *An Introduction to the Textual Criticism of the New Testament* (London: Hodder & Stoughton, 1925); F.G. Kenyon, *Handbook to the Textual Criticism of the New Testament* (London: Macmillan, 1926); J.H. Greenlee, *Introduction to New Testament Textual Criticism* (Grand Rapids: Eerdmans, 1964); B. Aland and K. Aland, *Der Text des Neuen Testaments* (Stuttgart: Deutsche Bibelgesellschaft, 2nd edn, 1981; ET *The Text of the New Testament: An Introduction to the Critical Editions and to the Theory and Practice of Modern Textual Criticism* [trans. E.F. Rhodes; Grand Rapids: Eerdmans, 2nd edn, 1989]); L. Vaganay and C.-B. Amphoux, *Initiation à la critique textuelle du Nouveau Testament* (Paris: Cerf, 2nd edn, 1986; ET *An Introduction to New Testament Textual Criticism* [trans. J. Heimerdinger; Cambridge: Cambridge University Press, 1991]); Metzger, *The Text of the New Testament, passim*. One also must note B.M. Metzger, *A Textual Commentary on the Greek New Testament* (London: United Bible Societies, 1971; Stuttgart: Deutsche Bibelgesellschaft/United Bible Societies, 2nd edn, 1994). Works on textual criticism of non-biblical sources that merit consideration as well include F.W. Hall, *A Companion to Classical Texts* (Oxford: Clarendon Press, 1913); R. Renehan, *Greek Textual Criticism: A Reader* (Cambridge, MA: Harvard University Press, 1969); M.L. West, *Textual Criticism and Editorial Technique Applicable to Greek and Latin Texts* (Teubner Studienbücher, Philologie; Stuttgart: Teubner, 1973). There is a wealth of valuable literature on manuscripts from the ancient world.

serious attention, especially in the light of the dependence of most critical New Testament study on the eclectic Nestle–Aland text. This text
has a number of drawbacks, including its practice of not following
a single-text tradition, its apparent confusion regarding its use of the
papyri, and its dependence upon a potentially misleading manuscript
classification system.[33] These limitations provide sufficient motivation
to explore further with reference to actual manuscripts the significant
variants in any given passage. Nevertheless, within the constrictions of
the eclectic text and its apparatus, just because a passage has a number
of textual variants does not mean that, in many instances, one cannot
judge between variants in order to establish with reasonable probability
the earliest reading of a text[34] (see Chapter 6, below, on discourse features as a criterion for authenticity). Where it is difficult to determine
the most plausible reading of a given text (whether due to internal or
external factors), this obviously lessens the probability that the wording
can be established by this criterion as authentic to Jesus.

If it can be shown that the text-critical issues can be decided satisfac-
torily, then one can move to the next stage of comparing traditions, to
determine textual variance. Textual variances are places where multiple
accounts (whether these be found in traditions or sources) have similar
wording, but wording which varies in some ways. Textual variances
clearly differ in their tendencies, but they all reveal that the tradition
has been altered at some stage in its transmission. The variations point
to attempts to harmonize disparate wording, in order to show Jesus as
saying the exact same thing in parallel accounts, or to smooth out awkward constructions or avoid difficult or troublesome words or phrases.
An instance with significant variance would indicate that, on the basis
of multiple traditions and the Greek language criterion, Jesus may have
said something like this, but without verbal agreement, it cannot be de-

33. See S.E. Porter, 'Why so Many Holes in the Papyrological Evidence for the
Greek New Testament?', in K. van Kampen and S. McKendrick (eds.), *The Bible as
Book: The Transmission of the Greek Text* (London: British Library Publications;
Grand Haven, MI: Scriptorium, forthcoming 2000).

34. Questions about the viability of using textual criticism to establish an original text, and the relation between a canonical and original text, are raised by K.D.
Clarke, 'Original Text or Canonical Text? Questioning the Shape of the New Testament Text We Translate', in S.E. Porter and R.S. Hess (eds.), *Translating the
Bible: Problems and Prospects* (JSNTSup, 173; Sheffield: Sheffield Academic Press,
1999), pp. 281-322.

termined exactly what he said. There are at least five major types of variances in the words of Jesus: addition/insertion (add), where words are added to a text; subtraction/omission (sub), where a word or more is not included in a text; lexical differentiation/replacement (lex), where differing lexical items are found in texts; morphological variance (morph), where the morphology of a word in the tradition differs; and syntactical word-order variation (synxWO), where the order of words, phrases, or even clauses has been changed.[35] Obviously, the strongest probability of authenticity rests with independent traditions that record the same statement of Jesus word for word, and the longer the passage even the more likely (lessening the chance of accidental similarity for a couple of words).

The various types of variance can compromise the reliability of the findings, though not all in the same ways. A useful initial distinction is to be made between content words and function words, that is, the difference between a noun or verb in a main clause, and such words as 'and' (καί) or 'but' (δέ). Function words include such words as conjunctions, and other words that might be used to place a statement in its larger context. In a given episode, these may well be changed by an author, for example inserting 'for' (γάρ) instead of 'and' (καί) or using no conjunction. One need not necessarily dismiss the rest of the words as inauthentic, however. The author may well have changed these function words in creating his narrative in order to make them fit better their Gospel context, and indicate the nature of their relation to the secondary material (see, for example, below on Mk 7.27). Content words are even more complex. Here too a distinction should be made between types of changes in content words. Radical changes in content, such that a decisively different meaning is conveyed by a sentence (for example, through change of lexical items), would in most instances compromise the authenticity of the statement more than would a morphological change (for example, the change of a verb from indicative to subjunctive mood). Addition and subtraction, if they can be clearly differentiated, may well point to an essential core of what was said, that is, by shedding the additions to a tradition, or accepting only the text that is left after subtractions from a tradition have occurred. Since, in dealing with this Greek language criterion, we are not concerned with trans-

---

35. These are adapted from Porter and O'Donnell, 'Authenticating the Words of Jesus', pp. 105-10, and are used below in the critical apparatus of the Synoptic parallels presented with each of the episodes analysed.

lation from Aramaic into Greek (or retroversion), this criterion cannot rely merely upon synonymous Greek words or those performing similar functions to provide the same level of probability regarding authenticity as the exact same wording would. In such an instance, where synonymous words or phrases are found, one cannot determine which is the original and which is the paraphrase, or at least cannot use them together to prove the authenticity of one or the other. If one has triple tradition, with two traditions agreed against the third, this criterion could serve as one indicator to determine the probability of which reading is authentic, especially if one can explain the origin of the variance in the third.

In each of the following episodes, a Synoptic parallel of the passage, but with only the spoken words of Jesus included, is presented. Along with this is an abbreviated critical apparatus indicating the textual variants in the Nestle–Aland 27th edn, categorized according to the scheme noted above. The parallels are presented in their typical Synoptic format, with Matthew, Mark, Luke and then John. However, the discussion usually begins with Mark, and then treats Matthew and Luke, and then John, according to the usual Synoptic discussions.

a. *Mk 7.25-30 = Mt. 15.21-28: Jesus' Conversation with the Syrophoenician or Canaanite Woman*

Table 3. *Mt. 15.21-28 = Mk 7.25-30*

Mt. 15.21-28	Mk 7.25-30
15.24 οὐκ ἀπεστάλην εἰ μὴ εἰς τὰ πρόβατα []^a τὰ ἀπολωλότα οἴκου Ἰσραήλ.	
15.26 οὐκ [ἔστιν καλὸν]^b λαβεῖν τὸν ἄρτον τῶν τέκνων καὶ βαλεῖν τοῖς κυναρίοις.	7.27 ἄφες πρῶτον χορτασθῆναι τὰ τέκνα, οὐ γάρ [ἔστιν καλὸν]^c λαβεῖν τὸν ἄρτον τῶν τέκνων καὶ τοῖς κυναρίοις βαλεῖν.
15.28 ὦ γύναι, μεγάλη σου ἡ πίστις· γενηθήτω σοι ὡς θέλεις.	7.29 διὰ τοῦτον τὸν λόγον ὕπαγε, ἐξελήλυθεν ἐκ τῆς θυγατρός σου τὸ δαιμόνιον.

^{a} add D ταῦτα
^{b} synxWO 544 καλόν ἐστιν | lex D ἔξεστιν | sub 1293 ἐστιν
^{c} synxWO A W f13 𝔐 καλόν ἐστιν

The first episode is Jesus' conversation with the Syrophoenician or Canaanite woman. This passage is often treated as a Markan episode, since Matthew places the story in Mark's order. However, at only two places in the stories are there significant verbal parallels, and these are Jesus' parabolic words to the woman and her reply (Mk 7.27-28 = Mt. 15.26-27). Independence of the two accounts has already been discussed in Chapter 4, in terms of how the woman is described. Bundy notes further differences between the two accounts, however, drawing attention to features peculiar to Matthew such as the different approach to whether Jesus did or did not enter the region of Tyre and Sidon, Jesus' entering the woman's house, Jesus' travelling without being known or recognized, the heightened dramatic level of Matthew's recording of the event, the role of the disciples in Matthew's account, and the Jewish elements of the Matthaean story (Old Testament language, the title 'son of David' used of Jesus, and Jesus' use of Old Testament imagery with sheep).[36] There are also differences in development, with Matthew having a longer section that establishes the setting and Mark having a fuller description of the dialogue. On the basis of these differences, it is plausible that there are two independent accounts here, possibly a Markan and a Q account of these events.[37] If this independence of the two accounts is accepted, a further analysis of the textual variance can be made.

There is one block of words of Jesus that overlaps between the two Gospel accounts. There are surprisingly few textual variants in this block of words. In Mt. 15.26 and Mk 7.27, there is the text-critical question of whether one should read ἐστιν καλόν or καλόν ἐστιν, a slight alteration in word order. The former is certainly the better attested reading in Matthew,[38] and virtually certainly the better attested reading in Mark.[39] There is also a slight shift in word order in the two

36. Bundy, *Jesus and the First Three Gospels*, pp. 280-81.

37. See Bundy, *Jesus and the First Three Gospels*, p. 280; F.W. Beare, *The Earliest Records of Jesus* (Oxford: Basil Blackwell, 1964), p. 132: 'Here we find for the first time a story which is longer and more vivid in Matthew than in Mark. We can hardly imagine that in this one instance Matthew has expanded his Marcan source, after consistently abbreviating it up to this point. The explanation is rather that he has had at his disposal a second account of the same incident, independently transmitted, and has conflated this with the Marcan story.'

38. καλόν ἐστιν is read in 544 and 1010. D has ἔξεστιν, and 1293 has only ἔστιν.

39. ἐστιν καλόν is read in ℵ B D L Δ Θ *f*¹ 565 700 892 1241 and 1424, with καλόν ἐστιν read in A W *f*¹³ Majority text.

accounts between βαλεῖν τοῖς κυναρίοις and τοῖς κυναρίοις βαλεῖν, with no textual variants noted in Nestle–Aland (27th edn). Apart from these two instances, there is very little significant textual variance between the two blocks of wording. One is on firm ground in noting that Jesus probably used the following words: οὐκ[40] ἔστιν καλὸν λαβεῖν τὸν ἄρτον τῶν τέκνων καὶ τοῖς κυναρίοις βαλεῖν (or βαλεῖν τοῖς κυναρίοις). The invariant words are virtually certainly to be considered authentic by this criterion, with some uncertainty as to word order but not content for the remaining words. Numerous scholars have noted the parabolic nature of these words of Jesus. That they are appropriate to the context of confrontation between a Jewish man and a Canaanite or Syrophoenician woman is further confirmed by the use of the terminology regarding dogs, here a term of derogation (cf. Phil. 3.2).[41]

b. *Mk 12.13-17 = Mt. 22.16-22 = Lk. 20.20-26: Jesus' Conversation with Pharisees and Herodians over the Roman Coin of Caesar*

Table 4. *Mt. 22.16-22 = Mk 12.13-17 = Lk. 20.20-26*

Mt. 22.16-22	Mk 12.13-17	Lk. 20.20-26
22.18 τί με πειράζετε, ὑποκριταί;	12.15 τί με πειράζετε; []ᵇ	
22.19 ἐπιδείξατέ μοι τὸ νόμισμα τοῦ κήνσου.	φέρετέ μοι δηνάριον ἵνα ἴδω.	20.24 δείξατέ μοι [δηνάριον]ᶜ.
22.20 τίνος ἡ εἰκὼν αὕτη καὶ ἡ ἐπιγραφή;	12.16 τίνος ἡ εἰκὼν αὕτη καὶ ἡ ἐπιγραφή;	τίνος ἔχει εἰκόνα καὶ ἐπιγραφήν;
22.21 ἀπόδοτε οὖν τὰ Καίσαρος []ᵃ Καίσαρι καὶ τὰ τοῦ θεοῦ τῷ θεῷ.	12.17 τὰ Καίσαρος ἀπόδοτε Καίσαρι καὶ τὰ τοῦ θεοῦ τῷ θεῷ.	20.25 τοίνυν ἀπόδοτε τὰ []ᵈ Καίσαρος []ᵉ Καίσαρι καὶ τὰ τοῦ θεοῦ τῷ θεῷ.

ᵃ add D K Δ Θ 565 700c 892 τῷ
ᵇ add 𝔓⁴⁵ N W Θ f1 f13 28 33 565 579 2542 ὑποκριταί
ᶜ lex D τὸ νόμισμα
ᵈ add D τοῦ
ᵉ add C* D L f13 892 1241 τῷ

40. Mark 7.27 has the conjunction γάρ, probably included by the author to make a logical transition from the previous words of Jesus that he records. These words are not found in Matthew, and so no conjunction is necessary. On γάρ, see S.E. Porter, *Idioms of the Greek New Testament* (BLG, 2; Sheffield: JSOT Press, 2nd edn, 1994), pp. 207-208.

The second episode to consider is Jesus' conversation with the Pharisees and Herodians over the Roman coin (Mk 12.13-17 = Mt. 22.16-22 = Lk. 20.20-26). This is usually treated as a Markan episode almost wholly taken over by Matthew and Luke.[42] If that is so, then this episode would not qualify for assessment by this criterion, since there is only a single source. However, there are some variances in the wording, especially the words of Jesus, with Matthew and Luke agreeing against Mark (Mt. 22.19 = Lk. 20.24 against Mk 12.15). These variences *might* indicate that there were two independent traditions of this episode, with Mark forming the basis, but with Matthew and Luke knowing the other tradition. If that is the case, then this episode would qualify for assessment by this criterion. I will proceed along those lines, recognizing that most scholars would not agree on this point.[43] In any event, there are a number of textual variants in the pericopes, virtually all of them apparently later attempts to harmonize the accounts.[44]

41. See P. Pokorný, 'From a Puppy to the Child: Problems of Contemporary Biblical Exegesis Demonstrated from Mark 7.24-30/Matt 15.21-8', *NTS* 41 (1995), pp. 321-37.

42. Bundy, *Jesus and the First Three Gospels*, p. 440; Beare, *Earliest Records of Jesus*, p. 212; T. Schramm, *Der Markus-Stoff bei Lukas: Eine literarkritische und redaktionsgeschichtliche Untersuchung* (SNTSMS, 14; Cambridge: Cambridge University Press, 1971), pp. 168-70.

43. W.D. Davies and D.C. Allison, Jr (*A Critical and Exegetical Commentary on the Gospel According to Saint Matthew* [3 vols.; ICC; Edinburgh: T. & T. Clark, 1988–97], III, p. 210) dismiss the minor agreements of Matthew and Luke against Mark as 'insignificant', but do not offer an explanation of their origins. Cf. M.D. Goulder, *Luke: A New Paradigm* (2 vols.; JSNTSup, 20; Sheffield: JSOT Press, 1989), p. 696, who is not so quick to dismiss the differences. See also M.D. Goulder, 'Luke's Knowledge of Matthew', in G. Strecker (ed.), *Minor Agreements: Symposium Göttingen 1991* (Göttinger theologische Arbeiten, 50; Göttingen: Vandenhoeck & Ruprecht, 1993), pp. 143-62. The minor agreements are a notorious problem in source criticism of the Gospels. For a recent study, beside the collection of essays noted above, see A. Ennulat, *Die 'Minor Agreements': Untersuchungen zu einer offenen Frage des synoptischen Problems* (WUNT, 2.62; Tübingen: Mohr Siebeck, 1994), esp. pp. 269-73 on this episode.

44. For example, Lk. 20.23 has τί με πειράζετε in A C D W Θ Ψ f^{13} Majority text, with ὑποκριταί in C, but ℵ B L 0266^vid f^1 892 1241 1424 are without these words; Mt. 22.21 adds the article τῷ before Καίσαρι in D K Δ Θ 565 700^c 892; and Lk. 20.25 adds the same article in C* D L f^{13} 892 1241, and the article τοῦ before Καίσαρος in D. Mark 12.15 also has ὑποκριταί in 𝔓^45 N W Θ $f^{1, 13}$ 28 33 565 579 2542, which is probably too quickly dismissed by Nestle–Aland (27th edn), by not

If these objections regarding independent traditions are put aside and the Synoptic accounts are examined, three blocks of words of Jesus are worth considering. The first is the question Jesus asks his disputants, the second is the wording regarding the coin and inscription, and the third is Jesus' pronouncement. There is only agreement in two of the sources in most instances. Matthew 22.18 and Mk 12.15 agree that Jesus asks the Pharisees and Herodians τί με πειράζετε;, but Luke records neither who Jesus' specific disputants are nor this question. All three Gospels agree that Jesus then asks to be shown a coin, but again there is textual variance. Mark 12.15 and Lk. 20.24 use the term Denarius, while Mt. 22.19 uses a general term for coin (νόμισμα); and Mt. 22.19 and Lk. 20.24 use two different forms of δείκνυμι, ἐπιδείξατε and δείξατε respectively, while Mk 12.15 uses φέρω. The Gospels also all agree that Jesus asks a question regarding the coin. However, Mt. 22.20 and Mk 12.16 have τίνος ἡ εἰκὼν αὕτη καὶ ἡ ἐπιγραφή;, while Lk. 20.24 has τίνος ἔχει εἰκόνα καὶ ἐπιγραφήν;. Lastly, the Gospels all agree that Jesus gave instructions to those listening. Here all three Gospels do generally agree regarding the wording, with a few minor exceptions. Matthew 22.21 and Lk. 20.25 have connecting words (οὖν and τοίνυν) —which Mk 12.17 does not—but they are different ones. Matthew and Luke also have similar textual variants, with the article added to Caesar before the second reference in Matthew and both the second and first references in Luke.[45] The third variance is in word order, with Matthew and Luke having a more usual Greek order of verb followed by object.[46] The essential wording of Jesus' pronouncement is ἀπόδοτε τὰ Καίσαρος Καίσαρι καὶ τὰ τοῦ θεοῦ τῷ θεῷ (with Mark having τὰ Καίσαρος ἀπόδοτε etc.).

---

providing the manuscript evidence for the text they print without this word. A.W. Argyle ('"Hypocrites" and the Aramaic Theory', *ExpTim* 75 [1963–64], pp. 113-14; 'Greek among the Jews of Palestine in New Testament Times', *NTS* 20 [1974], pp. 87-89, esp. p. 89) argues that use of ὑποκριτής in Mt. 6.2, 15, 16 indicates authentic tradition. The use of the word alone, however, does not seem to be able to show authentic tradition, since it may be argued that it is simply a loanword taken over into Aramaic, not evidence of clear bilingualism. See G.H.R. Horsley, *New Documents Illustrating Early Christianity*. V. *Linguistic Essays* (New South Wales, Australia: Macquarie University, 1989), p. 21.

45. This evidence is limited and in the Western tradition (D, etc.), and so is rightly dismissed.

46. Porter, *Idioms of the Greek New Testament*, pp. 292-95.

In other words, if we have grounds for arguing that this conversation took place in Greek (the criterion developed in Chapter 4, above), and if we have two independent traditions (an item of far less certainty), then we have a reasonable knowledge of what those words may have been. We know that Jesus probably asked a question about being tested, asked for a coin, asked a question regarding the image and inscription on it, and made a pronouncement regarding Caesar. However, we have less foundation on the basis of the criterion of textual variance to say with certainty what those actual words were, apart from in a few instances of tripartite agreement as noted above, especially regarding Jesus' final pronouncement.

c. *Mk 8.27-30 = Mt. 16.13-20 = Lk. 9.18-21: Jesus' Conversation with his Disciples at Caesarea Philippi*

Table 5. *Mt. 16.13-20 = Mk 8.27-30 = Lk. 9.18-21*

Mt. 16.13-20	Mk 8.27-30	Lk. 9.18-21
16.13 τίνα []ᵃ [λέγουσιν οἱ ἄνθρωποι εἶναι]ᵇ [τὸν]ᶜ υἱὸν ἀνθρώπου;	8.27 τίνα με λέγουσιν οἱ ἄνθρωποι εἶναι;	9.18 τίνα με [λέγουσιν οἱ ὄχλοι]ˡ εἶναι;
16.15 ὑμεῖς δὲ τίνα με λέγετε εἶναι;	8.29 ὑμεῖς δὲ τίνα με λέγετε εἶναι;	9.20 ὑμεῖς δὲ τίνα με λέγετε εἶναι;

16.17 μακάριος εἶ, Σίμων [Βαριωνᾶ]ᵈ, ὅτι σὰρξ καὶ αἷμα οὐκ ἀπεκάλυψέν σοι ἀλλ᾽ ὁ πατήρ μου ὁ [ἐν τοῖς οὐρανοῖς]ᵉ.

16.18 καγὼ δέ σοι λέγω ὅτι σὺ εἶ Πέτρος, καὶ ἐπὶ ταύτῃ τῇ πέτρᾳ οἰκοδομήσω μου τὴν ἐκκλησίαν καὶ πύλαι ἅδου οὐ κατισχύσουσιν αὐτῆς.

16.19 [δώσω σοι]ᶠ τὰς [κλεῖδας]ᵍ τῆς βασιλείας τῶν οὐρανῶν, καὶ [ὃ ἐάν]ʰ δήσῃς ἐπὶ τῆς γῆς ἔσται [δεδεμένον]ⁱ ἐν τοῖς οὐρανοῖς, καὶ [ὃ ἐάν]ʲ λύσῃς ἐπὶ τῆς γῆς ἔσται [λελυμένον]ᵏ ἐν τοῖς οὐρανοῖς.

ᵃ add D L Θ f1 f13 33 𝔐 με
ᵇ synxWO ℵ² D 579 700 οἱ ἄνθρωποι λέγουσιν εἶναι l synxWO ℵ* οἱ ἄνθρωποι εἶναι λέγουσιν l synxWO f1 λέγουσιν εἶναι οἱ ἄνθρωποι
ᶜ sub D
ᵈ lex L G f1 f13 33 565 700 892 1241 1424 Βὰρ Ιωνᾶ
ᵉ sub B ἐν οὐρανοῖς l sub 0281 f13 565 579 οὐρανοῖς
ᶠ add B2 C* C³ W f13 𝔐 καὶ δώσω σοι l add Θ 0281 1424 δώσω δέ σοι l synxWO D σοὶ δώσω
ᵍ morph ℵ² B² C D f1 f13 33 𝔐 κλεῖς
ʰ morph Θ f1 ὅσα ἄν

ⁱ morph Θ f1 δεδεμένα
^j morph Θ f1 ὅσα ἄν
^k morph Θ f1 λελυμένα
^l synxWO א* B L Ξ f1 892 2542 οἱ ὄχλοι λέγουσιν | lex A 579 1241 1424 λέγουσιν οἱ ἄνθρωποι | *txt* 𝔓⁷⁵ א² C D W Θ Ψ f13 33 𝔐

The third episode for examination is Jesus' conversation with his disciples at Caesarea Philippi (Mk 8.27-30 = Mt. 16.13-20 = Lk. 9.18-21). If the arguments for Matthaean independence presented in Chapter 4, above, are not accepted, then the material in this section derives from a single source, Mark, and there are no multiply attested traditions to compare. However, as noted above, there are significant reasons for seeing at least parts of the Matthaean account as having priority, and hence being independent of Mark, especially for Mt. 16.17-19. If the arguments for Matthaean priority regarding this passage are accepted, the criterion of multiple traditions still limits examination here to two clusters of wording (but not Mt. 16.17-19).[47] I find those arguments for Matthaean independence in this episode at least plausible,[48] and will proceed to examine the variance in the wording.

The first cluster of words has a number of textual variants, and the second has none. The first cluster is Jesus' question to his disciples regarding who he is (Mk 8.27 = Mt. 16.13 = Lk. 9.18). There are textual variants here in all three Gospels.[49] Nevertheless, the core of the question comes through: τίνα λέγουσιν οἱ ἄνθρωποι/ὄχλοι εἶναι;. Matthew alone also has τὸν υἱὸν τοῦ ἀνθρώπου.[50] The variance between ἄνθρωποι in Matthew and Mark and ὄχλοι in Luke is one of lexical replacement, but not one of sense (there is also a change of word order in some manucripts—see Table 5). Probably the word uttered

47. See Beare, *Earliest Records of Jesus*, p. 137; J.A. Fitzmyer, *The Gospel According to Luke* (2 vols.; AB, 28, 28A; Garden City, NY: Doubleday, 1981, 1985), I, pp. 770-71.

48. The arguments for independence, and even priority, of Matthew are presented in S.E. Porter, 'Vague Verbs, Periphrastics, and Matthew 16:19', *FN* 1 (1988), pp. 154-73, esp. pp. 171-72; repr. in *idem, Studies in the Greek New Testament: Theory and Practice* (SBG, 6; New York: Peter Lang, 1996), pp. 103-123, esp. pp. 121-23; following B.F. Meyer, *The Aims of Jesus* (London: SCM Press, 1979), pp. 185-97.

49. For example, there are some alterations in word order in Mt. 16.13, especially in א. See Table 5, above.

50. There are no significant textual variants in the other Gospels to harmonize with this.

would have been ἄνθρωποι, following Matthaean or Markan priority, but one cannot say for certain. The second cluster of words (Mk 8.29 = Mt. 16.15 = Lk. 9.20) has all three Gospels agreeing that then Jesus asked ὑμεῖς δὲ τίνα με λέγετε εἶναι;.

One can conclude on the basis of this criterion that, if we have independent traditions in Matthew and Mark, it is probable that we have the words of Jesus captured fairly certainly in the first question, and virtually certainly in the second. The block of words that Jesus speaks in Mt. 16.17-19 falls outside consideration by this criterion, since there is no multiple attestation.

d. *Mk 15.2-5 = Mt. 27.11-14 = Lk. 23.2-4 = Jn 18.29-38: Jesus' Trial before Pilate*

Table 6. *Mt. 27.11-14 = Mk 15.2-5 = Lk. 23.2-4 = Jn 18.29-38*

Jn 18.29-38			
18.34 [ἀπὸ σεαυτοῦ]a [σὺ]b τοῦτο λέγεις ἢ ἄλλοι [εἶπόν σοι]c περὶ ἐμοῦ;			
18.36 ἡ [βασιλεία ἡ ἐμή]d οὐκ ἔστιν ἐκ τοῦ κόσμου τούτου· εἰ ἐκ τοῦ κόσμου τούτου ἦν ἡ [βασιλεία ἡ ἐμὴ]d, οἱ ὑπηρέται [οἱ ἐμοὶ ἠγωνίζοντο [ἂν]]d ἵνα μὴ παραδοθῶ τοῖς Ἰουδαίοις· νῦν δὲ ἡ [βασιλεία ἡ ἐμὴ]d οὐκ ἔστιν ἐντεῦθεν.			
Mt. 27.11-14	Mk 15.2-5	Lk. 23.2-4	
27.11 σὺ λέγεις.	15.2 σὺ λέγεις.	23.3 σὺ λέγεις.	18.37 σὺ λέγεις ὅτι βασιλεύς εἰμι []f. ἐγὼ εἰς τοῦτο γεγέννημαι καὶ εἰς τοῦτο ἐλήλυθα εἰς τὸν κόσμον, ἵνα μαρτυρήσω τῇ ἀληθείᾳ· πᾶς ὁ ὢν ἐκ τῆς ἀληθείας ἀκούει μου τῆς φωνῆς.

a lex A C² D⁵ W Θ 087 f1 f13 33 𝔐 ἀφ' ἑαυτοῦ | txt 𝔓⁶⁶ ℵ B C* L N Ψ 0109 579 l844

b sub 𝔓⁶⁶* ℵ* Dˢ

c synxWO 𝔓⁶⁰ᵛⁱᵈ ℵ A C³ N Θ Ψ 087 0109 f1 f13 33 𝔐 σοι εἶπον | txt 𝔓⁶⁶ B C* Dˢ L W

d synxWO, sub Dˢ N Θ 0109 0250 𝔐 ἐμὴ βασιλεία

e synxWO A Dˢ Θ 0250 𝔐 ἂν οἱ ἐμοὶ ἠγωνίζοντο | sub B* οἱ ἐμοὶ ἠγωνίζοντο | txt 𝔓⁶⁰ᵛⁱᵈ 𝔓⁹⁰ᵛⁱᵈ ℵ B² L W Ψ 0109 f13 1 33 579 l844

f add A Θ 0109 0250 𝔐 ἐγώ | txt 𝔓⁶⁰ᵛⁱᵈ ℵ B Dˢ L W Ψ f1 f13 33 l844

The fourth and final episode to consider is Jesus' trial before Pilate (Mk 15.2-5 = Mt. 27.11-14 = Lk. 23.2-4 = Jn 18.29-38). The question of Pilate to Jesus and the answer of Jesus to Pilate are the only spoken wording that is multiply attested in the tradition.[51] The Gospels all agree that Pilate's question was σὺ εἶ ὁ βασιλεὺς τῶν Ἰουδαίων; (Mk 15.2 = Mt. 27.11 = Lk. 23.3 = Jn 18.33), with no textual variants or variance in wording. The non-Jewish phrasing 'of the Jews',[52] in conjunction with this criterion, indicates that this was probably Pilate's question to Jesus (whether it was conveyed to Jesus by means of an interpreter or not!— so on any account, we probably have the authentic words of Pilate).[53] Similarly, Jesus' answer, σὺ λέγεις, in the Synoptic Gospels given immediately but in John's Gospel given after elucidation by Jesus and expanded with ὅτι βασιλεύς εἰμι (Jn 18.36-37),[54] has no textual variants

51. See J.A.T. Robinson, *The Priority of John* (ed. J.F. Coakley; London: SCM Press, 1985; Oak Park, IL: Meyer-Stone, 1987), p. 259.

52. See C.E.B. Cranfield, *The Gospel According to Saint Mark* (Cambridge: Cambridge University Press, 1959), p. 457; note that 'king of Israel' would have been more Jewish phrasing. However, as R.H. Gundry points out (*Mark: A Commentary on his Apology for the Cross* [Grand Rapids: Eerdmans, 1993], p. 924), Jews could use 'king of the Jews' in addressing Gentiles, as seen in Josephus, *War* 1.282; *Ant.* 14.36; 15.373, 409; 16.291, 311. The same wording, 'king of the Jews', is found in the *titulus* placed by Pilate, mentioned in all four Gospels (Mk 15.26 = Mt. 27.37 = Lk. 23.38 = Jn 19.19). On the *titulus*, see E. Bammel, 'The *titulus*', in E. Bammel and C.F.D. Moule (eds.), *Jesus and the Politics of his Day* (Cambridge: Cambridge University Press, 1984), pp. 353-64.

53. This might be thought to be a trivial example. However, when the problems with determining the actual words of ancient figures are considered, the conclusion is of greater importance than at first appears. The most well-known instance of this difficulty in New Testament studies is perhaps the speeches in Acts, and their relation to the speeches of other ancients. On this subject, see S.E. Porter, 'Thucydides 1.22.1 and Speeches in Acts: Is there a Thucydidean View?', *NovT* 30 (1990), pp. 121-42; repr. in *idem, Studies in the Greek New Testament*, pp. 173-93; cf. *idem, The Paul of Acts: Essays in Literary Criticism, Rhetoric, and Theology* (WUNT, 115; Tübingen: Mohr Siebeck, 1999), esp. pp. 98-171.

54. See P. Gardner-Smith, *Saint John and the Synoptic Gospels* (Cambridge: Cambridge University Press, 1938), pp. 62-63; C.K. Barrett, *The Gospel According to St John* (London: SPCK; Philadelphia: Westminster Press, 2nd edn, 1978 [1955]), p. 537; G.R. Beasley-Murray, *John* (WBC, 36; Dallas: Word Books, 1987), p. 329. Cf. R.T. Fortna, *The Fourth Gospel and its Predecessor: From Narrative Source to Present Gospel* (Philadelphia: Fortress Press, 1988), pp. 163-64. On the possible meanings of Jesus' words, see R. Bultmann, *Das Evangelium des Johannes* (MeyerK; Göttingen: Vandenhoeck & Ruprecht, 1947; 2nd edn, 1964; supplement

and no variance among the Gospel accounts (Mk 15.2 = Mt. 27.11 = Lk. 23.3 = Jn 18.37). The words themselves, σὺ λέγεις, are only found in these three places in the Synoptic Gospels, clearly indicating that they are not a part of any of the Synoptic Gospels' redactional tendency. The same two words appear also in Jn 8.33, 52, 9.17 and 14.9, but in these Johannine instances they are used, not in a statement, but only in a question, and all of these but 14.9 are not on the lips of Jesus.[55]

Scholarship on the relation between the Synoptic Gospels and John's Gospel, especially in the Passion account, has tended to maintain the independence of the Johannine account, even if, as in recent scholarship, there is seen to be an interlocking of tradition at points.[56] There is also a

1966; ET *The Gospel of John: A Commentary* [trans. G.R. Beasley-Murray; Oxford: Basil Blackwell, 1971]), p. 654.

55. These eight instances are the only ones in the entire New Testament with these two word forms collocated. The plural, ὑμεῖς λέγετε, is used in Lk. 22.70, its only use in the Synoptic Gospels. The construction with an aorist verb form, σὺ εἶπας, appears only at Mt. 26.25, 64. On the meaning of such phrasing, see D.R. Catchpole, 'The Answer of Jesus to Caiaphas (Matt. xxvi.64)', *NTS* 17 (1970–71), pp. 213-26; and R.E. Brown, *The Death of the Messiah: From Gethsemane to the Grave* (2 vols.; ABRL; New York: Doubleday; London: Chapman, 1994), I, pp. 488-93, 733; cf. Davies and Allison, *Matthew*, III, pp. 581-82.

56. There has been much debate by scholars over the independence of the Johannine account, especially whether John's Gospel has an independent Passion tradition. The clear trend over the last 60 years has been to assert the independence of John from the Synoptics. The history of discussion began with belief in the dependence of John on the Synoptics (e.g. B.W. Bacon, *The Fourth Gospel in Research and Debate: A Series of Essays on Problems Concerning the Origin and Value of the Anonymous Writings Attributed to the Apostle John* [London: T. Fisher Unwin, 1919], pp. 356-84; B.H. Streeter, *The Four Gospels: A Study of Origins* [London: Macmillan, 1926], pp. 393-426), but the important work of Gardner-Smith (*Saint John, passim*), followed by Bultmann (*Gospel of John, passim*) and C.H. Dodd (*Historical Tradition in the Fourth Gospel* [Cambridge: Cambridge University Press, 1963], esp. pp. 21-151), turned the tide significantly, if not irretrievably (see D.A. Carson, 'Historical Tradition in the Fourth Gospel: After Dodd, What?', in R.T. France and D. Wenham [eds.], *Gospel Perspectives: Studies of History and Traditon in the Four Gospels*, II [Sheffield: JSOT Press, 1981], pp. 85-145). Although there are those who continue to argue for dependence (e.g. Barrett, *John*, esp. pp. 42-54; R.H. Lightfoot, *St John's Gospel: A Commentary* [ed. C.F. Evans; Oxford: Clarendon Press, 1956], pp. 26-42; F. Neirynck, 'John and the Synoptics: Response to P. Borgen', in M. de Jonge [ed.], *L'évangile de Jean: Sources, rédaction, théologie* [BETL, 44; Gembloux: Duculot, 1977], pp. 73-106; repr. in F. Neirynck, *Evangelica: Gospel Studies—Etudes d'évangile. Collected Essays* [ed.

significant amount of research, recently re-articulated, that the Lukan Passion account is also independent of that of Mark and Matthew.[57] On the basis of the multiple Passion traditions (at least two, if not three

F. Van Segbroeck; BETL, 60; Leuven: Leuven University Press/Peeters, 1982], pp. 365-400; T.L. Brodie, *The Quest for the Origin of John's Gospel: A Source-Oriented Approach* [New York: Oxford University Press, 1993]), those who have argued for independence have continued to prevail (e.g. Robinson, *Priority of John*, who builds on his earlier 'The New Look on the Fourth Gospel', in K. Aland [ed.], *Studia Evangelica* [TU, 73; Berlin: Akademie-Verlag, 1958], pp. 338-50; repr. in Robinson, *Twelve New Testament Studies* [SBT, 34; London: SCM Press, 1962], pp. 94-106; D.M. Smith, *Johannine Christianity: Essays on its Setting, Sources, and Theology* [Durham: University of South Carolina, 1984; Edinburgh: T. & T. Clark, 1987], pp. 95-172; P. Borgen, 'John and the Synoptics', in D. Dungan [ed.], *The Interrelations of the Gospel* [BETL, 95; Leuven: Leuven University Press/ Peeters, 1990], pp. 408-37; *idem*, 'The Independence of the Gospel of John: Some Observations', in F. Van Segbroeck, C.M. Tuckett, G. Van Belle and J. Verheyden [eds.], *The Four Gospels 1992: Festschrift Frans Neirynck* [3 vols.; BETL, 100; Leuven: Leuven University Press/Peeters, 1992], III, pp. 1815-33; cf. on this specific episode R. Schnackenburg, *Das Johannesevangelium* [4 vols.; HTK, 4.1-4; Freiburg: Herder, 1965–84; ET *The Gospel According to St John* (trans. K. Smyth; 3 vols.; New York: Crossroad, 1982)], III, pp. 247-48; R.E. Brown, *The Gospel According to John* [2 vols.; AB, 29, 29A; Garden City, NY: Doubleday, 1966, 1970], II, p. 861). A recent development, still endorsing Johannine independence, is to see a variety of independent pre-Synoptic traditions available, which the Gospel writers, including that of John's Gospel, might have used (e.g. M.E. Glasswell, 'The Relationship between John and Mark', *JSNT* 23 [1985], pp. 99-115; B. Lindars, *John* [NTG; Sheffield: JSOT Press, 1990], pp. 27-29, 44; D.A. Carson, *The Gospel According to John* [Leicester: Inter-Varsity Press; Grand Rapids: Eerdmans, 1991], pp. 49-58). The most recent discussion, and one that sees John using Mark and Luke, is found in M. Lang, *Johannes und die Synoptiker: Eine redaktionsgeschichtliche Analyse von Joh 18–20 vor dem markinischen und lukanischen Hintergrund* (FRLANT, 182; Göttingen: Vandenhoeck & Ruprecht, 1999). Surveys of research include W.F. Howard, *The Fourth Gospel in Recent Criticism and Interpretation* (rev. C.K. Barrett; London: Epworth Press, 1931; 4th edn, 1955), pp. 128-43; R. Kysar, *The Fourth Evangelist and his Gospel: An Examination of Contemporary Scholarship* (Minneapolis: Augsburg, 1975), pp. 54-65; G. Burge, *Interpreting the Gospel of John* (Guides to New Testament Exegesis; Grand Rapids: Baker Book House, 1992), pp. 15-35, esp. pp. 27-28; and J.D. Dvorak, 'The Relationship between John and the Synoptic Gospels', *JETS* 41 (1998), pp. 201-13.

57. These include, e.g., V. Taylor, *Behind the Third Gospel: A Study of the Proto-Luke Hypothesis* (Oxford: Clarendon Press, 1926), pp. 52-54; *idem, The Passion Narrative of St Luke* (SNTSMS, 19; Cambridge: Cambridge University Press, 1972), pp. 86-87 (excluding Lk. 23.3 = Mk 15.2); W. Grundmann, *Das Evangelium*

independent traditions), and this criterion, it is probable that these two words, σὺ λέγεις, are authentic Greek words of Jesus.[58]

4. *Conclusion*

For this second criterion, that of textual variance, to be applied to the words of Jesus, three other criteria or conditions must be operative. The first is that of Greek language and its context, established in Chapter 4, above, or a similar criterion. The second is that of multiple attestation, in a revised form that selects those incidents where there is multiply attested wording, ostensibly uttered in Greek. The third is that there must be words of Jesus in common for analysis as to their textual variance. As a result of applying this criterion, the conclusion can be drawn that there are almost certainly one, and quite possibly a total of four, incidents in which the authentic words of Jesus are arguably preserved. In all four of them, there is a context in which Greek would have been the expected language of communication by Jesus and his conversational partners. In one of the episodes—Jesus' trial before Pilate—there is clear multiple tradition that supports the Greek-language context. In the other three episodes—Jesus' conversation with the Syrophoenician or Canaanite woman, his conversation with the Pharisees and Herodians, and his conversation with his disciples at Caesarea Philippi—there are

---

nach Lukas (THKNT; Berlin: Evangelische Verlagsanstalt, 6th edn, 1971), p. 421; I.H. Marshall, *The Gospel of Luke* (NIGTC; Grand Rapids: Eerdmans, 1978), p. 852 (excluding Lk. 23.3 = Mk 15.2); and J.B. Green, *The Death of Jesus: Tradition and Interpretation in the Passion Narrative* (WUNT, 2.33; Tübingen: Mohr Siebeck, 1988), pp. 9-19 on the history of research and his method, and esp. pp. 77-79, 102-104, 285-87 (cf. p. 327), where he argues that Luke almost assuredly had a source separate from Mark in the Passion narrative, and that Luke knew and used such a source specifically in Lk. 23.1-5 (= Mk 15.1b-5), since, apart from in Lk. 23.3, there are only six words shared by Luke and Mark. However, if v. 3 is removed from the Lukan account, there is a serious break in the continuity of the Lukan account. For a summary of the majority opinion, see Brown, *Death of the Messiah*, I, pp. 737-43. Earlier in the century, and resisting the forces of form criticism, a few scholars argued for clear earlier sources for the Markan account. See, e.g., W.L. Knox, *The Sources of the Synoptic Gospels. I. St Mark* (ed. H. Chadwick; Cambridge: Cambridge University Press, 1953), esp. pp. 115-47.

58. Cf. the similar conclusion regarding the antiquity of the tradition (as well as the independence of the Johannine tradition from that of Mark) in Brown, *Death of the Messiah*, I, p. 727.

plausible arguments to be made for multiple tradition. In all four of the incidents, there are words of Jesus to be analysed for their textual variance. Text-critical variants affect some of these words, and the failure to have verbal parallels in all sources affects others. Once the texts to be compared are established, one must consider the textual variances between them in order to establish the probability of the words reflecting the actual Greek words of Jesus. The results are that we have firm evidence for the actual words of Jesus (and of Pilate) in Jesus' trial before Pilate. We probably have some of the actual words of Jesus in his conversations with the Syrophoenician or Canaanite woman and with his disciples in Caesarea Philippi. In Jesus' conversation with the Pharisees and Herodians we may know the content of Jesus' words, but we cannot establish the exact wording to the same extent. These results are, in some respects, minimal in that the number of words that meet this criterion are not plentiful, but they are nevertheless significant. This criterion is designed to go beyond simply noting that Jesus may have said something in Greek in a given context, and to determine the authenticity of specific words uttered. In that sense, any number of words, no matter how small, that meet the criterion are noteworthy, and need to be weighed in future discussion of the words of Jesus.

EXCURSUS: CORRECTIONS TO TWO RECENT PAPERS

Corrections to S.E. Porter and M.B. O'Donnell, 'The Implications of Textual Variants for Authenticating the Words of Jesus', in B. Chilton and C.A. Evans (eds.), *Authenticating the Words of Jesus* (NTTS, 28.1; Leiden: E.J. Brill, 1998), pp. 97-133.

p. 104, para. 2, line 13: for Larry *read* Lincoln
p. 110, para. 2, lines 9, 12: for ἀσκοὺς *read* ἀσκούς
p. 125, Mk 2.19: for μεθ᾽ ἑαυτῶν *read* μεθ᾽ ἑαυτῶν
p. 125, Mk 2.22: for ῥήξει ὁ οις τοὺς *read* ῥήξει ὁ οἶνος τοὺς
p. 127, Mk 4.28: for ει *read* εἶτα (twice)
p. 127, Mk 4.30: for παραβολὴ *read* παραβολῇ
p. 128, Mk 6.4: for ἑαυτοῦ *read* ἑαυτοῦ (twice)
p. 128, Mk 6.11: for ὃ ς *read* ὃς
p. 128, Mk 7.8: for εντολήν *read* ἐντολήν
p. 131, Mk 9.43: for βληθῆαι *read* βληθῆναι
p. 131, Mk 9.43: for γένενναν *read* γέενναν
p. 131, Mk 9.49: for θυσίᾳ *read* θυσία (three times)
p. 132, Mk 10.43: for ει *read* εἶναι

p. 132, Mk 12.7: for ει read εἶπαν (twice)
p. 132, Mk 12.29: for πάτων read πάντων
p. 132, Mk 13.7: for θοευβεῖσθε read θορευβεῖσθε

Corrections to S.E. Porter and M.B. O'Donnell, 'The Implications of Textual Variants for Authenticating the Activities of Jesus', in B. Chilton and C.A. Evans (eds.), *Authenticating the Activities of Jesus* (NTTS, 28.2; Leiden: E.J. Brill, 1998), pp. 121-51.

p. 122, para. 2, line 7 from bottom: for η *read* ἦλθεν and for ει *read* εἶδεν
p. 122, para. 2, line 2 from bottom: for η *read* ἦλθεν
p. 123, para. 1, line 5: for *14224 read l4224*
p. 123, note 1, line 3: for *subject* (S) *predicate read subject* (S), *predicate*
p. 130, note 15, line 3: for *Testament. read Testament,*
p. 130, note 18, line 2: for ει *read* εἶπεν
p. 131, list line 2 at 6.37: for ει *read* εἶπεν
p. 131, list line 7 at 10.3: for ει *read* εἶπεν
p. 131, list line 10 at 11.14: for ει *read* εἶπεν
p. 131, note 20, line 1: for ὅ ς *read* ὅς
p. 131, note 20, line 2: for ει *read* εἶπεν
p. 132, list line 4 at 14.48: for ει *read* εἶπεν
p. 132, note 24, line 2: for ει *read* εἰπόντι
p. 140, para. 1, line 4: for ει *read* εἶπεν
p. 140, para. 3, line 2 from bottom: for η *read* ἦσαν
p. 144, Mk 2.19: for ειαὐτοῖς *read* εἶπεν αὐτοῖς (twice)
p. 148, Mk 7.17: for οι *read* οἶκον (twice)
p. 148, Mk 6.41: for τοῦς *read* τοὺς (twice)
p. 150, Mk 6.47: for ητὸ *read* ἦν τὸ (twice)
p. 150, Mk 6.47: for μέσωτῆς *read* μέσῳ τῆς
p. 150, Mk 6.47: for ηπάλαι *read* ἦν πάλαι
p. 151, Mk 15.25: for ηδὲ *read* ἦν δὲ (twice)
p. 151, Mk 11.13: for ησύκων *read* ἦν σύκων
p. 151, Mk 11.13: for ηκαιρὸς *read* ἦν καιρὸς

Chapter 6

THE CRITERION OF DISCOURSE FEATURES

1. *Introduction*

The third and final criterion to discuss in this monograph is that of discourse features. Discourse analysis (or textlinguistics) is a fairly recent
development in the field of linguistics.[1] In some ways, it is the multi-
disciplinary development in linguistics that corresponds with the (almost
inherently) multi-disciplinary nature of biblical studies. Drawing upon
the full resources of recent linguistic research, discourse analysis moves
beyond the earlier confinement of linguistics to units no larger than the
sentence, and considers larger units of material, up to and including
entire discourses.[2] Discourse analysis is related to the field of stylistics,

---

1.   For surveys of the major avenues of research, see D. Schiffrin, *Approaches
to Discourse* (Oxford: Basil Blackwell, 1994); and S.E. Porter, 'Discourse Analysis
and New Testament Studies: An Introductory Survey', in S.E. Porter and D.A.
Carson (eds.), *Discourse Analysis and Other Topics in Biblical Greek* (JSNTSup,
113; SNTG, 2; Sheffield: Sheffield Academic Press, 1995), pp. 14-35. Some of the
significant works on discourse analysis in New Testament studies that have appeared
since this article was written, and are not mentioned below in this chapter, include
H. Boers, *The Justification of the Gentiles: Paul's Letters to the Galatians and
Romans* (Peabody, MA: Hendrickson, 1994); D. Hellholm, 'Substitutionelle Gliederungsmerkmale und die Komposition des Matthäusevangeliums', and F. Siegert, 'Die
Makrosyntax des Hebräerbriefs', both in T. Fornberg and D. Hellholm (eds.), *Texts
and Contexts: Biblical Texts in their Textual and Situational Contexts. Essays in
Honor of Lars Hartman* (Oslo: Scandinavian University Press, 1995), pp. 11-76 and
305-16, respectively; E.A. Nida, *The Sociolinguistics of Interlingual Communication* (Collection Traductologie; Brussels: Editions du Hansard, 1996); J. Holmstrand, *Markers and Meaning in Paul: An Analysis of 1 Thessalonians, Philippians
and Galatians* (ConBNT, 28; Stockholm: Almqvist & Wiksell, 1997); cf. S.E. Porter
and J.T. Reed (eds.), *Discourse Analysis and the New Testament: Approaches and
Results* (JSNTSup, 170; SNTG, 4; Sheffield: Sheffield Academic Press, 1999).
2.   See Schiffrin, *Approaches to Discourse*, pp. 23-31. Introductions to dis-

or the study of the definable and quantifiable linguistic tendencies and characteristics that describe or define a given writer's use of language, often in terms of a particular discourse or subject matter. Stylistics is an area of investigation that is often mentioned as important in the standard textual-criticism handbooks, but has not figured into textual criticism in a particularly rigorous way.[3] The reasons for this are several. One is the limitation of the way that most textual criticism is done, that is, on an *ad hoc* and instance by instance basis that does not allow for analysis of the larger patterns of linguistic usage that are so important for stylistic study. Another is the limitations in the field of stylistics itself, especially as it has traditionally been practised in biblical studies. Only within the last 40 years or so has stylistics developed in its own right into a discipline that is capable of appreciating differences between authors and among works.[4] Those who have used it in biblical studies,

course analysis abound. The best is probably still G. Brown and G. Yule, *Discourse Analysis* (CTL; Cambridge: Cambridge University Press, 1983).

3. See, e.g., B.M. Metzger, *The Text of the New Testament: Its Transmission, Corruption, and Restoration* (New York: Oxford University Press, 3rd edn, 1992), p. 210; K. Aland and B. Aland, *Der Text des Neuen Testaments* (Stuttgart: Deutsche Bibelgesellschaft, 2nd edn, 1981; ET *The Text of the New Testament: An Introduction to the Critical Editions and to the Theory and Practice of Modern Textual Criticism* [trans. E.F. Rhodes; Grand Rapids: Eerdmans, 2nd edn, 1989]), p. 280. The school of textual criticism that places most emphasis on stylistic features is that of so-called thorough-going eclecticism. See J.K. Elliott, 'Thoroughgoing Eclecticism in New Testament Textual Criticism', in B.D. Ehrman and M.W. Holmes (eds.), *The Text of the New Testament in Contemporary Research: Essays on the Status Quaestionis* (SD, 46; Grand Rapids: Eerdmans, 1995), pp. 321-35, esp. p. 321; cf. *idem*, *Essays and Studies in New Testament Textual Criticism* (EFN, 3; Córdoba: Ediciones El Almendro, 1992).

4. Major linguistic works in stylistics include T. Sebeok (ed.), *Style in Language* (New York: Wiley, 1960); N.E. Enkvist, J. Spencer and M.J. Gregory, *Linguistics and Style* (Language and Language Learning; Oxford: Oxford University Press, 1964); R. Fowler (ed.), *Essays on Style and Language: Linguistic and Critical Approaches to Literary Style* (London: Routledge & Kegan Paul, 1966); D. Crystal and D. Davy, *Investigating English Style* (ELS, 1; London: Longman, 1969); G.W. Turner, *Stylistics* (Harmondsworth: Penguin Books, 1973); A. Cluysenaar, *Introduction to Literary Stylistics: A Discussion of Dominant Structures in Verse and Prose* (London: Batsford, 1976); I.R. Galperin, *Stylistics* (Moscow: Vyssaja Skola, 1977; 3rd edn, 1981); G.N. Leech and M.H. Short, *Style in Fiction: A Linguistic Introduction to English Fictional Prose* (ELS, 13; London: Longman, 1981); R. Bradford, *Stylistics* (New Critical Idiom; London: Routledge, 1997).

and the related area of classical studies, have lagged behind even this slow progress.[5] A last limitation has been in terms of the body of data available for examination. Recent research, especially utilizing computer technology, has resulted in the development of much larger corpora that now are machine readable and retrievable.[6] Along with this increase in available data has come the realization, however, that certain corpora are simply too small for the kinds of lexical counting so often done in some kinds of stylistic studies (with which New Testament scholars are often all too familiar).[7] Nevertheless, the limitations of stylistics, at least as utilized in New Testament studies, do not mean

---

5.   Major works on style in Greek, some of which are not linguistically so phisticated, include the following: J.D. Denniston, *Greek Prose Style* (Oxford Clarendon Press, 1952); K. Dover, *The Evolution of Greek Prose Style* (Oxford: Clarendon Press, 1997); E.A. Nida *et al.*, *Style and Discourse: With Special Reference to the Text of the Greek New Testament* (Roggebaai, South Africa: Bible Society, 1983); A.B. Spencer, *Paul's Literary Style: A Stylistic and Historical Comparison of II Corinthians 11:16–12:13, Romans 8:9-39, and Philippians 3:2–4:13* (Lanham, MD: University Press of America, 1984; 2nd edn, 1998). For a recent assessment, see J.E. Botha, 'Style in the New Testament: The Need for Serious Reconsideration', *JSNT* 43 (1991), pp. 71-87 (repr. in S.E. Porter and C.A. Evans [eds.], *New Testament Text and Language: A Sheffield Reader* [BibSem, 44; Sheffield: Sheffield Academic Press, 1997], pp. 114-29). This list does not include numerous studies that are focused primarily on questions of authorship (see note 7, below). Perhaps the best study in this area is A. Kenny, *A Stylometric Study of the New Testament* (Oxford: Clarendon Press, 1986). Jesus' style has been occasionally used as a criterion in historical-Jesus research, although the use has often been linguistically rudimentary. See J. Jeremias, 'Kennzeichen der ipsissima vox Jesu', in *Synoptische Studien Alfred Wikenhauser zum siebzigsten Geburtstag dargebracht* (Munich: Zink, 1954), pp. 86-93; ET 'Characteristics of the *Ipsissima Vox Jesu*', in *idem*, *The Prayers of Jesus* (SBT, 2.6; London: SCM Press, 1967), pp. 108-15; N.J. McEleney, 'Authenticating Criteria and Mark 7:1-23', *CBQ* 34 (1972), pp. 431-60, esp. pp. 444-45.

6.   See M.B. O'Donnell, 'The Use of Annotated Corpora for New Testament Discourse Analysis: A Survey of Current Practice and Future Prospects', in Porter and Reed (eds.), *Discourse Analysis and the New Testament*, pp. 71-117.

7.   See M.B. O'Donnell, 'Linguistic Fingerprints or Style by Numbers: The Use of Statistics in the Discussion of Authorship of New Testament Documents', in S.E. Porter and D.A. Carson (eds.), *Linguistics and the New Testament: Critical Junctures* (JSNTSup, 168; SNTG, 5; Sheffield: Sheffield Academic Press, 1999), pp. 206-62; cf. also W. Smith, 'Computers, Statistics and Disputed Authorship', in J. Gibbons (ed.), *Language and the Law* (LSLS; London: Longman, 1994), pp. 374-413.

that principles of discourse analysis cannot be applied to the New Testament, in particular to issues related to authenticating Jesus tradition. To the contrary, the recent developments in discourse analysis, both of non-biblical and of biblical texts, provide a foundation for developing a principled means of advancing discussion of such issues.

2. *Defining the Criterion of Discourse Features*

How then is this criterion of discourse features to be defined and used in terms of authenticating the words of Jesus? A recent development in discourse studies has been the utilization of discourse analysis to ask questions regarding authorship and authenticity of testimony taken down by police. In a number of recent instances, discourse analysts have been enlisted to examine what the police have purported to be the accurate, and even verbatim, testimonies of suspects in crimes. However, linguistic analysis has shown that the use of the language by the purported criminal does not fit the profile of that kind of language user or of that particular language user.[8] In these instances, questions of authenticity

---

8.   See, e.g., M. Coulthard, '*Power*ful Evidence for the Defence: An Exercise in Forensic Discourse Analysis', and 'Forensic Analysis of Personal Written Texts: A Case Study', both in Gibbons (ed.), *Language and the Law*, pp. 414-27 and 362-73 respectively; cf. M. Coulthard, 'On Beginning the Study of Forensic Texts: Corpus Concordance Collocation', in M. Hoey (ed.), *Data, Description, Discourse: Papers on the English Language in Honour of John McH. Sinclair* (London: HarperCollins, 1993), pp. 86-97; *idem*, 'On the Use of Corpora in the Analysis of Forensic Texts', *Forensic Linguistics* 1 (1994), pp. 27-43; *idem*, 'The Official Version: Audience Manipulation in Police Records of Interviews with Suspects', in C.R. Caldas-Coulthard and M. Coulthard (eds.), *Texts and Practices: Readings in Critical Discourse Analysis* (London: Routledge, 1996), pp. 166-78; H. Kniffka with S. Blackwell and M. Coulthard (eds.), *Recent Developments in Forensic Linguistics* (Frankfurt: Peter Lang, 1996). The field of critical discourse analysis has made an important contribution to this area of study, because of its concern for power structures manipulated through discourse. For an introduction to critical discourse analysis, see N. Fairclough, *Critical Discourse Analysis: The Critical Study of Language* (LSLS; London: Longman, 1995); the essays in Caldas-Coulthard and Coulthard (eds.), *Texts and Practices*, esp. pp. 3-104; N. Fairclough and R. Wodak, 'Critical Discourse Analysis', in T.A. van Dijk (ed.), *Discourse as Social Interaction. II. Discourse Studies: A Multidisciplinary Introduction* (London: Sage, 1997), pp. 258-84; and an application to New Testament studies, with reservations, in S.E. Porter, 'Is Critical Discourse Analysis Critical? An Evaluation

have been very important, to say the least, since they have resulted in convictions being overturned or miscarriages of justice being corrected. In the light of these developments, along with the recognition that there are a number of limitations in dealing with a 'purely epigraphic language'[9] such as ancient Greek (for example, the samples are not large, there often is no other text available for comparison, and no analyst is a native speaker of the language being examined), there is potential for developing a method of discourse analysis that could be applied to examination of an ancient document, such as the Greek New Testament, with questions of authenticity in mind.

There are several possible ways that the criterion of discourse features could be used in historical-Jesus research. These uses would, first of all, depend upon the model of discourse analysis employed. What is clearly needed is both a model of discourse study that will provide for analysis beyond the level of the sentence, in order to appreciate features of discourse, and one that will avoid the pitfalls of previous stylistic research. The Hallidayan model of sociolinguistically based discourse analysis provides at least potential for being such a model.[10] A way to proceed

Using Philemon as a Test Case', in Porter and Reed (eds.), *Discourse Analysis and the New Testament*, pp. 47-70.

9.   The language is that of N.E. Collinge, 'Some Reflexions on Comparative Historical Syntax', *Archivum Linguisticum* 12 (1960), pp. 79-101 (79). Some of these problems are addressed in S.E. Porter, 'Studying Ancient Languages from a Modern Linguistic Perspective: Essential Terms and Terminology', *FN* 2 (1989), pp. 147-72; cf. also *idem, Studies in the Greek New Testament: Theory and Practice* (SBG, 6; New York: Peter Lang, 1996), pp. 7-20, esp. p. 19; and J.T. Reed, 'Modern Linguistics and the New Testament: A Basic Guide to Theory, Terminology, and Literature', in S.E. Porter and D. Tombs (eds.), *Approaches to New Testament Study* (JSNTSup, 120; Sheffield: JSOT Press, 1995), pp. 222-65. See also D. Biber, *Variation across Speech and Writing* (Cambridge: Cambridge University Press, 1988), who shows that many of the supposed differences between speech and writing fall along a continuum, rather than being a disjunction, and thus can be accommodated with proper methodology.

10.   The Hallidayan bibliography is large. His most important works with bearing on register and discourse analysis include M.A.K. Halliday, *Explorations in the Functions of Language* (EILS; London: Arnold, 1973); *idem, Language as Social Semiotic: The Social Interpretation of Language and Meaning* (London: Arnold, 1978); *idem, An Introduction to Functional Grammar* (London: Arnold, 1985; 2nd edn, 1994); and *idem* and R. Hasan, *Cohesion in English* (ELS, 9; London: Longman, 1976) and Halliday and Hasan, *Language, Context, and Text: Aspects of Language in a Social-Semiotic Perspective* (Geelong, Victoria, Australia: Deakin Uni-

would be, for each of the Gospels, to take the words of Jesus and isolate them from the other words of the Gospel (narrative and authorial exposition), and identify a number of linguistic features in these bodies of material. On the basis of these findings, one could establish from the narrative and expository material the linguistic tendencies of a given Gospel writer. Against this one could then test the wording of a passage purportedly uttered by Jesus. The results of such a comparison could then be analysed in terms of the Hallidayan concept of register.[11] Reg-

versity Press, 1985). See also M.A.K. Halliday and R.P. Fawcett (eds.), *New Developments in Systemic Linguistics*. I. *Theory and Description* (London: Pinter, 1987); R.P. Fawcett and D.J. Young (eds.), *New Developments in Systemic Linguistics*. II. *Theory and Application* (London: Pinter, 1988); M. Davies and L. Ravelli (eds.), *Advances in Systemic Linguistics: Recent Theory and Practice* (London: Pinter, 1992); M. Coulthard (ed.), *Advances in Written Text Analysis* (London: Routledge, 1994). Examples of a Hallidayan discourse model applied to the Greek New Testament, though none applied to authentication criteria in historical-Jesus research, include J.T. Reed, *A Discourse Analysis of Philippians: Method and Rhetoric in the Debate over Literary Integrity* (JSNTSup, 136; Sheffield: Sheffield Academic Press, 1997), esp. pp. 16-122; *idem*, 'Discourse Analysis', in S.E. Porter (ed.), *Handbook to Exegesis of the New Testament* (NTTS, 25; Leiden: E.J. Brill, 1997), pp. 189-217; G. Martín-Asensio, 'Foregrounding and its Relevance for Interpretation and Translation, with Acts 27 as a Case Study', in S.E. Porter and R.S. Hess (eds.), *Translating the Bible: Problems and Prospects* (JSNTSup, 173; Sheffield: Sheffield Academic Press, 1999), pp. 189-223; *idem*, 'Participant Reference and Foregrounded Syntax in the Stephen Episode', and T. Klutz, 'Naked and Wounded: Foregrounding, Relevance and Situation in Acts 19.13-20', both in Porter and Reed (eds.), *Discourse Analysis and the New Testament*, pp. 235-57 and 258-79, respectively; cf. S.E. Porter, *Idioms of the Greek New Testament* (BLG, 2; Sheffield: JSOT Press, 2nd edn, 1994), esp. pp. 298-307. A full critique of Halliday's model is not made in this chapter, but the above literature contains references to such discussion. Other methods of discourse analysis have been applied to the Greek New Testament. See P. Cotterell and M. Turner, *Linguistics and Biblical Interpretation* (London: SPCK; Downers Grove, IL: InterVarsity Press, 1989), pp. 230-92. One of the most promising studies is L. Hartman, *Text-Centered New Testament Studies: Text-Theoretical Essays on Early Jewish and Early Christian Literature* (ed. D. Hellholm; WUNT, 102; Tübingen: Mohr Siebeck, 1997), who utilizes the categories of E. Gülich and W. Raible, *Linguistische Textmodelle: Grundlagen und Möglichkeiten* (UTb, 130; Munich: Fink, 1977).

11. Recent studies on register include M. Ghadessy (ed.), *Register Analysis: Theory and Practice* (London: Pinter, 1993); D. Biber, *Dimensions of Register Variation: A Cross-Linguistic Comparison* (Cambridge: Cambridge University Press, 1995); D. Biber and E. Finegan (eds.), *Sociolinguistic Perspectives on Register*

ister consists of the three features of the context of situation—the field, tenor and mode of discourse—which categories are realized by the informational, interpersonal, and textual meta-functions of the semantic system of the language.[12] Register does not directly determine the specific lexico-grammatical realizations that may be used in a given utterance, but it constrains a number of semantic or functional components. Halliday has applied his register analysis to a number of texts, including some that are quite short (e.g. 1500 words),[13] and contends that he is able to establish the context of situation of the discourse on the basis of analysis of linguistic features brought to the fore by register analysis. One of the problems in much previous stylistic analysis has been that of the sample size involved. Traditional discussions, such as those of authorship of the Pauline letters, flounder on the fact that the kinds of stylistic tests performed require much larger samples than are available in the individual letters.[14] The Hallidayan register analysis contends to have overcome this limitation, because, according to Halliday's method, sample size is not necessarily a determining factor.

In such analysis, the key would rest in providing criteria by which one can determine the field, tenor and mode of a discourse, and being able to express these in terms of specific linguistic features that could

(Oxford Studies in Sociolinguistics; New York: Oxford University Press, 1995). Applications of Hallidayan register to the Greek of the New Testament have been few. Besides Reed (*Discourse Analysis*, pp. 34-122), one such set of studies is S.E. Porter, 'Dialect and Register in the Greek of the New Testament: Theory', and *idem*, 'Register in the Greek of the New Testament: Application with Reference to Mark's Gospel', in M.D. Carroll R. (ed.), *Rethinking Contexts, Rereading Texts: Contributions from the Social Sciences to Biblical Interpretation* (JSOTSup, 299; Sheffield: Sheffield Academic Press, 2000), pp. 190-208 and 209-29.

12. See Reed, *Discourse Analysis*, p. 61, for a graphic display of these relations. The concept of context is a highly complex one. For a recent discussion of some of its dimensions, see the essays in A. Duranti and C. Goodwin (eds.), *Rethinking Context: Language as an Interactive Phenomenon* (Studies in the Social and Cultural Foundations of Language, 11; Cambridge: Cambridge University Press, 1992).

13. This is the approximate length of his selections from W. Golding's *The Inheritors*, used in Halliday, *Explorations*, pp. 135-38; cf. M.A.K. Halliday, 'The Construction of Knowledge and Value in the Grammar of Scientific Discourse, with Reference to Charles Darwin's *The Origin of Species*', in Coulthard (ed.), *Advances in Written Text Analysis*, pp. 136-56, where he analyses two excerpts from Darwin's work of approximately 500 words each.

14. See O'Donnell, 'Linguistic Fingerprints or Style by Numbers', where he analyses and criticizes such attempts.

distinguish one text from another analysed in this way. Then the comparison could be made between the significant linguistic features of the narrative and the significant linguistic features of the words of Jesus in a particular pericope. The field of discourse specifically examines the subject matter and purpose of the discourse by examining lexical choice and the transitivity network (how 'who does what to whom' is grammaticalized), the tenor of discourse by the participant structure and interpersonal semantics (including personal reference, and mood and modality), and the mode of discourse by the features of the text as text (including channel of conveyance and theme, cohesion and informational structure). The major question here is whether any of these functions, developed to describe differences in discourse (and possibly reconstructing the original context of situation),[15] is sufficient for determination of authenticity in an ancient text. Unlike with a modern text, the firm points of comparison in the context of culture for an ancient text are few and far between.[16] If the linguistic tests are thought to be sufficiently precise, it may not matter if material is compared across literary types (e.g. narrative of the Gospel and expository words of Jesus); nevertheless, it might still be appropriate to begin with similar literary types (e.g. narrative of the Gospel and narrative words of Jesus, such as a parable). If the words of Jesus are determined to be significantly different from those of the surrounding Gospel, and especially if these words are consistent from one segment to another, then the presumption is that the author, and by extension any later redactors, of the Gospel have preserved the words of Jesus in an earlier form, ostensibly a form that could well be authentic, rather than redacting them as the Gospel was constructed and transmitted. In several ways, this criterion resembles the traditional criterion of change against the redactional tendency (see Chapter 3, above), arguing that wording not reflecting the style of the Gospel's author, yet preserved in the tradition, has a greater probability of authenticity. However, as will be demonstrated below, this new criterion of discourse features attempts to utilize, in a far more linguisti-

15. This is a potentially problematic issue for an ancient text. See Porter, 'Register in the Greek of the New Testament: Application with Reference to Mark's Gospel'.

16. Note, e.g., that when dealing with the Gospels one has a single, anonymous text for each author (apart from the possibility of combining Luke and Acts, two anonymous writings), with little to no firm information regarding the date or provenance of composition.

cally rigorous way, a variety of data, placing them in an appropriate discourse analytic framework. These data may be gathered from traditional stylistic analysis (as is done below), or they may consist of new types of data specially derived for a given analysis (a desideratum for future research). Comparison of Synoptic parallels could also support the hypothesis if they preserve similar wording against their Gospel contexts (see Chapter 5, above, for the criterion of textual variance).

To test the sufficiency of this criterion fully, one would need to begin with a complete analysis of a given Gospel, and of all of the passages that contain the words of Jesus (in other words, a corpus similar to the one needed for the study of textual variants and variance—see Chapter 5, above). A potential area of investigation might be a narrative parable of Jesus, as compared to the Gospel in which it is found. However, besides the difficulty of not having the database sufficiently developed for comparison against an entire Gospel,[17] there are other difficulties as well in parable studies that merit brief mention.[18] First concerns what constitutes a parable. This has been debated among scholars, resulting in various conclusions.[19] Most would agree on the core parables, but the edges are fragmented, introducing difficulties for any attempt at a

17. The data that could be used for such a project, and many others as well, is being compiled by the *Hellenistic Greek Text Annotation Project* of the Centre for Advanced Theological Research, University of Surrey Roehampton. Preliminary findings growing from this project are scheduled to be published in S.E. Porter and M.B. O'Donnell, *The Words and Activities of Jesus: Textual Variants and Register Analysis* (Texts and Editions, 1; Leiden: E.J. Brill, forthcoming).

18. For a recent survey of parable research, see C.L. Blomberg, 'The Parables of Jesus: Current Trends and Needs in Research', in B. Chilton and C.A. Evans (eds.), *Studying the Historical Jesus: Evaluations of the State of Current Research* (NTTS, 19; Leiden: E.J. Brill, 1994), pp. 231-54.

19. A sample of some lists of the parables is to be found in S. Goebel, *Die Parabeln Jesu*; ET *The Parables of Jesus: A Methodical Exposition* (trans. Professor Banks; Edinburgh: T. & T. Clark, 1913), pp. 457-58; J. Jeremias, *Die Gleichnisse Jesu* (Zürich: Zwingli-Verlag, 1947; Göttingen: Vandenhoeck & Ruprecht, 10th edn, 1984; ET *The Parables of Jesus* [trans. S.H. Hooke; London: SCM Press; New York: Charles Scribner's Sons, 3rd edn, 1972]), pp. 247-48; P.B. Payne, 'The Authenticity of the Parables of Jesus', in R.T. France and D. Wenham (eds.), *Gospel Perspectives: Studies of History and Tradition in the Four Gospels*, II (Sheffield: JSOT Press, 1981), pp. 329-44; C.L. Blomberg, *Interpreting the Parables* (Downers Grove, IL: InterVarsity Press, 1990), pp. 6-7; C.W. Hedrick, *Parables as Poetic Fictions: The Creative Voice of Jesus* (Peabody, MA: Hendrickson, 1994), pp. 252-53.

complete study. Second is that so few of the parables have multiple forms for productive comparison. According to many scholars, only four parables are found in two Gospels (those of the faithful and unfaithful servants, children in the marketplace, two builders [only three or four verses], and householder and the thief [only two verses]), and only three parables are found in Matthew, Mark and Luke (those of the sower, the wicked tenants [only two or three verses], and the mustard seed). The third, and perhaps most important, concerns how the parables are viewed by scholars. Blomberg lists as his first two (of ten) remaining questions in parables research, first, that of the extent the Gospel writers have redacted their material, and, secondly, the relation of the parables of the Gospels to rabbinic parallels.[20] In parables research, the tendencies are for those who examine the Semitic (rabbinic) backgrounds of the parables to look at conceptual (not verbal) and literary parallels.[21] At the same time, those who look to the Greek literary backgrounds tend to examine the parables a-contextually, giving no literary context or comparative literary analysis, even if they examine the wording.[22] Each of

20. Blomberg, 'Parables of Jesus', p. 253. Cf. C.A. Evans, 'Reconstructing Jesus' Teaching: Problems and Possibilities', in J.H. Charlesworth and L.L. Johns (eds.), *Hillel and Jesus: Comparative Studies of Two Major Religious Leaders* (Minneapolis: Fortress Press, 1997), pp. 397-426, who, in studying selected parables, contends that 'the challenge faced by those engaged in Jesus research lies not so much in the task of identifying tradition that originated with Jesus, but in ascertaining what the tradition originally meant' (p. 398).

21. See, e.g., C.A. Evans, 'Early Rabbinic Sources and Jesus Research', in B. Chilton and C.A. Evans, *Jesus in Context: Temple, Purity, and Restoration* (AGJU, 39; Leiden: E.J. Brill, 1997), pp. 27-57, esp. pp. 44-50; *idem, Noncanonical Writings and New Testament Interpretation* (Peabody, MA: Hendrickson, 1992), pp. 227-31. Evans ('Early Rabbinic Sources', p. 49) notes 'significant common terminology' between the parables of Jesus and of the rabbis. However, all of these features either find parallels in contemporary and earlier Greek literature, or are not linguistically distinct items, as some of his own examples show in 'Reconstructing Jesus' Teaching: Problems and Possibilities', in Chilton and Evans, *Jesus in Context*, pp. 145-76, esp. pp. 158-59, 167-68 (I wish to thank Craig Evans for drawing my attention to these examples). Cf. W.O.E. Oesterley, *The Gospel Parables in the Light of their Jewish Background* (London: SPCK, 1936), for a more detailed study within this framework.

22. Hedrick (*Parables as Poetic Fictions, passim*) examines the periodic structure, assonance and consonance, and other literary features of parables, but does not compare his findings with what might be found elsewhere in the Gospel. In fact, he treats the Gospel writer as just one of the interpreters of the parables, followed by

these problems is to some extent overcome by this new authentication criterion, however. This criterion is based upon comparing material of similar literary type, whether labelled a parable or not, although ideally the material should be suitable for analysis of Jesus' spoken words against a Gospel narrative itself. If Halliday is correct, length of excerpt is not in itself a limiting factor, especially if comparison is being done in terms of an entire Gospel. Since comparison of a single episode is to be against the whole of the Gospel, the particular placement of the parable in its context may well prove to be less important.

In the light of requiring a larger sample in order to perform the analysis noted above, I will instead attempt to test this criterion for authenticity, that of discourse features, on another type of discourse, by utilizing data gathered by other scholars in the course of their study of the passage. Nevertheless, if this attempt is at all successful, it is hoped that larger stretches and other types of texts can soon be included in such analysis.

3. *Discourse Features of Mark 13*

Instead of examining a parable, I will analyse in broad terms one large episode in Mark's Gospel in comparison with the rest of the Gospel. This will serve as a guide to determining the feasibility of this criterion of discourse features. Mark 13.5-37 is the single largest discourse in Mark's Gospel, but may not have been delivered as an entire discourse, if it was delivered by Jesus at all.[23] In analysing passages of this sort,

others, including modern interpreters. A similar perspective is found in R.W. Funk, *Parables and Presence: Forms of the New Testament Tradition* (Philadelphia: Fortress Press, 1982), esp. pp. 19-28 (originally published as 'The Narrative Parables: The Birth of a Language Tradition', *St Andrew's Review* [spring–summer 1974], pp. 299-323).

23. Discourse analysis is not a tool that can be used to determine textual integrity, although it can provide a means of structuring evidence for those wishing to argue for or against it. This is shown by Reed, *Discourse Analysis*, pp. 412-18. It does not actually matter to what is being tested here whether the words in Mk 13.5-37, if spoken by Jesus, were delivered at the same time or not. This criterion is attempting to determine authenticity, not co-temporality. The range of critical opinion on Mk 13 is usefully surveyed in G.R. Beasley-Murray, *Jesus and the Last Days: The Interpretation of the Olivet Discourse* (Peabody, MA: Hendrickson, 1993), pp. 1-349. See also D.E. Aune, *Prophecy in Early Christianity and the Ancient Mediterranean World* (Grand Rapids: Eerdmans, 1983), esp. pp. 184-87;

recent work in computational stylistics has made some impressive gains in terms of the statistical methods that can be used in future linguistic research on the text of the New Testament.[24] Despite the gains from a statistical standpoint, the discourse framework in which such work is

G. Theissen, *Lokalkolorit und Zeitgeschichte in den Evangelien: Ein Beitrag zur Geschichte der synoptischen Tradition* (NTOA, 8; Göttingen: Vandenhoeck & Ruprecht, 1989; ET *The Gospels in Context: Social and Political History in the Synoptic Tradition* [trans. L.M. Maloney; Edinburgh: T. & T. Clark, 1992]), esp. pp. 125-65; M.D. Hooker, *The Gospel According to Saint Mark* (BNTC; Peabody, MA: Hendrickson, 1991), pp. 297-324; C.C. Black, 'An Oration at Olivet: Some Rhetorical Dimensions of Mark 13', in D.F. Watson (ed.), *Persuasive Artistry: Studies in New Testament Rhetoric in Honor of George A. Kennedy* (JSNTSup, 50; Sheffield: JSOT Press, 1991), pp. 66-92; A.Y. Collins, *The Beginning of the Gospel: Probings of Mark in Context* (Minneapolis: Fortress Press, 1992), pp. 73-91; R.H. Gundry, *Mark: A Commentary on his Apology for the Cross* (Grand Rapids: Eerdmans, 1993), pp. 733-800; B.M.F. van Iersel, *Marcus, uitgelegd aan andere lezers* (Baarn: Gooi en Sticht; Kampen: Kok, 1997; ET *Mark: A Reader-Response Commentary* [trans. W.H. Bisscheroux; JSNTSup, 164; Sheffield: Sheffield Academic Press, 1998]), pp. 387-412; and W.A. Such, *The Abomination of Desolation in the Gospel of Mark: Its Historical Reference in Mark 13:14 and its Impact in the Gospel* (Lanham, MD: University Press of America, 1999). My examination of Beasley-Murray's study, as well as a number of other analyses of this passage, indicates that even those studies that examine the language of the passage are not interested in developing a criterion for authenticity, even if they wish to maintain it. Instead, such issues are decided on the basis of a number of other factors, such as the nature of the teaching, especially regarding the future. I will therefore not engage in detailed discussion with or respond to the wide range of critical opinion on this passage, except as necessary.

24. For example, among recent studies, see D.L. Mealand, 'The Extent of the Pauline Corpus: A Multivariate Approach', *JSNT* 59 (1995), pp. 61-92; *idem*, 'Correspondence Analysis of Luke', *Literary and Linguistic Computing* 10 (1995), pp. 171-82; *idem*, 'Measuring Genre Differences in Mark with Correspondence Analysis', *Literary and Linguistic Computing* 12 (1997), pp. 227-45; A.J.M. Linmans, *Onderschikking in de synoptische evangeliën: Syntaxis, discourse-functies en stilometrie* (Leiden: FSW, 1995); *idem*, 'Correspondence Analysis of the Synoptic Gospels', *Literary and Linguistic Computing* 13 (1998), pp. 1-13. Linmans responds in his 1998 article to Mealand's latter 1995 article, stressing the role of discourse types in accounting for differences between discourse units, and thus mitigating Mealand's contention in his 1997 article that differences in variables are reflected in genre types. Although Linmans argues for use of register analysis, he does not perform such an analysis, merely specifying a number of discourse features that merit further investigation. He also admits that the current electronic tools are inadequate for the requirements.

done is still in its infancy, however, raising many intriguing questions of how discourse segments relate to each other, the implications of these relations for source theories, and the influence of discourse type on stylistic variation. To this point, there are far more questions than answers in statistically based approaches, however, especially with regard to the issues that are raised in this monograph regarding issues of authenticity. A sustained use of functional linguistics in such statistical studies, noted as an appropriate way forward in some of this research, is also lacking. In the light of serious disagreement regarding appropriate statistical tests, and the lack of what I consider the requisite data for such studies, I have avoided any type of sustained statistical analysis. In approaching this discourse, therefore, I have begun my analysis with the results of several standard studies of the Gospel of Mark, in particular those that have been concerned to analyse various linguistic features of the text.[25] None of these studies categorizes such features into

25. Major works on Markan style, not all of equal value for this study, include J.C. Hawkins, *Horae Synopticae: Contributions to the Study of the Synoptic Problem* (Oxford: Clarendon Press, 1899; 2nd edn, 1909), *passim*; C.H. Turner, 'Marcan Usage: Notes, Critical and Exegetical, on the Second Gospel', *JTS* OS 25 (1924), pp. 377-86; OS 26 (1924–25), pp. 12-20, 145-56, 225-40, 337-46; OS 27 (1926), pp. 58-62; OS 28 (1926–27), pp. 9-30, 349-62; OS 29 (1928), pp. 275-89, 346-61 (repr. in J.K. Elliott [ed.], *The Language and Style of the Gospel of Mark: An Edition of C.H. Turner's 'Notes on Marcan Usage' Together with Other Comparable Studies* [NovTSup, 71; Leiden: E.J. Brill, 1993], pp. 3-146, with additional notes); J.C. Doudna, *The Greek of the Gospel of Mark* (JBLMS, 12; Philadelphia: Society of Biblical Literature and Exegesis, 1961); J. Lambrecht, *Die Redaktion der Markus-Apokalypse: Literarische Analyse und Strukturuntersuchung* (AnBib, 289; Rome: Pontifical Biblical Institute, 1967); A.J. Pryke, *Redactional Style in the Marcan Gospel: A Study of Syntax and Vocabulary as Guides to Redaction in Mark* (SNTSMS, 33; Cambridge: Cambridge University Press, 1978), esp. pp. 139-76 for classification of redaction and reconstruction of the Markan redacted text; E.C. Maloney, *Semitic Interference in Marcan Syntax* (SBLDS, 51; Chico, CA: Scholars Press, 1981); R.A. Martin, *Syntax Criticism of the Synoptic Gospels* (Studies in the Bible and Early Christianity, 10; Lewiston: Edwin Mellen Press, 1987); D.B. Peabody, *Mark as Composer* (New Gospel Studies, 1; Macon, GA: Mercer University Press/Peeters, 1987); F. Neirynck, *Duality in Mark: Contributions to the Study of the Markan Redaction* (BETL, 31; Leuven: Leuven University Press/ Peeters, 1988); K.D. Dyer, *The Prophecy on the Mount: Mark 13 and the Gathering of the New Community* (International Theological Studies: Contributions of Baptist Scholars, 2; Bern: Peter Lang, 1998), pp. 49-65, 67-92, 131-50, 293-310. Recent studies of Mark have been critically analysed by F. Neirynck, 'The Redactional Text of

the three contextual functions of register that I have outlined above, but they have provided the basic information, nonetheless. I have used this procedure so as to avoid the charge of unfair subjectivity in the selection of tests and the assemblage of data for them, since all of the material has been suggested by others who do not have the same critical framework in mind.[26] My application of the concept of register, it seems to me, allows for these data to be put to an extended conceptual use not fully realized in this previous research. Rather than simply comparing each factor independently and as of equal weight with any other, the register framework allows for a categorization of data in terms of their major discourse functions. The results can then be compared in a more meaningful way in terms of the discourse itself. As a result of this study, several features of this discourse show that it has been left relatively unedited by Mark, indicating that it came to him as an earlier source, and hence it possibly represents authentic Jesus tradition. This conclusion runs against much of the critical consensus regarding this passage. The factors that I analyse here are merely a beginning of what might be done in more detail on the Markan style of discourse in terms of register and authenticity, and would need to be done in extending and developing this criterion further.

Mark', *ETL* 57 (1981), pp. 144-62; repr. in *idem, Evangelica: Gospel Studies—Etudes d'évangile. Collected Essays* (ed. F. Van Segbroeck; BETL, 60; Leuven: Leuven University Press/Peeters, 1982), pp. 618-36; C.C. Black, *The Disciples According to Mark: Markan Redaction in Current Debate* (JSNTSup, 27; Sheffield: JSOT Press, 1989), esp. pp. 184-218 (pp. 205-12 devoted to Pryke), illustrating the need to develop independent databases and criteria. Commentaries with useful information on Markan style include H.B. Swete, *The Gospel According to Mark* (London: Macmillan, 1898), pp. xliv-l; M.-J. Lagrange, *Evangile selon Saint Marc* (EB; Paris: J. Gabalda, 1929), pp. lxvii-lxxxiii; and V. Taylor, *The Gospel According to St Mark* (London: Macmillan, 1959), pp. 44-54.

26. I am not alone in suggesting new approaches to Mark's Gospel, including ch. 13. See C. Breytenbach, *Nachfolge und Zukunftserwartung nach Markus: Eine methodenkritische Studie* (ATANT, 71; Zürich: Theologischer Verlag, 1984), esp. pp. 85-132, 280-330; P.L. Danove, *The End of Mark's Story: A Methodological Study* (BIS, 3; Leiden: E.J. Brill, 1993); J.G. Cook, *The Structure and Persuasive Power of Mark: A Linguistic Approach* (Semeia Studies; Atlanta: Scholars Press, 1995); and W. Schenk, 'The Testamental Disciple-Instruction of the Markan Jesus (Mark 13): Levels of Communication and its Rhetorical Structures', in Porter and Reed (eds.), *Discourse Analysis and the New Testament*, pp. 197-222, esp. pp. 211-13 for a survey of research.

I will treat the three components of register and their functions in terms of the mode and textual function, tenor and interpersonal function, and field and informational function. This provides a logical order that allows for the proper categorization of the data and the drawing of pertinent conclusions.

a. *Mode of Discourse and Textual Function*
With regard to textual features of discourse, I will concentrate on cohesion, or the objective means by which the text displays its unity as a whole.[27] One of the noteworthy (and often commented upon) features of Mark's Gospel is the use of the conjunction καί ('and') to introduce sections and sub-sections of the Gospel.[28] For example, of the 88 sections in the Westcott–Hort edition of the Greek New Testament, according to Hawkins, 80 sections begin with καί, while δέ begins (postpositively) 6, a much more frequent usage of καί against δέ than in Matthew and Luke.[29] Mark apparently uses this conjunction as a means of uniting together his episodes/pericopes and signalling when a new one begins.[30] Whether one accepts this feature of Markan syntax as simply a feature of Koine Greek (perhaps enhanced in Markan usage), whether one treats it as a distinctive characteristic of Markan style, or whether one considers it a clear Semitism,[31] a noteworthy feature of Mark 13 is

27. See Halliday and Hasan, *Cohesion in English*, pp. 1-2.
28. Conjunctions are a common feature for analysis in studies of cohesion. See Halliday and Hasan, *Cohesion in English*, pp. 226-73; D. Schiffrin, *Discourse Markers* (Studies in Interactional Sociolinguistics, 5; Cambridge: Cambridge University Press, 1987), esp. pp. 128-90. See also S.H. Levinsohn, *Textual Connections in Acts* (SBLMS, 31; Atlanta: Scholars Press, 1987), esp. pp. 83-156; *idem, Discourse Features of New Testament Greek: A Coursebook* (Dallas: Summer Institute of Linguistics, 1992), esp. pp. 13-30; and D.A. Black *et al.* (eds.), *Linguistics and New Testament Interpretation: Essays on Discourse Analysis* (Nashville: Broadman, 1992), where various essays touch on this topic. However, it has recently been argued that lexis organizes text. See M. Hoey, *Patterns of Lexis in Text* (Describing English Language; Oxford: Oxford University Press, 1991). This theory requires further testing on the Greek of the New Testament.
29. Hawkins, *Horae Synopticae*, p. 151. There are numerous internal uses of conjunctive καί as well. See Maloney, *Semitic Interference*, p. 66, who notes the frequency of use of καί over δέ throughout Mark's Gospel.
30. To use the functional language of Levinsohn (*Discourse Features*, pp. 13-31), Mark's use of καί usually seems to indicate continuity or points of departure.
31. On the use of conjunctive καί as a feature of Greek, see S. Trenkner, *Le style καί dans le récit attique oral* (Cahiers, 1; Brussels: Editions de l'Institut d'Etudes

significantly *reduced* use of introductory conjunctive καί. According to the sub-sections in the Nestle–Aland Greek New Testament (27th edn), καί is used to open 114 of 143 sub-sections of Mark's Gospel, including Mk 13.1 and 3, both narrative portions outside of the words of Jesus, but is used in only one of nine sub-sections within vv. 5-37—at v. 21.[32] In other words, roughly 80 per cent of all of the sub-sections of the Gospel begin with καί (that is, four out of five), while within Mk 13.5-37, only about 11 per cent of the sections begin with καί (the percentage of the sub-sections of the Gospel as a whole beginning with καί would increase if Mk 13.5-37 were not entered into the calculation).[33] Within Mk 13.5-37, rather than καί, two other linguistic features are apparently used to create textual cohesion. One of these is conjunctive δέ, used in vv. 9, 14, and 28, that is, in one out of three instances. Although the sample is too small to speak definitively, the ratios for usage of καί and δέ in Mark's Gospel are here apparently reversed. The other linguistic feature of textual cohesion in the discourse is asyndeton. Six of 22

Polonaises en Belgique, 1948), esp. pp. 5-7 on the New Testament; E. Mayser, *Grammatik der griechischen Papyri aus der Ptolemäerzeit* (3 vols.; Berlin: W. de Gruyter, 1906–1934; 2nd edn of vol. 1, 1970), II.3, pp. 184-86; M. Reiser, *Syntax und Stil des Markusevangeliums im Licht der hellenistischen Volksliteratur* (WUNT, 2.11; Tübingen: Mohr Siebeck, 1984), pp. 99-137. On the use of καί as a characteristic of Markan style, see Hawkins, *Horae Synopticae*, pp. 150-52; Taylor, *Mark*, pp. 48-49; and so many commentators. On the use of καί as a Semitism, see M. Black, *An Aramaic Approach to the Gospels and Acts* (Oxford: Clarendon Press, 1946; 2nd edn, 1954; 3rd edn, 1967; repr. with 'Introduction: An Aramaic Approach Thirty Years Later', by C.A. Evans, pp. v-xxv; Peabody, MA: Hendrickson, 1998), pp. 61-69; Maloney, *Semitic Interference*, pp. 66-74; cf. S.P. Brock, review of *Aramaic Approach*, by Black, in *JTS* NS 20 (1969), pp. 274-78.

    32. Some later manuscripts do attempt to add καί, however; see D at Mk 13.15.

    33. This coincides with overall instances of καί in Mark's Gospel. Chapter 13 has the lowest frequency per verse of use of καί (1.1 per verse compared to a range of 1.2 in ch. 15 to 2.0 in chs. 5 and 6), whether vv. 1-5a are included or not (without these verses the frequency is 1.0 per verse). Mark 13 also has the lowest frequency of verse-initial καί of any chapter in Mark's Gospel (0.35 per verse compared to 0.40 in ch. 10 to 0.83 in ch. 3), whether vv. 1-5a are included or not (without these verses the frequency is 0.31 per verse); this is roughly half that of the frequency of verse-initial καί for the entire Gospel (0.65 per verse). The frequency of καί per 1000 words in the whole of Mark's Gospel is 84.45, with ch. 13 having a frequency of only 59.42 per 1000 words. It is clearly of more significance for the textual component of cohesion to examine uses of καί that connect sub-sections of discourse, than simply counting instances.

instances of Mark's instances of asyndeton—changed in Matthew and Luke (if Markan priority is to be believed)[34]—occur in Mk 13.5-37 (vv. 6, 7, 8 [2×], 9, 34).[35]

Another textual feature is information flow. The vocabulary of a discourse is often analysed in an undifferentiated way. One of the advantages of Hallidayan register analysis is that the choice of lexical items is seen to contribute to different dimensions of the discourse. For the most part, vocabulary is often treated as indicating the subject matter of the discourse, which will be discussed briefly below regarding the field of discourse. The choice of lexical items is also a means by which an author structures and shapes the textual component, and directs the flow of information. In terms of the characteristics of Markan vocabulary, by which he creates the textual component of his discourse, one can see some interesting patterns in Mark 13. The characteristic vocabulary of an author is that set of lexical items that is regularly drawn upon to shape the discourse and convey the flow of information. Of the 41 words that Hawkins determines are characteristic of Mark's Gospel, there are only four instances of these words occurring in the words of Jesus in Mk 13.5-37 (out of 357 uses of this characteristic vocabulary throughout the Gospel).[36] Whereas the characteristic vocabulary appears at a rate of

34. This follows the majority of thought in current Synoptic scholarship, but the point is not dependent upon it and has value no matter what model of Synoptic origins one maintains (see Chapter 2, above, for discussion of the competing views). One could simply rephrase and speak of the 6 of 22 instances of Mark's instances of asyndeton that are not found in Matthew and Luke but occur in Mk 13.5-37. Sensitive to the misuse of linguistic arguments in discussion of the Synoptic Gospels is D.A. Black, 'Some Dissenting Notes on R. Stein's *The Synoptic Problem* and Markan "Errors"', *FN* 1 (1988), pp. 95-101; *idem*, 'Discourse Analysis, Synoptic Criticism, and Markan Grammar: Some Methodological Considerations', in Black *et al.* (eds.), *Linguistics and New Testament Interpretation*, pp. 90-98 (though he is not without some of his own odd linguistic judgments).

35. Hawkins, *Horae Synopticae*, pp. 137-38. On asyndeton, see Levinsohn, *Discourse Features*, pp. 49-68; on Markan asyndeton, see Maloney, *Semitic Interference*, pp. 77-81, to some extent refuting Black, *Aramaic Approach*, pp. 55-61.

36. These include εὐαγγέλιον in Mk 13.10, οὔπω in 13.7, πρωΐ in 13.35 and τοιοῦτος in 13.19. See Hawkins, *Horae Synopticae*, pp. 12-13. Pryke (*Redactional Style*, pp. 136-38) presents a list of 140 Markan redactional vocabulary (1423 occurrences), but the list cannot be used, because, reflective of its problems, it includes words that have a single occurrence, it includes syntactical units, and seems to be determined on the basis of sometimes questionable and subjective syntactical analysis. For a reconsideration of some issues related to Markan vocabulary, see

roughly one in every 31 words over the entire Gospel (11,099 words in Mk 1.1–16.8), these words only appear at the rate of roughly one in every 132 words in Mk 13.5-37 (530 words). The characteristic vocabulary is approximately more than four times as frequent in the Gospel as it is in Mk 13.5-37. In other words, there appears to be a shift in the information flow, since this Markan section must rely upon highly non-characteristic vocabulary. There is also the use of what some have considered odd or unusual vocabulary and phrasing in Mk 13.5-37, which has arguably been changed in the other Gospels.[37] These odd or unusual features are, by definition, ones that the author does not use elsewhere to constitute the textual component of the discourse. For example, the word προμεριμνᾶτε ('trouble') in 13.11 is not found elsewhere in the New Testament, and changed to the unprefixed form in Mt. 10.19 and Lk. 12.11; the articular prepositional phrase (ὁ εἰς τὸν ἀγρόν) in 13.16 is changed to use of ἐν in Mt. 24.18 and Lk. 17.31; the phrase ἔσονται γὰρ αἱ ἡμέραι ἐκεῖναι ψλῖψις in 13.19 is avoided in Mt. 24.21 and Lk. 21.23; and the pronouns οἵα…τοιαύτη in 13.19 are not found elsewhere in Mark, in the Matthaean parallel or in Daniel, to which is being alluded.[38] These odd features become components of the pattern of information flow of Mk 13.5-37, avoided in the other Gospels, as well as elsewhere in Mark.

Placing vocabulary analysis, as well as other factors, within this register category helps to isolate their function within Mark's Gospel. Thus, on the basis of the data gathered and analysed above, there are several clear indications with regard to cohesion and information flow that Mk 13.5-37 is constructed at the textual level differently than the rest of Mark's Gospel.

b. *Tenor of Discourse and Interpersonal Function*
The tenor of the discourse is concerned with the interpersonal relations of the discourse. This includes how interpersonal relations are gram-

R. Mackowski, 'Some Colloquialisms in the Gospel According to Mark', in R.F. Sutton, Jr (ed.), *Daidalikon: Studies in Memory of Raymond V. Schoder, SJ* (Wauconda, IL: Bolchazy-Carducci, 1989), pp. 229-38.

37. This point as formulated is dependent upon Markan priority in Synoptic origins; however, it is not necessarily such. One could simply note that in Mk 13.5-37 certain less usual lexical and syntactical choices are made. On issues in lexicography with regard to the Greek of the New Testament, see Porter, *Studies in the Greek New Testament*, pp. 49-74.

38. See Hawkins, *Horae Synopticae*, pp. 133-34.

maticalized by such linguistic features as names and reduced forms, such as pronouns, and how the actions of the participants are related to reality (mood and modality).[39] The tenor of this discourse can be analysed on several levels, including in terms of the interaction of Jesus and his listeners, and in terms of the interaction of those depicted in the discourse itself. I will concentrate on the former here. Before Jesus' speech itself begins (Mk 13.1-4), the directive focus of the discourse is moving from the disciples to Jesus. The disciples address him with commands, demanding information from him about the Temple and when its destruction will occur (vv. 1, 4), while Jesus simply uses a question and a statement in return (v. 2), before he begins the discourse in v. 5. However, within the discourse itself, Jesus clearly is instigating and directing comments to his listeners by means of use of the imperative.[40] As Vorster states, 'It is remarkable that almost everything which is said to, and thus about the four [disciples] to whom the speech is directed, is done by way of imperatives...'[41] Indeed, Mark 13 has a larger number of imperatives than any other single chapter in Mark (21 in total and 19 in vv. 5-37 [1 per 1.7 verses], with the two in vv. 1 and 4 used by the disciples).[42] This is the case even though it is much smaller than several other chapters that have large numbers of imperatives (e.g. Mark 9 has 11 imperatives in 50 verses [1 per 4.5 verses], ch. 10 has 15 in 52 verses [1 per 3.5 verses], and ch. 14 has 18 in 65 verses [1 per 3.6 verses]). The ratios indicate that the frequency of imperatives in Mk 13.5-37 is

39. On participant reference, see Levinsohn, *Discourse Features*, pp. 113-26; Martín-Asensio, 'Participant Reference and Foregrounded Syntax', esp. p. 240; on mood and modality, see S.E. Porter, *Verbal Aspect in the Greek of the New Testament, with Reference to Tense and Mood* (SBG, 1; New York: Peter Lang, 1989), pp. 163-78; *idem, Idioms of the Greek New Testament*, pp. 50-61.

40. On the directive function of the imperative form, see Porter, *Verbal Aspect*, pp. 335-61; *idem, Idioms of the Greek New Testament*, pp. 53-56.

41. W.S. Vorster, 'Literary Reflections on Mark 13:5-37: A Narrated Speech of Jesus', in *idem, Speaking of Jesus: Essays on Biblical Language, Gospel Narrative and the Historical Jesus* (NovTSup, 92; ed. J.E. Botha; Leiden: E.J. Brill, 1999), pp. 395-413 (410) (revised from *Neot* 21.2 [1987], pp. 91-112). The use of the imperative βλέπετε (found in Mk 4.24 [= Lk. 8.18]; 12.36; 13.5 [= Mt. 24.4; Lk. 21.8], 9, 33) is cited by P. Vassiliadis to argue for a Markan sayings-of-Jesus source (ΛΟΓΟΙ ΙΗΣΟΥ: *Studies in Q* [University of South Florida International Studies in Formative Christianity and Judaism; Atlanta: Scholars Press, 1999], pp. 153-59).

42. The imperative in Mk 13.1 is ἴδε. On this form, see Doudna, *Greek of the Gospel of Mark*, pp. 63-65.

roughly more than twice that of any other chapter in the Gospel. Mark 13.5-37, according to Dyer, also has 5.1 per cent of the total verses of Mark's Gospel, but 13.6 per cent of the imperatives.[43] In other words, in this discourse, the frequency of imperatives, which were not necessary to use (as evidenced by Jesus' mode of speaking with the disciples before the discourse proper begins, and as his communication elsewhere in the Gospel indicates), is out of keeping with Markan usage elsewhere in the Gospel. Part of the result of this usage is a sense of urgency created by the commanding posture of the discourse, in which Jesus is seen to be the one who instigates directive pronouncement. This is not a conversation or a dialogue, but a direct address.[44] This mode of discourse is not characteristic of how Jesus is elsewhere depicted as speaking in Mark's Gospel,[45] however, and sets the depiction of Jesus in relation to others into significant relief in Mark 13.

Mood is only one feature of the tenor of the discourse that could be analysed. In itself, however, it is instructive for helping to isolate and quantify a particular orientation to communication between Jesus and his conversational partners that is not so readily found elsewhere in Mark's Gospel.

c. *Field of Discourse and Informational Function*
The field of discourse is concerned with what the discourse is about, that is, its subject matter, and the information conveyed. The recognition that syntax conveys meaning has been fully adopted by Hallidayan linguistics,[46] so much so that it has been institutionalized as part of the

43. Dyer, *Prophecy on the Mount*, p. 81 n. 49. Our statistics vary slightly, but the point is the same. Dyer also notes that Mk 13.5-37 contains 22.6 per cent of the future tense-form verbs in Mark's Gospel (26 out of 115 instances), even though it contains only 5.1 per cent of the total words.

44. See Gundry, *Mark*, p. 752; contra Aune, *Prophecy in Early Christianity*, pp. 186-87, 399-400.

45. Note how typical it is for Jesus to begin his speaking in Mark's Gospel (in passages longer than one verse that are not simple instructions) with questions that lead directly to his statements (e.g. Mk 2.8-9, 19, 25; 3.24; 4.13, 21, 30; 7.18; 8.17; 10.18, 36; 12.24, 35). He virtually never is seen to follow a question with a command (or imperative) (except Mk 14.6). See Mk 4.3; 6.8; 8.15, 33; 9.39; 12.38, where he begins with an imperative.

46. Although from a different framework, note the perspective in C. Ferris, *The Meaning of Syntax: A Study in the Adjectives of English* (LLL; London: Longman, 1993), esp. p. 1-18.

analysis of informational structure. The development of the transitivity network has been a means of quantifying who does what action to whom, and how.[47] Short of performing a complete analysis of the transitivity system in Mk 13.5-37 and the rest of the Gospel (something not done by any of the studies I am relying upon), the following more traditional features merit attention.

The first feature is Markan syntactical style. Mark 13 does not conform to typical Markan stylistic syntactical features. Of 14 syntactical features that are considered by Pryke to be guides to Mark the editor and redactor's style,[48] Mk 13.5-37 has only five instances of three of these features.[49] In other words, Mk 13.5-37 does not have a very large number of the redactional features that are said to characterize Markan style, but it has more of the style of non-Markan material, which must have originated from earlier sources. This non-Markan material may of course have come from a number of different sources, with the words spoken by Jesus possibly being construed as authentic source material by this criterion. These three Markan linguistic features include the following. (1) The first is two uses of parenthetical clauses, in 13.10 and 14b, both instances of what Pryke calls catechetical, liturgical and biblical usage.[50] In Mk 13.10, the parenthetical statement—καὶ εἰς πάντα τὰ ἔθνη πρῶτον δεῖ κηρυχθῆναι τὸ εὐαγγέλιον—is called by Pryke 'a Marcan redactional passage which the evangelist believes ex-

---

47. See Halliday, *Functional Grammar*, pp. 144-57. The transitivity system involves the question of voice, a problematic one in ancient Greek, especially for the middle voice (see Porter, *Idioms of the Greek New Testament*, pp. 62-73). A useful exposition of the concept of transitivity will be found in G. Martín-Asensio, *Transitivity-Based Foregrounding in the Acts of the Apostles: A Functional-Grammatical Approach* (JSNTSup; SNTG; Sheffield: Sheffield Academic Press, forthcoming).

48. See Pryke, *Redactional Style*, pp. 32-135. His study is much more satisfactory than that of Neirynck (*Duality in Mark*), since Pryke attempts to analyse the relative frequencies of the syntactical tendencies, and account for redactional influence.

49. Those features listed by Pryke that are not to be found in Mk 13.5-37 include: genitive absolute, participle as a main verb, πολλά accusative, ἄρχομαι + infinitive, εὐθύς and καὶ εὐθύς, πάλιν, 'redundant' participle, periphrastic tenses, 'impersonals', ὥστε + infinitive, and two or more participles before or after the main verb.

50. Pryke, *Redactional Style*, p. 53; cf. Turner, 'Marcan Usage', *JTS* os 26 (1924–25), pp. 145-46.

presses the mind of Christ, although it may not be His exact words. The main reasons for regarding this verse as parenthetical and redactional are the vocabulary and the fact that the poetry of the passage and its main theme are interrupted by the parenthetical phrase...'[51] In Mk 13.14b, the parenthetical statement is ὁ ἀναγινώσκων νοείτω, for which there is a diversity of scholarly opinion on its origins.[52] (2) The second feature is two uses of λέγω ὅτι in 13.6 and 30. According to Pryke, relying on the work of others before him, the author of the Gospel avoids indirect speech and prefers direct speech, of which these are two instances.[53] (3) The last feature is the use of explanatory γάρ in 13.11b.[54] If the first and second features are clearly redactional, as Pryke contends, these two portions of verses in v.11 can perhaps be seen to have been edited when the discourse was placed within its surrounding narrative, without necessarily affecting one's view of the authenticity of the remaining material. In any event, this leaves at most one supposed Markan syntactical redactional feature unexplained within Mk 13.5-37, the γάρ in 13.11—one at least arguably necessary to its discursive nature. By this analysis, there is very little evidence of Markan syntactical redaction of Mk 13.5-37.

Dyer has approached the issue of syntax from a different angle. In a response to the challenges of stylometry, he has chronicled the instances of unique clusters of three-word syntax sequences in Mark 13 and the rest of the Gospel. In response to the work of Peabody, as well as noting the features cited by Neirynck,[55] Dyer has also plotted recurrent six-

51. Pryke, *Redactional Style*, p. 53, citing the vocabulary of ἔθνη, πρῶτον, δεῖ, κηρύσσω, εὐαγγέλιον.

52. Pryke, *Redactional Style*, p. 56. See Collins, *Beginning of the Gospel*, p. 78.

53. Pryke, *Redactional Style*, p. 73, citing Turner, 'Marcan Usage', *JTS* OS 28 (1926), pp. 9-15; J. Sundwall, 'Die Zusammensetzung des Markusevangeliums', in *Acta Academiae Aboensis, Humaniora*, IX (Åbo: Åbo Academy, 1934), pp. 1-86, here p. 8; M. Zerwick, *Untersuchungen zum Markus-Stil: Ein Beitrag zur Durcharbeitung des Neuen Testamentes* (Rome: Pontifical Biblical Institute, 1937), pp. 4ff., 45.

54. Pryke, *Redactional Style*, p. 126.

55. Peabody, *Mark as Composer, passim*; Neirynck, *Duality in Mark, passim*. Dyer (*Prophecy on the Mount*) rightly draws attention to the shortcomings of the work of Neirynck and Peabody. He notes that Neirynck provides abundant lists, but does not answer the question of how these indicate redaction (p. 139). He notes that Peabody has a mix of vocabulary and grammatical features in his lists (p. 147). Neirynck's lists are a mix of features, all evidencing some form of duality, but this

word syntactical sequences in Mark's Gospel. According to him, unique syntax ostensibly indicates 'distinctive traditions', whereas recurrent syntax indicates 'inter-connected traditions or Markan redaction'.[56] It is not entirely clear, however, what linguistic status these three- and six-word syntactical sequences have; much more research is necessary to quantify what they might indicate. Dyer uses them in an attempt to isolate redactional and non-redactional syntax within Mark 13, differentiating the influence of the author on particular groups of verses. Thus, his analysis of recurrent syntax shows a particularly high concentration in Mk 13.24-27 (71.8 per cent recurrent syntax). What is worth noting here, however, is that regarding his three-word syntactical sequences, there is a larger percentage of unique syntax in Mk 13.3-37 (21.7 per cent), especially vv. 14-23 (35.3 per cent), than there is in any other section of the Gospel (other sections that are close are Mk 1.1-16 with 20.3 per cent and 10.32-34 20.5 per cent, but the latter may be too small for meaningful calculation).[57] As interesting as these indicators are, one must be cautious in attributing more status to them than is warranted at this stage in research, since there is no cross-correlation with other Greek writers, or even detailed exploration of their meaning within Mark's Gospel.

The second feature of the field of discourse is the subject matter. The subject matter is usually indicated by the choice of vocabulary items. In terms of the subject matter of this discourse, there has been much debate over the origins of the apocalyptic imagery and thought, and whether it is possible or likely that Jesus could have stated what he does about the impending troubles, which seem so much like the destruction of Jerusalem that occurred in 70 CE.[58] In a brief study of the vocabulary of Mark

---

includes a wide range of features. Many, but not all, are found in Mk 13, while others are not (2. Adverbs in θεν; 12. Double statement; 14. Translation; 15. Substantive followed by apposition; 17. Series of three; 18. Correspondence in narrative; 19. Exposition in discourse; 20. Narrative in discourse; 22. Request and realization; 23. Direct discourse preceded by qualifying verb; 24. Quotation and comment; 28. Sandwich arrangement). Many of the samples are clearly too small to work with (e.g. 2; 24; 28), while most are probably too small. The same criticisms can be made of Peabody's work as well.

56. Dyer, *Prophecy on the Mount*, p. 147.

57. Dyer, *Prophecy on the Mount*, p. 88.

58. Cf. T.R. Hatina, 'The Focus of Mark 13:24-27: The Parousia, or the Destruction of the Temple?', *BBR* 6 (1996), pp. 43-66; N.H. Taylor, 'Palestinian Christianity and the Caligula Crisis. Part II. The Markan Eschatological Discourse',

13, Perrin noted that 'of the 165 words in the Nestle text of Mark 13.5-27, 35 (= 21.2 per cent) do not occur elsewhere in the Gospel, and of these 35 words 15 are to be found in the Book of Revelation'. Similarly, 'investigation of the vocabulary of Mark 13.28-37 reveals a total vocabulary of 79 words, of which 13 (= 16.4 per cent) do not occur elsewhere in the Gospel. Of these 13 words only 2 are to be found again in Revelation.'[59] Although Perrin uses this evidence as it is to argue for the secondary nature or inauthenticity of the discourse, this conclusion does not necessarily follow, especially when the data are placed within the larger Hallidayan framework. All that Perrin's findings tend to show (the size of the chapter is too small to argue for far-reaching conclusions) is that Mark 13 has a higher proportion of unique, and possibly apocalyptic, vocabulary than elsewhere in the Gospel.[60] These statistics have been called into question by Dyer.[61] He notes that Perrin, using Morgenthaler, only counts a lexical item once, regardless of its number of occurrences. When the total number of words is used in the calculations, the proportion of unique words falls. Dyer's recalculated figures are that Mk 13.5-27 has 41 unique words out of 381 total words (= 10.8 per cent), and Mk 13.28-37 has 14 of 152 (= 11.7 per cent). To show that these figures are not as distinctive as Perrin claimed, Dyer draws parallels with Mark 4, the other major discourse of Jesus in Mark's Gospel (with 493 words in vv. 3-32). According to Dyer, there are 60 unique words out of 493 words (= 12.2 per cent) in Mk 4.3-32. Dyer is correct in noting that one cannot challenge the authenticity of Mark 13 simply on the basis of Perrin's statistics. His conclusion is that 'the vocabulary of Mk 13 is no more distinctive than the other major discourse

JSNT 62 (1996), pp. 13-41; and the provocative integrative proposal of E. Adams, 'Historical Crisis and Cosmic Crisis in Mark 13 and Lucan's *Civil War*', *TynBul* 48.2 (1997), pp. 329-44.

59. N. Perrin, *The Kingdom of God in the Teaching of Jesus* (London: SCM Press, 1963), p. 131, using R. Morgenthaler, *Statistik des neutestamentlichen Worschatzes* (Zürich: Gotthelf-Verlag, 1958), pp. 186-87. Cf. M.E. Boring, *Sayings of the Risen Jesus: Christian Prophecy in the Synoptic Tradition* (SNTSMS, 46; Cambridge: Cambridge University Press, 1982), pp. 186-95, esp. pp. 193-95, who cites and expands on Perrin's statistics, citing more parallels with Revelation.

60. There is question whether the apocalyptic vocabulary shared by Mk 13 and Revelation comes from Mark, Revelation, common apocalyptic tradition, or where. See Dyer, *Prophecy on the Mount*, p. 77.

61. Dyer, *Prophecy on the Mount*, pp. 75-77.

in the Gospel, Mk 4'.[62] Although he uses this to argue against the uniqueness of Mark 13, the evidence that he has gathered could also be interpreted to show, at least in a limited way, that Mark 13 and Mark 4, both with vocabulary distinct from that of the rest of the Gospel and discourses of Jesus, are independent from the general subject matter of the Gospel. The nature of the subject matter of Mark 13 is no doubt responsible in large part for various theories on the origins of this discourse prior to the Gospel's author receiving it.[63]

At this point in the investigation, and with the limited resources currently available, a Hallidayan register analysis does not look like it is able to resolve this issue definitively. However, the data regarding syntax and subject matter indicate that the field of discourse of Mark 13 also has a number of distinctive features when compared to the rest of the Gospel.[64]

4. *Conclusion*

Scholarship is far from a consensus on the origin of the so-called apocalyptic discourse of Mark 13.[65] Nevertheless, the features analysed above have been gathered from a number of standard treatments of Markan linguistic features, and supplemented by several of my own. When placed within a different conceptual model—that of Hallidayan register analysis—they provide evidence for a possible way forward in the debate over criteria. There is clear evidence in terms of all dimensions of register—field, tenor and mode—that much of Mk 13.5-37 does not conform to the Markan register elsewhere. In other words, the results here confirm that the context of situation out of which this discourse arose seems to be decidedly different from that of the Gospel as a whole. So little is known of the origins of Mark's Gospel, or, more

62. Dyer, *Prophecy on the Mount*, p. 77.

63. The major theories have revolved around the apocalyptic dimension of the discourse, and in particular whether a written source, often labelled the 'little apocalypse', lies behind what is found in Mk 13.5-37. As Collins points out (*Beginning of the Gospel*, pp. 81-88), there is no necessity to accept the 'little apocalypse' theory, nor to deny the origins of the discourse with Jesus (pp. 88-91). Perhaps this new criterion will add further evidence to the discussion.

64. See D. Wenham, *The Rediscovery of Jesus' Eschatological Discourse* (Gospel Perspectives, 4; Sheffield: JSOT Press, 1984), esp. pp. 359-64, 373-74.

65. See G.R. Beasley-Murray, *Jesus and the Kingdom of God* (Grand Rapids: Eerdmans; Exeter: Paternoster Press, 1986), pp. 322-23, for a survey of opinion.

particularly, of the individual discourses within it,[66] that it is fruitless to try to speculate on these matters here,[67] except to recognize that the features noted above point clearly toward an earlier origin of the discourse than the Gospel itself. As noted above, discourse analysis cannot decide textual integrity, but works from the premise of unity (or disunity). If we take the discourse in Mark 13 as a unity—and that is the basis upon which the analysis above has been made—the evidence points to Mark having taken an earlier unitary tradition and placed it within his Gospel. He has made only a few adaptations according to his style, but left many if not most of the features of the earlier tradition untouched. If we accept Markan priority in Synoptic source criticism, further support for this hypothesis can be found in terms of how Matthew and Luke have made further changes to this discourse. This confluence of situational factors would point to this discourse being possibly authentic Jesus tradition, in terms of how historical-Jesus research construes such a concept.

One question that has been in the background of this analysis of Mk 13.5-37 is that of the language of Jesus. So far, utilizing this criterion, no explicit statement has been made regarding whether one can determine whether Jesus delivered this discourse in Greek or not. The analysis has been made on the basis of the Greek language of the Gospel, requiring, as has been noted in Chapter 5, above, that close attention be paid to the Greek text that has been the subject of scrutiny. However, this criterion, although it relies upon analysis of the Greek text and is, therefore, in this sense a Greek language criterion for authenticity, does not necessarily rely upon the original discourse being delivered in Greek to prove effective. The reasonable presumption, however, is that, even in translation, the significant number of discourse features that are distinct in the discourse from the narrative of the Gospel indicate a separate source. This translated source may have originally been given

---

66. See M. Hengel, 'Entstehungszeit und Situation des Markusevangeliums', in H. Cancik (ed.), *Markus-Philologie: Historische, literargeschichtliche und stilistische Untersuchungen zum zweiten Evangelium* (WUNT, 33; Tübingen: Mohr Siebeck, 1984), pp. 1-45; ET in M. Hengel, *Studies in the Gospel of Mark* (trans. J. Bowden; London: SCM Press, 1985), pp. 1-30, who links Mk 13 to the discussion of authorship.

67. I have made an attempt to describe the Markan context of situation along other, related lines in Porter, 'Register in the Greek of the New Testament: Application with Reference to Mark's Gospel'.

in Aramaic, with a significant number of textual linguistic features of the translation (not necessarily Semitisms, but Greek discourse features) distinguishing the selection from its surrounding discourse. This criterion would still apply whether the narrative in which the discourse is embedded were originally written in Greek, or whether it were written (as is unikely) in another language, such as Aramaic. However, this is not the full extent of the use of this criterion. If it could be shown, on the basis of the first criterion above—that of Greek language and its context—or a similar criterion or method, that the analysed discourse were originally probably delivered in Greek, this criterion could serve as a useful check upon that presumption. If the features of the discourse were significantly distinct from those of its surrounding narrative, this criterion could serve to confirm that the discourse was originally delivered in Greek. If the features were not, then one would not necessarily have disproved that the discourse was originally delivered in Greek, but one would not be able to appeal to this criterion in support of such a presumption. So far, this criterion is not able to determine on its own whether a discourse was originally delivered in Greek.

To make this criterion more useful, it requires much further refinement in a number of areas. One of these is in terms of the corpora studied. When a sufficient database has been prepared, it will be possible to study a far greater number of linguistic features in this, and other, texts of the New Testament and the Graeco-Roman world, and to draw conclusions that extend over a much larger corpus. Another refinement is in terms of the linguistic features studied and the explanations given of the results. The larger body of material in machine processable form will allow for greater experimentation in terms of not only a larger number of features for analysis, but a higher level of complexity in those features themselves. It will have been noted, I am sure, that I have not compared my results of the above study in any systematic way with the results of other studies of authenticity of this passage, apart from those few studies utilized above that address similar issues. It might be instructive to do so, in order to compare the results and see whether further clarification of issues comes from other quarters. However, this new criterion, along with the other two presented in Chapters 4 and 5, above, is not meant simply as a further supplement to decisions made according to other criteria. This criterion is designed to break new ground in exploration of what is meant by criteria for authenticity in historical-Jesus research. This third criterion of discourse features may have the greatest potential because of its possible extension over a larger body of material to develop linguistic indicators to aid in determining which portions of a Gospel are earlier than other portions, and hence could reflect the authentic words of Jesus.

CONCLUSION

At the beginning of this all-too-brief study, I began with a question. That question was whether the term 'third quest' was merited as a descriptive label of current historical-Jesus research, in particular in terms of the criteria for authenticity that are often invoked in such research. Even though this study has been a relatively short one, I believe that we have come a long way from that question in the ensuing discussion. I have first surveyed the history of historical-Jesus research. Although the vast majority of scholars wish to divide the scholarly study of Jesus into several discrete approach-based units, I have not been convinced by such divisions. These divisions seem to mask as much as, if not more than, they reveal. One of the major historical facts that they hide is that there has been a consistent and sustained scholarly discussion of who Jesus was and what he said and did that has extended from the eighteenth to the twentieth centuries. This discussion may not always have been equally actively maintained in various countries or by various language groups, or have approached the issues in the same methodological ways, but it has seemed to be consistently present for virtually all of the twentieth century, and the nineteenth before it. It seems, however, that much historical-Jesus research has been seduced into focusing its attention on a small band of discussion, in particular the treatments of Jesus that were being written in Germany in the early part of the twentieth century, and whether they utilized form-critical methods. But even in the Germany of the first half of that century there was more discussion of Jesus than those who advocate the 'no quest' period seem willing to admit, to say nothing of the research being done elsewhere. In the light of the international nature of current scholarly research, as well as the relation between this subject matter and the activity of the Christian Church, my conclusion is that we should not speak of historical-Jesus research in terms of the conceptual framework of only one nationality or approach, but take note of its consistent and ongoing development in various quarters. There is no denying that there have been a number of crucial developments in method and approach along the way, but I do not believe that the segmented scenario usually advocated is warranted.

In particular, in the light of such discussion, I have been interested in tracing the criteria for authenticity, as they were developed and utilized in historical-Jesus research. Part of the evidence for seeing one continuous and ongoing history of Jesus research is the fact that the criteria for authenticity have themselves transcended any rigid boundaries in their own origins and development. Although several of the major criteria had their origins around the turn of the nineteenth to twentieth centuries, as I have tried to note, most of them were originally formulated in the light of the development of form criticism. Again, one of the possible reasons that the history of Jesus research has been written as it has been, may well be that form criticism found its greatest initial support, and resulted in several of its major formative statements, in German-speaking circles. It is entirely logical that form criticism led to the positing of criteria for authenticity, since one of the major goals of form criticism was to be able to differentiate between earliest Church tradition and its development. Several of the more surprising features of the development of these criteria, however, are that their formulation often lacked a systematic nature in the work of their earliest advocates, but that more definitive statements as to the formulation and use of these criteria often came from those who are associated with the so-called 'new' or 'second quest' for the historical Jesus. This development in the criteria seems to move in the opposite direction from the way some have wished to characterize the 'new' or 'second quest'. When one realizes that the quest for the historical Jesus has been an ongoing and continuous one, one can understand this tendency towards codification of the criteria by those responsible.

These developments have led me to investigate several recent attempts to redeem, expand or transform the criteria for authenticity. In terms of those who are advocating a 'third quest' for the historical Jesus along what they claim are significantly different lines than previous quests, the development of such criteria would seem to be a sine qua non of their efforts. It is surprising, therefore, that more attention has not been given to the development of such criteria among 'third quest' advocates. My examination of two major recent attempts to redefine the traditional criteria and appropriate them in terms of the development of new criteria has not resulted in the kind of optimistic view of these criteria that others have, however. The shortcomings are several, and merit repeating here. One is the failure to sufficiently formulate the criteria in terms that avoid falling victim to the criticisms of the traditional criteria that these new or refined criteria are attempting to correct. Another shortcoming is the misguided notion that something new and different has been developed, when in fact the result is simply a reformulation, often with new language, of criteria that were formulated earlier and, in fact, criticized and corrected along similar lines. The result is a sense that the newest criteria advocated by some for the 'third quest' have failed once more to push forward discussion of the criteria for authenticity.

In the light of these developments—or lack of them, even among a number of historical-Jesus scholars who merit much respect in the work that they have done—I have taken what some might well see as the bold step of attempting to develop new criteria for authenticity. As much as is possible (although admittedly, not entirely), I have tried to develop these criteria independently of the traditional criteria. Since several of these traditional criteria appeal to basic common sense, or even standard principles of logic, it has of course been impossible—and it would, indeed, be unwise—to attempt to work outside of these parameters. Nevertheless, I have begun from a very different point in developing these criteria, and tried to be consistent and faithful to my presuppositions in their development. Taking note of recent comments by other scholars (both positive and negative), I have gone outside of the Gospels themselves and begun with a view of the world of first-century Roman Palestine. My view of this world is, apparently, quite different from that of many other New Testament scholars, some of whom I have directly responded to in the course of this work. I am convinced, on the basis of what I see as virtually undeniable evidence, that there was widespread use of the Greek language in first-century Palestine. Further, I believe that there is good evidence and reason for believing that Jesus and many of his closest followers probably also used Greek. I do not wish to deny that they also knew and used Aramaic (and even perhaps knew some Hebrew), and probably used Aramaic in the majority of their communication. Nevertheless, there is substantial evidence that they also would have known Greek. Of course, we do not have the kind of access to their linguistic usage that we have in modern linguistic contexts. We must work on the basis of the remains available, but interpreted within a linguistically sound methodological framework. I have tried to utilize such a framework, in terms of concepts of multilingualism and prestige languages, as well as what is known of Greek as the *lingua franca* of the Graeco-Roman world. I do not think that all who have entered into this discussion have been as precise in this regard as they might have been. I do not consider for a moment that I have got all of the facts and perspectives correct either, but I do think that this research is moving in the proper direction for such discussion, and I hope that I and others will have a chance to continue and advance such work.

On the basis of this starting point within the Greek-speaking world of first-century Palestine (without the disjunctive presupposition of denying the use of other languages), I have developed the criterion of Greek language and its context. I have done this by examining the Gospel accounts in an attempt to find situations where it is likely that Jesus and his conversational partners would have used Greek. A number of such contexts have been suggested by others, and I may well have excluded some that merit further attention. I have tried to be rigorous and restrained in my use of my method, and believe that I have found an essential minimum number of episodes, where it is plausible to suggest that Greek was the language of conversation on that occasion. I have started from this point, and extended the criterion by analysing the subject matter as also consistent with the use of Greek. On the basis of these two sub-criteria, it is possible to note seven Gospel episodes where it is possible that Jesus spoke in Greek with others. This first new criterion of Greek language and its context establishes that Jesus probably spoke in Greek on particular, definable occasions, but it does not determine with certainty what those words might have been.

The second new criterion is that of Greek textual variance. This criterion is a further extension of the one above on Greek language and its context. This criterion also relies upon recent work regarding textual variants in the words of Jesus to develop a principle for differentiating authentic tradition. In those contexts where it has been established by the first criterion or some other means that Greek was the language of communication between Jesus and his conversational partners, this criterion attempts to determine what those words might have been. This criterion relies upon there being multiple independent traditions, but overcomes the limitations of this traditional criterion by applying it at the point that it has been especially criticized—to determine specific wording. It is able to do this because of the use of Greek language as the linguistic medium of communication. On this basis, it is probable that we have the very words of Jesus in at least one, if not up to four episodes in the Gospels. Some will dispute these individual episodes, and others will resist the force of the conclusions (perhaps because they have pre-decided that Jesus could not have spoken Greek, despite the overwhelming evidence to the contrary), but the minimalist conclusions seem to me to be secure.

The third and final criterion is that of discourse features. This criterion departs the furthest from the traditional criteria for authenticity and relies upon recent work in discourse analysis. Discourse analysis, a new area of linguistic investigation especially for the New Testament, has much to offer biblical scholars. In developing this criterion, I have attempted to combine this new method with the traditional stylistic findings of other scholars. By examining the findings of others within this new interpretive framework, I believe that a third criterion can be developed that allows us to determine whether a given episode may well be authentic to the Jesus tradition. This criterion, I believe, has the most potential for further development as the resources available for study increase, and as the linguistic features examined are further refined. Its application to a larger number of major pericopes in the Gospels has the promise of determining whether larger chunks of Jesus material, rather than simply individual sentences, have a claim to authenticity.

The results of this study have, in many respects, been negative in the sense that I have concluded that much of the conceptual framework of previous historical-Jesus research has been imprecisely and inaccurately formulated. Part of my work has been to call for historical-Jesus scholars to re-assess our interpretive framework. My development of new criteria has been a major part of this attempt. Rather than leaving the negative critique, I have attempted to develop and utilize these new criteria for authenticity as a way forward in historical-Jesus research. Again, the number of passages that have been analysed and the conclusions promoted have been small. As I have stated at several points in the research above, however, just because a passage does not fulfil these criteria does not mean that a given episode was not uttered in Greek or that it is not authentic. There are clear and distinct limitations to these criteria that must be respected. However, there is a potential for further research that may well lead others to extend the results to a larger number of passages. In any event, this work has been an attempt to broaden and extend the scope of historical-Jesus research, as we enter a new century of continued discussion of the fascinating man from Galilee.

BIBLIOGRAPHY

Abbott, T.K., *Essays, Chiefly on the Original Texts of the Old and New Testaments* (London: Longmans, Green, 1891).

Abel, F.-M., *Grammaire du grec biblique: Suivie d'un choix de papyrus* (EB; Paris: J. Gabalda, 1927)

Achtemeier, P.J., *'Omne verbum sonat*: The New Testament and the Oral Environment of Late Western Antiquity', *JBL* 109 (1990), pp. 3-27.

Adams, E., 'Historical Crisis and Cosmic Crisis in Mark 13 and Lucan's *Civil War*', *TynBul* 48.2 (1997), pp. 329-44.

Adinolfi, M., 'L'ellenizzazione della Palestina', in M. Adinolfi and P. Kaswalder (eds.), *Entrarono a Cafarnao: Lettura interdisciplinare di Mc 1. Studi in onore di P. Virginio Ravanelli* (Studium Biblicum Franciscanum, 44; Jerusalem: Franciscan Printing Press, 1997), pp. 29-35.

Aland, K., and B. Aland, *Der Text des Neuen Testaments* (Stuttgart: Deutsche Bibelgesellschaft, 2nd edn, 1981; ET *The Text of the New Testament: An Introduction to the Critical Editions and to the Theory and Practice of Modern Textual Criticism* [trans. E.F. Rhodes; Grand Rapids: Eerdmans, 2nd edn, 1989]).

Allison, D.C., Jr, 'Matthew 23.39 = Luke 13.35B as a Conditional Prophecy', *JSNT* 18 (1983), pp. 75-84; repr. in Evans and Porter (eds.), *The Historical Jesus*, pp. 262-70.

Anderson, H., *Jesus and Christian Origins: A Commentary on Modern Viewpoints* (New York: Oxford University Press, 1964).

Argyle, A.W., 'Did Jesus Speak Greek?', *ExpTim* 67 (1955–56), pp. 92-93, 383.

—'Greek among the Jews of Palestine in New Testament Times', *NTS* 20 (1974), pp. 87-89.

— '"Hypocrites" and the Aramaic Theory', *ExpTim* 75 (1963–64), pp. 113-14.

Atkinson, K., 'On Further Defining the First-Century CE Synagogue: Fact or Fiction?', *NTS* 43 (1997), pp. 491-502.

Aulén, G., *Jesus i nutida historisk forskning* (Stockholm: Verbum, 1973; 2nd edn, 1974; ET *Jesus in Contemporary Historical Research* [trans. I.H. Hjelm; Philadelphia: Fortress Press, 1976]).

Aune, D.E., 'Jesus and Cynics in First-Century Palestine: Some Critical Considerations', in Charlesworth and Johns (eds.), *Hillel and Jesus*, pp. 176-92.

—*Prophecy in Early Christianity and the Ancient Mediterranean World* (Grand Rapids: Eerdmans, 1983).

Bacon, B.W., *The Fourth Gospel in Research and Debate: A Series of Essays on Problems Concerning the Origin and Value of the Anonymous Writings Attributed to the Apostle John* (London: T. Fisher Unwin, 1919).

Baetens Beardsmore, H., *Bilingualism: Basic Principles* (Multilingual Matters, 1; Clevedon: Multilingual Matters, 1982; 2nd edn, 1986).

Baird, J.A., *Audience Criticism and the Historical Jesus* (NTL; Philadelphia: Westminster Press; London: SCM Press, 1969).

—*The Justice of God in the Teaching of Jesus* (Philadelphia: Westminster Press, 1963).

Bammel, E., 'The *titulus*', in Bammel and Moule (eds.), *Jesus and the Politics of his Day*, pp. 353-64.

Bammel, E., and C.F.D. Moule (eds.), *Jesus and the Politics of his Day* (Cambridge: Cambridge University Press, 1984).

Banks, R.J., 'Setting "The Quest for the Historical Jesus" in a Broader Framework', in France and Wenham (eds.), *Gospel Perspectives*, II, pp. 61-82.

Barbour, R.S., *Traditio-Historical Criticism of the Gospels* (Studies in Creative Criticism, 4; London: SPCK, 1972).

Bardy, G., *La question des langues dans l'église ancienne* (Etudes de théologie historique, 1; Paris: Beauchesne, 1948).

Bar-Kochva, B., *Pseudo-Hecataeus, 'On the Jews': Legitimizing the Jewish Diaspora* (Berkeley: University of California Press, 1996).

Barr, J., 'Hebrew, Aramaic and Greek in the Hellenistic Age', in W.D. Davies and L. Finkelstein (eds.), *The Cambridge History of Judaism. II. The Hellenistic Age* (Cambridge: Cambridge University Press, 1989), pp. 79-114.

— *The Typology of Literalism in Ancient Biblical Translations* (Nachrichten der Akademie der Wissenschaften in Göttingen I. Philologisch-Historische Klasse. Mitteilungen des Septuaginta-Unternehmens, 15; Göttingen: Vandenhoeck & Ruprecht, 1979).

—'Which Language Did Jesus Speak?—Some Remarks of a Semitist', *BJRL* 53 (1970), pp. 9-29.

Barrett, C.K., *The Gospel According to St John* (London: SPCK; Philadelphia: Westminster Press, 2nd edn, 1978 [1955]).

— *Jesus and the Gospel Tradition* (London: SPCK, 1967).

Bassnett, S., *Translation Studies* (London: Routledge, rev. edn, 1991 [1980]).

Bassnett, S., and H. Trivedi (eds.), *Post-Colonial Translation: Theory and Practice* (Translation Studies; London: Routledge, 1999).

Beare, F.W., *The Earliest Records of Jesus* (Oxford: Basil Blackwell, 1964).

Beasley-Murray, G.R., *Jesus and the Kingdom of God* (Grand Rapids: Eerdmans; Exeter: Paternoster Press, 1986).

—*Jesus and the Last Days: The Interpretation of the Olivet Discourse* (Peabody, MA: Hendrickson, 1993).

—*John* (WBC, 36; Dallas: Word Books, 1987).

Beattie, D.R.G., and M.J. McNamara (eds.), *The Aramaic Bible: Targums in their Historical Context* (JSOTSup, 166; Sheffield: JSOT Press, 1994).

Beker, J., *Jesus von Nazaret* (Berlin: W. de Gruyter, 1995).

Bell, G.K.A., and A. Deissmann (eds.), *Mysterium Christi: Christological Studies by British and German Theologians* (London: Longmans, Green; Berlin: Furche-Verlag, 1930).

Bell, R.T., *Translation and Translating: Theory and Practice* (Applied Linguistics and Language Study; London: Longman, 1991).

Bellinzoni, A.J., Jr (ed.), *The Two-Source Hypothesis: A Critical Appraisal* (Macon, GA: Mercer University Press, 1985).

Benoit, P., J.T. Milik and R. de Vaux (eds.), *Les grottes de Murabba'at* (DJD, 2; Oxford: Clarendon Press, 1961).

Berger, K., *Einführung in die Formgeschichte* (UTb, 1444; Tübingen: Franke, 1987).

—*Exegese des Neuen Testaments: Neue Wege vom Text zur Auslegung* (UTb, 658; Heidelberg: Quelle & Meyer, 1977).

—'Hellenistische Gattungen im Neuen Testament', *ANRW* 2.25.2, pp. 1031-1432.

Betz, H.D., *Antike und Christentum: Gesammelte Aufsätze IV* (Tübingen: Mohr Siebeck, 1998).

—'Jesus and the Cynics: Survey and Analysis of a Hypothesis', *JR* 74 (1994), pp. 453-75; repr. in *idem, Antike und Christentum,* pp. 32-56.

—'Wellhausen's Dictum "Jesus was not a Christian, but a Jew" in Light of Present Scholarship', *ST* 45 (1991), pp. 83-110; repr. in *idem, Antike und Christentum,* pp. 1-31.

Betz, O., *Was Wissen wir von Jesus?* (Stuttgart: Kreuz, 1965; ET *What Do We Know about Jesus?* [trans. M. Kohl; London: SCM Press, 1968]).

Beyer, K., *Die aramäische Texte vom Toten Meer* (Göttingen: Vandenhoeck & Ruprecht, 1984).

Biber, D., *Dimensions of Register Variation: A Cross-Linguistic Comparison* (Cambridge: Cambridge University Press, 1995).

—*Variation across Speech and Writing* (Cambridge: Cambridge University Press, 1988).

Biber, D., and E. Finegan (eds.), *Sociolinguistic Perspectives on Register* (Oxford Studies in Sociolinguistics; New York: Oxford University Press, 1995).

Bilde, P., *Flavius Josephus between Jerusalem and Rome: His Life, his Works, and their Importance* (JSPSup, 2; Sheffield: JSOT Press, 1988).

Birkeland, H., *The Language of Jesus* (Avhandlinger utgitt av Det Norske Videnskaps-Akademie I. II. Historish-Filosofisk Klasse I; Oslo: Dybwad, 1954).

Black, C.C., *The Disciples According to Mark: Markan Redaction in Current Debate* (JSNTSup, 27; Sheffield: JSOT Press, 1989).

—'An Oration at Olivet: Some Rhetorical Dimensions of Mark 13', in D.F. Watson (ed.), *Persuasive Artistry: Studies in New Testament Rhetoric in Honor of George A. Kennedy* (JSNTSup, 50; Sheffield: JSOT Press, 1991), pp. 66-92.

Black, D.A., 'Discourse Analysis, Synoptic Criticism, and Markan Grammar: Some Methodological Considerations', in Black *et al.* (eds.), *Linguistics and New Testament Interpretation,* pp. 90-98.

—*It's Still Greek to Me: An Easy-to-Understand Guide to Intermediate Greek* (Grand Rapids: Baker Book House, 1998).

—'Some Dissenting Notes on R. Stein's *The Synoptic Problem* and Markan "Errors"', *FN* 1 (1988), pp. 95-101.

Black, D.A., and D.S. Dockery (eds.), *New Testament Criticism and Interpretation* (Grand Rapids: Zondervan, 1991).

Black, D.A., *et al.* (eds.), *Linguistics and New Testament Interpretation: Essays on Discourse Analysis* (Nashville: Broadman, 1992).

Black, M., *An Aramaic Approach to the Gospels and Acts* (Oxford: Clarendon Press, 1946; 2nd edn, 1954; 3rd edn, 1967; repr. with 'Introduction: An Aramaic Approach Thirty Years Later', by C.A. Evans, pp. v-xxv; Peabody, MA: Hendrickson, 1998).

Blass, F., *Philology of the Gospels* (London: Macmillan, 1898).

Blass, F., and A. Debrunner, *A Greek Grammar of the New Testament and Other Early Christian Literature* (trans. R.W. Funk; Chicago: University of Chicago Press, 1961).

Blomberg, C.L., 'Historical Criticism of the New Testament', in D.S. Dockery, K.A. Mathews and R.B. Sloan (eds.), *Foundations for Biblical Interpretation* (Nashville: Broadman & Holman, 1994), pp. 414-33.

—*The Historical Reliability of the Gospels* (Leicester: Inter-Varsity Press, 1987).

—*Interpreting the Parables* (Downers Grove, IL: IVP, 1990).

—'Interpreting the Parables of Jesus: Where Are We and Where Do We Go from Here?', *CBQ* 53 (1991), pp. 50-78.

—'The Parables of Jesus: Current Trends and Needs in Research', in Chilton and Evans (eds.), *Studying the Historical Jesus*, pp. 231-54.

Boccaccini, G., *Middle Judaism: Jewish Thought 300 B.C.E. to 200 C.E.* (Minneapolis: Fortress Press, 1991).

Bock, D.L., 'Form Criticism', in Black and Dockery (eds.), *New Testament Criticism and Interpretation*, pp. 175-96.

—*Luke* (2 vols.; Baker Exegetical Commentary on the New Testament, 3A, B; Grand Rapids: Baker Book House, 1994, 1996).

Bockmuehl, M., *This Jesus: Martyr, Lord, Messiah* (Edinburgh: T. & T. Clark; Downers Grove, IL: InterVarsity Press, 1994).

Boers, H., *The Justification of the Gentiles: Paul's Letters to the Galatians and Romans* (Peabody, MA: Hendrickson, 1994).

Bond, H.K., *Pontius Pilate in History and Interpretation* (SNTSMS, 100; Cambridge: Cambridge University Press, 1998).

Borg, M.J., *Conflict, Holiness and Politics in the Teachings of Jesus* (Lewiston, NY: Edwin Mellen Press, 1984; repr. Harrisburg, PA: Trinity Press International, 1998).

—*Jesus in Contemporary Scholarship* (Valley Forge, PA: Trinity Press International, 1994).

—*Jesus a New Vision: Spirit, Culture, and the Life of Discipleship* (San Francisco: HarperSanFrancisco, 1987).

Borgen, P., 'The Independence of the Gospel of John: Some Observations', in Van Segbroeck, Tuckett, Van Belle and Verheyden (eds.), *The Four Gospels 1992*, III, pp. 1815-33.

—'John and the Synoptics', in Dungan (ed.), *The Interrelations of the Gospels*, pp. 408-37.

Boring, M.E., 'The Historical-Critical Method's "Criteria of Authenticity": The Beatitudes in Q and Thomas as a Test Case', *Semeia* 44 (1988), pp. 9-44.

—*Sayings of the Risen Jesus: Christian Prophecy in the Synoptic Tradition* (SNTSMS, 46; Cambridge: Cambridge University Press, 1982).

Bornkamm, G., 'Die Sturmstillung im Matthäusevangelium', *Wort und Dienst: Jahrbuch der Theologischen Schule Bethel* NS 1 (1948), pp. 49-54; repr. in Bornkamm, Barth and Held, *Tradition and Interpretation in Matthew*, pp. 52-57.

—'Enderwartung und Kirche im Matthäusevangelium', in W.D. Davies and D. Daube (eds.), *The Background of the New Testament and its Eschatology: Studies in Honour of C.H. Dodd* (Cambridge: Cambridge University Press, 1954), pp. 222-60.

—*Jesus von Nazareth* (Urban-Bücher, 19; Stuttgart: W. Kohlhammer, 1956; 10th edn, 1975; ET *Jesus of Nazareth* [trans. I. McLuskey and F. McLuskey with J.M. Robinson; London: Hodder & Stoughton, 1960]).

Bornkamm, G., G. Barth and H.J. Held, *Überlieferung und Auslegung im Matthäusevangelium* (Neukirchen–Vluyn: Neukirchener Verlag, 1960; ET *Tradition and Interpretation in Matthew* [trans. P. Scott; NTL; London: SCM Press; Philadelphia: Westminster Press, 1963]).

Botha, J.E., 'Style in the New Testament: The Need for Serious Reconsideration', *JSNT* 43 (1991), pp. 71-87.

Bousset, W., *Jesus* (Halle: Gebauer-Schwetschke, 1904; Tübingen: Mohr Siebeck, 3rd edn, 1907; ET *Jesus* [CThL; trans. J.P. Trevelyan; London: Williams & Norgate; New York: Putnam's Sons, 1906]).

—*Kyrios Christos: Geschichte des Christusglaubens von den Anfängen des Christentums bis Irenaeus* (FRLANT, 4; Göttingen: Vandenhoeck & Ruprecht, 1913; 5th edn, 1964; ET *Kyrios Christos: A History of the Belief in Christ from the Beginnings of Christianity to Irenaeus* [trans. J.E. Steely; Nashville: Abingdon Press, 1970]).

Bowden, J.S., *Jesus: The Unanswered Questions* (London: SCM Press, 1988).

Braaten, C.E., and R.A. Harrisville (eds.), *The Historical Jesus and the Kerygmatic Christ: Essays on the New Quest of the Historical Jesus* (Nashville: Abingdon Press, 1964).

Bradford, R., *Stylistics* (New Critical Idiom; London: Routledge, 1997).

Braun, F.-M., *Jésus: Histoire et critique* (Tournai: Casterman, 1947).

Braun, H., *Jesus: Der Mann aus Nazareth und seine Zeit* (Berlin: Kreuz-Verlag, 1969).

Breech, J., *The Silence of Jesus: The Authentic Voice of the Authentic Man* (Philadelphia: Fortress Press, 1980).

Brehm, H.A., 'The Meaning of Ἑλληνιστής in Acts in Light of a Diachronic Analysis of ἑλληνίζειν', in Porter and Carson (eds.), *Discourse Analysis and Other Topics*, pp. 180-99.

Breytenbach, C., *Nachfolge und Zukunftserwartung nach Markus: Eine methodenkritische Studie* (ATANT, 71; Zürich: Theologischer Verlag, 1984).

Brixhe, C., *Essai sur le Grec Anatolien: Au début de notre ère* (TMEA, 1; Nancy: Presses Universitaires de Nancy, 1984).

Brixhe, C. (ed.), *La koiné grecque antique* (3 vols.; TMEA, 10, 14, 17; Nancy: Presses Universitaires de Nancy, 1993–98).

Brock, S.P., review of *Aramaic Approach*, by Black, in *JTS* NS 20 (1969), pp. 274-78.

Brodie, T.L., *The Quest for the Origin of John's Gospel: A Source-Oriented Approach* (New York: Oxford University Press, 1993).

Brown, C., 'Historical Jesus, Quest of', in Green, McKnight and Marshall (eds.), *Dictionary of Jesus and the Gospels*, pp. 326-41.

Brown, G., and G. Yule, *Discourse Analysis* (CTL; Cambridge: Cambridge University Press, 1983).

Brown, R.E., *The Death of the Messiah: From Gethsemane to the Grave* (2 vols.; ABRL; New York: Doubleday; London: Chapman, 1994).

—*The Gospel According to John* (2 vols.; AB 29, 29A; Garden City, NY: Doubleday, 1966, 1970).

—*An Introduction to the New Testament* (ABRL; New York: Doubleday, 1997).

Browning, R., *Medieval and Modern Greek* (Cambridge: Cambridge University Press, 2nd edn, 1983), pp. 19-52.

—'Von der Koine bis zu den Anfängen des modernen Griechisch', in H.-G. Nesselrath (ed.), *Einleitung in die griechische Philologie* (Stuttgart: Teubner, 1997), pp. 156-68.

Bruce, F.F., 'Render to Caesar', in Bammel and Moule (eds.), *Jesus and the Politics of his Day*, pp. 249-63.

—*Tradition Old and New* (Exeter: Paternoster Press, 1970).

Büchsel, F., 'Die griechische Sprache der Juden in der Zeit der Septuaginta und des Neuen Testaments', *ZAW* 60 (1944), pp. 132-49.

Bultmann, R., *Das Evangelium des Johannes* (MeyerK; Göttingen: Vandenhoeck & Ruprecht, 1947; 2nd edn, 1964; supplement 1966; ET *The Gospel of John: A Commentary* [trans. G.R. Beasley-Murray; Oxford: Basil Blackwell, 1971]).

—*Das Verhältnis der urchristlichen Christusbotschaft zum historischen Jesus* (Sitzungsberichte der Heidelberger Akademie der Wissenschaften phil.-hist. Klasse; Heidelberg: Winter, 1960; 3rd edn, 1962); ET 'The Primitive Christian Kerygma and the

Historical Jesus', in Braaten and Harrisville (eds.), *The Historical Jesus and the Kerygmatic Christ*, pp. 15-42.

—*Die Geschichte der synoptischen Tradition* (FRLANT, 29; Göttingen: Vandenhoeck & Ruprecht, 1921; 2nd edn, 1931; 6th edn, 1957; ET *History of the Synoptic Tradition* [trans. J. Marsh; Oxford: Basil Blackwell, 1963; 2nd edn, 1968]).

—*Jesus* (Berlin: Deutsche Bibliothek, 1926; 2nd edn, 1934; ET *Jesus and the Word* [trans. L.P. Smith and E. Huntress; New York: Charles Scribner's Sons, 1934; London: Ivor Nicholson & Watson, 1935]).

—'Neues Testament und Mythologie: Das Problem der Entmythologisierung der neutesta-mentlichen Verkündigung', in H.W. Bartsch (ed.), *Kerygma und Mythos: Ein theo-logisches Gespräch* (Hamburg: H. Reich, 1948; 2nd edn, 1951), pp. 15-48; ET 'New Testament and Mythology: The Mythological Element in the Message of the New Testament and the Problem of its Re-Interpretation', in H.W. Bartsch (ed.), *Kerygma and Myth: A Theological Debate* (trans. R.H. Fuller; London: SPCK, 1953; 2nd edn, 1964), pp. 1-44.

—'The New Approach to the Synoptic Problem', *JR* 6 (1926), pp. 337-62; repr. in S. Ogden (ed.), *Existence and Faith: Shorter Writings of Rudolf Bultmann* (New York: Merid-ian, 1960; London: Hodder & Stoughton, 1961), pp. 35-54.

—*Theologie des Neuen Testaments* (Tübingen: Mohr Siebeck, 1948; 7th edn ed. O. Merk, 1977; ET *Theology of the New Testament* [2 vols.; trans. K. Grobel; London: SCM Press; New York: Charles Scribner's Sons, 1951, 1955]).

Bundy, W.E., *Jesus and the First Three Gospels: An Introduction to the Synoptic Tradition* (Cambridge, MA: Harvard University Press, 1955).

Burge, G., *Interpreting the Gospel of John* (Guides to New Testament Exegesis; Grand Rapids: Baker Book House, 1992).

Burkitt, F.C., *The Gospel History and its Transmission* (Edinburgh: T. & T. Clark, 1906; 3rd edn, 1911).

—*Jesus Christ: An Historical Outline* (London: Blackie, 1932).

Burney, C.F., *The Aramaic Origin of the Fourth Gospel* (Oxford: Clarendon Press, 1922).

—*The Poetry of Our Lord* (Oxford: Clarendon Press, 1925).

Byrskog, S., *Jesus the Only Teacher: Didactic Authority and Transmission in Ancient Israel, Ancient Judaism and the Matthean Community* (ConBNT, 24; Stockholm: Almqvist & Wiksell, 1994).

Cadoux, C.J., *The Historic Mission of Jesus: A Constructive Reexamination of the Escha-tological Teaching in the Synoptic Gospels* (London: Lutterworth, 1941).

Caldas-Coulthard, C.R., and M. Coulthard (eds.), *Texts and Practices: Readings in Critical Discourse Analysis* (London: Routledge, 1996).

Calvert, D.G.A., 'An Examination of the Criteria for Distinguishing the Authentic Words of Jesus', *NTS* 18 (1971–72), pp. 209-19.

Caragounis, C.C., *The Son of Man: Vision and Interpretation* (WUNT, 38; Tübingen: Mohr Siebeck, 1986).

Carpenter, H., *Jesus* (Past Masters; Oxford: Oxford University Press, 1980).

Carlston, C.E., 'A *Positive* Criterion of Authenticity?', *BR* 7 (1962), pp. 33-44.

Carrington, P., *According to Mark: A Running Commentary on the Oldest Gospel* (Cam-bridge: Cambridge University Press, 1960).

—*The Primitive Christian Calendar: A Study in the Making of the Marcan Gospel* (Cam-bridge: Cambridge University Press, 1952).

Carson, D.A., *The Gospel According to John* (Leicester: Inter-Varsity Press; Grand Rapids: Eerdmans, 1991).

—'Historical Tradition in the Fourth Gospel: After Dodd, What?', in France and Wenham (eds.), *Gospel Perspectives*, II, pp. 85-145.

—'Redaction Criticism: On the Legitimacy and Illegitimacy of a Literary Tool', in D.A. Carson and J.D. Woodbridge (eds.), *Scripture and Truth* (Grand Rapids: Zondervan, 1983), pp. 119-42.

Cartlidge, D.R., and D.L. Dungan, *Documents for the Study of the Gospels* (Philadelphia: Fortress Press; London: Collins, 1980).

Cary, M., *A History of Rome down to the Reign of Constantine* (London: Macmillan, 1935; 2nd edn, 1954).

—*The Legacy of Alexander: A History of the Greek World from 323 to 146 B.C.* (New York: Dial, 1932).

Case, S.J., *The Historicity of Jesus* (Chicago: University of Chicago Press, 1912; 2nd edn, 1928).

—*Jesus: A New Biography* (Chicago: University of Chicago Press, 1927).

Casey, M., 'An Aramaic Approach to the Synoptic Gospels', *ExpTim* 110.7 (1999), pp. 275-78.

—*Aramaic Sources of Mark's Gospel* (SNTSMS, 102; Cambridge: Cambridge University Press, 1998).

—'In Which Language Did Jesus Teach?', *ExpTim* 108.11 (1997), pp. 326-28.

Catchpole, D.R., 'The Answer of Jesus to Caiaphas (Matt. xxvi.64)', *NTS* 17 (1970–71), pp. 213-26.

—'The Centurion's Faith and its Function in Q', in Van Segbroeck, Tuckett, Van Bekke and Verheyden(eds.), *The Four Gospels 1992*, I, pp. 517-40; repr. in D.R. Catchpole, *The Quest for Q* (Edinburgh: T. & T. Clark, 1993), pp. 280-308.

—'Tradition History', in Marshall (ed.), *New Testament Interpretation*, pp. 165-80.

Charlesworth, J.H., 'The Historical Jesus in Light of Writings Contemporaneous with Him', *ANRW* 2.25.1 (Berlin: W. de Gruyter, 1982), pp. 451-76.

—*Jesus within Judaism: New Light from Exciting Archaeological Discoveries* (ABRL; New York: Doubleday, 1988).

Charlesworth, J.H., and C.A. Evans, 'Jesus in the Agrapha and Apocryphal Gospels', in Chilton and Evans (eds.), *Studying the Historical Jesus*, pp. 479-533.

Charlesworth, J.H., and L.L. Johns (eds.), *Hillel and Jesus: Comparative Studies of Two Major Religious Leaders* (Minneapolis: Fortress Press, 1997).

Chilton, B., 'Assessing Progress in the Third Quest', in Chilton and Evans (eds.), *Authenticating the Words of Jesus*, pp. 15-25.

—*A Galilean Rabbi and his Bible: Jesus' Use of the Interpreted Scripture of his Time* (GNS, 8; Wilmington, DE: Michael Glazier, 1984).

—*The Glory of Israel: The Theology and Provenience of the Isaiah Targum* (JSOTSup, 23; Sheffield: JSOT Press, 1982).

—*God in Strength: Jesus' Announcement of the Kingdom* (SNTU, B.1; Freistadt: Plöchl, 1979; repr. BibSem, 8; Sheffield: JSOT Press, 1987).

—'The Kingdom of God in Recent Discussion', in Chilton and Evans (eds.), *Studying the Historical Jesus*, pp. 255-80.

—*Profiles of a Rabbi: Synoptic Opportunities in Reading about Jesus* (BJS, 177; Atlanta: Scholars Press, 1989).

—*Pure Kingdom: Jesus' Vision of God* (SHJ; Grand Rapids: Eerdmans; London: SPCK, 1996).

—*The Temple of Jesus: His Sacrificial Program within a Cultural History of Sacrifice* (University Park: Pennsylvania State University Press, 1992).

—'Traditio-Historical Criticism and Study of Jesus', in J.B. Green (ed.), *Hearing the New Testament: Strategies for Interpretation* (Grand Rapids: Eerdmans; Carlisle: Paternoster Press, 1995), pp. 37-60.

Chilton, B., and C.A. Evans, *Jesus in Context: Temple, Purity, and Restoration* (AGJU, 39; Leiden: E.J. Brill, 1997).

Chilton, B. (ed.), *The Kingdom of God in the Teaching of Jesus* (IRT, 5; Philadelphia: Fortress Press; London: SPCK, 1984).

Chilton, B., and C.A. Evans (eds.), *Authenticating the Activities of Jesus* (NTTS, 28.2; Leiden: E.J. Brill, 1998).

—*Authenticating the Words of Jesus* (NTTS, 28.1; Leiden: E.J. Brill, 1998).

—*Studying the Historical Jesus: Evaluations of the State of Current Research* (NTTS, 19; Leiden: E.J. Brill, 1994).

Chomsky, W., 'What Was the Jewish Vernacular during the Second Commonwealth?', *JQR* 42 (1951–52), pp. 193-212.

Clarke, K.D., 'Original Text or Canonical Text? Questioning the Shape of the New Testament Text We Translate', in Porter and Hess (eds.), *Translating the Bible*, pp. 281-322.

Clarke, W.K.L., *New Testament Problems: Essays—Reviews—Interpretations* (London: SPCK, 1929).

Cluysenaar, A., *Introduction to Literary Stylistics: A Discussion of Dominant Structures in Verse and Prose* (London: Batsford, 1976).

Collinge, N.E., 'Some Reflexions on Comparative Historical Syntax', *Archivum Linguisticum* 12 (1960), pp. 79-101.

Collins, A.Y., *The Beginning of the Gospel: Probings of Mark in Context* (Minneapolis: Fortress Press, 1992).

Collins, R.F., *Introduction to the New Testament* (Garden City, NY: Doubleday, 1983).

Colwell, E.C., 'The Greek Language', in G. Buttrick (ed.), *The Interpreter's Dictionary of the Bible*, II (Nashville: Abingdon Press, 1962), pp. 479-87.

—*The Greek of the Fourth Gospel: A Study of its Aramaisms in the Light of Hellenistic Greek* (Chicago: University of Chicago Press, 1931).

—*Jesus and the Gospel* (New York: Oxford University Press, 1963).

Conzelmann, H., *Die Mitte der Zeit: Studien zur Theologie des Lukas* (BHT, 17; Tübingen: Mohr Siebeck, 1953; 2nd edn, 1957; 4th edn, 1962; ET *The Theology of St Luke* [trans. G. Buswell; New York: Harper & Brothers; London: Faber & Faber, 1960]).

—'Jesus Christus', *RGG*, III (Tübingen: Mohr Siebeck, 3rd edn, 1959), cols. 619-53; ET *Jesus* (trans. J.R. Lord; Philadelphia: Fortress Press, 1973).

—'Zur Methode der Leben-Jesu-Forschung', *ZTK* 56 (1959), pp. 2-13; ET 'The Method of the Life-of-Jesus Research', in Braaten and Harrisville (eds.), *The Historical Jesus and the Kerygmatic Christ*, pp. 54-68.

Conzelmann, H., and A. Lindemann, *Arbeitsbuch zum Neuen Testament* (Tübingen: Mohr Siebeck, 8th edn, 1985; ET *Interpreting the New Testament: An Introduction to the Principles and Methods of New Testament Exegesis* [trans. S.S. Schatzmann; Peabody, MA: Hendrickson, 1988]).

Cook, J.G., *The Structure and Persuasive Power of Mark: A Linguistic Approach* (Semeia Studies; Atlanta: Scholars Press, 1995).

Corley, B. (ed.), *Colloquy on New Testament Studies: A Time for Reappraisal and Fresh Approaches* (Macon, GA: Mercer University Press, 1983).

Corrington, G.P., 'Redaction Criticism', in S.R. Haynes and S.L. McKenzie (eds.), *To Each its Own Meaning: An Introduction to Biblical Criticisms and their Application* (Louisville, KY: Westminster/John Knox Press, 1993), pp. 87-99.

Costas, P.W., *An Outline of the History of the Greek Language, with Particular Emphasis on the Koine and the Subsequent Periods* (Chicago: Ukrainian Society of Sciences of America, 1936; repr. Chicago: Ares, 1979).

Cotterell, P., and M. Turner, *Linguistics and Biblical Interpretation* (London: SPCK; Downers Grove, IL: InterVarsity Press, 1989).

Cotton, H.M., and J. Geiger, *Masada, The Y. Yadin Excavations 1963–65. II. The Latin and Greek Documents* (Jerusalem: Israel Exploration Society, 1989).

Cotton, H.M., W.E.H. Cockle and F.G.B. Millar, 'The Papyrology of the Roman Near East: A Survey', *JRS* 85 (1995), pp. 214-35.

Cotton, H.M., and A. Yardeni (eds.), *Aramaic, Hebrew and Greek Documentary Texts from Nahal Hever and Other Sites* (DJD, 27; Oxford: Clarendon Press, 1997).

Coulthard, M., 'The Official Version: Audience Manipulation in Police Records of Interviews with Suspects', in Caldas-Coulthard and Coulthard (eds.), *Texts and Practices*, pp. 166-78.

—'On Beginning the Study of Forensic Texts: Corpus Concordance Collocation', in M. Hoey (ed.), *Data, Description, Discourse: Papers on the English Language in Honour of John McH. Sinclair* (London: HarperCollins, 1993), pp. 86-97.

—'On the Use of Corpora in the Analysis of Forensic Texts', *Forensic Linguistics* 1 (1994), pp. 27-43.

—'*Power*ful Evidence for the Defence: An Exercise in Forensic Discourse Analysis', in Gibbons (ed.), *Language and the Law*, pp. 414-27.

Coulthard, M. (ed.), *Advances in Written Text Analysis* (London: Routledge, 1994).

Cranfield, C.E.B., *The Gospel According to Saint Mark* (Cambridge: Cambridge University Press, 1959).

Cross, A.R., 'Historical Methodology and New Testament Study', *Themelios* 22.3 (1997), pp. 28-51.

Crossan, J.D., *The Historical Jesus: The Life of a Mediterranean Jewish Peasant* (San Francisco: HarperSanFrancisco, 1992).

—*In Parables: The Challenge of the Historical Jesus* (New York: Harper & Row, 1973).

Crossan, J.D., L.T. Johnson and W.H. Kelber, *The Jesus Controversy: Perspectives in Conflict* (Harrisburg, PA: Trinity Press International, 1999).

Crystal, D., 'Some Current Trends in Translation Theory', *The Bible Translator* 27 (1976), pp. 322-29.

Crystal, D., and D. Davy, *Investigating English Style* (London: Longman, 1969).

Cullmann, O., *Heil als Geschichte: Heilsgeschichtliche Existenz im Neuen Testament* (Tübingen: Mohr Siebeck, 1965; ET *Salvation in History* [NTL; trans. S.G. Sowers; London: SCM Press, 1967]).

—*Petrus: Jünger—Apostel—Märtyrer* (Berlin: Evangelische Verlagsanstalt, 2nd edn, 1961; ET *Peter: Disciple, Apostle, Martyr: A Historial and Theological Study* [trans. F.V. Filson; London: SCM Press, 1962]).

Culpepper, R.A., *Anatomy of the Fourth Gospel: A Study in Literary Design* (Philadelphia: Fortress Press, 1983).

Dahl, N.A., 'Der historische Jesus als geschichtswissenschaftliches und theologisches Problem', *KD* 1 (1955), pp. 104-32; ET 'The Problem of the Historical Jesus', in C.E. Braaten and R.A. Harrisville (eds.), *Kerygma and History: A Symposium on the Theology of Rudolf Bultmann* (Nashville: Abingdon Press, 1962), pp. 138-71; repr. in N.A. Dahl, *The Crucified Messiah and Other Essays* (Minneapolis: Augsburg, 1974), pp. 48-89, 173-74.

Dalman, G., *Die Worte Jesu: Mit Berücksichtigung des nachkanonischen jüdischen Schrifttums und der aramäistischen Sprache erörtert* (Leipzig: Hinrichs, 1898; rev. edn, 1930; ET *The Words of Jesus: Considered in the Light of Post-Biblical Jewish Writings and the Aramaic Language* [trans. D.M. Kay; Edinburgh: T. & T. Clark, 1909]).

—*Grammatik des jüdisch-palästinischen Aramäisch* (Leipzig: J.C. Hinrichs, 1894; 2nd edn, 1905; repr. Darmstadt: Wissenschaftliche Buchgesellschaft, 1960).

—*Jesus–Jeschua: Die drei Sprachen Jesu, Jesus in der Synagoge, auf dem Berge beim Passahmahl, am Kreuz* (Leipzig: J.C. Hinrichs, 1922; ET *Jesus–Jeshua: Studies in the Gospels* [trans. P.P. Levertoff; London: SPCK, 1929]).

—*Orte und Wege Jesu* (Leipzig: J.C. Hinrichs, 3rd edn, 1924; ET *Sacred Sites and Ways: Studies in the Topography of the Gospels* [trans. P.P. Levertoff; London: SPCK, 1935]).

Daniel-Rops, H., *Jésus en son temps* (Paris: Fayard, 1945; ET *Jesus in his Time* [trans. R.W. Millar; London: Eyre & Spottiswoode, 1955; 2nd edn, 1956]).

Danove, P.L., *The End of Mark's Story: A Methodological Study* (BIS, 3; Leiden: E.J. Brill, 1993).

Daube, D., *The New Testament and Rabbinic Judaism* (London: Athlone Press, 1956).

Davids, P.H., 'The Gospels and Jewish Tradition: Twenty Years after Gerhardsson', in France and Wenham (eds.), *Gospel Perspectives*, I, pp. 75-99.

Davies, M., and L. Ravelli (eds.), *Advances in Systemic Linguistics: Recent Theory and Practice* (London: Pinter, 1992).

Davies, W.D., 'Reflections on a Scandinavian Approach to "The Gospel Tradition"', in *Neotestamentica et Patristica: Eine Freudesgabe, Herrn Professor Dr Oscar Cullmann zu seinem 60. Geburtstag überreicht* (NovTSup, 6; Leiden: E.J. Brill, 1962), pp. 14-34; repr. in W.D. Davies, *The Setting of the Sermon on the Mount* (Cambridge: Cambridge University Press, 1964), pp. 464-80.

Davies, W.D., and D.C. Allison, Jr, *A Critical and Exegetical Commentary on the Gospel According to Saint Matthew* (3 vols.; ICC; Edinburgh: T. & T. Clark, 1988–97).

Davis, C.W., *Oral Biblical Criticism: The Influence of the Principles of Orality on the Literary Structure of Paul's Epistle to the Philippians* (JSNTSup, 172; Sheffield: Sheffield Academic Press, 1999).

Debrunner, A., *Geschichte der griechischen Sprache*. II. *Grundfragen und Grundzüge des nachklassischen Griechisch* (ed. A. Scherer; Sammlung Göschen, 114/114a; Berlin: W. de Gruyter, 2nd edn, 1969).

De Waard, J. and E.A. Nida, *From One Language to Another: Functional Equivalence in Bible Translating* (Nashville: Nelson, 1986).

Deissmann, A., *Bibelstudien* (Marburg: Elwert, 1895).

—*Bible Studies* (trans. A. Grieve; Edinburgh: T. & T. Clark, 1901).

—'Hellenistisches Griechisch', in A. Hauck (ed.), *Realencyklopädie für protestantische Theologie und Kirche*, VII (Leipzig: J.C. Hinrichs, 3rd edn, 1899), pp. 627-39; ET in Porter (ed.), *Language of the New Testament*, pp. 39-59.

—*Licht vom Osten* (Tübingen: Mohr Siebeck, 1908; 4th edn, 1923; ET *Light from the Ancient East* [trans. L.R.M. Strachan; London: Hodder & Stoughton, 1910; 4th edn, 1927]).

—*Neue Bibelstudien* (Marburg: Elwert, 1897).

—*Philology of the Greek Bible: Its Present and Future* (trans. L.R.M. Strachan; London: Hodder & Stoughton, 1908).

Denniston, J.D., *Greek Prose Style* (Oxford: Clarendon Press, 1952).

Dibelius, M., *Die Formgeschichte des Evangeliums* (Tübingen: Mohr Siebeck, 1919; 2nd edn, 1933; 6th edn ed. G. Bornkamm; ET *From Tradition to Gospel* [trans. B. Woolf; London: Ivor Nicholson & Watson, 1934]).

—*Gospel Criticism and Christology* (London: Ivor Nicholson & Watson, 1935).

—*Jesus* (Sammlung Göschen; Berlin: W. de Gruyter, 1939; ET *Jesus* [trans. C.B. Hedrick and F.C. Grant; Philadelphia: Westminster Press, 1949; London: SCM Press, 1963]).

Dodd, C.H., *The Apostolic Preaching and its Developments* (London: Hodder & Stoughton, 1936).

—*The Founder of Christianity* (New York: Macmillan, 1970; London: Collins, 1971).

—'The Framework of the Gospel Narrative (1932)', in *idem*, *New Testament Studies* (Manchester: Manchester University Press, 1953), pp. 1-11.

—*Historical Tradition in the Fourth Gospel* (Cambridge: Cambridge University Press, 1963).

—*History and the Gospel* (London: Nisbet, 1938).

—*The Parables of the Kingdom* (London: Nisbet, 1935; New York: Charles Scribner's Sons, rev. edn, 1961).

—'The Primitive Catechism and the Sayings of Jesus', in A.J.B. Higgins (ed.), *New Testament Essays: Studies in Memory of Thomas Walter Manson 1893–1958* (Manchester: Manchester University Press, 1959), pp. 106-18.

Donahue, J.R., 'Redaction Criticism: Has the *Hauptstrasse* Become a *Sackgasse*?', in E.S. Malbon and E.V. McKnight (eds.), *The New Literary Criticism and the New Testament* (JSNTSup, 109; Sheffield: JSOT Press, 1994), pp. 27-57.

Doty, W.G., 'The Discipline and Literature of New Testament Form Criticism', *ATR* 51 (1969), pp. 257-321.

Doudna, J.C., *The Greek of the Gospel of Mark* (JBLMS, 12; Philadelphia: Society of Biblical Literature and Exegesis, 1961).

Dover, K., *The Evolution of Greek Prose Style* (Oxford: Clarendon Press, 1997).

Downes, W., *Language and Society* (London: Fontana, 1984).

Downing, F.G., *The Church and Jesus: A Study in History, Philosophy and Theology* (SBT, 10; London: SCM Press, 1968).

—'Compositional Conventions and the Synoptic Problem', *JBL* 107 (1988), pp. 69-85.

Dufton, F., 'The Syrophoenician Woman and her Dogs', *ExpTim* 100 (1988–89), p. 417.

Duncan, G.S., *Jesus, Son of Man: Studies Contributory to a Modern Portrait* (London: Nisbet, 1947).

Dungan, D.L., *A History of the Synoptic Problem: The Canon, the Text, the Composition, and the Interpretation of the Gospels* (ABRL; New York: Doubleday, 1999).

Dungan, D.L. (ed.), *The Interrelations of the Gospels* (BETL, 95; Leuven: Leuven University Press/Peeters, 1990).

Dunkerley, R., *The Unwritten Gospel: Ana and Agrapha of Jesus* (London: George Allen & Unwin, 1925).

Dunn, J.D.G., 'Can the Third Quest Hope to Succeed?', in Chilton and Evans (eds.), *Authenticating the Activities of Jesus*, pp. 31-48.

—*The Evidence for Jesus: The Impact of Scholarship on our Understanding of How Christianity Began* (London: SCM Press, 1985).

—'Jesus and Factionalism in Early Judaism', in Charlesworth and Johns (eds.), *Hillel and Jesus*, pp. 156-75.

Dupont, J. (ed.), *Jésus aux origines de la christologie* (BETL, 40; Gembloux: Duculot, 1975; Leuven: Leuven University Press/Peeters, 2nd edn, 1989).

Duranti, A., and C. Goodwin (eds.), *Rethinking Context: Language as an Interactive Phenomenon* (Studies in the Social and Cultural Foundations of Language, 11; Cambridge: Cambridge University Press, 1992).

Dvorak, J.D., 'The Relationship between John and the Synoptic Gospels', *JETS* 41 (1998), pp. 201-13.

Dyer, K.D., *The Prophecy on the Mount: Mark 13 and the Gathering of the New Community* (International Theological Studies: Contributions of Baptist Scholars, 2; Bern: Peter Lang, 1998).

Eagleson, R., 'Forensic Analysis of Personal Written Texts: A Case Study', in Gibbons (ed.), *Language and the Law*, pp. 362-73.

Edersheim, A., *The Life and Times of Jesus the Messiah* (2 vols.; London: Longmans, Green; New York: Randolph, 1883; 7th edn, 1892).

Edwards, D., 'First Century Urban/Rural Relations in Lower Galilee: Exploring the Archaeological and Literary Evidence', in D.J. Lull (ed.), *Society of Biblical Literature 1988 Seminar Papers* (SBLSP, 27; Atlanta: Scholars Press, 1988), pp. 169-82.

—'The Socio-Economic and Cultural Ethos of the Lower Galilee in the First Century: Implications for the Nascent Jesus Movement', in Levine (ed.), *The Galilee in Late Antiquity*, pp. 53-73.

Edwards, D.R., and C.T. McCollough (eds.), *Archaeology and the Galilee: Texts and Contexts in the Graeco-Roman and Byzantine Periods* (South Florida Studies in the History of Judaism, 143; Atlanta: Scholars Press, 1997).

Elliott, J.K., *The Apocryphal New Testament* (Oxford: Clarendon Press, 1993).

—*Essays and Studies in New Testament Textual Criticism* (Estudios de Filología Neotestamentaria, 3; Córdoba: Ediciones El Almendro, 1992).

—'Thoroughgoing Eclecticism in New Testament Textual Criticism', in B.D. Ehrman and M.W. Holmes (eds.), *The Text of the New Testament in Contemporary Research: Essays on the Status Quaestionis* (SD, 46; Grand Rapids: Eerdmans, 1995), pp. 321-35.

Ellis, E.E., 'Gospels Criticism: A Perspective on the State of the Art', in Stuhlmacher (ed.), *Gospel and the Gospels*, pp. 26-52.

—'The Historical Jesus and the Gospels', in J. Ådna, S.J. Hafemann and O. Hofius (eds.), *Evangelium Schriftauslegung Kirche: Festschrift für Peter Stuhlmacher zum 65. Geburtstag* (Göttingen: Vandenhoeck & Ruprecht, 1997), pp. 94-106.

—'New Directions in Form Criticism', in Strecker (ed.), *Jesus Christus in Historie und Theologie*, pp. 299-315; repr. in E.E. Ellis, *Prophecy and Hermeneutic in Early Christianity* (WUNT, 18; Tübingen: Mohr Siebeck, 1978; repr. Grand Rapids: Eerdmans, 1980), pp. 237-53.

Emerton, J.A., 'Did Jesus Speak Hebrew?', *JTS* NS 12 (1961), pp. 189-202.

—'The Problem of Vernacular Hebrew in the First Century AD and the Language of Jesus', *JTS* NS 24 (1973), pp. 1-23.

Enkvist, N.K., J. Spencer and M.J. Gregory, *Linguistics and Style* (Oxford: Oxford University Press, 1964).

Ennulat, A., *Die 'Minor Agreements': Untersuchungen zu einer offenen Frage des synoptischen Problems* (WUNT, 2.62; Tübingen: Mohr Siebeck, 1994).

Enslin, M.S., *The Prophet from Nazareth* (New York: McGraw–Hill, 1961).

Epp, E.J., 'Textual Criticism in the Exegesis of the New Testament, with an Excursus on Canon', in Porter (ed.), *Handbook to Exegesis*, pp. 45-97.

Epp, E.J., and G.W. MacRae (eds.), *The New Testament and its Modern Interpreters* (The Bible and its Modern Interpreters; Atlanta: Scholars Press, 1989).

Evans, C.A., 'Authenticating the Activities of Jesus', in Chilton and Evans (eds.), *Authenticating the Activities of Jesus*, pp. 3-29.

—'Authenticity Criteria in Life of Jesus Research', *CSR* 19 (1989), pp. 6-31.

—'From Gospel to Gospel: The Function of Isaiah in the New Testament', in C.C. Broyles and C.A. Evans (eds.), *Writing and Reading the Scroll of Isaiah: Studies of an Interpretive Tradition* (2 vols.; VTSup, 70.1–2; Formation and Interpretation of Old Testament Literature, 1; Leiden: E.J. Brill, 1997), II, pp. 651-91.

—'The Historical Jesus and Christian Faith: A Critical Assessment of a Scholarly Problem', *CSR* 18 (1988), pp. 48-63.

—'Introduction: An Aramaic Approach Thirty Years Later', in M. Black, *An Aramaic Approach to the Gospels and Acts* (Oxford: Clarendon Press, 1946; 2nd edn, 1954; 3rd edn, 1967; repr. Peabody, MA: Hendrickson, 1998), pp. v-xxv.

—*Jesus* (IBR Bibliographies, 5; Grand Rapids: Baker Book House, 1992).

—*Jesus and his Contemporaries: Comparative Studies* (AGJU, 25; Leiden: E.J. Brill, 1995).

—'Life of Jesus', in Porter (ed.), *Handbook to Exegesis*, pp. 427-75.

—*Life of Jesus Research: An Annotated Bibliography* (NTTS, 24; Leiden: E.J. Brill, rev. edn, 1996).

—*Noncanonical Writings and New Testament Interpretation* (Peabody, MA: Hendrickson, 1992).

—'Reconstructing Jesus' Teaching: Problems and Possibilities', in Charlesworth and Johns (eds.), *Hillel and Jesus*, pp. 397-426.

—'Source, Form and Redaction Criticism: The "Traditional" Methods of Synoptic Interpretation', in Porter and Tombs (eds.), *Approaches to New Testament Study*, pp. 17-45.

—*Word and Glory: On the Exegetical and Theological Background of John's Prologue* (JSNTSup, 89; Sheffield: JSOT Press, 1993).

Evans, C.A., and S.E. Porter (eds.), *The Historical Jesus: A Sheffield Reader* (BibSem, 33; Sheffield: Sheffield Academic Press, 1995).

Fairclough, N., *Critical Discourse Analysis: The Critical Study of Language* (SLSL; London: Longman, 1995).

Fairclough, N., and R. Wodak, 'Critical Discourse Analysis', in T.A. van Dijk (ed.), *Discourse as Social Interaction*. II. *Discourse Studies: A Multidisciplinary Introduction* (London: Sage, 1997), pp. 258-84.

Farmer, W.R., *The Gospel of Jesus: The Pastoral Relevance of the Synoptic Problem* (Louisville, KY: Westminster/John Knox Press, 1994).

—'An Historical Essay on the Humanity of Jesus Christ', in W.R. Farmer, C.F.D. Moule and R.R. Niebuhr (eds.), *Christian History and Interpretation: Studies Presented to John Knox* (Cambridge: Cambridge University Press, 1967), pp. 101-26.

—*The Synoptic Problem: A Critical Analysis* (New York: Macmillan; London: Collier–Macmillan, 1964).

Farmer, W.R. (ed.), *New Synoptic Studies: The Cambridge Gospel Conference and Beyond* (Macon, GA: Mercer University Press, 1983).

Farrer, A.M., 'On Dispensing with Q', in D.E. Nineham (ed.), *Studies in the Gospels: Essays in Memory of R.H. Lightfoot* (Oxford: Basil Blackwell, 1957), pp. 55-88.

—*St Matthew and St Mark* (London: Dacre Press, 1954).

—*A Study in St Mark* (London: Dacre Press, 1951).

Fawcett, R.P., and D.J. Young (eds.), *New Developments in Systemic Linguistics*. II. *Theory and Application* (London: Pinter, 1988).

Feldman, L., 'How Much Hellenism in Jewish Palestine?', *HUCA* 57 (1986), pp. 83-111.

Ferguson, C., 'Diglossia', *Word* 15 (1959), pp. 325-40.

Ferris, C., *The Meaning of Syntax: A Study in the Adjectives of English* (LLL; London: Longman, 1993).

Fiensy, D.A., 'Jesus' Socioeconomic Background', in Charlesworth and Johns (eds.), *Hillel and Jesus*, pp. 225-55.

Finegan, J., *The Archaeology of the New Testament: The Life of Jesus and the Beginnings of the Early Church* (Princeton, NJ: Princeton University Press, 1969).

Fishman, J.A. (ed.), *Readings in the Sociology of Jewish Languages* (Contributions to the Sociology of Jewish Languages, 1; Leiden: E.J. Brill, 1985).

Fitzmyer, J.A., 'The Contribution of Qumran Aramaic to the Study of the New Testament', *NTS* 20 (1973–74), pp. 383-407; repr. in *idem, A Wandering Aramean*, pp. 85-113.

—*The Gospel According to Luke* (2 vols.; AB, 28, 28A; Garden City, NY: Doubleday, 1981, 1985).

—'The Languages of Palestine in the First Century AD', *CBQ* 32 (1970), pp. 501-31; repr. with corrections and additions in Porter (ed.), *Language of the New Testament*, pp. 126-62.

—'Methodology in the Study of the Aramaic Substratum of Jesus' Sayings in the New Testament', in Dupont (ed.), *Jésus aux origines de la christologie*, pp. 73-102; repr. in Fitzmyer, *A Wandering Aramean*, pp. 1-27.

—*A Wandering Aramean: Collected Aramaic Essays* (SBLMS, 25; Missoula, MT: Scholars Press, 1979; repr. in *The Semitic Background of the New Testament* [Biblical Resource Series; Grand Rapids: Eerdmans; Livonia, MI: Dove Booksellers, 1997]).

Fitzmyer, J.A., and D.J. Harrington, *A Manual of Palestinian Aramaic Texts* (Biblica et Orientalia, 34; Rome: Biblical Institute Press, 1978).

Flender, H., *Heil und Geschichte in der Theologie des Lukas* (BEvT, 41; Munich: Chr. Kaiser Verlag, 1965; ET *St Luke: Theologian of Redemptive History* [trans. R.H. Fuller and I. Fuller; London: SPCK, 1967]).

Fletcher, P., and M. Garman (eds.), *Language Acquisition: Studies in First Language Development* (Cambridge: Cambridge University Press, 2nd edn, 1986).

Flusser, D., *Jesus in Selbstzeugnissen und Bilddocumenten* (Rowohlts Monographien, 140; Hamburg: Rowohlt, 1968; ET *Jesus* [in collaboration with R.S. Notley; New York: Herder & Herder, 1969; Jerusalem: Magnes Press, rev. edn, 1997]).

Fornberg, T., and D. Hellholm (eds.), *Texts and Contexts: Biblical Texts in their Textual and Situational Contexts. Essays in Honor of Lars Hartman* (Oslo: Scandinavian University Press, 1995).

Fortna, R.T., *The Fourth Gospel and its Predecessor: From Narrative Source to Present Gospel* (Philadelphia: Fortress Press, 1988).

Fosdick, H.E., *The Man from Nazareth as his Contemporaries Saw Him* (New York: Harper, 1949).

Fowl, S.E., 'Reconstructing and Deconstructing the Quest of the Historical Jesus', *SJT* 42 (1989), pp. 319-33.

Fowler, R. (ed.), *Essays on Style and Language: Linguistic and Critical Approaches to Literary Style* (London: Routledge & Kegan Paul, 1966).

France, R.T., 'The Authenticity of the Sayings of Jesus', in C. Brown (ed.), *History, Criticism and Faith* (Downers Grove, IL: InterVarsity Press, 1977), pp. 101-43.

—*Matthew—Evangelist and Teacher* (Exeter: Paternoster Press, 1989).

France, R.T., and D. Wenham (eds.), *Gospel Perspectives: Studies of History and Tradition in the Four Gospels*, I (Sheffield: JSOT Press, 1980).

—*Gospel Perspectives: Studies of History and Tradition in the Four Gospels*, II (Sheffield: JSOT Press, 1981).

Freyne, S., *Galilee from Alexander the Great to Hadrian 323 BCE to 135 CE: A Study of Second Temple Judaism* (Notre Dame: University of Notre Dame Press; Wilmington, DE: Michael Glazier, 1980; repr. Edinburgh: T. & T. Clark, 1998).

—'The Geography, Politics, and Economics of Galilee and the Quest for the Historical Jesus', in Chilton and Evans (eds.), *Studying the Historical Jesus*, pp. 75-121.

—'Jesus and the Urban Culture of Galilee', in Fornberg and Hellholm (eds.), *Texts and Contexts*, pp. 597-622.

Fuchs, E., 'Die Frage nach dem historischen Jesus', *ZTK* 53 (1956), pp. 210-29; repr. in *idem, Zur Frage nach dem historischen Jesus*, pp. 143-67; ET 'The Quest of the Historical Jesus (1956)', in *idem, Studies of the Historical Jesus*, pp. 11-31.

—*Studies of the Historical Jesus* (trans. A. Scobie; SBT, 42; London: SCM Press, 1964).

—*Zur Frage nach dem historischen Jesus* (Tübingen: Mohr Siebeck, 1960; ET *Studies of the Historical Jesus* (trans. A. Scobie; SBT, 42; London: SCM Press, 1964).

Fuller, R.H., *A Critical Introduction to the New Testament* (London: Gerald Duckworth, 1966).

—*The Mission and Achievement of Jesus: An Examination of the Presuppositions of New Testament Theology* (SBT, 12; London: SCM Press, 1954).

—*The New Testament in Current Study: Some Trends in the Years 1941–1962* (New York: Charles Scribner's Sons, 1962; London: SCM Press, rev. edn, 1963).

Funk, R.W., *Language, Hermeneutic, and Word of God* (New York: Harper & Row, 1966).

—*Parables and Presence: Forms of the New Testament Tradition* (Philadelphia: Fortress Press, 1982).

Funk, R.W., *et al.*, *The Parables of Jesus: Red Letter Edition* (Sonoma, CA: Polebridge Press, 1988).

Gagnon, R.A.J., 'Luke's Motives for Redaction in the Account of the Double Delegation in Luke 7:1-10', *NovT* 36 (1994), pp. 122-45.

—'The Shape of Matthew's Q Text of the Centurion at Capernaum: Did it Mention Delegations?', *NTS* 40 (1994), pp. 133-42.

—'Statistical Analysis and the Case of the Double Delegation in Luke 7:3-7a', *CBQ* 55 (1993), pp. 709-31.

Galperin, I.R., *Stylistics* (Moscow: Vyssaja Skola, 3rd edn, 1981).

Gardner-Smith, P., *Saint John and the Synoptic Gospels* (Cambridge: Cambridge University Press, 1938).

Gerhardsson, B., 'Der Weg der Evangelientradition', in Stuhlmacher (ed.), *Das Evangelium und die Evangelien*, pp. 79-102.

—*Memory and Manuscript: Oral Tradition and Written Transmission in Rabbinic Judaism and Early Christianity* (ASNU, 22; trans. E.J. Sharpe; Lund: C.W.K. Gleerup, 1961; repr. in Biblical Resources Series; Grand Rapids: Eerdmans; Livonia, MI: Dove Booksellers, 1998).

—*Tradition and Transmission in Early Christianity* (ConBNT, 20; trans. E.J. Sharpe; Lund: C.W.K. Gleerup, 1964; repr. in Biblical Resource Series; Grand Rapids: Eerdmans; Livonia, MI: Dove Booksellers, 1998).

Ghadessy, M. (ed.), *Register Analysis: Theory and Practice* (London: Pinter, 1993).

Gibbons, J. (ed.), *Language and the Law* (London: Longman, 1994).

Gibson, A., *Biblical Semantic Logic: A Preliminary Analysis* (Oxford: Basil Blackwell, 1981).

Gibson, E., *The 'Christians for Christians' Inscriptions of Phrygia* (HTS, 32; Atlanta: Scholars Press, 1978).

Gignac, F., *A Grammar of the Greek Papyri of the Roman and Byzantine Periods* (2 vols.; Milan: Cisalpino, 1976, 1981).

—'The Language of the Non-Literary Papyri', in D.H. Samuel (ed.), *Proceedings of the Twelfth International Congress of Papyrology* (Toronto: Hakkert, 1970), pp. 139-52.

—'The Papyri and the Greek Language', *Yale Classical Studies* 28 (1985), pp. 157-58.

Gilliard, F.D., 'More Silent Reading in Antiquity: *Non Omne Verbum Sonabat*', *JBL* 112 (1993), pp. 689-94.

Glasson, T.F., *Greek Influence in Jewish Eschatology* (London: SPCK, 1961).

—*His Appearing and his Kingdom: The Christian Hope in the Light of its History* (London: Epworth Press, 1953).

—'Schweitzer's Influence: Blessing or Bane?', *JTS* NS 28 (1977), pp. 289-302; repr. in Chilton (ed.), *The Kingdom of God in the Teaching of Jesus*, pp. 107-20.

—*The Second Advent: The Origin of the New Testament Doctrine* (London: Epworth Press, 1945; 2nd edn, 1947).

Glasswell, M.E., 'The Relationship between John and Mark', *JSNT* 23 (1985), pp. 99-115.

Glover, T.R., *The Jesus of History* (London: SCM Press, 1917).

—*Jesus of Nazareth* (York: William Sessions, 1912; repr. from *idem*, *The Conflict of Religions in the Early Roman Empire* [London: Methuen, 1909], pp. 113-40).

Goebel, S., *Die Parabeln Jesu*; ET *The Parables of Jesus: A Methodical Exposition* (trans. Professor Banks; Edinburgh: T. & T. Clark, 1913).

Goetz, S.C., and C.L. Blomberg, 'The Burden of Proof', *JSNT* 11 (1981), pp. 39-63.

Goguel, M., *La vie de Jésus* (Paris: Payot, 1932; ET *The Life of Jesus* [trans. O. Wyon; London: George Allen & Unwin; New York: Macmillan, 1933]).

Goodacre, M.S., *Goulder and the Gospels: An Examination of a New Paradigm* (JSNTSup, 133; Sheffield: Sheffield Academic Press, 1996).

Goodspeed, E.J., *A Life of Jesus* (New York: Harper & Brothers, 1950).

—'The Original Language of the New Testament', in *idem*, *New Chapters in New Testament Study* (New York: Macmillan, 1937), pp. 127-68.

Goppelt, L., *Theologie des Neuen Testaments.I.Jesu Wirken in seiner theologischen Bedeutung* (ed. J. Roloff; Göttingen: Vandenhoeck & Ruprecht, 1975; ET *Theology of the*

New Testament. I. *The Ministry of Jesus in its Theological Significance* [trans. J.E. Alsup; Grand Rapids: Eerdmans, 1981]).

Goulder, M.D., *The Evangelists' Calendar: A Lectionary Explanation of the Development of Scripture* (London: SPCK, 1978).

—*Luke: A New Paradigm* (2 vols.; JSNTSup, 20; Sheffield: JSOT Press, 1989).

—'Luke's Knowledge of Matthew', in G. Strecker (ed.), *Minor Agreements: Symposium Göttingen 1991* (Göttinger theologische Arbeiten, 50; Göttingen: Vandenhoeck & Ruprecht, 1993), pp. 143-62.

Grabbe, L.L., *Judaism from Cyrus to Hadrian* (Minneapolis: Augsburg–Fortress, 1992; London: SCM Press, 1994).

Grant, M., *Herod the Great* (London: Weidenfeld & Nicolson, 1971).

Green, J.B., *The Death of Jesus: Tradition and Interpretation in the Passion Narrative* (WUNT, 2.33; Tübingen: Mohr Siebeck, 1988).

Green, J.B., S. McKnight and I.H. Marshall (eds.), *Dictionary of Jesus and the Gospels* (Downers Grove, IL: InterVarsity Press, 1992).

Greenlee, J.H., *Introduction to New Testament Textual Criticism* (Grand Rapids: Eerdmans, 1964).

Gregg, R.C., and D. Urman, *Jews, Pagans, and Christians in the Golan Heights: Greek and Other Inscriptions of the Roman and Byzantine Eras* (South Florida Studies in the History of Judaism, 140; Atlanta: Scholars Press, 1996).

Grintz, J.M., 'Hebrew as the Spoken and Written Language in the Last Days of the Second Temple', *JBL* 79 (1960), pp. 32-47.

Grosjean, F., *Life with Two Languages: An Introduction to Bilingualism* (Cambridge, MA: Harvard University Press, 1982).

Gruen, E.S., *Heritage and Hellenism: The Reinvention of Jewish Tradition* (Berkeley: University of California Press, 1998).

Grundmann, W., *Das Evangelium nach Lukas* (THKNT; Berlin: Evangelische Verlagsanstalt, 6th edn, 1971).

—*Die Geschichte Jesu Christi* (Berlin: Evangelische Verlagsanstalt, 1956; 2nd edn, 1959).

Guelich, R., *Mark 1–8:26* (WBC, 34A; Dallas: Word Books, 1989).

Gülich, E., and W. Raible, *Linguistische Textmodelle: Grundlagen und Möglichkeiten* (UTb, 130; Munich: Fink, 1977).

Gundry, R.H., 'The Language Milieu of First-Century Palestine: Its Bearing on the Authenticity of the Gospel Tradition', *JBL* 83 (1964), pp. 404-408.

—*Mark: A Commentary on his Apology for the Cross* (Grand Rapids: Eerdmans, 1993).

—*Matthew: A Commentary on his Literary and Theological Art* (Grand Rapids: Eerdmans, 1982).

—'The Narrative Framework of Matthew XVI.17-19: A Critique of Professor Cullmann's Hypothesis', *NovT* 7 (1964), pp. 1-9.

Güttgemanns, E., *Offene Fragen zur Formgeschichte des Evangeliums: Eine methodologische Skizze der Grundlagenproblematik der Form- und Redaktionsgeschichte* (BEvTh, 54; Munich: Chr. Kaiser Verlag, 1970; 2nd edn, 1971; ET *Candid Questions Concerning Gospel Form Criticism: A Methodological Sketch of the Fundamental Problematics of Form and Redaction Criticism* [trans. W.G. Doty; Pittsburgh: Pickwick Press, 1979]).

Guy, H.A., *The Life of Christ: Notes on the Narrative and Teaching in the Gospels* (London: Macmillan, 1957).

Hachlili, R., 'The Goliath Family in Jericho: Funerary Inscriptions from a First Century A.D. Jewish Monumental Tomb', *BASOR* 235 (1979), pp. 31-65.

Hadas-Lebel, M., *Histoire de la langue hébraïque: Des origines à l'époque de la Mishna* (Paris: Peeters, 1995).

Haenchen, E., *Der Weg Jesu: Eine Erklärung des Markus-Evangeliums und der kanonischen Parallelen* (Berlin: Alfred Töpelmann, 1966; Berlin: W. de Gruyter, 2nd edn, 1968).

Hagner, D.A., *Matthew* (2 vols.; WBC, 33A, B; Dallas: Word Books, 1993, 1995).

Hahn, F., 'Methodologische Überlegungen zur Rückfrage nach Jesus', in Kertelge (ed.), *Rückfrage nach Jesus*, pp. 11-77; ET 'Methodological Reflections on the Historical Investigation of Jesus', in F. Hahn, *Historical Investigation and New Testament Faith: Two Essays* (trans. R. Maddox; Philadelphia: Fortress Press, 1983), pp. 35-105.

Hall, F.W., *A Companion to Classical Texts* (Oxford: Clarendon Press, 1913).

Halliday, M.A.K., 'The Construction of Knowledge and Value in the Grammar of Scientific Discourse, with Reference to Charles Darwin's *The Origin of Species*', in Coulthard (ed.), *Advances in Written Text Analysis*, pp. 136-56.

—*Explorations in the Functions of Language* (EISL; London: Arnold, 1973).

—*An Introduction to Functional Grammar* (London: Arnold, 1985; 2nd edn, 1994).

—*Language as Social Semiotic: The Social Interpretation of Language and Meaning* (London: Arnold, 1978).

Halliday, M.A.K., and R. Hasan, *Cohesion in English* (London: Longman, 1976).

—*Language, Context, and Text: Aspects of Language in a Social-Semiotic Perspective* (Geelong, Victoria, Australia: Deakin University Press, 1985).

Halliday, M.A.K., and R.P. Fawcett (eds.), *New Developments in Systemic Linguistics*. I. *Theory and Description* (London: Pinter, 1987).

Hamers, J.F., and M.H.A. Blanc, *Bilingualité et bilinguisme* (Brussels: Pierre Mardaga, 1983; ET *Bilinguality and Bilingualism* [Cambridge: Cambridge University Press, 1989]).

Harnack, A., *Das Wesen des Christentums* (Leipzig: J.C. Hinrichs, 1900; ET *What is Christianity?* [trans. T.B. Saunders; CThL; London: Williams & Norgate; New York: Putnam's Sons, 1900; 3rd edn, 1904]).

—*Sprüche und Reden Jesu: Die zweite Quelle des Matthäus und Lukas* (BENT, 2; Leipzig: J.C. Hinrichs, 1907; ET *The Sayings of Jesus: The Second Source of St Matthew and St Luke* [trans. J.R. Wilkinson; CThL; London: Williams & Norgate; New York: Putnam's Sons, 1908]).

Harris, J.R., 'The So-Called Biblical Greek', *ExpTim* 25 (1913), pp. 54-55.

Harris, W.V., *Ancient Literacy* (Cambridge, MA: Harvard University Press, 1989).

Harrisville, R.A., 'Representative American Lives of Jesus', in Braateu and Harrisville (eds.), *The Historical Jesus and the Kerygmatic Christ*, pp. 172-96

Hart, H.St.J., 'The Coin of "Render unto Caesar…" (A Note on Some Aspects of Mark 12:13-17; Matt. 22:15-22; Luke 20:20-26)', in Bammel and Moule (eds.), *Jesus and the Politics of his Day*, pp. 241-48.

Hartman, L., *Text-Centered New Testament Studies: Text-Theoretical Essays on Early Jewish and Early Christian Literature* (ed. D. Hellholm; WUNT, 102; Tübingen: Mohr–Siebeck, 1997).

Harvey, A.E., *Jesus and the Constraints of History* (London: Gerald Duckworth; Philadelphia: Westminster Press, 1982).

Harvey, V.A., and S.M. Ogden, 'How New is the "New Quest of the Historical Jesus"?', in Braaten and Harrisville (eds.), *The Historical Jesus and the Kerygmatic Christ*, pp. 197-242.

Hastings, J. (ed.), *A Dictionary of the Bible* (5 vols.; Edinburgh: T. & T. Clark, 1898–1904).

Hatim, B., and I. Mason, *Discourse and the Translator* (LSLS; London: Longman, 1990).

—*The Translator as Communicator* (London: Routledge, 1997).

Hatina, T.R., 'The Focus of Mark 13:24-27: The Parousia, or the Destruction of the Temple?', *BBR* 6 (1996), pp. 43-66.

Haugen, E., 'Dialect, Language, Nation', *American Anthropologist* 68 (1966), pp. 922-35; repr. in Pride and Holmes (eds.), *Sociolinguistics*, pp. 97-111.

—'Problems of Bilingualism', *Lingua* 2 (1950), pp. 271-90.

Hawkins, J.C., *Horae Synopticae: Contributions to the Study of the Synoptic Problem* (Oxford: Clarendon Press, 2nd edn, 1909).

Hawthorne, G.F. (ed.), *Current Issues inn Biblical and Patristic Interpretation* (Festschrift M.C. Tenney; Grand Rapids: Eerdmans, 1975).

Hayes, J.H., and S.R. Mandell, *The Jewish People in Classical Antiquity from Alexander to Bar Kochba* (Louisville, KY: Westminster/John Knox Press, 1998).

Headlam, A.C., *The Life and Teaching of Jesus the Christ* (London: John Murray, 1923; 2nd edn, 1927).

Hedrick, C.W., *Parables as Poetic Fictions: The Creative Voice of Jesus* (Peabody, MA: Hendrickson, 1994).

Heitmüller, W., *Jesus* (Tübingen: J.C.B. Mohr, 1913).

Hellholm, D., 'Substitutionelle Gliederungsmerkmale und die Komposition des Matthäus-evangeliums', in Fornberg and Hellholm (eds.), *Texts and Contexts*, pp. 11-76.

Hemer, C.J., 'Reflections on the Nature of New Testament Greek Vocabulary', *TynBul* 38 (1987), pp. 65-92.

Hengel, M., 'Der vorchristliche Paulus', in M. Hengel and U. Heckel (eds.), *Paulus und das antike Judentum* (WUNT, 58; Tübingen: Mohr Siebeck, 1991), pp. 177-291; ET *The Pre-Christian Paul* (with R. Deines; trans. J. Bowden; London: SCM Press; Philadelphia: Trinity Press International, 1991).

—'Entstehungszeit und Situation des Markusevangeliums', in H. Cancik (ed.), *Markus-Philologie: Historische, literargeschichtliche und stilistische Untersuchungen zum zweiten Evangelium* (WUNT, 33; Tübingen: Mohr Siebeck, 1984), pp. 1-45; ET in M. Hengel, *Studies in the Gospel of Mark* (trans. J. Bowden; London: SCM Press, 1985), pp. 1-30.

—'Jerusalem als jüdische *und* hellenistische Stadt', in B. Funck (ed.), *Hellenismus: Beiträge zur Erforschung von Akkulturation und politischer Ordnung in den Staaten des hellenistischen Zeitalters* (Tübingen: Mohr Siebeck, 1996), pp. 269-306.

—*Judentum und Hellenismus: Studien zu ihrer Begegnung unter besonderer Berücksichti-gung Palästinas bis zur Mitte des 2.Jh.s v. Chr.* (WUNT, 10; Tübingen: Mohr Siebeck, 1969; 2nd edn, 1973; ET *Judaism and Hellenism: Studies in their Encounter in Palestine during the Early Hellenistic Period* [2 vols.; trans. J. Bowden; London: SCM Press; Philadelphia: Fortress Press, 1974]).

—*Nachfolge und Charisma* (Berlin: W. de Gruyter, 1968; ET *The Charismatic Leader and his Followers* [trans. J.C.G. Greig; Edinburgh: T. & T. Clark, 1981; repr. 1996]).

—'Zwischen Jesus und Paulus', *ZTK* 72 (1975), pp. 151-206; ET in *idem, Between Jesus* and Paul: Studies in the Earliest History of Christianity (trans. J. Bowden; Philadelphia: Fortress Press, 1983), pp. 1-29.

Hengel, M., with C. Markschies, 'Zum Problem der "Hellenisierung" Judäas im 1. Jahrhundert nach Christus'; ET *The 'Hellenization' of Judaea in the First Century after Christ* (trans. J. Bowden; London: SCM Press; Philadelphia: Trinity Press International, 1989).

Herder, J.G., *Vom Erlöser der Menschen: Nach unsern drei ersten Evangelien* (Riga: Hartknoch, 1796).

—*Von Gottes Sohn, der Welt Heiland: Nach Johannes Evangelium* (Riga: Hartknoch, 1797).

Heyer, C.J. den, *Wie is Jezus? Balans van 150 jaar onderzoek naar Jesus* (Zoetermeer, The Netherlands: Uitgeverij Meinema, 1996; ET *Jesus Matters: 150 Years of Research* [trans. J. Bowden: London: SCM Press, 1996]).

Hill, C.C., *Hellenists and Hebrews: Reappraising Division within the Earliest Church* (Minneapolis: Fortress Press, 1992).

Hirsch, E.D., Jr, *Validity in Interpretation* (New Haven: Yale University Press, 1967).

Hoehner, H., *Herod Antipas* (SNTSMS, 17; Cambridge: Cambridge University Press, 1972).

Hoey, M., *Patterns of Lexis in Text* (Describing English Language; Oxford: Oxford University Press, 1991).

Hofius, O., ' "Unknown Sayings of Jesus" ', in Stuhlmacher (ed.), *Gospel and the Gospels*, pp. 336-60.

Holmén, T., 'Doubts about Double Dissimilarity: Restructuring the Main Criterion of Jesus-of-History Research', in Chilton and Evans (eds.), *Authenticating the Words of Jesus*, pp. 47-80.

Holmes, J., *An Introduction to Sociolinguistics* (London: Longman, 1992).

Holmstrand, J., *Markers and Meaning in Paul: An Analysis of 1 Thessalonians, Philippians and Galatians* (ConBNT, 28; Stockholm: Almqvist & Wiksell, 1997).

Hooker, M.D., 'Christology and Methodology', *NTS* 17 (1970), pp. 480-87.

—*The Gospel According to Saint Mark* (BNTC; Peabody, MA: Hendrickson, 1991).

—'In his Own Image?', in Hooker and Hickling (eds.), *What about the New Testament?*, pp. 28-44.

—'On Using the Wrong Tool', *Theology* 75 (1972), pp. 570-81.

Hooker, M.D., and C. Hickling (eds.), *What about the New Testament? Essays in Honour of Christopher Evans* (London: SCM Press, 1975).

Horrocks, G., *Greek: A History of the Language and its Speakers* (LLL; London: Longmans, 1997).

Horsley, G.H.R., 'Divergent Views on the Nature of the Greek of the Bible', *Bib* 65 (1984), pp. 393-403.

—*New Documents Illustrating Early Christianity. V. Linguistic Essays* (New South Wales, Australia: Macquarie University, 1989).

Horsley, R.A., *Archaeology, History and Society in Galilee: The Social Context of Jesus and the Rabbis* (Valley Forge, PA: Trinity Press International, 1996).

—*Galilee: History, Politics, People* (Valley Forge, PA: Trinity Press International, 1995).

—*Jesus and the Spiral of Violence* (San Francisco: HarperSanFrancisco, 1987).

—*Sociology and the Jesus Movement* (New York: Crossroad, 1989).

Horst, P.W. van der, *Ancient Jewish Epitaphs: An Introductory Survey of a Millennium of*

Jewish Funerary Epigraphy (300 BCE–700 CE) (Contributions to New Testament Exegesis and Theology, 2; Kampen: Kok Pharos, 1991).

—'Was the Synagogue a Place of Sabbath Worship before 70 CE?', in S. Fine (ed.), *Jews, Christians, and Polytheists in the Ancient Synagogue: Cultural Interaction during the Greco-Roman Period* (London: Routledge, 1999), pp. 18-43.

Hoskyns, E., and N. Davey, *The Riddle of the New Testament* (London: Faber & Faber, 1931).

Howard, W.F., *The Fourth Gospel in Recent Criticism and Interpretation* (rev. C.K. Barrett; London: Epworth Press, 1931; 4th edn, 1955).

Hudson, R.A., *Sociolinguistics* (CTL; Cambridge: Cambridge University Press, 2nd edn, 1996).

Hughes, P.E., 'The Languages Spoken by Jesus', in R.N. Longenecker and M.C. Tenney (eds.), *New Dimensions in New Testament Study* (Grand Rapids: Zondervan, 1974), pp. 127-43.

Humbert, J., *Histoire de la langue grecque* (Que sais-je?, 1483; Paris: Presses Universitaires de France, 1972).

Hunter, A.M., *Interpreting the New Testament 1900–1950* (London: SCM Press, 1951).

—*The Work and Words of Jesus* (Philadelphia: Westminster Press, 1950; London: SCM Press, 1951).

Hurst, L.D., 'The Neglected Role of Semantics in the Search for the Aramaic Words of Jesus', *JSNT* 28 (1986), pp. 63-80; repr. in Evans and Porter (eds.), *The Historical Jesus*, pp. 219-36.

Hurtado, L.W., 'Greco-Roman Textuality and the Gospel of Mark: A Critical Assesssment of Werner Kelber's *The Oral and the Written Gospel*', *BBR* 7 (1997), pp. 91-106.

Hyltenstam, K., and L.K. Obler (eds.), *Bilingualism across the Lifespan: Aspects of Acquisition, Maturity, and Loss* (Cambridge: Cambridge University Press, 1989).

Iersel, B.M.F. van, *Marcus, uitgelegd aan andere lezers* (Baarn: Gooi en Sticht; Kampen: Kok, 1997; ET *Mark: A Reader-Response Commentary* [trans. W.H. Bisscheroux; JSNTSup, 164; Sheffield: Sheffield Academic Press, 1998]).

Irmscher, J., 'Σὺ λέγεις (Mk. 15,2—Mt. 27,11—Lk. 23,3)', *Studii Clasice* 2 (1960), pp. 151-58.

Isaac, B., 'A Donation for Herod's Temple in Jerusalem', *IEJ* 33 (1983), pp. 86-92.

Iser, W., *Der Akt des Lesens: Theorie ästhetischer Wirkung* (Munich: Fink, 1976; ET *The Act of Reading: A Theory of Aesthetic Response* [trans. D.H. Wilson; Baltimore: The Johns Hopkins University Press, 1978]).

Jackson, B., *Twenty-Five Agrapha or Extra-Canonical Sayings of our Lord* (London: SPCK, 1900).

Jacoby, F., *Die Fragmente der griechischen Historiker* (3 vols. and 16 parts; Leiden: E.J. Brill, 1954–69).

James, M.R., *The Apocryphal New Testament* (Oxford: Clarendon Press, 1924).

Jellicoe, S., *The Septuagint and Modern Study* (Oxford: Clarendon Press, 1968).

Jeremias, J., 'Der gegenwärtige Stand der Debatte um das Problem des historischen Jesus', in H. Ristow and K. Matthiae (eds.), *Der historische Jesus und der kerygmatische Christus: Beiträge zum Christusverständnis in Forschung und Verkündigung* (Berlin: Evangelische Verlagsanstalt, 1960), pp. 12-25; ET 'The Present Position in the Controversy Concerning the Problem of the Historical Jesus', *ExpTim* 69 (1957–58), pp. 333-39.

—*Die Abendmahlsworte Jesu* (Göttingen: Vandenhoeck & Ruprecht, 1935; 3rd edn, 1960; ET *The Eucharistic Words of Jesus* [trans. A. Ehrhardt; Oxford: Basil Blackwell, 1955]).

—*Die Gleichnisse Jesu* (Zürich: Zwingli-Verlag, 1947; Göttingen: Vandenhoeck & Ruprecht, 10th edn, 1984; ET *The Parables of Jesus* [trans. S.H. Hooke; London: SCM Press, 3rd edn, 1972]).

—'Isolated Sayings of the Lord', in E. Hennecke and W. Schneemelcher (eds.), *Neutestamentliche Apokryphen*, I (2 vols.; Tübingen: Mohr Siebeck, 1959; ET *New Testament Apocrypha*, I [trans. R.McL. Wilson; London: Lutterworth; Philadelphia: Westminster Press, 1963]), pp. 85-90.

—'Kennzeichen der ipsissima vox Jesu', in *Synoptische Studien: Alfred Wikenhauser zum siebzigsten Geburtstag am 22. Februar 1953 dargebracht von Freunden, Kollegen und Schulern* (Munich: Zink, 1954), pp. 86-93; ET 'Characteristics of the *Ipsissima Vox Jesu*', in *idem, The Prayers of Jesus*, pp. 108-15.

—*Neutestamentliche Theologie. I. Die Verkündigung Jesu* (Gütersloh: Gerd Mohn, 1971; ET *New Testament Theology. I. The Proclamation of Jesus* [trans. J. Bowden; NTL; London: SCM Press; New York: Charles Scribner's Sons, 1971]).

—*The Prayers of Jesus* (trans. J. Bowden, C. Burchard and J. Reumann; SBT, 2.6; London: SCM Press, 1967).

—*Unbekannte Jesusworte* (Gütersloh: C. Bertelsmann, 2nd edn, 1951; Gütersloh: Gerd Mohn, 3rd edn, 1963; ET *Unknown Sayings of Jesus* [trans. R.H. Fuller; London: SPCK, 1957; 2nd edn, 1964]).

Johnson, L.T., *The Gospel of Luke* (SP, 3; Collegeville, MN: Liturgical Press, 1991).

—*The Real Jesus: The Misguided Quest for the Historical Jesus and the Truth of the Traditional Gospels* (San Francisco: HarperCollins, 1996).

Johnson, S.E., *The Griesbach Hypothesis and Redaction Criticism* (SBLMS, 41; Atlanta: Scholars Press, 1991).

Jones, A.H.M., *Cities of the Eastern Roman Provinces* (Oxford: Clarendon Press, 1937).

—*The Greek City from Alexander to Justinian* (Oxford: Clarendon Press, 1940).

Jonge, M. de, *God's Final Envoy: Early Christology and Jesus' Own View of his Mission* (SHJ; Grand Rapids: Eerdmans, 1998).

—*Jesus, the Servant-Messiah* (New Haven: Yale University Press, 1991).

Joüon, P., 'Quelques aramaïsmes: Sous-jacent au grec des Evangiles', *RSR* 17 (1927), pp. 210-29.

Jüngel, E., *Paulus und Jesus* (Tübingen: Mohr Siebeck, 1962).

Kahle, P.E., *The Cairo Geniza* (Oxford: Basil Blackwell, 2nd edn, 1959).

Kähler, M., *Der sogenannte historische Jesus und der geschichtliche, biblische Christus* (Leipzig: Deichert, 1892; 2nd edn, 1896; repr. Theologische Bücherei, 2; Munich: Chr. Kaiser Verlag, 1956; ET *The So-Called Historical Jesus and the Historic, Biblical Christ* [trans. C.E. Braaten; Philadelphia: Fortress Press, 1964]).

Kapsomenos, S.G., 'Das Griechische in Ägypten', *Museum Helveticum* 10 (1953), pp. 248-63.

Käsemann, E., 'Das Problem des historischen Jesus', *ZTK* 51 (1954), pp. 125-53; repr. in *idem, Exegetische Versuche und Besinnungen*, I, pp. 187-214; ET 'The Problem of the Historical Jesus', in *idem, Essays on New Testament Themes*, pp. 15-47.

—'Die neue Jesus-Frage', in Dupont (ed.), *Jésus aux origines de la christologie*, pp. 47-57.

—*Essays on New Testament Themes* (trans. W.J. Montague; SBT, 41; London: SCM Press, 1964; Philadelphia: Fortress Press, 1982).

—*Exegetische Versuche und Besinnungen*, I (Göttingen: Vandenhoeck & Ruprecht, 2nd edn, 1960).

—'Sackgassen im Streit um den historischen Jesus', in *idem, Exegetische Versuche und Besinnungen*, II (Göttingen: Vandenhoeck & Ruprecht, 1964; 2nd edn, 1965), pp. 31-68; ET 'Blind Alleys in the "Jesus of History" Controversy', in *idem, New Testament Questions of Today* (trans. W.J. Montague; London: SCM Press, 1969), pp. 23-65.

—'Zum Thema der Nichtobjektivierbarkeit', *EvT* 12 (1952–53), pp. 455-66; repr. in *idem, Exegetische Versuche und Besinnungen*, I, pp. 224-36; ET 'Is the Gospel Objective?', in *idem, Essays on New Testament Themes*, pp. 48-62.

Kasper, W., *Jesus der Christus* (Mainz: Matthias-Grünewald Verlag, 1974; ET *Jesus the Christ* [trans. V. Green; London: Burns & Oates; New York: Paulist Press, 1976]).

Kaufman, S., 'Dating the Language of the Palestinian Targums and their Use in the Study of First Century CE Texts', in Beattie and McNamara (eds.), *The Aramaic Bible*, pp. 118-41.

—'On Methodology in the Study of the Targums and their Chronology', *JSNT* 23 (1985), pp. 117-24.

Keck, L.E., *A Future for the Historical Jesus: The Place of Jesus in Preaching and Theology* (Nashville: Abingdon Press, 1971; London: SCM Press, 1972).

Kee, H.C., 'Defining the First-Century CE Synagogue: Problems and Progress', *NTS* 41 (1995), pp. 481-500.

—'Early Christianity in the Galilee: Reassessing the Evidence from the Gospels', in Levine (ed.), *The Galilee in Late Antiquity*, pp. 3-22.

—*Jesus in History: An Approach to the Study of the Gospels* (New York: Harcourt Brace Jovanovich, 1970; 2nd edn, 1977).

—'The Transformation of the Synagogue after 70 C.E.', *NTS* 36 (1990), pp. 1-24.

—*What Can We Know about Jesus?* (Understanding Jesus Today; Cambridge: Cambridge University Press, 1990).

Kenny, A., *A Stylometric Study of the New Testament* (Oxford: Clarendon Press, 1986).

Kenyon, F.G., *Handbook to the Textual Criticism of the New Testament* (London: Macmillan, 1926).

Kertelge, K. (ed.), *Rückfrage nach Jesus: Zur Methodik und Bedeutung der Frage nach dem historischen Jesus* (QD, 63; Freiburg: Herder, 1974).

Keylock, L.R., 'Bultmann's Law of Increasing Distinctness', in Hawthorne (ed.), *Current Issues in Biblical and Patristic Interpretation*, pp. 193-210.

Kilpatrick, G.D., 'Dura-Europos: The Parchments and the Papyri', *GRBS* 5 (1964), pp. 215-25.

—'Jesus, his Family and his Disciples', *JSNT* 15 (1982), pp. 3-19; repr. in Evans and Porter (eds.), *The Historical Jesus*, pp. 13-28.

Kirk, G.S., *Homer and the Epic* (Cambridge: Cambridge University Press, 1965).

Klausner, J., *Jesus of Nazareth: His Life, Times, and Teaching* [Hebrew 1925] (trans. H. Danby; London: George Allen & Unwin, 1925).

Klein, W., *Second Language Acquisition* (CTL; Cambridge: Cambridge University Press, 1986).

Kloppenborg, J.S., *The Formation of Q: Trajectories in Ancient Christian Wisdom Collections* (Studies in Antiquity and Christianity; Philadelphia: Fortress Press, 1987).

Klutz, T., 'Naked and Wounded: Foregrounding, Relevance and Situation in Acts 19.13-20', in Porter and Reed (eds.), *Discourse Analysis and the New Testament*, pp. 258-79.

Kniffka, H., with S. Blackwell and M. Coulthard (eds.), *Recent Developments in Forensic Linguistics* (Frankfurt: Peter Lang, 1996).

Knox, J., *The Church and the Reality of Christ* (New York: Harper & Row, 1962; London: Collins, 1963).

Knox, W.L., *The Sources of the Synoptic Gospels*. I. *St Mark* (ed. H. Chadwick; Cambridge: Cambridge University Press, 1953).

Koch, K., *Was ist Formgeschichte? Neue Wege der Bibelexegese* (Neukirchen–Vluyn: Neukirchener Verlag, 1964; 2nd edn, 1967; ET *The Growth of the Biblical Tradition: The Form-Critical Method* [trans. S.M. Cupitt; New York: Charles Scribner's Sons, 1969]).

Koester, H., *Ancient Christian Gospels: Their History and Development* (Philadelphia: Trinity Press International; London: SCM Press, 1990).

—*Introduction to the New Testament*. I. *History, Culture, and Religion of the Hellenistic Age* (Philadelphia: Fortress Press, 1982).

Kokkinos, N., *The Herodian Dynasty: Origins, Role in Society and Eclipse* (JSPSup, 30; Sheffield: Sheffield Academic Press, 1998).

Kraft, R.A., and G.W.E. Nickelsburg (eds.), *Early Judaism and its Modern Interpreters* (The Bible and its Modern Interpreters; Atlanta: Scholars Press; Philadelphia: Fortress Press, 1986).

Krentz, E., *The Historical-Critical Method* (GBS; Philadelphia: Fortress Press, 1975).

Kuhn, T., *The Structure of Scientific Revolutions* (International Encyclopedia of Unified Science; Chicago: University of Chicago Press, 1962; 2nd edn, 1970).

Kuhrt, A., and S. Sherwin-White (eds.), *Hellenism in the East* (London: Gerald Duckworth, 1987).

Kümmel, W.G., *Das Neue Testament: Geschichte der Erforschung seiner Probleme* (Munich: Alber, 1958; rev. edn, 1970; ET *The New Testament: The History of the Investigation of its Problems* [trans. S.M. Gilmour and H.C. Kee; Nashville: Abingdon Press, 1972]).

—*Dreissig Jahre Jesusforschung (1950–80)* (BBB, 60; ed. H. Merklein; Bonn: Hanstein, 1985).

—'Jesusforschung seit 1981', *TRu* 53 (1988), pp. 229-49; 54 (1989), pp. 1-53; 55 (1990), pp. 21-45; 56 (1991), pp. 27-53, 391-420.

—*Verheissung und Erfüllung* (Zürich: Zwingli-Verlag, 1956; ET *Promise and Fulfilment: The Eschatological Message of Jesus* [trans. D.M. Barton; London: SCM Press, 1957]).

Kutscher, E.Y., 'Hebrew Language: Mishnaic', *EncJud*, XVI, cols. 1592-93.

—*A History of the Hebrew Language* (ed. R. Kutscher; Leiden: E.J. Brill, 1982).

Kysar, R., *The Fourth Evangelist and his Gospel: An Examination of Contemporary Scholarship* (Minneapolis: Augsburg, 1975).

Ladd, G.E., *Jesus and the Kingdom: The Eschatology of Biblical Realism* (Grand Rapids: Eerdmans, 1964; London: SPCK, 1966).

Lagrange, M.-J., *L'évangile de Jésus-Christ* (Paris: J. Gabalda, 1928; ET *The Gospel of Jesus Christ* [2 vols.; London: Burns, Oates & Washbourne, 1938]).

—*Evangile selon Saint Marc* (EB; Paris: J. Gabalda, 1929).

Lakatos, I., 'Falsification and the Methodology of Scientific Research Programmes', in I. Lakatos and A. Musgrave (eds.), *Criticism and the Growth of Knowledge: Proceedings of the International Colloquium in the Philosophy of Science, London, 1965, volume 4* (Cambridge: Cambridge University Press, 1970), pp. 91-196.

Lang, M., *Johannes und die Synoptiker: Eine redaktionsgeschichtliche Analyse von Joh 18–20 vor dem markinischen und lukanischen Hintergrund* (FRLANT, 182; Göttingen: Vandenhoeck & Ruprecht, 1999).

Lapide, P., 'Insights from Qumran into the Languages of Jesus', *RevQ* 8 (1975), pp. 483-86.

Leaney, A.R.C., *The Jewish and Christian World 200 B.C. to A.D. 200* (Cambridge: Cambridge University Press, 1984).

Leclercq, H., 'Note sur le grec néo-testamentaire et la position du grec en Palestine au premier siècle', *Les études classiques* 42 (1974), pp. 243-55.

Lee, J.A.L., 'Some Features of the Speech of Jesus in Mark's Gospel', *NovT* 27 (1985), pp. 1-36.

Leech, G.N., and M.H. Short, *Style in Fiction: A Linguistic Introduction to English Fictional Prose* (London: Longman, 1981).

Lefort, L.-Th., 'Pour une grammaire des LXX', *Muséon* 41 (1928), pp. 152-60.

Lentzen-Deis, F., 'Kriterien für die historische Beurteilung der Jesusüberlieferung in den Evangelien', in Kertelge (ed.), *Rückfrage nach Jesus*, pp. 78-117.

Leon, H.J., *The Jews of Ancient Rome* (Philadelphia: Jewish Publication Society of America, 1960; Peabody, MA: Hendrickson, rev. edn, 1995).

Levine, L.I. (ed.), *The Galilee in Late Antiquity* (New York: Jewish Theological Seminary of America; Cambridge, MA: Harvard University Press, 1992).

Levinsohn, S.H., *Discourse Features of New Testament Greek: A Coursebook* (Dallas: Summer Institute of Linguistics, 1992).

—*Textual Connections in Acts* (SBLMS, 31; Atlanta: Scholars Press, 1987).

Lewis, N., *The Documents from the Bar Kokhba Period in the Cave of Letters: Greek Papyri* (Jerusalem: Israel Exploration Society, Hebrew University of Jerusalem, Shrine of the Book, 1989).

Lieberman, S., *Greek in Jewish Palestine: Studies in the Life and Manners of Jewish Palestine in the II–IV Centuries C.E.* (New York: Feldheim, 2nd edn, 1965).

—'How Much Greek in Jewish Palestine?', in A. Altmann (ed.), *Biblical and Other Studies* (Cambridge, MA: Harvard University Press, 1963), pp. 123-41.

Lifshitz, B., 'L'hellénisation de Juifs en Palestine: A propos des inscriptions de Besara (Beth-Shearim)', *RB* 72 (1965), pp. 520-38.

Lightfoot, R.H., *The Gospel Message of St Mark* (Oxford: Clarendon Press, 1950).

—*History and Interpretation in the Gospels* (London: Hodder & Stoughton; New York: Harper, 1935).

—*Locality and Doctrine in the Gospels* (London: Hodder & Stoughton, 1938).

—*St John's Gospel: A Commentary* (ed. C.F. Evans; Oxford: Clarendon Press, 1956).

Lindars, B., *John* (NTG; Sheffield: JSOT Press, 1990).

Linmans, A.J.M., 'Correspondence Analysis of the Synoptic Gospels', *Literary and Linguistic Computing* 13 (1998), pp. 1-13.

—*Onderschikking in de synoptische evangeliën: Syntaxis, discourse-functies en stilometrie* (Leiden: FSW, 1995).

Linnemann, E., *Jesus of the Parables* (trans. J. Sturdy; New York: Harper & Row, 1967 [= *Parables of Jesus* (London: SPCK, 1966)]).

Loisy, A., *La naissance du christianisme* (Paris: Nourry, 1933; ET *The Birth of the Christian Religion* [trans. L.P. Jacks; London: George Allen & Unwin, 1948]).

Longenecker, R.N., 'Literary Criteria in Life of Jesus Research: An Evaluation and Proposal', in Hawthorne (ed.), *Current Issues in Biblical and Patristic Interpretation*, pp. 217-29.

López Eire, A., 'Del ático a la *koiné*', *Emerita* 49 (1981), pp. 377-92.

Lord, A.B., *Epic Singers and Oral Tradition* (Myth and Poetics; Ithaca, NY: Cornell University Press, 1991).

Loveday, L., *The Sociolinguistics of Learning and Using a Non-Native Language* (Oxford: Pergamon Press, 1982).

Lührmann, D., 'Die Frage nach Kriterien für ursprüngliche Jesusworte: Eine Problemskizze', in Dupont (ed.), *Jésus aux origines de la christologie*, pp. 59-72.

Mackowski, R., 'Some Colloquialisms in the Gospel According to Mark', in R.F. Sutton, Jr (ed.), *Daidalikon: Studies in Memory of Raymond V. Schoder, SJ* (Wauconda, IL: Bolchazy-Carducci, 1989), pp. 229-38.

MacMullen, R., 'Provincial Languages in the Roman Empire', *AJP* 87 (1966); repr. in *Changes in the Roman Empire: Essays in the Ordinary* (New Haven: Yale University Press, 1990), pp. 32-40, 282-86.

Maloney, E.C., *Semitic Interference in Marcan Syntax* (SBLDS, 51; Chico, CA: Scholars Press, 1981).

Mann, C.S., *Mark* (AB, 27; Garden City, NY: Doubleday, 1986).

Manson, T.W., 'The Life of Jesus: A Study of the Available Materials', *ExpTim* 53 (1942), pp. 248-51; repr. in *idem, Studies in the Gospels and Epistles*, pp. 13-27.

—'The Life of Jesus: Some Tendencies in Present-day Research', in W.D. Davies and D. Daube (eds.), *The Background of the New Testament and its Eschatology* (Festschrift C.H. Dodd; Cambridge: Cambridge University Press, 1954), pp. 211-21.

—'The Quest of the Historical Jesus—Continued', repr. in *idem, Studies in the Gospels and Epistles*, pp. 3-12.

—*The Sayings of Jesus* (London: SCM Press, 1949 [first published in H.D.A. Major, T.W. Manson and C.J. Wright, *The Mission and Message of Jesus: An Exposition of the Gospels in the Light of Modern Research* (London: Ivor Nicholson & Watson, 1937), pp. 301-639]).

—*The Servant-Messiah: A Study of the Public Ministry of Jesus* (Cambridge: Cambridge University Press, 1953).

—*Studies in the Gospels and Epistles* (ed. M. Black; Manchester: Manchester University Press, 1962).

—*The Teaching of Jesus: Studies of its Form and Content* (Cambridge: Cambridge University Press, 1931; 2nd edn, 1935).

Manson, W., *Jesus the Messiah: The Synoptic Tradition of the Revelation of God in Christ with Special Reference to Form-Criticism* (London: Hodder & Stoughton, 1943; Philadelphia: Westminster Press, 1946).

Marrou, H.I., *Histoire de l'education dans l'antiquité* (Paris: Seuil, 3rd edn, 1948; *A History of Education in Antiquity* [trans. G. Lamb; London: Sheed & Ward, 1956]).

Marsh, J., *Jesus in his Lifetime* (London: Sidgwick & Jackson, 1981).

Marshall, I.H., *The Gospel of Luke* (NIGTC; Grand Rapids: Eerdmans, 1978).

—*I Believe in the Historical Jesus* (Grand Rapids: Eerdmans, 1977).

—*Luke: Historian and Theologian* (Exeter: Paternoster Press, 1970).

Marshall, I.H. (ed.), *New Testament Interpretation: Essays on Principles and Methods* (Exeter: Paternoster Press; Grand Rapids: Eerdmans, 1977).

Martin, R.A., *Syntax Criticism of the Synoptic Gospels* (Studies in the Bible and Early Christianity, 10; Lewiston, NY: Edwin Mellen Press, 1987).

Martin, R.P., 'The New Quest of the Historical Jesus', in C.F.H. Henry (ed.), *Jesus of Nazareth: Saviour and Lord* (London: Tyndale Press, 1966), pp. 23-45.

—'The Pericope of the Healing of the "Centurion's" Servant/Son (Matt 8:5-13 par. Luke 7:1-10): Some Exegetical Notes', in R.A. Guelich (ed.), *Unity and Diversity in New Testament Theology: Essays in Honor of George E. Ladd* (Grand Rapids: Eerdmans, 1978), pp. 14-22.

Martín-Asensio, G., 'Foregrounding and its Relevance for Interpretation and Translation, with Acts 27 as a Case Study', in Porter and Hess (eds.), *Translating the Bible*, pp. 189-223.

—'Participant Reference and Foregrounded Syntax in the Stephen Episode', in Porter and Reed (eds.), *Discourse Analysis and the New Testament*, pp. 235-57.

—*Transitivity-Based Foregrounding in the Arts of the Apostles: A Functional-Grammatical Approach* (JSNTSup; SNTG; Sheffield: Sheffield Academic Press, forthcoming).

Marxsen, W., *Anfangsprobleme der Christologie* (Gütersloh: Gerd Mohn, 1960; ET *The Beginnings of Christology: A Study in its Problems* [Facet Books, Biblical Studies, 22; Philadelphia: Fortress Press, 1969; 2nd edn, 1979]).

—*Der Evangelist Markus: Studien zur Redaktionsgeschichte des Evangeliums* (FRLANT, 67; Göttingen: Vandenhoeck & Ruprecht, 1956; 2nd edn, 1959; ET *Mark the Evangelist: Studies on the Redaction History of the Gospel* [trans. J. Boyce *et al.*; Nashville: Abingdon Press, 1969]).

Mason, S., *Josephus and the New Testament* (Peabody, MA: Hendrickson, 1992).

Masson, E., 'Translator's Prolegomena', in G.B. Winer, *A Grammar of the New Testament Diction* (trans. E. Masson; Edinburgh: T. & T. Clark, 1859; 6th edn, 1866), pp. i-x.

Matthews, S., *The Social Teaching of Jesus: An Essay in Christian Sociology* (New York: Macmillan, 1902).

Mayser, E., *Grammatik der griechischen Papyri aus der Ptolemäerzeit* (3 vols.; Berlin: W. de Gruyter, 1906–1934; 2nd edn of vol. 1, 1970).

McArthur, H.K., 'Basic Issues, A Survey of Recent Gospel Research', in *idem* (ed.), *In Search of the Historical Jesus*, pp. 139-44.

—'The Burden of Proof in Historical Jesus Research', *ExpTim* 82 (1970–71), pp. 116-19.

McArthur, H.K. (ed.), *In Search of the Historical Jesus* (New York: Charles Scribner's Sons, 1969).

McDonald, J.I.H., 'New Quest—Dead End? So What about the Historical Jesus', in E.A. Livingstone (ed.), *Studia Biblica 1978*. II. *Papers on the Gospels. Sixth International Congress on Biblical Studies* (JSNTSup, 2; Sheffield: JSOT Press, 1980), pp. 151-70.

McDonald, L.M., and S.E. Porter, *Early Christianity and its Sacred Literature* (Peabody, MA: Hendrickson, 2000).

McEleney, N.J., 'Authenticating Criteria and Mark 7:1-23', *CBQ* 34 (1972), pp. 431-60.

McKnight, E.V., 'Form and Redaction Criticism', in Epp and MacRae (eds.), *New Testament and its Modern Interpreters*, pp. 149-74.

—*What is Form Criticism?* (GBS; Philadelphia: Fortress Press, 1969).

McKnight, S., *Interpreting the Synoptic Gospels* (Guides to New Testament Exegesis; Grand Rapids: Baker Book House, 1988).

—*A New Vision for Israel: The Teachings of Jesus in National Context* (SHJ; Grand Rapids: Eerdmans, 1999).

—'Public Declaration or Final Judgment? Matthew 10:26-27 = Luke 12:2-3 as a Case of Creative Redaction', in Chilton and Evans (eds.), *Authenticating the Words of Jesus*, pp. 363-83.

McLaren, J.S., *Turbulent Times? Josephus and Scholarship on Judaea in the First Century CE* (JSPSup, 29; Sheffield: Sheffield Academic Press, 1998).

Mead, A.H., 'The βασιλικός in John 4.46-53', *JSNT* 23 (1985), pp. 69-72.

Mealand, D.L., 'Correspondence Analysis of Luke', *Literary and Linguistic Computing* 10 (1995), pp. 171-82.

—'The Dissimilarity Test', *SJT* 31 (1978), pp. 41-50.

—'The Extent of the Pauline Corpus: A Multivariate Approach', *JSNT* 59 (1995), pp. 61-92.

—'Measuring Genre Differences in Mark with Correspondence Analysis', *Literary and Linguistic Computing* 12 (1997), pp. 227-45.

Meecham, H.G., *Light from Ancient Letters: Private Correspondence in the Non-Literary Papyri of Oxyrhynchus of the First Four Centuries, and its Bearing on New Testament Language and Thought* (London: Allen & Unwin, 1923).

Meeks, W.A., *The First Urban Christians* (New Haven: Yale University Press, 1983).

Meier, J.P., *A Marginal Jew: Rethinking the Historical Jesus* (3 vols.; ABRL; New York: Doubleday, 1991–).

Meillet, A., *Aperçu d'une histoire de la langue grecque* (Paris: Hachette, 3rd edn, 1930).

Mendels, D., *The Rise and Fall of Jewish Nationalism: Jewish and Christian Ethnicity in Ancient Palestine* (ABRL; New York: Doubleday, 1992; repr. Grand Rapids: Eerdmans, 1997).

Metzger, B.M., *The Text of the New Testament: Its Transmission, Corruption, and Restoration* (New York: Oxford University Press, 3rd edn, 1992).

—*A Textual Commentary on the Greek New Testament* (London: United Bible Societies, 1971; Stuttgart: Deutsche Bibelgesellschaft/United Bible Societies, 2nd edn, 1994).

Meyer, A., *Jesu Muttersprache: Das galiläische Aramäisch in seiner Bedeutung für die Erklärung der Reden Jesu und der Evangelien überhaupt* (Freiburg: Mohr Siebeck, 1896).

Meyer, B.F., *The Aims of Jesus* (London: SCM Press, 1979).

Meyers, E.M., 'The Cultural Setting of Galilee: The Case of Regionalism and Early Judaism', *ANRW* 2.2.19, pp. 686-702.

—'Galilean Regionalism: A Reappraisal', in W.D. Green (ed.), *Approaches to Ancient Judaism. V. Studies in Judaism and its Greco-Roman Context* (Atlanta: Scholars Press, 1985), pp. 115-31.

—'Jesus and his Galilean Context', in Edwards and McCollough (eds.), *Archaeology and the Galilee*, pp. 57-66.

Meyers, E.M., and J.F. Strange, *Archaeology, the Rabbis and Early Christianity* (London: SCM Press, 1981), pp. 73-78.

Michaels, J.R., *Servant and Son: Jesus in Parable and Gospel* (Atlanta: John Knox Press, 1981).

Millar, F., *The Roman Near East 31 BC–AD 337* (Cambridge, MA: Harvard University Press, 1993).

Millard, A., 'Latin in First-Century Palestine', in Z. Zevit, S. Gitin and M. Sokoloff (eds.), *Solving Riddles and Untying Knots: Biblical, Epigraphic, and Semitic Studies in Honor of Jonas C. Greenfield* (Winona Lake, IN: Eisenbrauns, 1995), pp. 451-58.

Miller, R.J. (ed.), *The Complete Gospels: Annotated Scholars Version* (Sonoma, CA: Pole-bridge Press, 1992; 2nd edn, 1994; San Francisco: HarperSanFrancisco, 3rd edn, 1994).

Milligan, G., 'The Grammar of the Greek New Testament', *ExpTim* 31 (1919–20), pp. 420-24.

—*Here and There among the Papyri* (London: Hodder & Stoughton, 1922).

—*The New Testament Documents: Their Origin and Early History* (London: Macmillan, 1913).

Mitton, C.L., *Jesus: The Fact behind the Faith* (Grand Rapids: Eerdmans, 1973; London: Mowbrays, 1975).

Moore, S.D., *Literary Criticism and the Gospels: The Theoretical Challenge* (New Haven: Yale University Press, 1989).

Morgan, R., 'The Historical Jesus and the Theology of the New Testament', in L.D. Hurst and N.T. Wright (eds.), *The Glory of Christ in the New Testament: Studies in Christology* (Festschrift G.B. Caird; Oxford: Clarendon Press, 1987), pp. 187-206.

Morgan, R., with J. Barton, *Biblical Interpretation* (OBS; Oxford: Oxford University Press, 1988).

Morris, L.L., *The Gospel According to John* (NICNT; Grand Rapids: Eerdmans, 1971).

—'The Gospels and the Jewish Lectionaries', in R.T. France and D. Wenham (eds.), *Gospel Perspectives: Studies in Midrash and Historiography*, III (Sheffield: JSOT Press, 1983), pp. 129-56.

—*The New Testament and the Jewish Lectionaries* (London: Tyndale Press, 1964).

Moule, C.F.D., 'Once More, Who were the Hellenists?', *ExpTim* 70 (1958–59), pp. 100-102.

—*The Phenomenon of the New Testament* (London: SCM Press, 1967).

—' "The Son of Man": Some of the Facts', *NTS* 41 (1995), pp. 277-79.

Moulton, J.H., 'Characteristics of New Testament Greek', *Expositor* Sixth Series 9 (1904), pp. 67-75, 215-25, 310-20, 359-68, 461-72; 10 (1904), pp. 24-34, 168-74, 276-83, 353-64, 440-50.

—'Grammatical Notes from the Papyri', *Classical Review* 15 (1901), pp. 31-39, 434-42; 18 (1904), pp. 106-12, 151-55.

—'New Testament Greek in the Light of Modern Discovery', in H.B. Swete (ed.), *Essays on Some Biblical Questions of the Day: By Members of the University of Cambridge* (London: Macmillan, 1909), pp. 461-505.

—'Notes from the Papyri', *Expositor* Sixth Series 3 (1901), pp. 271-82; 7 (1903), pp. 104-21; 8 (1903), pp. 423-39.

—*Prolegomena*, to *A Grammar of New Testament Greek* (Edinburgh: T. & T. Clark, 1906; 3rd edn, 1908).

—*The Science of Language and the Study of the New Testament* (Inaugural Lecture; Manchester: Manchester University Press, 1906).

Moulton, J.H., and G. Milligan, *The Vocabulary of the Greek Testament Illustrated from the Papyri and Other Non-Literary Sources* (London: Hodder & Stoughton, 1914–29).

Müller, M., *The First Bible of the Church: A Plea for the Septuagint* (JSOTSup, 206; Copenhagen International Seminar, 1; Sheffield: Sheffield Academic Press, 1996).

Munro, W., 'The Pharisee and the Samaritan in John: Polar or Parallel?', *CBQ* 57 (1995), pp. 710-28.

Mussies, G., 'Greek as the Vehicle of Early Christianity', *NTS* 29 (1983), pp. 356-69.

—'Greek in Palestine and the Diaspora', in Safrai and Stern (eds.), *The Jewish People in the First Century*, pp. 1040-64.

—'Languages (Greek)', *ABD* 4 (1992), pp. 195-203.

Mussner, F., 'Der "historische" Jesus', *TTZ* 69 (1960), pp. 321-37; repr. in *idem, Jesus von Nazareth*, pp. 43-61.

—*Jesus von Nazareth im Umfeld Israels und der Urkirche: Gesammelte Aufsätze* (ed. M. Theobald; WUNT, 111; Tübingen: Mohr Siebeck, 1999).

—'Methodologie der Frage nach dem historischen Jesus', in Kertelge (ed.), *Rückfrage nach Jesus*, pp. 118-47; repr. in Mussner, *Jesus von Nazareth*, pp. 13-42.

Muysken, P., 'Are Creoles a Special Type of Language?', in F.J. Newmeyer (ed.), *Linguistics: The Cambridge Survey*. II. *Linguistic Theory: Extensions and Implications* (Cambridge: Cambridge University Press, 1988), pp. 285-301.

Neil, W., *The Life and Teaching of Jesus* (London: Hodder & Stoughton; Philadelphia: Lippincott, 1965).

Neill, S., and T. Wright, *The Interpretation of the New Testament 1861–1986* (Oxford: Oxford University Press, 2nd edn, 1988 [1964]).

Neirynck, F., 'The Apocryphal Gospels and the Gospel of Mark', in J.-M. Sevrin (ed.), *The New Testament in Early Christianity* (BETL, 86; Leuven: Leuven University Press/ Peeters, 1989), pp. 123-75; repr. in F. Neirynck, *Evangelica II: 1982–1991 Collected Essays* (BETL, 99; Leuven: Leuven University Press, 1991), pp. 715-72.

—*Duality in Mark: Contributions to the Study of the Markan Redaction* (BETL, 31; Leuven: Leuven University Press/Peeters, 1988).

—*Evangelica: Gospel Studies—Etudes d'évangile. Collected Essays* (ed. F. Van Segbroeck; BETL, 60; Leuven: Leuven University Press/Peeters, 1982).

—'John and the Synoptics', in M. de Jonge (ed.), *L'évangile de Jean: Sources, rédaction, théologie* (BETL, 44; Gembloux: Duculot, 1977), pp. 73-106; repr. in Neirynck, *Evangelica: Gospel Studies*, pp. 365-400.

—'The Redactional Text of Mark', *ETL* 57 (1981), pp. 144-62; repr. in *idem, Evangelica: Gospel Studies*, pp. 618-36.

Neirynck, F., *et al.*, *The Gospel of Mark: A Cumulative Bibliography 1950–1990* (BETL, 102; Leuven: Peeters/Leuven University Press, 1992).

Nestle, E., *Einführung in das griechische Neue Testament* (Göttingen: Vandenhoeck & Ruprecht, 2nd edn, 1899; ET *Introduction to the Textual Criticism of the Greek New Testament* [trans. W. Edie; Theological Translation Library; London: Williams & Norgate, 1901]).

—*Philologica Sacra: Bemerkungen über die Urgestalt der Evangelien und Apostelgeschichte* (Berlin: Reuther & Reichard, 1896).

New, D.S., *Old Testament Quotations in the Synoptic Gospels, and the Two-Document Hypothesis* (SBLSCS, 37; Atlanta: Scholars Press, 1993).

Newmark, P., *About Translation* (Multilingual Matters, 74; Clevedon: Multilingual Matters, 1991).

Nicklin, T., *Gospel Gleanings: Critical and Historical Notes on the Gospels* (London: Longmans, Green, 1950).

Nida, E.A., *Language Structure and Translation: Essays by Eugene A. Nida* (ed. A.S. Dil; Stanford: Stanford University Press, 1975).

—*The Sociolinguistics of Interlingual Communication* (Collection Traductologie; Brussels: Editions du Hansard, 1996).

—*Toward a Science of Translating with Special Reference to Principles and Procedures Involved in Bible Translating* (Leiden: E.J. Brill, 1964).

Nida, E.A., and C.R. Taber, *The Theory and Practice of Translation* (Leiden: E.J. Brill, 1969).

Nida, E.A., et al., *Style and Discourse: With Special Reference to the Text of the Greek New Testament* (Roggebaai, South Africa: Bible Society, 1983).

Norden, E., *Agnostos Theos: Untersuchungen zur Formengeschichte religiöser Rede* (Stuttgart: Teubner, 1913; repr. Darmstadt: Wissenschaftliche Buchgesellschaft, 1956).

Nunan, D., *Introducing Discourse Analysis* (Penguin English Applied Linguistics; Harmondsworth: Penguin Books, 1993).

O'Collins, G., *Interpreting Jesus* (Geoffrey Chapman Theology Library; London: Chapman, 1983).

O'Donnell, M.B., 'Linguistic Fingerprints or Style by Numbers: The Use of Statistics in the Discussion of Authorship of New Testament Documents', in S.E. Porter and D.A. Carson (eds.), *Linguistics and the New Testament: Critical Junctures* (JSNTSup, 168; SNTG, 5; Sheffield: Sheffield Academic Press, 1999), pp. 206-62.

—'The Use of Annotated Corpora for New Testament Discourse Analysis: A Survey of Current Practice and Future Prospects', in Porter and Reed (eds.), *Discourse Analysis and the New Testament*, pp. 71-117.

Oesterley, W.O.E., *The Gospel Parables in the Light of their Jewish Background* (London: SPCK, 1936).

Ogg, G., *The Chronology of the Public Ministry of Jesus* (Cambridge: Cambridge University Press, 1940).

O'Neill, J.C., *The Bible's Authority: A Portrait Gallery of Thinkers from Lessing to Bultmann* (Edinburgh: T. & T. Clark, 1991).

Orchard, B., and H. Riley, *The Order of the Synoptics: Why Three Synoptic Gospels?* (Macon, GA: Mercer University Press, 1987).

Orrieux, C., *Les papyrus de Zenon: L'horizon d'un grec en Egypte au IIIe siècle avant J.C.* (Paris: Macula, 1983).

Osborne, G.R., 'Redaction Criticism', in Black and Dockery (eds.), *New Testament Criticism and Interpretation*, pp. 199-224.

Overman, A., 'Recent Advances in the Archaeology of the Galilee in the Roman Period', *CR* 1 (1993), pp. 35-58.

Owens, E.J., *The City in the Greek and Roman World* (London: Routledge, 1991).

Palmer, H., *The Logic of Gospel Criticism: An Account of the Methods and Arguments Used by Textual, Document, Source, and Form Critics of the New Testament* (London: Macmillan; New York: St Martin's, 1968).

Palmer, L.R., *The Greek Language* (London: Faber & Faber, 1980).

Patterson, S.W., 'What Language Did Jesus Speak?', *The Classical Outlook* 23 (1946), pp. 65-67.

Paulus, H.E.G., *Das Leben Jesu, als Grundlage einer reinen Geschichte des Urchristentums* (2 vols.; Heidelberg: Winter, 1828).

Payne, P.B., 'The Authenticity of the Parables of Jesus', in France and Wenham (eds.), *Gospel Perspectives*, II, pp. 329-44.

Peabody, D.B., *Mark as Composer* (New Gospel Studies, 1; Macon, GA: Mercer University Press/Peeters, 1987).

Peabody, F.G., *The Social Teaching of Jesus Christ* (Philadelphia: University of Pennsylvania Press, 1924).

Perrin, N., *Jesus and the Language of the Kingdom: Symbol and Metaphor in New Testament Interpretation* (NTL; London: SCM Press; Philadelphia: Fortress Press, 1976).

—*The Kingdom of God in the Teaching of Jesus* (London: SCM Press, 1963).

—*Rediscovering the Teaching of Jesus* (NTL; London: SCM Press; New York: Harper & Row, 1967).

—*What is Redaction Criticism?* (GBS; Philadelphia: Fortress Press; London: SCM Press, 1970).

Phipps, W.E., *The Wisdom and Wit of Rabbi Jesus* (Louisville, KY: Westminster/John Knox Press, 1993).

Piper, R.A. (ed.), *The Gospel behind the Gospels: Current Studies on Q* (NovTSup, 75; Leiden: E.J. Brill, 1995).

Pokorný, P., 'From a Puppy to the Child: Problems of Contemporary Biblical Exegesis Demonstrated from Mark 7.24-30/Matt 15.21-8', *NTS* 41 (1995), pp. 321-37.

—*Jesus in the Eyes of his Followers: Newly Discovered Manuscripts and Old Christian Confessions* (Dead Sea Scrolls and Christian Origins Library; North Richland Hills, TX: Bibal Press, 1998).

Polkow, D., 'Method and Criteria for Historical Jesus Research', in K.H. Richards (ed.), *Society of Biblical Literature 1987 Seminar Papers* (SBLSP, 26; Atlanta: Scholars Press, 1987), pp. 336-56.

Polomé, E.C., 'The Linguistic Situation in the Western Provinces of the Roman Empire', *ANRW* 2.29.2, pp. 509-53.

Popper, K.R., *Conjectures and Refutations: The Growth of Scientific Knowledge* (London: Routledge & Kegan Paul, 1963; 4th edn, 1972).

Porter, S.E., 'The Adjectival Attributive Genitive in the New Testament: A Grammatical Study', *Trinity Journal* NS 4 (1983), pp. 3-17.

—'Dialect and Register in the Greek of the New Testament: Theory', and 'Register in the Greek of the New Testament: Application with Reference to Mark's Gospel', in M.D. Carroll R. (ed.), *Rethinking Contexts, Rereading Texts: Contributions from the Social Sciences to Biblical Interpretation* (JSOTSup, 299; Sheffield: Sheffield Academic Press, 2000), pp. 190-208 and 209-29.

—'Did Jesus Ever Teach in Greek?', *TynBul* 44.2 (1993), pp. 199-235; repr. in *idem, Studies in the Greek New Testament*, pp. 139-71.

—'Discourse Analysis and New Testament Studies: An Introductory Survey', in Porter and Carson (eds.), *Discourse Analysis and Other Topics*, pp. 14-35.

—'The Greek Language of the New Testament', in *idem* (ed.), *Handbook to Exegesis*, pp. 99-130.

—'The Greek Papyri of the Judaean Desert and the World of the Roman East', in S.E. Porter and C.A. Evans (eds.), *The Scrolls and the Scriptures: Qumran Fifty Years After* (JSPSup, 26; RILP, 3; Sheffield: Sheffield Academic Press, 1997), pp. 293-311.

—*Idioms of the Greek New Testament* (BLG, 2; Sheffield: JSOT Press, 2nd edn, 1994).

—'Introduction: The Greek of the New Testament as a Disputed Area of Research', in *idem* (ed.), *Language of the New Testament*, pp. 11-38; repr. with corrections in *idem, Studies in the Greek New Testament*, pp. 75-99.

—'Is Critical Discourse Analysis Critical? An Evaluation Using Philemon as a Test Case', in Porter and Reed (eds.), *Discourse Analysis and the New Testament*, pp. 47-70.

—'Jesus and the Use of Greek in Galilee', in Chilton and Evans (eds.), *Studying the Historical Jesus*, pp. 123-54.

—*The Paul of Acts: Essays in Literary Criticism, Rhetoric, and Theology* (WUNT, 115; Tübingen: Mohr Siebeck, 1999).

—review of *The Interpretation of the New Testament 1861–1986*, by Neill and Wright, in *JETS* 35 (1992), pp. 546-47.

—*Studies in the Greek New Testament: Theory and Practice* (SBG, 6; New York: Peter Lang, 1996).

—'Studying Ancient Languages from a Modern Linguistic Perspective: Essential Terms and Terminology', *FN* 2 (1989), pp. 147-72.

—'Thucydides 1.22.1 and Speeches in Acts: Is There a Thucydidean View?', *NovT* 30 (1990), pp. 121-42.

—'Vague Verbs, Periphrastics, and Matthew 16:19', *FN* 1 (1988), pp. 154-73; repr. in *idem, Studies in the Greek New Testament*, pp. 103-23.

—*Verbal Aspect in the Greek of the New Testament, with Reference to Tense and Mood* (SBG, 1; New York: Peter Lang, 1989).

—'Why so Many Holes in the Papyrological Evidence for the Greek New Testament?', in K. van Kampen and S. McKendrick (eds.), *The Bible as Book: The Transmission of the Greek Text* (London: British Library Publications; Grand Haven, MI: Scriptorium, forthcoming 2000).

Porter, S.E., and M.B. O'Donnell, 'The Implications of Textual Variants for Authenticating the Activities of Jesus', in Chilton and Evans (eds.), *Authenticating the Activities of Jesus*, pp. 121-51.

—'The Implications of Textual Variants for Authenticating the Words of Jesus', in Chilton and Evans (eds.), *Authenticating the Words of Jesus*, pp. 97-133.

—*The Words and Activities of Jesus: Textual Variants and Register Analysis* (Texts and Editions, 1; Leiden: E.J. Brill, forthcoming).

Porter, S.E., and B.W.R. Pearson, 'Ancient Understandings of the Christian–Jewish Split', in S.E. Porter and B.W.R. Pearson, *Christian–Jewish Relations through the Centuries* (RILP, 6; JSNTSup, 192; Sheffield: Sheffield Academic Press, forthcoming 2000).

—'Why the Split? Christians and Jews by the Fourth Century', *JGRChJ* 1 (2000), forthcoming.

Porter, S.E. (ed.), *Diglossia and Other Topics in New Testament Greek* (JSNTSup 193; SNTG, 6; Sheffield: Sheffield Academic Press, forthcoming 2000).

—*Handbook to Exegesis of the New Testament* (NTTS, 25; Leiden: E.J. Brill, 1997).

—*The Language of the New Testament: Classic Essays* (JSNTSup, 60; Sheffield: JSOT Press, 1991).

Porter, S.E., and D.A. Carson (eds.), *Discourse Analysis and Other Topics in Biblical Greek* (JSNTSup, 113; SNTG, 2; Sheffield: JSOT Press, 1995).

Porter, S.E., and D. Tombs (eds.), *Approaches to New Testament Study* (JSNTSup, 120; Sheffield: JSOT Press, 1995).

Porter, S.E., and R.S. Hess (eds.), *Translating the Bible: Problems and Prospects* (JSNTSup, 173; Sheffield: Sheffield Academic Press, 1999).

Porter, S.E., and J.T. Reed (eds.), *Discourse Analysis and the New Testament: Approaches and Results* (JSNTSup, 170; SNTG, 4; Sheffield: Sheffield Academic Press, 1999).

Powell, M.A., *Jesus as a Figure in History: How Modern Historians View the Man from Galilee* (Louisville, KY: Westminster/John Knox Press, 1998).

Pride, J.B., and J. Holmes (eds.), *Sociolinguistics* (Harmondsworth: Penguin Books, 1972).

Pryke, A.J., *Redactional Style in the Marcan Gospel: A Study of Syntax and Vocabulary as Guides to Redaction in Mark* (SNTSMS, 33; Cambridge: Cambridge University Press, 1978).

Rabin, C., 'Hebrew and Aramaic in the First Centry', in Safrai and Stern (eds.), *Jewish People in the First Century*, pp. 1007-1039.

Radermacher, L., *Neutestamentliche Grammatik: Das Griechisch des Neuen Testaments im Zusammenhang mit der Volkssprache* (HNT, 1; Tübingen: Mohr Siebeck, 1911; 2nd edn, 1925).

Rajak, T., *Josephus: The Historian and his Society* (London: Gerald Duckworth, 1983; Philadelphia: Fortress Press, 1984).

Rauschenbusch, W., *A Theology of the Social Gospel* (New York: Macmillan, 1922).

Redlich, E.B., *Form Criticism: Its Value and Limitations* (Studies in Theology; London: Gerald Duckworth, 1939).

Reed, J.T., 'Discourse Analysis', in Porter (ed.), *Handbook to Exegesis*, pp. 189-217.

—*A Discourse Analysis of Philippians: Method and Rhetoric in the Debate over Literary Integrity* (JSNTSup, 136; SNTG, 3; Sheffield: Sheffield Academic Press, 1997).

—'Modern Linguistics and the New Testament: A Basic Guide to Theory, Terminology, and Literature', in Porter and Tombs (eds.), *Approaches to New Testament Study*, pp. 222-65.

Reicke, B., *The Roots of the Synoptic Gospels* (Philadelphia: Fortress Press, 1986).

Reimarus, H.S., *Von dem Zwecke Jesu und seiner Jünger: Noch ein Fragment des Wolfen-büttelschen Ungenannten* (Fragment 7; ed. G.E. Lessing; Braunschweig: n.p., 1778; ET *Reimarus: Fragments* [ed. C.H. Talbert; trans. R.S. Fraser; LJ; Philadelphia: Fortress Press, 1970; London: SCM Press, 1971]).

Reiser, M., *Syntax und Stil des Markusevangeliums im Licht der hellenistischen Volksliter-atur* (WUNT, 2.11; Tübingen: Mohr Siebeck, 1984).

Renan, E., *La vie de Jésus* (Paris: Lévy, 1863; ET *The Life of Jesus* [London: Trübner, 1864]).

Rendsburg, G.A., 'The Galilean Background of Mishnaic Hebrew', in Levine (ed.), *The Galilee in Late Antiquity*, pp. 225-40.

Renehan, R., *Greek Textual Criticism: A Reader* (Cambridge, MA: Harvard University Press, 1969).

Resch, A., *Agrapha: Aussercanonische Schriftfragmenta* (TU, 15.3–4; J.C. Leipzig: Hinrichs, 2nd edn, 1906).

Reumann, J., 'Jesus and Christology', in Epp and MacRae (eds.), *New Testament and its Modern Interpreters*, pp. 501-64.

—*Jesus in the Church's Gospels: Modern Scholarship and the Earliest Sources* (Philadel-phia: Fortress Press, 1968; London: SPCK, 1970).

Rhoads, D., *Israel in Revolution: 6–74 C.E. A Political History Based on the Writings of Josephus* (Philadelphia: Fortress Press, 1976).

—'Jesus and the Syrophoenician Woman in Mark', *JAAR* 62 (1994), pp. 343-75.

Richardson, P., *Herod: King of the Jews and Friend of the Romans* (Columbia: University of South Carolina Press; Edinburgh: T. & T. Clark, 1996).

Riches, J.K., 'The Actual Words of Jesus', *ABD* 3 (1992), pp. 802-804.

—*A Century of New Testament Study* (Cambridge: Lutterworth, 1993).

—*Jesus and the Transformation of Judaism* (London: Darton, Longman & Todd; New York: Seabury, 1980).

Riches, J.K., and A. Millar, 'Conceptual Change in the Synoptic Tradition', in A.E. Harvey (ed.), *Alternative Approaches to New Testament Study* (London: SPCK, 1985), pp. 37-60.

Riesenfeld, H., *The Gospel Tradition* (trans. E.M. Rowley and R.A. Kraft; Philadelphia: Fortress Press; Oxford: Basil Blackwell, 1970).

—'The Gospel Tradition and its Beginnings', in K. Aland (ed.), *Studia Evangelica* (TU, 73; Berlin: Akademie-Verlag, 1958); repr. in Riesenfeld, *The Gospel Tradition*, pp. 1-29.

Riesner, R., *Jesus als Lehrer: Eine Untersuchung zum Ursprung der Evangelien-Überlieferung* (WUNT, 2.7; Tübingen: Mohr Siebeck, 1981; 4th edn, 1994).

—'Jesus as Preacher and Teacher', in H. Wansbrough (ed.), *Jesus and the Oral Gospel Tradition* (JSNTSup, 64; Sheffield: JSOT Press, 1991), pp. 185-210.

—'Jüdische Elementarbildung und Evangelienüberlieferung', in France and Wenham (eds.), *Gospel Perspectives*, I, pp. 209-223.

—'Synagogues in Jerusalem', in R. Bauckham (ed.), *The Book of Acts in its First Century Setting. IV. Palestinian Setting* (Grand Rapids: Eerdmans; Exeter: Paternoster Press, 1995), pp. 179-211.

Rist, J.M., *On the Independence of Matthew and Mark* (SNTSMS, 32; Cambridge: Cambridge University Press, 1978).

Ristow, H., and K. Matthiae (eds.), *Der historische Jesus und der kerygmatische Christus: Beiträge zum Christusverständnis in Forschung und Verkündigung* (Berlin: Evangelische Verlagsanstalt, 1960).

Robbins, V.K., 'Pragmatic Relations as a Criterion for Authentic Sayings', *Forum* 1.3 (1985), pp. 35-63.

—*The Tapestry of Early Christian Discourse: Rhetoric, Society and Ideology* (London: Routledge, 1996).

Roberts, A., *Greek: The Language of Christ and his Apostles* (London: Longmans, Green, 1888).

—*A Short Proof that Greek was the Language of Christ* (Paisley: Alexander Gardner, 1893).

Robertson, A.T., *Epochs in the Life of Jesus: A Study of Development and Struggle in the Messiah's Work* (London: Hodder & Stoughton, 1908).

—*A Grammar of the Greek New Testament in the Light of Historical Research* (New York: Hodder & Stoughton, 1914; Nashville: Broadman, 4th edn, 1934).

—*An Introduction to the Textual Criticism of the New Testament* (London: Hodder & Stoughton, 1925).

Robinson, J.A.T., 'The Destination and Purpose of St John's Gospel', *NTS* 6 (1960), pp. 117-31; repr. in *idem*, *Twelve New Testament Studies*, pp. 107-125.

—'The New Look on the Fourth Gospel', in K. Aland (ed.), *Studia Evangelica* (TU, 73; Berlin: Akademie Verlag, 1958), pp. 338-50; repr. in *idem*, *Twelve New Testament Studies*, pp. 94-106.

—*The Priority of John* (ed. J.F. Coakley; London: SCM Press, 1985; Oak Park, IL: Meyer–Stone, 1987).

—*Twelve New Testament Studies* (SBT, 34; London: SCM Press, 1962).

Robinson, J.M., 'The Formal Structure of Jesus' Message', in W. Klassen and G.F. Snyder (eds.), *Current Issues in New Testament Interpretation: Essays in Honor of Otto A. Piper* (London: SCM Press; New York: Harper & Row, 1962), pp. 91-110, 273-84.

—*A New Quest of the Historical Jesus* (SBT, 25; London: SCM Press, 1959; Missoula, MT: Scholars Press, 1979).

—*The Problem of History in Mark* (SBT, 21; London: SCM Press, 1957).

—'The Study of the Historical Jesus after Nag Hammadi', *Semeia* 44 (1988), pp. 45-55.

Rohde, J., *Die redaktionsgeschichtliche Methode: Einführung und Sichtung des Forschungestandes* (Hamburg: Furche-Verlag, 1966; rev. 1968; ET *Rediscovering the Teaching of the Evangelists* [trans. D.M. Barton; NTL; London: SCM Press, 1968]).

Roloff, J., 'Auf der Suche nach einem neuen Jesusbild: Tendenzen und Aspekte der gegenwärtigen Diskussion', *TLZ* 98 (1973), cols. 561-72.

—'G. Theissen and D. Winter, The Question of Criteria in Jesus Research: From Dissimilarity to Plausibility', *Review of Theological Literature* 1 (1999), pp. 54-58.

Romaine, S., *Language in Society: An Introduction to Sociolinguistics* (Oxford: Oxford University Press, 1994), pp. 55-64.

Ropes, J.H., 'Agrapha', in Hastings (ed.), *A Dictionary of the Bible*, V, pp. 343-52.

Rosner, B.S., 'Looking Back on the 20th Century 1. New Testament Studies', *ExpTim* 110 (1999), pp. 316-20.

Ross, J.M., 'Jesus's Knowledge of Greek', *IBS* 12 (1990), pp. 41-47.

Rostovtzeff, M., *Social and Economic History of the Roman Empire* (2 vols.; Oxford: Clarendon Press, 1926; 2nd edn rev. P.M. Fraser, 1957).

Rydbeck, L., 'ΕΥΣΕΒΕΙΑΝ ΕΔΕΙΞΕΝ ΤΟΙΣ ΑΝΘΡΩΠΟΙΣ', in Fornberg and Hellholm (eds.), *Texts and Contexts*, pp. 591-96.

—*Fachprosa, vermeintliche Volkssprache und Neues Testament: Zur Beurteilung der sprachlichen Niveauunterschiede im nachklassischen Griechisch* (Uppsala: University of Uppsala; Stockholm: Almqvist & Wiksell, 1967).

—'The Language of the New Testament', *TynBul* 49.2 (1998), pp. 361-68.

Safrai, S., and M. Stern (eds.), *The Jewish People in the First Century* (CRINT, 1.2; Assen: Van Gorcum; Philadelphia: Fortress Press, 1976).

Sanday, W., 'Jesus Christ', in Hastings (ed.), *A Dictionary of the Bible*, II, pp. 603-653.

—*The Life of Christ in Recent Research* (New York: Oxford University Press, 1907).

—*Outlines of the Life of Christ* (Edinburgh: T. & T. Clark, 1905).

Sanday, W. (ed.), *Studies in the Synoptic Problem* (Oxford: Clarendon Press, 1911).

Sanders, E.P., *The Historical Figure of Jesus* (London: Allen Lane/Penguin, 1993).

—*Jesus and Judaism* (London: SCM Press; Philadelphia: Fortress Press, 1985).

—*Jewish Law from Jesus to the Mishnah: Five Studies* (London: SCM Press; Philadelphia: Trinity Press International, 1990).

—*Judaism: Practice and Belief 63 BCE–66 CE* (London: SCM Press; Philadelphia: Trinity Press International, 1992).

—*The Tendencies of the Synoptic Tradition* (SNTSMS, 9; Cambridge: Cambridge University Press, 1969).

Sanders, E.P., and M. Davies, *Studying the Synoptic Gospels* (London: SCM Press; Philadelphia: Trinity Press International, 1989).

Schäfer, P., *The History of the Jews in Antiquity: The Jews of Palestine from Alexander the Great to the Arab Conquest* (Luxembourg: Harwood, 1995).

Schenk, W., *Das biographische Ich-Idiom 'Menschensohn' in den frühen Jesus-Biographien: Der Ausdruck, seine Codes und seine Rezeptionen in ihren Kotexten* (FRLANT, 177; Göttingen: Vandenhoeck & Ruprecht, 1997).

—'The Testamental Disciple-Instruction of the Markan Jesus (Mark 13): Levels of Communication and its Rhetorical Structures', in Porter and Reed (eds.), *Discourse Analysis and the New Testament*, pp. 197-222.

Schiffrin, D., *Approaches to Discourse* (Oxford: Basil Blackwell, 1994).

—*Discourse Markers* (Studies in Interactional Sociolinguistics, 5; Cambridge: Cambridge University Press, 1987).

Schille, G., 'Ein neuer Zugang zu Jesus? Das traditionsgeschichtliche Kriterium', *Zeichen und Zeit* 40 (1986), pp. 247-53.

Schillebeeckx, E., *Jezus, het verhaal van een levende* (Bloemendaal: Nelissen, 1974; ET *Jesus: An Experiment in Christology* [trans. H. Hoskins; New York: Seabury, 1979]).

Schlatter, A., *Die Geschichte des Christus* (Stuttgart: Calwer Verlag, 1921; 2nd edn, 1923; ET *The History of the Christ: The Foundation for New Testament Theology* [trans. A.J. Köstenberger; Grand Rapids: Baker Book House, 1997]).

Schmidt, K.L., *Der Rahmen der Geschichte Jesu: Literarkritische Untersuchungen zur ältesten Jesusüberlieferung* (Berlin: Trowitzsch, 1919).

—'Jesus Christus', *RGG*, III (Tübingen: Mohr Siebeck, 2nd edn, 1929), cols. 110-51.

Schmidt, T.E., 'Cry of Dereliction or Cry of Judgment? Mark 15:34', *BBR* 4 (1994), pp. 145-53.

Schmiedel, P.W., *Das vierte Evangelium gegenüber den drei ersten* (Tübingen: J.C.B. Mohr, 1906; ET *The Johannine Writings* [trans. M.A. Canney; London: A. & C. Black, 1908]).

—'Gospels', in T.K. Cheyne and J.S. Black (eds.), *Encyclopaedia Biblica: A Critical Dictionary of the Literary, Political and Religious History, the Archaeology, Geography and Natural History of the Bible* (4 vols.; London: A. & C. Black, 1899–1907), II, cols. 1761-898.

Schmitt, R., 'Die Sprachverhältnisse in den östlichen Provinzen des römischen Reiches', *ANRW* 2.29.2, pp. 554-86.

Schnackenburg, R., *Das Johannesevangelium* (4 vols.; HTK, 4.1-4; Freiburg: Herder, 1965–84; ET *The Gospel according to St John* [trans. K. Smyth; 3 vols.; New York: Crossroad, 1982]).

—*Gottes Herrschaft und Reich* (Freiburg: Herder, 1963; 4th edn, 1965; ET *God's Rule and Kingdom* [trans. J. Murray; London: Burns & Oates, 1963; 2nd edn, 1968]).

Schramm, T., *Der Markus-Stoff bei Lukas: Eine literarkritische und redaktionsgeschichtliche Untersuchung* (SNTSMS, 14; Cambridge: Cambridge University Press, 1971).

Schulz, S., 'Der historische Jesus: Bilanz der Fragen und Lösungen', in Strecker (ed.), *Jesus Christus in Historie und Theologie*, pp. 3-25.

—'Die neue Frage nach dem historischen Jesus', in H. Baltensweiler and B. Reicke (eds.), *Neues Testament und Geschichte: Historisches Geschehen und Deutung im Neuen Testament* (Festschrift O. Cullmann; Zürich: Theologischer Verlag; Tübingen: Mohr Siebeck, 1972), pp. 33-42.

Schürer, E., *The History of the Jewish People in the Age of Jesus Christ* (3 vols.; rev. G. Vermes, F. Millar and M. Black; Edinburgh: T. & T. Clark, 1973–87).

Schürmann, H., 'Kritische Jesuserkenntnis: Zur kritischen Handhabung des "Unähnlichkeitskriteriums"', in idem, *Jesus—Gestalt und Geheimnis: Gesammelte Beiträge* (Paderborn: Bonifatius, 1994), pp. 420-34.

Schüssler Fiorenza, E., *Jesus: Miriam's Child and Sophia's Prophet* (New York: Continuum, 1994).

Schwabe, M., and B. Lifshitz (eds.), *Beth She'arim*. II. *The Greek Inscriptions* (New Brunswick, NJ: Rutgers University Press, for the Israel Exploration Society and the Institute of Archaeology, Hebrew University, 1974).

Schwarz, G., 'ΣΥΡΟΦΟΙΝΙΚΙΣΣΑ—ΧΑΝΑΝΑΙΑ (Markus 7.26/Matthäus 15.22)', *NTS* 30 (1984), pp. 626-28.

—*'Und Jesu Sprach': Untersuchungen zur aramäischen Urgestalt der Worte Jesu* (BWANT, 118; Stuttgart: W. Kohlhammer, 2nd edn, 1987).

Schwarz, H., *Christology* (Grand Rapids: Eerdmans, 1998).

Schweitzer, A., *Das Messianitäts- und Leidensgeheimnis: Eine Skizze des Lebens Jesu* (Tübingen: Mohr Siebeck, 1901; 3rd edn, 1956; ET *The Mystery of the Kingdom of God: The Secret of Jesus' Messiahship and Passion* [trans. W. Lowrie; London: A. & C. Black, 1925]).

—*Von Reimarus zu Wrede: Eine Geschichte der Leben-Jesu-Forschung* (Tübingen: Mohr Siebeck, 1906; 2nd edn, 1910; 6th edn, 1951; ET *The Quest of the Historical Jesus: A Critical Study of its Progress from Reimarus to Wrede* [trans. W. Montgomery; London: A. & C. Black, 1910]).

Schweizer, E., *Jesus Christus im vielfältigen Zeugnis des Neuen Testaments* (Munich: Siebenstern, 1968; ET *Jesus* [trans. D.E. Green; London: SCM Press; Atlanta: John Knox Press, 1971]).

—*Jesus: The Parable of God. What Do We Really Know about Jesus?* (Alison Park, PA: Pickwick, 1994; Edinburgh: T. & T. Clark, 1997).

Schwyzer, E., *Griechische Grammatik* (2 vols.; Munich: Beck, 1939, 1950).

Scott, B.B., 'From Reimarus to Crossan: Stages in a Quest', *CR* 2 (1994), pp. 253-80.

Sebeok, T. (ed.), *Style in Language* (New York: Wiley, 1960).

Segal, M.H., *A Grammar of Mishnaic Hebrew* (Oxford: Clarendon Press, 1927).

—'Mishnaic Hebrew and its Relation to Biblical Hebrew and to Aramaic', *JQR* 20 (1908), pp. 670-700, 734-37.

Segal, P., 'The Penalty of the Warning Inscription from the Temple of Jerusalem', *IEJ* 39 (1989), pp. 79-84.

Selby, G.R., *Jesus, Aramaic and Greek* (Doncaster: Brynmill Press, 1989).

Seliger, H.W., and R.M. Vago (eds.), *First Language Attrition* (Cambridge: Cambridge University Press, 1991).

Sevenster, J.N., *Do You Know Greek? How Much Greek Could the First Jewish Christians Have Known?* (NovTSup, 19; Leiden: E.J. Brill, 1968).

Sharp, D., *Language in Bilingual Communities* (EISL; London: Edward Arnold, 1973).

Sherwin-White, A.N., *Roman Society and Roman Law in the New Testament* (Sarum Lectures, 1960–61; Oxford: Clarendon Press, 1963).

Siegert, F., 'Die Makrosyntax des Hebräerbriefs', in Fornberg and Hellholm (eds.), *Texts and Contexts*, pp. 305-16.

Silva, M., 'Bilingualism and the Character of Palestinian Greek', *Bib* 61 (1980), pp. 198-219; repr. in Porter (ed.), *Language of the New Testament*, pp. 205-26.

Smalley, S.S., 'Redaction Criticism', in Marshall (ed.), *New Testament Interpretation*, pp. 181-95.

Smith, D.M., *Johannine Christianity: Essays on its Setting, Sources, and Theology* (Durham: University of South Carolina, 1984; Edinburgh: T. & T. Clark, 1987).

Smith, M., 'Aramaic Studies and the Study of the New Testament', *JBR* 26 (1958), pp. 304-13.

Smith, W., 'Computers, Statistics and Disputed Authorship', in Gibbons (ed.), *Language and the Law*, pp. 374-413.

Smyth, H.W., *Greek Grammar* (rev. G.M. Messing; Cambridge, MA: Harvard University Press, 1929; rev. edn, 1956).

Soden, H.F., *Die wichtigsten Fragen im Leben Jesu* (Leipzig: J.C. Hinrichs, 2nd edn, 1909).

Soukup, P.A., and R. Hodgson (eds.), *From One Medium to Another: Basic Issues for Communicating the Scriptures in New Media* (New York: American Bible Society; Kansas City: Sheed & Ward, 1997).

Spencer, A.B., *Paul's Literary Style: A Stylistic and Historical Comparison of II Corinthians 11:16–12:13, Romans 8:9-39, and Philippians 3:2–4:13* (Lanham, MD: University Press of America, 1998 [1984]).

Spolsky, B., 'Bilingualism', in F.J. Newmeyer (ed.), *Linguistics: The Cambridge Survey. IV. Language: The Socio-Cultural Context* (Cambridge: Cambridge University Press, 1988), pp. 100-118.

—'Diglossia in Hebrew in the Late Second Temple Period', *Southwest Journal of Linguistics* 10.1 (1991), pp. 85-104.

—'Jewish Multilingualism in the First Century: An Essay in Historical Sociolinguistics', in Fishman (ed.), *Readings in the Sociology of Jewish Languages*, pp. 35-50.

Stanton, G.N., 'Form Criticism Revisited', in Hooker and Hickling (eds.), *What about the New Testament?*, pp. 13-27.

—*The Gospels and Jesus* (OBS; Oxford: Oxford University Press, 1989).

—'Jesus of Nazareth: A Magician and a False Prophet who Deceived God's People?', in J.B. Green and M. Turner (eds.), *Jesus of Nazareth: Lord and Christ. Essays on the Historical Jesus and New Testament Christology* (Grand Rapids: Eerdmans; Carlisle: Paternoster Press, 1994), pp. 164-80.

—*Jesus of Nazareth in New Testament Preaching* (SNTSMS, 27; Cambridge: Cambridge University Press, 1974).

Stauffer, E., *Jesus: Gestalt und Geschichte* (Bern: Francke, 1957; ET *Jesus and his Story* [trans. R. Winston and C. Winston; London: SCM Press; New York: Knopf, 1960]).

—'Jesus, Geschichte und Verkündigung', *ANRW* 2.25.1, pp. 3-130.

Stein, R.H., 'The "Criteria" for Authenticity', in France and Wenham (eds.), *Gospel Perspectives*, I, pp. 225-63.

—*Jesus the Messiah: A Survey of the Life of Christ* (Downers Grove, IL: InterVarsity Press, 1996).

—*The Method and Message of Jesus' Teachings* (Philadelphia: Westminster Press, 1978; Louisville, KY: Westminster/John Knox Press, rev. edn, 1994).

—*The Synoptic Problem: An Introduction* (Grand Rapids: Baker Book House, 1987).

—'What Is *Redaktionsgeschichte*?', *JBL* 88 (1969), pp. 45-56.

Sterling, G.E., 'Recluse or Representative? Philo and Greek-Speaking Judaism beyond Alexandria', in E.H. Lovering, Jr, *Society of Biblical Literature 1995 Seminar Papers* (SBLSP, 34; Atlanta: Scholars Press, 1995), pp. 595-616.

Stine, P.C. (ed.), *Issues in Bible Translation* (UBSMS, 3; London: United Bible Societies, 1988).

Stoker, W.D., *Extracanonical Sayings of Jesus* (SBLRBS, 18; Atlanta: Scholars Press, 1989).

Stoldt, H.-H., *Geschichte und Kritik der Markushypothese* (Göttingen: Vandenhoeck & Ruprecht, 1977; ET *History and Criticism of the Marcan Hypothesis* [trans. D.L. Niewyk; Macon, GA: Mercer University Press; Edinburgh: T. & T. Clark, 1980]).

Stonehouse, N.B., *The Witness of Matthew and Mark to Christ* (London: Tyndale Press, 1944; repr. Grand Rapids: Eerdmans, 1958).

Strange, J.F., 'First Century Galilee from Archaeology and from the Texts', in Edwards and McCollough (eds.), *Archaeology and the Galilee*, pp. 39-48.

Strauss, D.F., *Das Leben Jesu für das deutsche Volk bearbeitet* (Leipzig: Brockhaus, 1864; 3rd edn, 1874; ET *A New Life of Jesus* [London: Williams & Norgate, 1865]).

—*Das Leben Jesu kritisch bearbeitet* (2 vols.; Tübingen: Osiander, 1835–36; 4th edn, 1840; ET *The Life of Jesus, Critically Examined* [3 vols.; trans. G. Eliot; London: Chapman, 1846; repr. Philadelphia: Fortress Press, 1972; London: SCM Press, 1973]).

—*Der Christus des Glaubens und der Jesus der Geschichte: Eine Kritik des Schleiermacher'schen Lebens Jesu* (Berlin: Duncker, 1865; ET *The Christ of Faith and the Jesus of History: A Critique of Schleiermacher's Life of Jesus* [trans. L.E. Keck; Philadelphia: Fortress Press, 1977]).

—*Hermann Samuel Reimarus und seine Schutzschrift für die vernünftigen Verehrer Gottes* (Bonn: Strauss, 2nd edn, 1877 [1862]).

Strecker, G. (ed.), *Jesus Christus in Historie und Theologie* (Festschrift H. Conzelmann; Tübingen: Mohr Siebeck, 1975).

Streeter, B.H., *The Four Gospels: A Study of Origins* (London: Macmillan, 1926).

—'The Literary Evolution of the Gospels', in Sanday (ed.), *Studies in the Synoptic Problem*, pp. 209-27.

—'St Mark's Knowledge and Use of Q', in Sanday (ed.), *Studies in the Synoptic Problem*, pp. 165-83.

Stuckenbruck, L.T., 'An Approach to the New Testament through Aramaic Sources: The Recent Methodological Debate', *JSP* 8 (1991), pp. 3-29.

Stuhlmacher, P., *Jesus von Nazareth—Christus des Glaubens* (Stuttgart: Calwer Verlag, 1988; ET *Jesus of Nazareth—Christ of Faith* [trans. S.S. Schatzmann; Peabody, MA: Hendrickson, 1993).

Stuhlmacher, P. (ed.), *Das Evangelium und die Evangelien: Vorträge vom Tübinger Symposium 1982* (WUNT, 28; Tübingen: Mohr Siebeck, 1983; ET *The Gospel and the Gospels* [Grand Rapids: Eerdmans, 1991]).

Styler, G.M., 'The Priority of Mark', in C.F.D. Moule, *The Birth of the New Testament* (BNTC; London: A. & C. Black, 3rd edn, 1981; HNTC; New York: Harper & Row, 1982), pp. 285-316.

Such, W.A., *The Abomination of Desolation in the Gospel of Mark: Its Historical Reference in Mark 13:14 and its Impact in the Gospel* (Lanham, MD: University Press of America, 1999).

Sundwall, J., 'Die Zusammensetzung des Markusevangeliums', in *Acta Academiae Aboensis, Humaniora*, IX (Åbo: Åbo Academy, 1934), pp. 1-86.

Swete, H.B., *The Gospel According to Mark* (London: Macmillan, 1898).

Tarn, W., and G.T. Griffith, *Hellenistic Civilisation* (London: Edward Arnold, 1927; 3rd edn, 1952).

Taylor, N.H., 'Palestinian Christianity and the Caligula Crisis. Part II. The Markan Eschatological Discourse', *JSNT* 62 (1996), pp. 13-41.

Taylor, V., *Behind the Third Gospel: A Study of the Proto-Luke Hypothesis* (Oxford: Clarendon Press, 1926).

—*The Formation of the Gospel Tradition* (London: Macmillan, 1933; 2nd edn, 1935).

—*The Gospel According to St Mark* (London: Macmillan, 1959).

—*Jesus and his Sacrifice: A Study of the Passion-Sayings in the Gospels* (London: Macmillan, 1937).

—*The Life and Ministry of Jesus* (London: Macmillan, 1954; Nashville: Abingdon Press, 1955).

—*The Passion Narrative of St Luke* (SNTSMS, 19; Cambridge: Cambridge University Press, 1972).

—*The Work and Words of Jesus* (London: Macmillan, 1950).

Tcherikover, V., *Hellenistic Civilization and the Jews* (trans. S. Applebaum; 1959; repr. New York: Atheneum, 1975).

—'Palestine under the Ptolemies (A Contribution to the Study of the Zenon Papyri)', *Mizraim* 4–5 (1937), pp. 9-90.

Telford, W.R., 'Major Trends and Interpretive Issues in the Study of Jesus', in Chilton and Evans (eds.), *Studying the Historical Jesus*, pp. 33-74.

Teodorsson, S.-T., 'Phonological Variation in Classical Attic and the Development of Koine', *Glotta* 57 (1979), pp. 61-75.

—*The Phonology of Ptolemaic Koine* (Gothenburg: Acta Universitatis Gothoburgensis, 1977).

Thackeray, H.St.J., *A Grammar of the Old Testament in Greek According to the Septuagint* (Cambridge: Cambridge University Press, 1909).

—*Josephus: The Man and the Historian* (1929; repr. New York: Ktav, 1967).

Theissen, G., *Der Schatten des Galiläers: Historische Jesusforschung in erzählender Form* (Munich: Chr. Kaiser Verlag, 1986; ET *The Shadow of the Galilean: The Quest of the Historical Jesus in Narrative Form* [trans. J. Bowden; Philadelphia: Fortress Press, 1987]).

—'Historical Scepticism and the Criteria of Jesus Research *or* My Attempt to Leap across Lessing's Yawning Gulf', *SJT* 49 (1996), pp. 147-76.

—'Lokal- und Sozialkolorit in der Geschichte von der syrophönischen Frau (Mk 7:24-30)', *ZNW* 75 (1984), pp. 202-25.

—*Lokalkolorit und Zeitgeschichte in den Evangelien: Ein Beitrag zur Geschichte der synoptischen Tradition* (NTOA, 8; Göttingen: Vandenhoeck & Ruprecht, 1989; ET *The Gospels in Context: Social and Political History in the Synoptic Tradition* [trans. L.M. Maloney; Edinburgh: T. & T. Clark, 1992]).

—*Urchristliche Wundergeschichten: Ein Beitrag zur formgeschichtlichen Erforschung der synoptischen Evangelien* (SNT, 8; Gütersloh: Gerd Mohn, 1974; ET *The Miracle Stories of Early Christian Tradition* [trans. F. McDonagh; SNTW; Edinburgh: T. & T. Clark; Philadelphia: Fortress Press, 1983]).

Theissen, G., and A. Merz, *Der historische Jesus: Ein Lehrbuch* (Göttingen: Vandenhoeck & Ruprecht, 1996; ET *The Historical Jesus: A Comprehensive Guide* [trans. J. Bowden; London: SCM Press; Minneapolis: Fortress Press, 1998]).

Theissen, G., and D. Winter, *Die Kriterienfrage in der Jesusforschung: Vom Differenzkriterium zum Plausibilitätskriterium* (NTOA, 34; Freiburg: Universitätsverlag; Göttingen: Vandenhoeck & Ruprecht, 1997).

Thomson, G., *The Greek Language* (Cambridge: Heffer, 1972).

Thumb, A., *Die griechische Sprache im Zeitalter des Hellenismus: Beiträge zur Geschichte und Beurteilung der KOINH* (Strassburg: Trübner, 1901).

—*Handbuch der griechischen Dialekte* (Indogermanische Bibliothek; Heidelberg: Winter, 1909).

Torrey, C.C., *The Four Gospels: A New Translation* (New Haven: Yale University Press, 1958).

—*Our Translated Gospels: Some of the Evidence* (Cambridge, MA: Harvard University Press, 1916).

—'The Translations Made from the Original Aramaic Gospels', in D.G. Lyon and G.F. Moore (eds.), *Studies in the History of Religions* (Festschrift C.H. Toy; New York: Macmillan, 1912), pp. 269-317.

Tov, E., 'Did the Septuagint Translators Always Understand their Hebrew Text?', in A. Pietersma and C. Cox (eds.), *De Septuaginta: Studies in Honour of John William Wevers on his Sixty-Fifth Birthday* (Ontario: Benben, 1984), pp. 53-70.

Tov, E. (ed.), *The Greek Minor Prophets Scroll* (DJD, 8; Oxford: Clarendon Press, 1990).

Travis, S.H., 'Form Criticism', in Marshall (ed.), *New Testament Interpretation*, pp. 153-64.

Trenkner, S., *Le style καὶ dans le récit attique oral* (Cahiers, 1; Brussels: Editions de l'Institut d'Etudes Polonaises en Belgique, 1948).

Treu, K., 'Die Bedeutung des Griechischen für die Juden im römischen Reich', *Kairos* 15 (1973), pp. 123-44.

Trocmé, E., *Jésus de Nazareth vu par les témoins de sa vie* (Neuchâtel: Delachaux & Niestlé, 1972; ET *Jesus and his Contemporaries* [trans. R.A. Wilson; London: SCM Press, 1973]).

Tuckett, C.M., *Q and the History of Early Christianity: Studies on Q* (Edinburgh: T. & T. Clark, 1996).

—*Reading the New Testament: Methods of Interpretation* (London: SPCK, 1987).

—*The Revival of the Griesbach Hypothesis: An Analysis and Appraisal* (SNTSMS, 44; Cambridge: Cambridge University Press, 1983).

Tuckett, C.M. (ed.), *Synoptic Studies: The Ampleforth Conferences of 1982 and 1983* (JSNTSup, 7; Sheffield: JSOT Press, 1984).

Turner, C.H., 'Marcan Usage: Notes, Critical and Exegetical, on the Second Gospel', *JTS* OS 25 (1924), pp. 377-86; 26 (1924–25), pp. 12-20, 145-56, 225-40, 337-46; 27 (1926), pp. 58-62; 28 (1926–27), pp. 9-30, 349-62; 29 (1928), pp. 275-89, 346-61; repr. in J.K. Elliott (ed.), *The Language and Style of the Gospel of Mark: An Edition of C.H. Turner's 'Notes on Marcan Usage' Together with Other Comparable Studies* (NovTSup, 71; Leiden: E.J. Brill, 1993), pp. 3-146.

Turner, G.W., *Stylistics* (Harmondsworth: Penguin Books, 1973).

Turner, H.E.W., *Historicity and the Gospels: A Sketch of Historical Method and its Application to the Gospels* (London: Mowbrays, 1963).

Turner, N., *Grammatical Insights into the New Testament* (Edinburgh: T. & T. Clark, 1965).

—'The Language of the New Testament', in M. Black and H.H. Rowley (eds.), *Peake's Commentary on the Bible* (London: Nelson, 1962), pp. 659-62.

Vaganay, L., and C.-B. Amphoux, *Initiation à la critique textuelle du Nouveau Testament* (Paris: Cerf, 2nd edn, 1986; ET *An Introduction to New Testament Textual Criticism* [trans. J. Heimerdinger; Cambridge: Cambridge University Press, 1991]).

Van Segbroeck, F., C.M. Tuckett, G. Van Belle and J. Verheyden (eds.), *The Four Gospels 1992: Festschrift Frans Neirynck* (3 vols; BETL, 100; Leuven: Leuven University Press/Peeters, 1992).

Vassiliadis, P., ΛΟΓΟΙ ΙΗΣΟΥ: *Studies in Q* (University of South Florida International Studies in Formative Christianity and Judaism; Atlanta: Scholars Press, 1999).

Venuti, L. (ed.), *Rethinking Translation: Discourse, Subjectivity, Ideology* (London: Rout-
    ledge, 1992).
Vergote, J., 'Grec biblique', in *DBSup*, III, cols. 1353-60.
Vermes, G., *Jesus the Jew: A Historian's Reading of the Gospels* (London: Collins; Phil-
    adelphia: Fortress Press, 1973).
—*The Religion of Jesus the Jew* (Minneapolis: Fortress Press, 1993).
Via, D.A., Jr, *The Parables: Their Literary and Existential Dimension* (Philadelphia:
    Fortress Press, 1967).
Vledder, E.-J., *Conflict in the Miracle Stories: A Socio-Exegetical Study of Matthew 8 and
    9* (JSNTSup, 152; Sheffield: Sheffield Academic Press, 1996).
Voelz, J.W., 'The Linguistic Milieu of the Early Church', *CTQ* 56.2–3 (1992), pp. 81-97.
Vögtle, A., 'Die griechische Sprache und ihre Bedeutung für die Geschichte des Urchris-
    tentums', in H. Gundert (ed.), *Der Lebenswert des Griechischen* (Karlsruhe: Badenia,
    1973), pp. 77-93.
Vorster, W.S., *Speaking of Jesus: Essays on Biblical Language, Gospel Narrative and the
    Historical Jesus* (NovTSup, 92; ed. J.E. Botha; Leiden: E.J. Brill, 1999).
Wacholder, B.Z., *Eupolemus: A Study of Judaeo-Greek Literature* (Cincinnati: Hebrew
    Union College, Jewish Institute of Religion, 1974).
—*Nicolaus of Damascus* (Berkeley: University of California Press, 1962).
Walker, W.O., 'The Quest for the Historical Jesus: A Discussion of Methodology', *ATR* 51
    (1969), pp. 38-56.
Wardhaugh, R., *An Introduction to Sociolinguistics* (Oxford: Basil Blackwell, 1986; 2nd
    edn, 1992).
Watt, J.M., *Code-Switching in Luke and Acts* (Berkeley Insights in Linguistics and Semi-
    otics, 31; New York: Peter Lang, 1997).
—'Of Gutturals and Galileans: The Two Slurs of Matthew 26.73', in S.E. Porter (ed.),
    Diglossia and Other Topics in New Testament Greek (JSNTSup, 193; SNTG, 6;
    Sheffield: Sheffield Academic Press, forthcoming 2000).
Weaver, W.P., *The Historical Jesus in the Twentieth Century: 1900–1950* (Harrisburg, PA:
    Trinity Press International, 1999).
Weinreich, U., *Languages in Contact: Findings and Problems* (Publications of the Lin-
    guistic Circle of New York, 1; New York: Linguistic Circle of New York, 1953).
Weiss, B., *Das Leben Jesu* (2 vols.; Berlin: Wilhelm Herz, 1888).
Weiss, J., *Die Predigt Jesu vom Reiche Gottes* (Göttingen: Vandenhoeck & Ruprecht,
    1892; 2nd edn, 1900; De Waard, J. and E.A. Nida, *From One Language to Another:
    Functional Equivalence in Bible Translating* (Nashville: Nelson, 1986).
Jesus' Proclamation of the Kingdom of God [trans. R.H. Hiers and D.L. Holland; LJ;
    Philadelphia: Fortress Press; London: SCM Press, 1971]).
Weiss, Z., 'Social Aspects of Burial in Beth She'arim: Archeological Finds and Talmudic
    Sources', in Levine (ed.), *The Galilee in Late Antiquity*, pp. 357-71.
Welles, C.B., *Alexander and the Hellenistic World* (Toronto: Hakkert, 1970).
Wellhausen, J., *Das Evangelium Lucae* (Berlin: G. Reimer, 1904).
—*Das Evangelium Marci* (Berlin: G. Reimer, 1903).
—*Das Evangelium Matthaei* (Berlin: G. Reimer, 1904).
—*Einleitung in die drei erste Evangelien* (Berlin: G. Reimer, 1905; 2nd edn, 1911).
Wenham, D., *The Rediscovery of Jesus' Eschatological Discourse* (Gospel Perspectives, 4;
    Sheffield: JSOT Press, 1984).

Wenham, D. (ed.), *Gospel Perspectives: The Jesus Tradition outside the Gospels*, V (Shef-
    field: JSOT Press, 1985).
West, M.L., *Textual Criticism and Editorial Technique Applicable to Greek and Latin
    Texts* (Teubner Studienbücher, Philologie; Stuttgart: Teubner, 1973).
Westcott, B.F., *An Introduction to the Study of the Gospels* (London: Macmillan, 1851; 8th
    edn, 1895).
Westcott, B.F., and F.J.A. Hort, *The New Testament in the Original Greek*. II. *Introduction,
    Appendix* (Cambridge: Macmillan, 1881; repr. Peabody, MA: Hendrickson, 1988).
Westerholm, S., *Jesus and Scribal Authority* (ConBNT, 10; Lund: C.W.K. Gleerup, 1978).
Wexler, P., 'Recovering the Dialects and Sociology of Judeo-Greek in Non-Hellenic
    Europe', in Fishman (ed.), *Readings in the Sociology of Jewish Languages*, pp. 227-40.
Wiefel, W., *Das Evangelium nach Matthäus* (THKNT; Berlin: Evangelische Verlagsanstalt,
    1998).
Wilamowitz-Moellendorff, U., *Die griechische Literatur des Altertums* (Stuttgart: Teubner,
    3rd edn, 1912; repr. 1995).
Wilcox, M., 'The Aramaic Background of the New Testament', in Beattie and McNamara
    (eds.), *The Aramaic Bible*, pp. 362-78.
—'Jesus in the Light of his Jewish Environment', *ANRW* 2.25.1, pp. 131-95.
—'Peter and the Rock: A Fresh Look at Matthew 16:17-19', *NTS* 22 (1975), pp. 73-88.
—'Semitisms in the New Testament', *ANRW* 2.25.2, pp. 978-1029.
Willis, W. (ed.), *The Kingdom of God in 20th-Century Interpretation* (Peabody, MA: Hen-
    drickson, 1987).
Winton, A.P., *The Proverbs of Jesus: Issues of History and Rhetoric* (JSNTSup, 35;
    Sheffield: JSOT Press, 1990).
Wise, M.O., 'Languages of Palestine', in Green, McKnight and Marshall (eds.), *Dictionary
    of Jesus and the Gospels*, pp. 434-44.
Witherington, IB., II, *The Christology of Jesus* (Minneapolis: Fortress Press, 1991).
—*The Jesus Quest: The Third Search for the Jew of Nazareth* (Downers Grove, IL: Inter-
    Varsity Press, 1995).
Wood, H.G., *Jesus in the Twentieth Century* (London: Lutterworth, 1960).
Wrede, W., *Das Messiasgeheimnis in den Evangelien: Zugleich ein Beitrag zum Ver-
    ständnis des Markusevangeliums* (Göttingen: Vandenhoeck & Ruprecht, 1901; ET
    The Messianic Secret [trans. J.C.G. Greig; Cambridge: J. Clarke, 1971]).
Wright, N.T., *Jesus and the Victory of God* (Minneapolis: Fortress Press, 1996).
—*The New Testament and the People of God* (London: SPCK, 1992).
—'Quest for the Historical Jesus', *ABD* 3 (1992), pp. 796-802.
Zahrnt, H., *Es begann mit Jesus von Nazareth: Die Frage nach dem historischen Jesus*
    (Stuttgart: Kreuz, 1960; ET *The Historical Jesus* [trans. J.S. Bowden; London: Collins;
    New York: Harper & Row, 1963]).
Zeitlin, I.M., *Jesus and the Judaism of his Time* (Cambridge: Polity Press, 1988).
Zerwick, M., *Untersuchungen zum Markus-Stil: Ein Beitrag zur Durcharbeitung des
    Neuen Testamentes* (Rome: Pontifical Biblical Institute, 1937).
Zimmermann, F., *The Aramaic Origin of the Four Gospels* (New York: Ktav, 1979).
Zimmermann, H., *Neutestamentliche Methodenlehre: Darstellung der historisch-kritischen
    Methode* (Stuttgart: Katholische Bibelwerk, 1967; 2nd edn, 1968).
Zlateva, P. (ed.), *Translation as Social Action: Russian and Bulgarian Perspectives*
    (Translation Studies; London: Routledge, 1993).

OTHER ANCIENT REFERENCES

1.258	176	279	170	Polybius	
1.333	176	336-60	170	39.12	170
3.252	176	359	147		
6.22	176	390-93	170	Suetonius	
7.67	176	410	170	*Aug.*	
9.290	176			89	176
10.8	176	*War*			
10.218	169	1.3	169	*Claud.*	
11.148	176	1.282	204	42	176
11.159	176	2.117-18	162		
11.286	176	2.253-58	162	*Titus*	
12.145	168	5.193-94	168	3.2	176
14.36	204	5.360-61	176		
15.342-43	146	6.96	178	Ostraca, Papyri	
15.373	204	6.97	176	and Tablets	
16.6	146	6.124-25	168	*P. Egerton*	
16.203	146	6.129	178	2	146
16.242-43	146	6.327	178		
16.291	204	9.97	177	Inscriptions	
16.311	204			*CIJ II*	
17.20-21	146	Christian Authors		1400	168
17.52-53	147	*Gos. Thom.*		1404	177
17.94	147	100	146		
18.1-10	162			*IG II*	
18.23-25	162	Classical Authors		90.135	146
18.143	147	Aulus Gellius			
19.360	147	*N.A.*		*IG III*	
20.102	162	11.8.2	170	550	146
20.263-65	169			551	146
174	146	Cicero			
		Brut.		*OGIS II*	
Apion		81	170	598	168
1.50	169				
1.69-72	151	Dionysius of		*SEG VIII*	
		Halicarnassus		13	168
Life		1.7.2	170	169	168
11-13	170			244	177
13	153	*Ep. Arist.*		95	153
34-42	170	32	139	96	153
65	170	39	139		
88	170	46	139		
175-78	170	47–50	139		
186	170				

INDEX OF AUTHORS

JOURNAL FOR THE STUDY OF THE NEW TESTAMENT
SUPPLEMENT SERIES